The Write Start
Sentences to Paragraphs

WITH PROFESSIONAL AND STUDENT READINGS

Fourth Edition

D1411129

Gayle Feng-Checkett

St. Charles Community College

Lawrence Checkett

St. Charles Community College

WADSWORTH
CENGAGE Learning

Australia • Brazil • Japan • Korea • Mexico • Singapore • Spain • United Kingdom • United States

The Write Start: Sentences to Paragraphs with Professional and Student Readings, Fourth Edition

Gayle Feng-Checkett and Lawrence Checkett

Director of Developmental English: Annie Todd

Senior Development Editor: Kathy Sands-Boehmer

Associate Editor: Janine Tangney

Editorial Assistant: Melanie Opacki

Associate Media Editor: Emily Ryan

Marketing Manager: Kirsten Stoller

Marketing Coordinator: Ryan Ahern

Content Project Manager: Alison Eigel Zade

Art Director: Marissa Falco

Manufacturing Manager: Marcia Locke

Senior Rights Acquisition Account Manager-Text: Katie Huha

Production Service: Pre-Press PMG

Senior Photo Editor: Jennifer Meyer Dare

Photo Researcher: Bruce Carson

Cover Designer: Len Massiglia

Cover Photo: © Digital Vision / Getty Images

Compositor: Pre-Press PMG

For product information and technology assistance, contact us at **Cengage Learning Customer & Sales Support, 1-800-354-9706**

For permission to use material from this text or product, submit all requests online at **www.cengage.com/permissions.** Further permissions questions can be e-mailed to **permissionrequest@cengage.com.**

ISBN-13: 978-0-547-20131-3

ISBN-10: 0-547-20131-1

Wadsworth
20 Channel Center
Boston, MA 02210
USA

Cengage Learning products are represented in Canada by Nelson Education, Ltd.

For your course and learning solutions, visit **www.cengage.com.**

Purchase any of our products at your local college store or at our preferred online store **www.ichapters.com.**

Printed in the United States of America
1 2 3 4 5 6 7 13 12 11 10 09

BRIEF CONTENTS

PART THREE

DETAILED CONTENTS

PART 2

Writing Effective Paragraphs   127

Chapter 9

The Paragraph   133

Chapter 10

Description   159

The Writer's Resources   311

GRAMMAR   312

Readings   415

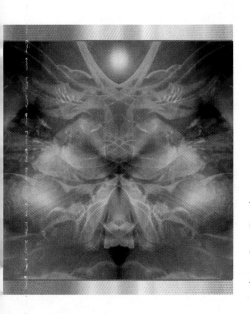

PREFACE

We are very pleased at how well the first three editions of *The Write Start with Readings: Sentences to Paragraphs* and its companion title, *The Write Start with Readings: Paragraphs to Essays*, have been received. Many schools from across the country have adopted *The Write Start* as their developmental writing texts, both individually and as a series.

Developmental writing teachers who used the first three editions are unanimously positive in their comments. They praise the texts' organization, which combines grammar instruction and writing instruction from the start; the varied and focused practices and writing assignments, which allow students of various backgrounds—including students for whom English is a second language (ESL)—to write about topics of interest to them; The Writer's Resources, which provide additional grammar instruction and practice for those who need it; and the book's design, which is attractive, simple, and functional. Such praise from fellow developmental writing teachers is both gratifying and energizing. They kind expressions continue to feed our commitment to the teaching of writing even more steadfast and resolute.

In this regard, we have taken the suggestions of our colleagues from across the country, and we have added to and refined the contents and organization of the fourth edition of *The Write Start: Sentences to Paragraphs*. In this edition, we have made improvements while retaining the basic strengths of the previous three editions.

What's New in the Fourth Edition

We have kept the fourth edition's basic approach, but we have added new features to make the text more flexible, clear, and useful.

- ■ *New Reorganized Chapters.* At the suggestion of many instructors using *The Write Start with Readings: Sentences to Paragraphs*, we have reorganized the chapters to better reflect how most instructors are teaching the material. Although the chapters are still modular and are easily adapted to any syllabus, combining many of the chapters having easily relatable material was both logical and sensible. Chapters 1 and 2 have been combined, Chapters 7 and 8 have been combined, and Chapters 10, 11, and 12 have been combined.

- ■ *More Exercises.* At the urging of instructors using the text, we have added more exercises for sentence combining in Chapters 3 and 5, and we have added more exercises for sentence combining and sentence fragments in The Writer's Resources section.

- ■ *New Chapter-ending Self-Assessment Tests.* In order to help developing writing students retain what they have read and practiced in each chapter, we have designed "Self-Assessment Tests" at the end of chapters. The assessment tools replace the old "Chapter Review" lists. The tests are more interactive, and they help to reinforce the material to which the writing student has been introduced.

- ■ *New Readings.* To facilitate instruction and to generate student interest, several professional and student readings have been replaced with more current and appropriate selections in the Readings section. Also, we have kept examples of both professional and student essays in each mode of development section.

Overview

Unlike most texts for developing writers, *The Write Start* begins with sentence formation, moves to paragraph organization, and ends with one chapter on the full essay. Although this is one suggestion for a course outline, the chapters are self-contained units allowing for flexibility of design, depending on the instructor's own needs and that of the class. Within the text, references are made to other chapters and to The Writer's Resources section when appropriate.

Organization of the Text

To the Student: Chapter 1

This section introduces developing writers to the importance of writing well. It stresses the idea that writing is difficult but, like other life skills, it can be mastered with the proper attitude, information, and hard work.

Writing Effective Sentences: Chapters 2–8

This section helps developing writers understand the fundamentals of good sentence building and establishes the importance of sentence variety in writing. Ten different sentence types are each given their own chapter. Each chapter contains examples to illustrate instruction. Multiple practice sets allow for the transference of specific skill-building ideas into clear, concise, and complete sentences.

Writing Effective Paragraphs: Chapters 9–17

This section teaches developing writers how to organize and construct body paragraphs in a variety of rhetorical modes. The chapters incorporate both professional and student paragraph models, as well as technique questions that focus on the elements necessary for effective paragraphs. Specific detail and sentence variety are an integral part of each paragraph chapter.

Writing Effective Essays: Chapter 18

The final product of most writing programs—developmental programs included—is the essay. For instructors who wish to include the essay in their courses, Chapter 18 introduces developing writers to the process of constructing a clear, concise essay. Using the skills learned in preceding sections on sentence variety and paragraph development, the demands of the essay are taught: writing the introductory paragraph, organizing and developing support in the body paragraphs, and coming to a conclusion that is appropriate for the essay's approach.

The Writer's Resources

The Writer's Resources are more than a listing of tables on parts of speech. Rather, to keep the instructional chapters "clean" so that students remain focused on the specific topic under discussion, The Writer's Resources section is a veritable warehouse of information on parts of speech, usage, punctuation, mechanics, and spelling. Examples and exercises accompany the material for illustration, clarification, and additional practice. References to The Writer's Resources are made in the text chapters where appropriate. Material helpful to ESL students is included in The Writer's Resources.

Additional Readings and "Read All About It"

An exciting feature of *The Write Start* is that most professional paragraph examples excerpted in the text can be found in full—with accompanying apparatus—in the Readings section. Instructors have the flexibility of showing their students the full context of specific paragraphs and how they are integrated into the whole essay. This feature is invaluable in showing student writers how developing specific subtopics works in developing the major topic. The essays were chosen to serve as models for the modes being taught in the text. Look in the margins for the "Read All About It" label.

Answer Section

At the end of *The Write Start,* an answer key contains half of the answers to the in-text Practice exercises. This approach allows for ultimate flexibility: Students can check half their answers to gauge their development, and instructors can use the remaining questions for homework or in-class work.

Special Features of *The Write Start*

The features embedded in *The Write Start* make it an invaluable tool for both instructors and students.

■ *Clarity and Simplicity.* Writing, mechanics, and grammar instruction are taught as quickly and simply as possible without losing core content, focusing on valuable insights and meaningful suggestions. Key terms and concepts are boldfaced and defined in each chapter as they are introduced, with ample examples for clarification. Key terms and definitions are repeated in the glossary.

■ *English as a Second Language Instruction.* Material aimed at students for whom English is not the first language is embedded throughout the text. The Write Start uses current ESL research and pedagogy to reach all developing writers. In addition, The Writer's Resources includes specific lists, charts, and exercises for ESL-specific concerns, such as verb form/tense, phrasal verbs, irregular verbs, articles, and idiomatic prepositional phrases. Finally, ESL icons point out the basic material most needed by ESL students throughout the text.

■ *Things You Need to Know.* In anticipation of instructors choosing to teach Chapters 2–8 in a different order than they appear in the book, prerequisites are mentioned at the beginning of certain chapters. These prerequisites, labeled "You Need to Know," direct instructors and students to specific information in preceding chapters that is necessary for a clearer understanding of the material under discussion. Visiting the prerequisite material first will make the current chapter material easier to understand.

■ *Student Writing.* The Write Start uses both professional and student writing. Although professional writing models often are engaging and prove that good writers actually do use the techniques and processes taught in writing classes, developing writers sometimes view professional writing with suspicion. They simply don't believe they will ever approach that level of expertise. *The Write Start* uses both student-generated and professional writing to make an important point: that developing writers use the same rules, processes, and techniques as their professional counterparts.

■ *Vocabulary.* Most developmental writing textbooks have vocabulary lists following the readings. In *The Write Start,* each essay is prefaced by a list of challenging words found in the essay. Readers are asked to look up the definitions of these words prior to reading the essay, so they can focus more easily on the essay's content.

■ *Ample Grammar and Writing Practice.* Brief segments of instruction are immediately followed by Practice exercises that reinforce the concepts taught. Topic Bank writing suggestions and Writing Opportunities based on photographs give students both verbal and visual subject matter for their paragraphs and essays.

■ *Reading and Analyzing to Improve Writing Skill.* Throughout Parts 2, 3, and the Readings, students are given "real" paragraphs and essays to read. By answering the questions following each reading, students learn the techniques that other writers use to communicate effectively.

The Write Start Series

More and more two- and four-year colleges are identifying levels of developmental writing students and are instituting developmental writing course sequences. *The Write Start* is a two-book series whose aim is to answer this need. Although the content of the two books is complementary for sequenced instruction, each book can be used effectively as a stand-alone text for different levels of instruction.

The series is designed for students with a variety of skill levels and for students with a variety of challenges in learning standard American English. *The Write Start with Readings: Sentences to Paragraphs* focuses primarily on sentence variety and paragraph development, with essay writing as the concluding section. *The Write Start with Readings: Paragraphs to Essays* begins with a review of paragraph construction in the rhetorical modes and moves to the thorough development of longer essays in the rhetorical modes, followed by a review of sentence grammar and variety. Both books share the same features, pedagogy, and easy-to-read format.

The Teaching and Learning Package

Each component of the teaching and learning package has been crafted to ensure that the course is rewarding for both instructors and students.

Annotated Instructor's Edition: A replica of the student text but includes all answers printed directly on the fill-in lines provided in the text. It also includes teaching suggestions and activities as an aid to instructors. (0-547-20158-3)

Instructor's Manual/Test Bank: Provides information on the following: *Using the Text, Syllabus Preparation, Answer Keys, Student and Professional Reading Selections, Thesis Sentences, Outlining, Proofreading Checklists, Peer Editing, English as a Second Language/English as a Foreign Language (ESL/EFL), Diagnostic Pre-Test,* and *Transparency Masters.* The test bank section provides a wealth of printed quizzes and additional practice exercises for each chapter in the text. The test bank is formatted in a way that simplifies copying and distribution. (0-547-20178-8)

Companion Websites: For additional content and interactive activities, be sure to visit our student and instructor companion websites. The *Write Start Online* provides a wealth of resources, including:

■ Online Quizzes

■ Additional Grammar Help and Exercises

■ Links to Online Writing Centers and Online Writing Assistants

■ Links to Online Writing Handbooks and Guides to Writing

■ . . . and more!

Multimedia Offerings

WriteSpace, Cengage Learning's online writing program, benefits students at all skill levels and saves time for instructors. This flexible, interactive, customizable, and comprehensive classroom management system includes diagnostic testing, personalized learning plans, practice exercises, writing modules (tutorials), visual literacy, an online handbook, and a powerful gradebook. WriteSpace resides in Eduspace and is powered by Blackboard.

Acknowledgments

We would like to thank everyone who has helped us write and publish *The Write Start*. Senior Sponsoring Editor Joann Kozyrev for her help and guidance. Our Development Editor, Kathy Sands-Boehmer, Editorial Assistant, Daisuke Yasutake and the team at Cengage Learning for all their help. Our students contributed paragraphs and essays to the text and demonstrated through their own writing that our techniques work, while challenging us to keep improving them. Finally, many thanks to the devoted English instructors around the country who reviewed our text and made valuable suggestions for improvement. Reviewers for this edition include: Fawcett Dunstan The Community College of Baltimore County, Essex Campus; Dr. Cynthia Edwards, Gallaudet University; Eric Hibbison, J. Sargeant Reynolds Community College;Tamara Kuzmenkov, Tacoma Community College; Dr. Jessica G. Rabin, Anne Arundel Community College; Catherine Rusco Muskegon Community College; Christy Shannon, Dalton State College; and Mary McCaslin Thompson, Anoka Ramsey Community College

Gayle Feng-Checkett
Lawrence Checkett

The Important Elements of Good Writing

The first question most students ask when starting to read a book on writing is, Why is writing that important? The simple answer is that being able to write well and express yourself will help you throughout the rest of your life. Consider the three situations in which you'll find yourself most often: school, work, and home.

- For school, you will be called on to write essays, reports, analyses, and research papers to show what you've learned.
- For work, you'll be asked to write memos, business letters, and reports to communicate clearly with coworkers, your boss, and even employees at other companies. Moreover, before getting that job, you'll need to write résumés and cover letters to your prospective employers.
- For personal business, you will need to write notes, letters, and e-mail to everyone from your children's teachers to local politicians and even your family and friends.

People sometimes work together on writing projects.

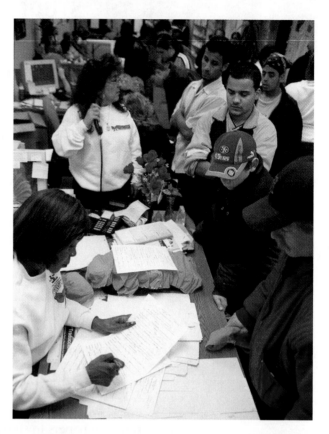

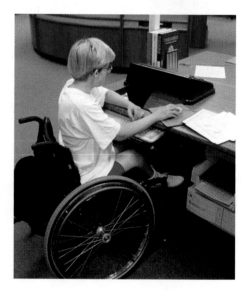

People need to write for school, work, community service, and personal reasons.

Whatever form your writing takes, and wherever you use it, you must learn to write well. Your writing for school, work, or personal business will have to express your ideas clearly. Organizing and developing your writing to achieve this clarity is one of the most important skills you can learn.

The key words in the previous paragraph are *learn* and *skills*. No one is born with good writing skills. Just as you must learn how to keyboard, balance a checkbook, or cook a simple meal, you also must learn how to write well.

How do you learn to write well? You learn how to write well in the same way you develop any other skill. Consider some of your other talents:

- Are you a good free-throw shooter in basketball?
- Are you a whiz at setting up a new program on a computer?
- Can you make a loaf of French bread from scratch?

Why are you so successful at a particular skill? Why does it seem so easy? Is the answer "a little hard work and practice"? If so, then why should learning how to write well be any different? Remember, writing is a skill just like any other skill. If you make a commitment to learn the skill of writing, you will learn how to write and do it well.

Avoiding the Two Major Problems of Poor Writing

There are two obvious problems arising from a poor piece of writing. The first problem is one of understanding. For example, what do the following sentences mean?

1. The chef, made primarily of noodles, served the fettuccine Alfredo to his customers.
2. The truck hit the wall, and it was damaged.
3. Throwing confetti, the parade floats moved slowly down the boulevard.

Can you understand these sentences? In the first sentence, the chef seems to be made of noodles, instead of the fettuccine Alfredo. In the second sentence, the pronoun *it* does not refer clearly to either truck or wall, so the reader cannot know which of the two was damaged. In the third sentence, the confetti was thrown by revelers (not mentioned), not by the parade floats.

In each of these sentences, the meaning is confused and unclear because of poor writing, but the problems are not difficult to correct. A bit of rearranging or the addition of a key word should do the trick:

1. The chef served fettuccine Alfredo, made primarily of noodles, to his customers.
2. The truck hit the wall, and the wall was damaged.
3. The revelers on the floats threw confetti as the parade floats moved slowly down the boulevard.

The second problem arising from poor writing is one of perception. When people read writing that is difficult to understand or that contains punctuation errors, poorly constructed sentences, and misspelled words, they think less of the writer. They think that the writer is either not very intelligent or at least careless (for not proofreading the writing for errors), or possibly both. When the people making such assessments are bosses, professors, school principals, coworkers, human resource managers, and admissions directors, the consequences can be devastating.

Poor writing can lead to not being admitted to college or to a failing grade on an assignment. It can mean not getting the job interview or receiving a poor performance review. It can be the reason an issue is not taken seriously by your local city council or your children are not getting the help they need at school. Learning to write well can help open those same doors that now seem closed.

Understanding Good Versus Poor Writing

What does it take to write well? Like many students, you might find that writing assignments are time-consuming, difficult, and no fun at all. If so, you're not alone. Many writers, including well-known professionals, find that writing is a chore. A good number of writers, though, find writing to be a joy, and by mastering some of the basic elements of good writing, perhaps you can, too.

Good Writing: Four Misconceptions

There are four basic misconceptions about good writing that can make it seem like a chore:

■ Good writing has to be complicated.
■ Good writing has to be long.
■ Good writing means writing just like you talk.
■ Good writing means good ideas—punctuation is of secondary importance.

In reality, the first two of these misconceptions are often misunderstood, whereas the last two are simply wrong. After all, the whole point of writing is to get information across clearly and concisely to someone else.

Good Writing Doesn't Have to Be Complicated

When people say "complicated," what they really mean is "developed." Keep your writing as simple as possible without leaving out any important information, and make certain you explain each idea fully. Concentrate on details that clearly express the main idea, not on words that the reader has to run to a dictionary to look up.

> **Complicated/Unclear**
> Televised educational programming should facilitate the pedagogical manifestations embedded in the internalized psyche of the community's concern for children's edification in discrete categories.

It would take twenty minutes using a dictionary and a thesaurus to figure out the meaning of this sentence.

> **Developed/Clear**
> Children's educational television shows, such as *Sesame Street,* *Reading Rainbow,* and *Mister Rogers' Neighborhood,* should reflect parents' concerns in regard to math, reading, and writing. The instruction should reflect the proper age and level of children's development.

Notice how simple the language is, yet the meaning is clear.

Good Writing Doesn't Have to Be Long

Some assignments dictate length by their very nature. For example, a research paper on the causes of World War II would necessarily be long. However, in most cases, short and simple writing is better. Most people in the business world and academia do not have unlimited time to read incoming communications. They want information that is clear and as short as possible without leaving out any important facts or ideas. However, you don't want your writing to be so brief that it becomes monotonous, immature, and uninformative.

> **Too Short**
>
> Tom is a Democrat. Yuri is a Republican. Yasheef is an Independent. Tom voted. Yuri voted. Yasheef voted. Senator Brown was reelected.

Here, the sing-song rhythm of the sentences is immature, and the information is insufficient. For example, is Senator Brown a Democrat, a Republican, or an Independent?

> **Too Long**
>
> Tom, a Democrat, likes chocolate ice cream and riding his bicycle in the countryside on weekends, whereas Yuri, a Republican, enjoys reading science articles and owns a two-story brick house. Furthermore, Yasheef, an Independent, has a red convertible and started his own business two years ago. Tom, Yuri, and Yasheef all voted in last Tuesday's election. Because it was a bright, sunny day and the forecast predicted a continuation of good weather, many other people came out to vote as well. Most of the voters in the district—a full 62 percent—were Democrats, whereas 34 percent were Republican and 4 percent were Independent. Senator Brown, a Democrat, received the most votes and was reelected.

Here, the inference is clear that Senator Brown was reelected because Democrats were the majority of voters in the district and the good weather boosted the voter turnout, but the sentences are too long and meandering. Also, most of the information has nothing to do with the topic.

> **Clear/Concise**
>
> Tom, a Democrat like the majority of voters in the district, voted along with Yuri, a Republican, and Yasheef, an Independent. Many other voters turned out because of the good weather. Later that evening, it was announced that the Democratic incumbent, Senator Brown, was reelected.

Here, all the necessary information is present, using clear, simplified language.

Good Writing Is More Formal than Talking

Writing, with the possible exception of short notes and memos to family members, friends, and coworkers, is more formal than talking. When you talk, you use slang, intonation, facial expressions, and other body language to get your point across. As a result, the exact words you use can be informal or imprecise, and your audience will still understand you. With writing, though, words are all you have to get your point across, so those words need to be more precise and more formal. Therefore, word choice, sentence structure, and paragraph organization become more important. In business and academia, do not use slang and confusing expressions that do not mean what their individual words suggest.

Slang

John F. Kennedy was a *cool* president, and he never *disrespected* his *posse*.

Appropriate Language

John F. Kennedy was *an effective* president, and he never *showed disrespect for his supporters*.

Confusing Expression

After the batter struck out, the coach *had a cow*.

Appropriate Language

After the batter struck out, the coach *became angry*.

The purpose of good writing is to get across information to someone in a clear and concise manner. Slang and confusing expressions are unacceptable in formal writing for several reasons.

Slang and confusing expressions are often used by a select group of people, usually belonging to a particular social group, profession, age group, or culture. The meaning of slang and confusing expressions is usually understood only by the select group. Also, slang and confusing expressions do not have an exact meaning, making it difficult for the reader to understand the intended meaning. You might use a word or an expression to mean one thing, and your reader might interpret it to mean something else. When someone says, "That song is bad," to one group, bad might mean "awful," whereas to another group, it might mean "good." A good example is the expression "The man was so angry, he had a cow." To a foreigner or to a person outside of the group familiar with its actual meaning, "having a cow" would certainly be confusing; the reader would have no way to figure out the cause-and-effect relationship between a man being angry and his having a cow.

When you write, try to use exact language that is easy to understand and clarifies ideas, not confuses them. Omit slang and confusing expressions, and use precise language to get your points across.

Good Writing Needs Proper Punctuation

Proper punctuation is essential to attain clear meaning. Punctuation has two prime functions: First, it divides information into smaller groups, making it easier for the reader to understand; and second, it creates rhythm so that the sentences flow easily together.

By way of comparison, think of punctuation as having a similar function in writing as traffic signals do on the road. Traffic signals keep the traffic (like words in writing) moving with a coordinated ease. The signals also divide traffic into smaller, more manageable groups to regulate flow and allow everyone to travel at a reasonable rate. For instance, you might think of a period as a red light (full stop), a semicolon as a flashing red light (a full stop but not quite as long as a nonflashing red light), and a comma as a flashing yellow light (a slowing down but not a full stop).

> **Without Punctuation**
>
> The secretary having finished at least for the day her stack of communications was then confronted with another set of demands without help from an assistant it would take her at least another four hours consequently she called with permission from her boss a temporary employment agency.

This sentence is difficult to follow, and finding a place to take a breath is almost impossible.

> **With Punctuation**
>
> The secretary, having finished at least for the day her stack of communications, was then confronted with another set of demands. Without help from an assistant, it would take her at least another four hours; consequently, she called, with permission from her boss, a temporary employment agency.

Notice how the punctuation helps to clarify the content by breaking the information into smaller units. Punctuation also helps to create rhythm in the writing by making the reader slow down and pause at certain places.

The Computer, Writing, and You

Now that you're in college, many instructors will expect you to use a computer on which to do your writing. Some courses will require you to submit your papers and essays on a disk or even to send them electronically to a folder for the instructor's or your classmates' comments. But don't panic. If your instructor doesn't spend time in class teaching you how to accomplish this, your school probably has an instructional center where tutors can instruct you individually or in special classes. In a few short weeks, you'll become comfortable with using the computer to help you with all your writing assignments.

Although you may have heard a few horror stories about students losing entire papers because of a computer crash or a file being destroyed by an Internet virus, millions of students just like you are discovering how computers can help them write their papers more efficiently, more accurately, and more professionally.

Computers can help you with a multitude of tasks that are necessary to complete a variety of writing assignments. You can use a computer to help you during all phases of the writing process.

Writing

- Brainstorming
- Freewriting
- Rough drafts (save multiple drafts for comparison)
- Inserting and/or deleting sentences (also helps you achieve sentence variety)
- Moving paragraphs (to help you organize and develop your ideas)

■ Thesaurus (to help you find synonyms and antonyms)
■ Spellchecker
■ Grammar checker
■ Format (italics, boldface, font size, highlighting, and many other features)

Research

■ Use the Internet and World Wide Web to find information.
■ Access online library catalogs and databases.
■ Write to others about your assignment using e-mail.
■ Talk live in "chat" rooms.
■ Exchange files and folders.
■ Post assignments to class archives and forums.

Using a computer to write can offer many advantages when working on your assignments. As you gain experience, you will learn to access information more quickly, focus your research, organize your ideas and communicate a developed point of view, and produce a professional-looking final draft. The new tools available to writers today can make many writing tasks and processes easier and quicker to accomplish.

We hope the examples you've been shown have erased some misconceptions about the writing process. Yes, writing can be difficult—but don't get discouraged, we're just getting started. The instructional chapters of this book have been designed to give you information and present techniques in a clear and concise manner so that your writing experience will be as productive as possible.

You don't have to be a professional to write well. This book also presents the thoughts and styles of many student writers just like you. The finished student writings that you will read are the product of the instructional chapters that went into the making of this book. These students were just like you when they began, and with work and dedication, you will be writing just like them in a relatively short time. There is a voice within you that is waiting to be discovered and developed. Let's go!

 Visit *The Write Start* Online!

For additional practice with the materials in this chapter, go to

http://www.cengage.com/devenglish/checkett/writestartSP4e.

Chapter Self-Assessment Test

Check either True or False on the blank next to the statement.

T   F

____   ____   Good writing is always complicated.

____   ____   Good writing does not have to be long.

____   ____   Good writing, like talking, is informal.

____   ____   It is permissible to use slang in academic writing.

____   ____   In writing, word choice, sentence structure, and paragraph organization are important.

____   ____   Punctuation does not influence clear meaning. It just divides information.

PART ONE

Writing Effective Sentences

In the following chapters, you will learn the basic rules of grammar and the basic sentence types. You also will learn the technique known as "sentence combining" that allows writers to create a more interesting and mature style of writing. Almost every aspect of your life at home, school, and work demands longer pieces of writing (memos, letters, reports, essays, research papers) with which to communicate to family, friends, teachers, and colleagues. All of these forms of writing are created using the grammar rules that make up Standard English. Without these rules, neither sentence variety nor longer pieces of writing would be possible.

2

The Simple Sentence and the Independent Clause

The sentence is the building block of all writing. Paragraphs, memos, letters, reports, and even essays and books are constructed from sentences. But what are sentences built out of? A properly constructed sentence must have a **subject,** a **verb,** and sufficient meaning.

In this chapter, we will practice identifying subjects and verbs in **simple sentences.** A simple sentence has one subject and one verb. This is also called an **independent clause.** Sentences can have more than one subject and one verb, as we will see in the next chapter.

ESL The Subject

The subject of a sentence is usually a noun (John, car, politics) or a pro-noun (I, you, he, she, it, we, they). It is usually located near the beginning of a sentence.

Nouns

A **noun** names persons, places, and things. Nouns can be either *common* (not capitalized) or *proper* (always capitalized). Notice that common nouns name general persons, places, and things, whereas proper nouns name particular persons, places, and things.

Common Nouns	Proper Nouns
(general)	(particular)
city	Los Angeles
boy	Peter
photocopier	Xerox

The subject nouns in the following examples are *italicized*.

Examples of Subject Nouns

Proper Noun/Person: *Fred* drove to the store.

Common Noun/Person: The *manager* counted the day's receipts.

Proper Noun/Place: *New York* is a city with many tall buildings.

Common Noun/Place: The *countryside* was very open but very quiet.

Proper Noun/Thing: The *Washington Monument* was circled by tourists.

Common Noun/Thing: The large *table* was filled with birthday gifts.

Pronouns

Pronouns are used to take the place of nouns.

Commonly Used Pronouns

I	we	me	it
you	they	this	that
everyone	something	nobody	which

For a complete list of pronouns, see The Writer's Resources (page 315). Subject pronouns in the following examples are *italicized*.

Examples of Subject Pronouns

I am a mechanic.

You should go to the job fair next week.

He will never graduate because he has poor study habits.

She uses public transportation to get to the office.

It is a large, white, furry, carnivorous bear living near the North Pole.

We can achieve world peace if we work together.

They should invest in mutual funds for their baby's future college education.

Using Pronouns to Eliminate Repetition

When we want to avoid using the same noun too many times, we use a pronoun to reduce repetition.

In the following sentence, the repetition of the nouns *children, soda,* and *potato chips* makes the sentence sound awkward and almost like it was written for a very young child's reader.

The children wanted to have a party, but the children did not have enough soda and potato chips. The children ran to the store and bought more soda and potato chips.

In the next sentence, noun repetition is eliminated by substituting pronouns for nouns. The pronoun substitutions are *italicized*.

The children wanted to have a party, but *they* did not have enough soda and potato chips. *They* ran to the store and bought *them*.

Once the main nouns have been established, we can use pronouns to eliminate repetition. However, overuse of pronouns can lead to the common problem called *pronoun reference error*. A pronoun reference error occurs when the pronoun that is replacing a noun does not clearly refer to that noun.

> **Example**
> The girl saw her mother at the store, and *she* was surprised.

Which noun, *girl* or *mother,* does the pronoun *she* refer to? There is no way for the reader to understand which reference the writer meant. Always be sure that when you substitute a pronoun for a noun, the pronoun refers clearly to that noun.

Identifying Subjects

The subject identifies *who* or *what* is *doing something* or *being something.*

> **Example**
> *Teachers educate students*. In this sentence, *Teachers* is the subject noun doing an activity—educating students.
>
> *Teachers are educators*. In this sentence, *Teachers* is the subject, but now it is not doing an action or activity. Rather, the "state of being" or "state of existence" of teachers is being explained.

PRACTICE 1   Identifying Subjects

Underline the subject in each of the following sentences.

Example: <u>Heathrow Airport</u> was crowded with vacationers returning home.

1. The airliner was flying the "red eye" from London to New York.

2. A thick fog had settled over New York's JFK airport.

3. The runway lights flashed blue and yellow.

4. The jet circled JFK for over an hour.

5. The air traffic controller gave the pilot landing clearance.

6. The pilot landed the aircraft successfully.

7. Passengers emptied into the large terminal.

8. Flight attendants helped children and senior citizens.

9. Signs written in many languages helped passengers find their way.

10. Luggage was picked up from the baggage carousel.

PRACTICE 2   Identifying Subjects

Underline the subject in each of the following sentences.

1. Frank Lloyd Wright wanted to study architecture at the University of Wisconsin.

2. It did not offer architecture courses.

3. Civil engineering became his major area of study.

4. The Adler and Sullivan Company hired him as a designer.

5. "Organic architecture" was a style he created.

6. This philosophy held that a building should develop out of its natural surroundings.

7. He created many wonderful buildings using this idea.

8. The carport was one of his inventions.

9. Air conditioning was first used in a Frank Lloyd Wright building.

10. Frank Lloyd Wright became a pioneer in modern architecture.

PRACTICE 3   Identifying Subjects

Underline the subject(s) in each of the following sentences.

1. The Yukon Territory is located in northwestern Canada.

2. The vast area (186,300 sq mi) is bordered by Alaska and British Columbia.

3. Its mineral wealth and scenic vistas are two of its main attractions.

4. The name Yukon is taken from an Indian expression meaning "great river."

5. High plateaus occupy most of the south and central portions of the territory.

6. The St. Elias Mountains separate the Yukon from the Pacific Ocean.

7. Forests cover about 40 percent of the total land area.

8. White spruce is the most common species of tree.

9. A subarctic climate prevails with severe winters and hot summers.

10. The annual precipitation ranges from nine to thirteen inches.

PRACTICE 4   Supplying Subjects

Supply a person, place, thing, or pronoun for the subject in the following sentences.

1. _____ called to his friend Oscar to see if he wanted to go for a

   walk.

2. The _____ sped down the road at breakneck speed.

3. _____ enjoyed going to the movies every Saturday.

4. Three _____ landed on the deck of the aircraft carrier.

5. _____ sparkled in the clear, evening sky.

6. The thick, wool _____ kept the camper warm while she slept.

7. Many _____ visit the Grand Canyon every year.

8. _____ read many books every summer.

9. _____ listened to rock, jazz, and classical music.

10. _____ is a popular Italian pasta dish.

PRACTICE 5   Writing Sentences

Write a sentence using the subject provided.

1. Tornado— _____

   _____

2. Cab driver— _____

   _____

3. Actors— _____

   _____

4. Apartment— _____

   _____

5. Detective— _____

   _____

6. Table— _____

   _____

7. Grapefruit— _____

_____

8. Motorcycle— _____

_____

9. Movie— _____

_____

10. DVD player— _____

_____

(ESL) Subjects and Prepositional Phrases

There is an old saying in writing: All subjects are nouns, but not all nouns are subjects. When looking for subjects, you might be confused by the noun in a prepositional phrase.

A **prepositional phrase** is a group of words containing a preposition, such as *in, of, on,* or *to,* and a noun as its object.

Preposition	+	Object	=	Prepositional Phrase
in	+	a minute	=	in a minute
of	+	the nation	=	of the nation
on	+	the roof	=	on the roof
to	+	the moon	=	to the moon

Many sentences contain prepositional phrases at or near the beginning where the subject noun is located. It is sometimes confusing to figure out which of the two nouns is the subject. The object noun of a preposition is never the subject.

> In the morning, coffee is my favorite beverage.
>   ↑   ↑
>   noun   noun

Two nouns side by side in front of the verb can be confusing. One method of identifying the subject noun is to cross out the prepositional phrase (and the noun in it); the noun that remains is the subject.

> ~~In the morning~~, coffee is my favorite beverage.

Once "in the morning" is crossed out, the noun *coffee* is easily identified as the subject.

Learn to recognize prepositions so that you can eliminate their object nouns as possible subjects.

Here is a list of commonly used prepositions you should become familiar with:

Commonly Used Prepositions

about	beside	off
above	between	on
across	by _concerning_	over
after	during	through
against	except	to
along	for	toward
among	from	under
around	in	until
at	into	up
before	like	with
behind	of	without

For a complete list of prepositions, see The Writer's Resources, page 352.

PRACTICE 6   Identifying Subjects and Prepositional Phrases

In each of the following sentences, cross out the prepositional phrases. Then underline the subjects.

Example: At the zoo, most animals are still kept in cages.

1. In the wind, kites are unpredictable.

2. The carton of oranges floated in the water.

3. Bill was safe in the space under the bridge.

4. Between the two hills, the houses are made from cedar logs.

5. The microwave on the counter in the kitchen was very clean.

6. During the week and on the weekend, homework is a constant activity.

7. Except on casual day, the workers always wore suits to the office.

8. Over the river and through the woods, the wolf raced to Grandmother's house.

9. The couple arrived at the wedding reception without a gift.

10. Three of the guitarists are alternative musicians.

PRACTICE 7   Identifying Subjects and Prepositional Phrases

In each of the following sentences, cross out the prepositional phrases. Then underline the subjects.

1. In a presidential election, the challenger has to choose a running mate.

2. Until the process ends, the party's campaigning cannot start.

3. At the beginning of the process, many candidates are considered.

4. Before the interviews, the candidates' party credentials are inspected.

5. After the elimination of some candidates, a short list is assembled.

6. From the short list, interviews are scheduled.

7. Without the interview process, the final choice cannot be made.

8. During the interview, the candidate must clarify specific positions.

9. By the end of the process, the challenger can make a clear choice for the party.

10. Behind each political partnership, a lot of work has to be done.

PRACTICE 8   Identifying Subjects and Prepositional Phrases

In each of the following sentences, cross out the prepositional phrases. Then underline the subjects.

1. In the plane, the tour passengers slept lightly.

2. The rocking motion of the plane was somewhat disturbing.

3. Many of the passengers slept with a pillow under their heads.

4. Outside the cabin, the stars shone like small fireflies in the dark.

5. There was a hushed silence inside the cabin.

6. In most cases, smaller children slept on their parents' laps.

7. The people with older children were free to roll over on their sides if they wanted to.

8. After the flight landed, the passengers walked to the baggage carousel.

9. On the waiting ramp, the passengers were required to show tickets to the skycaps.

10. During the trip to the hotel, their bags were carried on the top of the bus.

ESL **The Verb**

As a developing writer, you should become familiar with three types of verbs: *action verbs, linking verbs,* and *helping verbs.*

Action Verbs

Action verbs describe an activity the subject is performing:

Commonly Used Action Verbs		
arrive	soar	eat
study	run	smile
speak	construct	race
climb	called	leave

Examples

The mail carrier *arrives* with a package.
The dog *races* the squirrel to the tree.
The eagle *soars* high above the cliffs.
The defense lawyer *speaks* with a Southern drawl.

PRACTICE 9   **Identifying Action Verbs**

Underline the action verb in each of the following sentences. To help you find the action verb, circle the subject. Cross out any prepositional phrases.

Example: On average, (Tiger Woods) hits a golf ball over 290 yards off the tee.

1. As a young child, he learned the proper mechanics of the swing.

2. His father guided his golf instruction.

3. The youngster progressed rapidly as a golfer.

4. He garnered three Junior Amateur championships in a row.

5. Without hesitation, Woods won three straight Amateur championships.

6. On the professional tour, Tiger arrived at the Masters tournament as a tour rookie.

7. He regularly launched 300-yard drives on the longer holes.

8. His length off the tee catapulted him to victory again.

Tiger Woods

9. Tigers stunned the golfing world with his outstanding and exciting play.

10. Woods earned over a million dollars his first full year on the professional tour.

PRACTICE 10   Identifying Action Verbs

Underline the action verb in each of the following sentences. To help you find the action verb, circle the subject. Cross out any prepositional phrases.

1. A letter arrived at Marjorie's apartment.

2. She opened the letter on the kitchen table.

3. A handwritten note fell from the envelope.

4. She unfolded the piece of paper.

5. For no apparent reason, She read the message aloud.

6. Tears of happiness flowed from her eyes.

7. A major airline had selected her name from a list of contest entrants.

8. After calming down, Marjorie called her mother and father on the phone.

9. She told them the happy news.

10. She had won round-trip tickets for four to London.

PRACTICE 11 Identifying Action Verbs

Underline the action verb in each of the following sentences. To help you find the action verb, circle the subject. Cross out any prepositional phrases.

1. Most people participate in outdoor activities.

2. One person scuba dives in the Caribbean.

3. Another skis in the mountains of Colorado.

4. People on both Florida coasts fish for trophy marlin and swordfish.

5. A group from Vermont searches for rare birds in the deep forests.

6. "Spelunkers" crawl through narrow caves.

7. Missourians ride bikes on the scenic Katy Trail.

8. Individuals connected with ropes climb the faces of steep cliffs.

9. Others leap from bridges with bungee cords attached to their ankles.

10. Small groups in military garb play paintball in the woods.

PRACTICE 12 Writing Sentences

Write a sentence using the action verb provided.

1. Starts— _____

_____

2. Jumps— _____

_____

3. Study— _____

_____

4. Bake— _____

_____

5. Swerves— _____

_____

6. Builds— _____

_____

7. Travels— _____

_____

8. Speaks— _____

_____

9. Looks— _____

_____

10. Crashes— _____

_____

Linking Verbs

Linking verbs indicate a condition or state of being. The linking verb connects the subject with a word or phrase identifying or describing something about the subject:

Commonly Used Linking Verbs		
act	feel	look
appear	grow	seem
be (am, is, are, was, were, have been)	become	taste

Examples

Dr. Smith _is_ a surgeon.
The wool sweater _feels_ rough.
The desert sand _becomes_ cool in the evening.
Aretha _appears_ tired and sluggish.

PRACTICE 13   Identifying Linking Verbs

There is a linking verb in each of the following sentences. To help identify the linking verb, circle the subject, and draw a line to the word or words that describe the subject. Then circle that word or group of words. Finally, underline the linking verb between the two circles.

Examples: The building is a skyscraper.

The player seems nervous.

Nurses are intelligent and caring.

1. The concert was very exciting.

2. The foyer looked buffed and polished from floor to ceiling.

3. The hall felt cold and stuffy.

4. People in the audience seemed nervous.

5. Members of the orchestra were relaxed.

6. The symphony orchestra sounded confident and well-rehearsed.

7. The cookies served during intermission smelled heavenly.

8. The music remained controlled throughout the evening.

9. The conductor appeared pleased with the orchestra members' effort.

10. At the concert's end, the applause became louder with each bow.

PRACTICE 14   Identifying Linking Verbs

There is a linking verb in each of the following sentences. To help identify the linking verb, circle the subject, and draw a line to the word or words describing the subject. Then circle that word or group of words. Finally, underline the linking verb between the two circles.

1. My life was not wonderful.

2. I appeared surly and cantankerous to my friends.

3. My family said I looked depressed.

4. My job became boring and uninteresting.

5. Even food smelled dull and tasteless.

6. I had become lazy and indifferent.

7. I felt disassociated from my true self.

8. These unproductive states of mind were not acceptable.

9. I turned to a counselor for help.

10. After many months, the therapy seems to be helping.

PRACTICE 15   Writing Sentences

Write a sentence using the linking verb provided.

1. Was— _____

_____

2. Seem— _____

_____

3. Is— _____

_____

4. Feel— _____

_____

5. Become— _____

_____

6. Am— _____

_____

7. Appear— _____

_____

8. Were— _____

_____

9. Have been— _____

_____

10. Are— _____

_____

Helping Verbs

Helping verbs combine with a main verb to form a group of words called a *verb phrase*. The helping verb gives the main verb a specific time reference or meaning.

Commonly Used Helping Verbs

can	could	may
might	must	shall
should	will	woul

forms of the irregular verbs *be*, *do*, and *have*

For a list of irregular verbs, see The Writer's Resources, pages 328–333.

Examples

The manager *can* fire employees if they break regulations.
Keeping a diary *might* help you better understand yourself.
Studying *will* enhance your grade point average.
A positive attitude *should* make your day more enjoyable.

PRACTICE 16   Identifying Helping Verbs and Verb Phrases

There is a helping verb and a main verb in each of the following sentences. To help identify the helping verb, circle the subject. Then cross out any prepositional phrases. Finally, underline the entire verb phrase.

Example: Studies ~~of all ages~~ indicate that (exercising) can help overall mental and physical health ~~for most people~~.

1. People of all ages should exercise.

2. However, exercising must be done on a regular basis.

3. Working out three times a week can create a more healthy person.

4. On the other hand, exercising too much may be detrimental to your health.

5. An effective workout must include exercises for both muscles and the cardiovascular system.

6. Lifting weights should be accompanied by an aerobic exercise.

7. Some experts think walking might be as beneficial as jogging.

8. Mental health also will be stimulated by physical exercise.

9. Good mental health could facilitate success in other areas of your life.

10. Regular exercising would lower health-related costs nationally.

PRACTICE 17   Identifying Helping Verbs and Verb Phrases

There is a helping verb and a main verb in each of the following sentences. To help identify the helping verb, circle the subject. Then cross out any prepositional phrases. Finally, underline the entire verb phrase.

1. How do you start a hobby?

2. First, you can buy a hobby magazine and learn the varieties of hobbies available.

3. Then, you should ask your friends and neighbors what hobbies they have.

4. You will need to figure out how much time and money you have to invest in the hobby.

5. Budgeting may help you narrow your choices.

6. Of course, you must ask for advice at a hobby shop near you.

7. This could put you in touch with other enthusiasts interested in the same hobby as you.

8. A hobby club will be an invaluable resource for furthering your enjoyment.

9. Being a member of a club also might get you discounts on materials and publications.

10. Also, other members would assist you with difficult aspects of your hobby.

PRACTICE 18   Writing Sentences

Write a sentence using the helping verb provided. You also will have to choose a main verb to combine with the helping verb as you create each sentence.

Examples: Can—I can *ride* a unicycle for five minutes before losing my balance.

                  ↑ ↑
          helping main
           verb   verb

1. Could— _____

_____

2. May— _____

_____

3. Can— _____

_____

4. Might— _____

_____

5. Must— _____

_____

⬭ESL⬭ Verb Tense (Time)

In writing, time is called *tense*. Because tense is shown primarily through the *verb*, time is more accurately called **verb tense.** It is important to know whether an action or linking verb is in the past, present, or future tense. After all, you would certainly react differently if something had already happened, was happening at present, or was not going to happen until later. This section deals with the simplest forms of past, present, and future verb tense in regard to the action and linking verbs we have already studied.

For additional information regarding verb tense, see The Writer's Resources, page 327.

Examples of Simple Past, Present, and Future Verb Tense	
Past	I <u>talked</u> yesterday.
	I <u>worked</u> last Saturday.
	He <u>talked</u> for two hours.
	He <u>worked</u> last summer.
Present	I <u>talk</u> now.
	I <u>work</u> all the time.
	She <u>talks</u> in her sleep.
	She <u>works</u> at Benny's.
Future	I <u>will talk</u> later.
	I <u>will work</u> tomorrow.
	They <u>will talk</u> next Monday.
	They <u>will work</u> after dinner.

For a complete list of tenses, see The Writer's Resources, Grammar, Verbs (pages 326-332).

Examples

Past Tense Linking Verb: Juan *was* a student at USC last year.

Present Tense Linking Verb: Juan *is* a student at USC this year.

Future Tense Linking Verb: Juan *will be* a student at USC next year.

Past Tense Action Verb: Amy *skated* yesterday.

Present Tense Action Verb: Amy *skates* today.

Future Tense Action Verb: Amy *will skate* tomorrow.

PRACTICE 19   Using Verb Tenses

Complete the following sentences by filling in the blank spaces with the past tense form, the present tense form, and the future tense form of the verb provided.

1. Verb: practice

Past Tense: The girls' soccer team _____ for the tournament.

Present Tense: The girls' soccer team _____ for the tournament.

Future Tense: The girls' soccer team _____ for the tournament.

2. Verb: dance

Past Tense: The ballerina _____ *Swan Lake* for the first time.

Present Tense: The ballerina _____ *Swan Lake* for the first time.

Future Tense: The ballerina _____ *Swan Lake* for the first time.

3. Verb: cook

Past Tense: I _____ seafood gumbo for my guests.

Present Tense: I _____ seafood gumbo for my guests.

Future Tense: I _____ seafood gumbo for my guests.

4. Verb: play

Past Tense: Jasmine _____ the guitar for her boyfriend.

Present Tense: Jasmine _____ the guitar for her boyfriend.

Future Tense: Jasmine _____ the guitar for her boyfriend.

5. Verb: clean

Past Tense: Melvin _____ his school locker.

Present Tense: Melvin _____ his school locker.

Future Tense: Melvin _____ his school locker.

PRACTICE 20   Using Verb Tenses

Complete the following sentences by filling in the blank spaces with the past tense form, the present tense form, and the future tense form of the verb provided.

1. Verb: corner

   Past Tense: The dog _____ the cat in the alley.

   Present Tense: The dog _____ the cat in the alley.

   Future Tense: The dog _____ the cat in the alley.

2. Verb: assume

   Past Tense: The professor _____ the students had read the chapter.

   Present Tense: The professor _____ the students had read the chapter.

   Future Tense: The professor _____ the students had read the chapter.

3. Verb: consume

   Past Tense: The crocodile _____ a large portion of meat for its daily meal.

   Present Tense: The crocodile _____ a large portion of meat for its daily meal.

   Future Tense: The crocodile _____ a large portion of meat for its daily meal.

4. Verb: type

   Past Tense: The secretary _____ a letter for the vice president.

   Present Tense: The secretary _____ a letter for the vice president.

   Future Tense: The secretary _____ a letter for the vice president.

5. Verb: camp

   Past Tense: The scientist _____ deep in the Amazon rain forest.

   Present Tense: The scientist _____ deep in the Amazon rain forest.

   Future Tense: The scientist _____ deep in the Amazon rain forest.

PRACTICE 21   Using Verb Tenses

Complete the following sentences by filling in the blank spaces with the past tense form, the present tense form, and the future tense form of the verb provided.

1. Verb: trust

Past Tense: The employees _____ their boss.

Present Tense: The employees _____ their boss.

Future Tense: The employees _____ their boss.

2. Verb: coordinate

Past Tense: The manager _____ all cleaning responsibilities.

Present Tense: The manager _____ all cleaning responsibilities.

Future Tense: The manager _____ all cleaning responsibilities.

3. Verb: exercise

Past Tense: Felicia _____ every morning at 4 a.m.

Present Tense: Felicia _____ every morning at 4 a.m.

Future Tense: Felicia _____ every morning at 4 a.m.

4. Verb: juggle

Past Tense: The executive _____ a long list of activities.

Present Tense: The executive _____ a long list of activities.

Future Tense: The executive _____ a long list of activities.

5. Verb: jump

Past Tense: The kangaroo _____ over the fence guarding the field.

Present Tense: The kangaroo _____ over the fence guarding the field.

Future Tense: The kangaroo _____ over the fence guarding the field.

■ **PRACTICE 22**   **Using Verb Tenses**

Supply a present, past, or future tense verb in the space provided in each of the following sentences. In the parentheses, identify the tense for the verb you wrote.

Example: The eagle <u>glides (present tense)</u> over the river searching for salmon.

1. The girls _____ (_____) on the freshly mowed lawn.

2. The space shuttle _____ (_____) into the sky over Florida.

3. The college student_____ (_____) for the History 101 final exam.

4. The cyclist _____ (_____) toward the finish line.

5. The kittens _____ (_____) together in the warmth of the sunbeam.

6. All one hundred senators _____ (_____) the health care legislation.

7. Jennifer _____ (_____) the customer choose the correct pair of glasses.

8. The judge _____ (_____) the gavel on her desk to restore order.

9. José _____ (_____) three dozen fajitas for the party.

10. The choir _____ (_____) the gospel song with feeling and emotion.

PRACTICE 23   Using Verb Tenses

Supply a present, past, or future tense verb in the space provided in each of the following sentences. In the parentheses, identify the tense for the verb you wrote.

1. The skater _____ (_____) on the frozen pond.

2. Kitaro _____ (_____) the chemistry exam.

3. Tina _____ (_____) lifting weights during gym class.

4. The bird _____ (_____) its feathers after a dip in the bird bath.

5. The engine _____ (_____) as the dragster reached the start line.

6. The senator _____ (_____) at the fundraiser banquet.

7. Icebergs _____ (_____) as they float aimlessly in the ocean.

8. The grasshopper _____ (_____) in the field of golden corn.

9. The severe storms _____ (_____) across the Midwest.

10. Donny _____ (_____) while riding the roller coaster.

Compound Subjects

To this point, we have been using single subjects and single verbs. However, compound subjects and compound verbs also can be used in simple sentences. First, we explore compound subjects. A **compound subject** consists of two or more nouns or pronouns connected by *and, or, either/or,* or *neither/ nor.* Some special relationships exist between certain compound subjects and their verb complements. For a discussion with exercises, see The Writer's Resources, pages 342–345.

> **Examples**
>
> *Bill and Raul* drove to the cineplex.
> *Either you or I* will have to pick Melanie up at the train station.
> *Neither Venice nor Rome* is ignored by tourists.

Compound subjects can be separated by other words, but they are still considered one subject as long as they are doing the same action or being the same thing.

> **Examples**
>
> *Charles* the dentist, *Clyde* the doctor, and *Phylis* the chiropractor met for dinner.
> In this sentence, Charles, Clyde, and Phylis are having dinner together.
> Large, powerful *St. Bernards*, sleek, fast *Russian greyhounds*, and small, aggressive *English terriers* are popular pets around the world.
> In this sentence, the various types of dogs share a common experience.

PRACTICE 24   Identifying Compound Subjects

Underline the compound subjects in the following sentences. To help you identify the subjects, cross out any prepositional phrases you find, and circle the verb.

1. The child's ears and nose looked just like its mother's.

2. Neither my golf coach nor my swimming coach was ever a professional.

3. Jupiter, Mars, and Venus are planets in our solar system.

4. After the dance, Joan and Jillian drove to a private party.

5. The antique sofa, the art deco clock, and the abstract painting were sold at auction.

6. At Chicago's Navy Pier, Fred and Dianna bought three sweaters and a necklace.

7. The slithery snake, the prickly hedgehog, and the colorful parrot are the most popular animals at the children's zoo.

8. In the middle of the room, the food, the drinks, and the cake covered the table.

9. *Hamlet* and *Macbeth* are are two of Shakespeare's most famous plays.

10. Either the cat or dog knocked the lamp and vase onto the floor.

PRACTICE 25   Identifying Compound Subjects

Underline the compound subjects in the following sentences. To help you identify the subjects, cross out any prepositional phrases you find, and circle the verb.

1. For their new business venture, Jamal and Nerita purchased two computers.

2. Brad Pitt, George Clooney, and Julia Roberts are popular movie stars.

3. At the auto show, neither Mick, Tina, nor Jacki bought a car.

4. The lawn mower, the edger, and the cultivator sat unused in the garage.

5. His and Hers are popular monograms on bath towels.

6. Either you or I will have to make dinner for the Cub Scouts.

7. Chrysler, General Motors, and Ford are known as the "Big Three" auto makers.

8. In the middle of the night, snoring, cat calls, and crying infants can reduce sleep.

9. The yellow finch, the aptly named red-breasted grosbeak, and the red-winged blackbird are favorite subjects for bird watching clubs.

10. Nike, Adidas, and Reebok are best-selling athletic shoes.

Compound Verbs

Like subjects, verbs also can be compound. A **compound verb** consists of more than one verb. With few exceptions, compound verbs are almost always connected by the conjunction *and*.

> **Examples**
> Janet *laughed and cried* during the movie.
> The horse *ran and jumped* as part of the rodeo contest.
> Paris *dazzles and excites* visiting tourists.

In the sentences above, notice that the subject is not repeated in front of the second verb. We do not write: *Paris dazzles* and *Paris excites* visiting tourists. Writing *Paris* twice is unnecessarily repetitive, and it makes the rhythm of the sentence choppy and awkward.

PRACTICE 26   Identifying Compound Verbs

Underline the compound verbs in the following sentences.

1. The horse trotted and galloped around the track.

2. The mechanic tuned the engine and lubricated the chassis of the car.

3. The audience laughed and cried at the actor's performance.

4. The broker bought and sold the investor's energy stocks.

5. The motel room was clean and smelled of lilacs and roses.

6. A fax machine can save money and hasten communications.

7. In New York City, skateboarders ride on subways and skate in parking garages.

8. Ramon caught and cleaned a bucketful of fish.

9. The legislature argued and voted on fifty-three bills this current session.

10. The police chased and arrested the bank robber.

PRACTICE 27   Identifying Compound Verbs

Underline the compound verbs in the following sentences.

1. Lightning cracked and popped in the darkened sky.

2. In the auditorium, students clapped their hands and stomped their feet.

3. The two elk rivals snorted and brandished their antlers at one another.

4. The old fire engine jiggled and rattled down the cobblestone street.

5. A distant waterfall roared and thundered across the plain.

6. After the huge meal, the diners moaned and groaned.

7. The truck skidded, jackknifed, and crashed into the barrier.

8. Seabirds fly, dive, swim, and float while searching for food.

9. The bull lowered its head, scraped its hooves, and charged the matador.

10. The dancers twirled and leaped in time with the music.

PRACTICE 28   **Writing Sentences with Compound Subjects and Verbs**

Write sentences for the following compound subjects and verbs. Provide compound subjects for the compound verbs listed and compound verbs for the compound subjects when given.

Examples: Bill/Ted—Bill and Ted <u>laughed and cried</u> during the movie.

dribbled/shot—<u>Jill and Teiko</u> dribbled and shot during the game.

1. flight attendant/passenger— _____

_____

2. swam/lifted weights— _____

_____

3. truck/car— _____

_____

4. shivered/trembled— _____

_____

5. Ira/Sheila— _____

_____

6. camped/hiked— _____

_____

7. flower/tree— _____

_____

8. ate/drank— _____

_____

9. teacher/student— _____

_____

10. stumbled/fell— _____

_____

Correcting Sentence Fragments

A simple sentence consists of a single **independent clause.** An independent clause is a series of words with a subject, verb, and complete meaning. This means that the independent clause can stand on its own as a simple sentence. When you are writing sentences, be certain that each independent clause has a subject, a verb, and complete meaning. If the subject, verb, or complete meaning is missing from the independent clause, then a sentence fragment error has occurred.

> **Examples of Sentence Fragments**
>
> **1.** Kicked the football. (no subject—who or what kicked the football?)
>
> To correct, add a subject:
> The football player kicked the football.
>
> **2.** The chef the fettuccine Alfredo. (no verb—what did the chef do in relation to the fettuccine Alfredo?)
>
> To correct, add a verb:
> The chef prepared the fettuccine Alfredo.
>
> **3.** The announcement of the new dress code caused all the employees. (insufficient meaning—what did the dress code cause the employees to do?)
>
> To correct, add additional information to create complete meaning:
> The announcement of the new dress code caused all the employees to buy uniforms.

PRACTICE 29   Correcting Sentence Fragments

Correct and rewrite the following sentence fragments using the three techniques listed above.

1. Marathon runners, training for the Olympics, as many as one hundred miles every week.

_____

2. Build nests and lay eggs.

_____

3. It was time for the archaeologists.

_____

4. Cooks in a short amount of time.

_____

5. The man wearing the red vest.

_____

6. The gigantic iceberg a hole in *Titanic*'s hull.

_____

7. George a computer at a discount store to save money.

_____

8. Can earn money by investing in mutual funds.

_____

9. Broken racket strings was the reason for her.

_____

10. Spilled the platter of ravioli on her Aunt Vidalia's new dress.

_____

PRACTICE 30   Correcting Sentence Fragments

Correct and rewrite the following sentence fragments using the three techniques listed on page 36.

1. Ate the delicious apple strudel for dessert.

_____

2. Ramon fourteen hours a day to save enough tuition money for school.

_____

3. The rugby team rode a bus for fourteen hours in order.

_____

4. A chipped tooth caused the movie star to.

_____

5. The wine steward the list of the restaurant's entire stock.

_____

6. Measured the foundation before pouring the concrete.

_____

7. The entered the dark cave looking for a place to sleep.

_____

8. The baker sifted the flour before.

_____

9. The security guard to the third floor to make certain the doors were locked.

_____

10. The cleaned all the desks, mopped the floors, and emptied the waste-baskets.

_____

PRACTICE 31　　Correcting Sentence Fragments

Correct and rewrite the following sentence fragments using the three techniques listed above.

1. The mechanic and his assistant as many as fifty cars every week.

_____

2. Leap out of the lake to catch bugs.

_____

3. The basketball team need to.

_____

4. The woman walking down the aisle.

_____

5. Melts in only a few minutes if left out at room temperature.

_____

6. The fire the entire forest.

_____

7. Can make better grades by studying every night.

_____

8. A week voice was the reason she didn't.

_____

9. Spilled the stack of CDs all over the desk.

_____

10. Joanne a coffee maker at the discount store.

_____

PRACTICE 32   Correcting Sentence Fragments

Correct and rewrite the following sentence fragments using the three techniques listed above.

1. The doctor and the nurse the patient.

_____

2. Run one hundred yards in less than ten seconds.

_____

3. The engineer designed the plans in order to.

_____

4. After the rain stopped.

_____

5. The cab driver the couple off at the nightclub.

_____

6. Used the computer to surf the Net.

_____

7. The dog the cat up a tree.

_____

8. Was disappointed that she wasn't accepted into art school.

_____

9. The record crowd stayed until.

_____

10. The police the suspect's.

_____

PRACTICE 33   **Editing Proper and Common Nouns and Pronoun References**

In the following paragraph, underline once all proper nouns that are not capitalized, and underline twice all common nouns that are capitalized. Then correct any capitalization errors that you have marked. Next, draw a line through all pronouns that do not clearly refer to a specific noun or nouns. If the reference is not clear, make the necessary changes. Finally, write your correctly edited paragraph on the lines provided.

Mike could have been a better Student. He was a senior at martin luther king High School and planned to go to college after Graduation. His work wasn't always done on time, and sometimes he forgot it altogether. Mike didn't always study, and he partied too much. It was the reason for his poor grades. Mike always seemed to know where and when good parties were going to happen. He always brought popular goodies to the parties, so he was always welcome. His favorite party snacks were hostess ding dongs and wild turkey bourbon. It was a big hit. One weekend, Mike was killed when the ford mustang Mike was driving smashed into a dodge caravan. His blood-alcohol level was above the Legal Amount, and he had been driving over the speed limit. The police said it was the reason for the crash. Mike had become a victim of his own drunk driving.

_____

_____

_____

_____

_____

_____

_____

_____

_____

_____

_____

_____

_____

_____

PRACTICE 34   Editing Subjects and Prepositional Phrases

Nouns in prepositional phrases are often mistaken for the subject of the sentence. In the following paragraph, draw a line through the prepositional phrases, and underline the subject nouns. Punctuate the sentences correctly, and rewrite the paragraph on the lines provided.

During a tornado wind and lightning cause most destruction. In high winds buildings can be destroyed. As it passes a tornado causes a sudden drop in air pressure on the outside of the building. Inside the building air cannot escape fast enough to equalize the pressure on the walls and roof. Before the high winds tornadoes also create lightning. Along with the wind lightning can cause additional death and destruction. In a storm lightning can strike buildings, trees, and power lines. Without electricity, fires can rage out of control.

_____

_____

_____

_____

_____

_____

_____

| PRACTICE 35 | Editing Sentence Fragments |

In the following paragraph, identify and underline sentence fragments. Then correct the sentence fragments and rewrite the paragraph on the lines provided.

Young children have difficulty adjusting to new environments. Moving to a different community. And living in a new house. Lead to more uncertainty. Unfamiliar bedrooms and neighbors. Often cause crying and real and imagined illness. Going to a new school also can be stressful. Because of the pressure of new friends and fitting in. Meeting new friends and being accepted by them can be a challenge. Comparing new friends to old friends can definitely. A reason for feeling abandoned and alone. However, taking part in activities with new acquaintances can help relieve stress and the uncertainty of new experiences.

_____

_____

_____

_____

_____

_____

_____

_____

 Visit *The Write Start* Online!

For additional practice with the materials in this chapter, go to

http://www.cengage.com/devenglish/checkett/writestartSP4e.

Chapter Self-Assessment Test

Check either True or False on the blank next to the statement.

T   F

____ ____   A simple sentence must contain both a subject and a verb.

____ ____   The subject of a sentence can be a noun but never a pronoun.

____ ____   Nouns can be replaced by pronouns to avoid repetition.

____ ____   Subject nouns are often confused with nouns in prepositional phrases.

____ ____   Crossing out prepositional phrases can help find subject nouns.

____ ____   There are three types of verbs: action, linking, and helping.

____ ____   Action verbs connect the subject with an idea that describes the subject.

____ ____   Helping verbs describe what the subject is doing.

____ ____   Helping verbs combine with the main verb to form a *verb phrase*.

____ ____   Helping verbs give the main verb a specific time reference, called *tense*.

____ ____   Subjects can be compound, consisting of more than one noun.

____ ____   Verbs can never be compound.

____ ____   The three simplest forms of verb tense are *never*, *soon*, and *sometimes*.

____ ____   Sentence fragments occur when the subject, verb, or sufficient meaning are missing from the sentence.

3

Linking Independent Clauses Using the Comma and Coordinators

ESL Coordinating Conjunctions

Simple sentences are the basis for most writing; however, writing with only simple sentences can lead to dull writing, and complex ideas often need a more complex sentence format for developed expression. For the sake of variety and more complex ideas, a writer connects one simple sentence to another simple sentence by **using a comma (,)** and one of the following **coordinating conjunctions: B**ut, **O**r, **Y**et, **F**or, **A**nd, **N**or, **S**o. We remember the coordinating conjunctions by **BOYFANS** (taken from the first letter of each word). The BOYFANS conjunctions link simple sentences together to create *compound sentences.* Therefore, a **compound sentence** consists of two simple sentences (two independent clauses) linked together with a coordinating conjunction and a comma. We will learn about forming compound sentences using the BOYFANS conjunctions in this chapter. (There are other methods of forming compound sentences: using a semicolon, and using a semicolon and adverbial conjunction. These will be discussed in Chapters 4 and 5.)

The list below explains the meaning of each of the coordinating conjunctions in BOYFANS. They are not interchangeable. Note that the comma is placed before each coordinating conjunction to signal the start of the second complete sentence.

Using Coordinating Conjunctions

But—Use to connect two simple sentences that have contrasting meanings:

Jawan hit the ball, **but** *Christie caught the ball.*

Or—Use to combine two simple sentences that involve a choice:

Christie could have thrown the ball to Jose, **or** *she could have thrown it to home plate.*

Yet—Use to combine two simple sentences that have contrasting meanings:

Jawan hit the ball, **yet** *Christie caught the ball.*

For—Use to combine two simple sentences that involve a reason:

Malik tried to score from second base, **for** *there were already two outs.*

And—Use to combine two simple sentences that involve adding one idea to another:

Jason hit the ball, **and** *Latoya caught the ball.*

Nor—Use when the first simple sentence is in the negative and you want to combine it with another simple sentence:

Mark does not like striking out, **nor** *does Hakeem like sliding into a base.*

So—Use to combine two simple sentences that show a result:

Isabel scored a run, **so** *her team won the game.*

Instead of expressing ideas using all simple sentences, like this:

Jawan hit the ball. Christie caught the ball. Christie could throw the ball to first base. She could throw the ball to third. Pang ran quickly to third base. Chinua tagged him out.

We can add variety and connect ideas, like this:

Jawan hit the ball, **but** Christie caught the ball. Christie could throw the ball to first base, **or** she could throw the ball to third. Pang ran quickly to third base, **yet** Chinua tagged him out.

Notice that the coordinating conjunctions not only combine the shorter sentences into longer, more rhythmical ones, but they also help connect two different ideas, making them easier for the reader to understand.

PRACTICE 1   **Using Coordinating Conjunctions**

Practice *coordinating* using *conjunctions*. Combine the following pairs of simple sentences by using a comma and the BOYFANS in the parentheses ( ).

1. (but) Jawan hit the ball. Christie caught the ball.

_____

2. (or) Christie could throw the ball to first base. She could throw the ball to third.

_____

_____

3. (yet) Pang ran quickly to third base. Chinua tagged him out.

_____

4. (for) Jefferson struck out three times. The pitcher threw a wicked curve-ball.

_____

5. (and) Tom singled four times. Angie hit two home runs.

_____

6. (nor) Yoshi did not have a base on balls. Sarita did not bunt during the game.

_____

7. (so) Joe caused three errors. The other team scored five runs.

_____

PRACTICE 2   **Using Coordinating Conjunctions**

Combine some more simple sentences, but this time you choose which BOYFANS you think works the best. Try not to use the same coordinating conjunction twice. Choose from the list:

But **O**r **Y**et **F**or **A**nd **N**or **S**o

Examples: Mel wanted to go hiking. Shonda wanted to read a book.

Mel wanted to go hiking, <u>but</u> Shonda wanted to read a book.

1. Some friends wanted to go to the park. _____ Others wanted to go to the zoo.

2. Bicycling is good exercise. _____ Try to ride at least three times each week.

3. Salads are not only great tasting. _____ They are also healthy.

4. Morning is the best time to exercise. _____ There is less heat and humidity.

5. Genetics does not guarantee good health. _____ Eating only fruit is not the solution.

6. Fish is very tasty. _____ Too much sauce can mask its taste.

7. Broccoli is a tasty and nutritious choice. _____ Asparagus also is a good choice.

PRACTICE 3   Using Coordinating Conjunctions

Try some more. Choose a different BOYFANS for each sentence, and remember to place a comma before each coordinating conjunction.

Examples: Flowers are very beautiful. Buying them can be expensive.

Flowers are very beautiful, <u>but</u> buying them can be expensive.

1. Jets travel to Chicago. Trains travel there, as well.

   _____

2. Reading a book can be exciting. Listening to music can be soothing.

   _____

3. Good grades are important. Study hard and do all homework.

   _____

4. The car did not get good gas mileage. It did not ride smoothly either.

   _____

5. John did not like the restaurant. He continued eating there.

   _____

6. Jenny enjoyed hiking. The woods were both beautiful and quiet.

   _____

7. Snakes can make interesting pets. They can be dangerous.

   _____

PRACTICE 4   Combining Simple Sentences

Combine the following ten simple sentences. You can try different combinations in the spaces between the sentences. Write your finished effort on the blank lines provided below the sentences. You should finish with five combined sentences instead of ten single sentences.

The camping trip was exciting.

The trip to the national forest took thirteen hours.

Everyone was tired but happy when they arrived.

The tents were easy to set up.

They had running water and electricity.

Dave did not bring mosquito repellant.

Juan did not bring extra blankets.

Camping in the woods

Everyone was hungry.

Pilar went to gather firewood.

The full moon emerged from the clouds later that evening.

Write your finished combined sentences below:

1. _____

2. _____

3. _____

4. _____

5. _____

PRACTICE 5   Combining Simple Sentences

Combine the following ten simple sentences. You can try different combinations in the spaces between the sentences. Write your finished effort on the blank lines provided below the sentences. You should finish with five combined sentences instead of ten single sentences.

The game was exciting

The score was tied at halftime.

Both teams scored two goals during the second half.

The forwards seemed confused by the defense in the first half.

Both coaches substituted for forwards in the second half.

The weather was cold and rainy.

The star of the home team, Sheila Brown, scored in overtime.

The winning goal was a header near the far post.

The game was tied after regulation.

The crowd cheered throughout the entire game.

Write your finished sentences below.

1. _____

2. _____

3. _____

4. _____

5. _____

PRACTICE 6   Combining Simple Sentences

Combine the following ten simple sentences. You can try different combinations in the spaces between the sentences. Write your finished effort on the blank lines provided below the sentences. You should finish with five combined sentences instead of ten single sentences.

The paleontologists arrived in China during early summer.

They traveled to Mongolia for the best places to dig.

The team included three graduate students.

They struck camp late in the afternoon.

Their first meal consisted of canned Spam and nuts.

The first dinosaur was discovered on the second day.

A small bone was found sticking out of the ground.

The small bone was just the tip of a front claw.

It took eight days to uncover the full skeleton.

It turned out to be a *T-Rex*.

Write your finished sentences below.

1. _____

2. _____

3. _____

4. _____

5. _____

PRACTICE 7   Combining Simple Sentences

Try combining pairs of sentences with a variety of coordinating conjunctions. You can use the spaces between the sentences to try different BOYFANS. Write your finished sentences on the blank lines provided below the sentences. You should finish with seven combined sentences instead of fourteen single sentences.

Maurice loved to fish.

He went to the lake as often as possible.

His girlfriend Liz did not like to fish.

She did find riding in the boat fun.

They both liked camping.

It was restful sitting around the campfire.

Liz enjoyed cooking the fish.

She took responsibility for packing the cooking equipment.

Cleaning fish was not her favorite activity.

She did not like the taste.

Sometimes Liz would sit in the boat and read.

She would also apply lotion and try tanning in the afternoon sun.

The ride back home was long.

Both Maurice and Liz could not wait to return.

Write your finished combined sentences below:

1. _____

2. _____

3. _____

4. _____

5. _____

6. _____

7. _____

PRACTICE 8   Combining Simple Sentences

Try combining pairs of sentences with a variety of coordinating conjunctions. You can use the spaces between the sentences to try different BOYFANS. Write your finished sentences on the blank lines provided below the sentences. You should finish with seven combined sentences instead of fourteen single sentences.

Linda and Deirdre decided to go out for sports their sophomore year.

There were many sports to choose from.

It was a hard decision.

They did not like swimming.

They did not like soccer.

They liked volleyball.

They enjoyed basketball.

Many of their friends played all four.

Linda's favorite sport was volleyball.

Deirdre's favorite sport was basketball.

They compromised and went out for the track.

They were both fast runners.

They went to the sports store.

They both bought new track shoes.

Write your finished combined sentences below:

1. _____

2. _____

3. _____

4. _____

5. _____

6. _____

7. _____

PRACTICE 9   **Combining Simple Sentences**

Try combining pairs of sentences with a variety of coordinating conjunctions. You can use the spaces between the sentences to try different BOYFANS. Write your finished sentences on the blank lines provided below the sentences. You should finish with seven combined sentences instead of fourteen single sentences.

Carl has always wanted to be a chef.

He began by watching his grandmother cook.

His favorite type was spicy and hot.

Carl did not like bland food.

He did not like full food.

Salsa with red hot chili peppers was his favorite sauce.

He used plenty of habeñero peppers.

His girlfriend preferred making pastries.

They opened a restaurant.

Carl concentrated on the entrees.

Maria made all the desserts from scratch.

Their restaurant was a big hit.

They decided to open another.

They developed a chain of restaurants over the next ten years.

Write your finished sentences below.

1. _____

2. _____

3. _____

4. _____

5. _____

6. _____

7. _____

ESL Correcting Run-on and Comma Splice Sentences

Now that you have practiced combining simple sentences to create compound sentences, there are two pitfalls you should avoid: run-on sentences and comma splice sentences.

Run-on

A **run-on sentence** commonly occurs when two independent clauses (complete ideas) are combined without a comma and a coordinating conjunction.

> **Example**
> Joan rides the subway to work the bus is too slow.
> This sentence announces two complete ideas:
> *Joan rides the subway to work—the bus is too slow.*

Here are two methods to correct a run-on sentence:

1. Create two separate sentences.

> Joan rides the subway to work. The bus is too slow.

2. Use a comma and a coordinating conjunction (**b**ut, **o**r, **y**et, **f**or, **a**nd, **n**or, **s**o) to link the two ideas together to create a correctly punctuated compound sentence.

> Joan rides the subway to work, **for** the bus is too slow.

Comma Splice

A **comma splice** sentence occurs when two independent clauses are joined with a comma but without a coordinating conjunction.

> **Example**
>
> Brian plays the cello, David plays the piano.
>
> This sentence announces two complete ideas joined (or spliced together—hence the name *comma splice*) by only a comma.
>
> *Brian plays the cello, David plays the piano.*

Correct the comma splice by adding a coordinating conjunction after the comma to create a correctly punctuated compound sentence.

> Brian plays the cello, **and** David plays the piano.

PRACTICE 10   Correcting Run-on and Comma Splice Errors

Most of the following sentences contain run-on or comma splice errors. If you find a correct sentence, write **C** in the left-hand column. If the sentence contains a run-on or comma splice error, write either **RO** or **CS.** Then correct the error using any of the techniques you have learned. Use all methods at least once.

Example: __RO__ The space shuttle program has been very expensive it has also been very successful.

The space shuttle program has been very expensive, but it has also been very successful. (coordinating conjunction added)

1. _____ The shuttle is designed to carry large payloads, there are accommodations for up to seven crew members.

_____

2. _____ The orbiter stage of the spacecraft has a lifetime of one hundred missions, the winged orbiter can make unpowered landings on its return to earth.

_____

3. _____ The shuttle is very flexible, for it can deploy and retrieve satellites.

_____

4. _____ Its supporters saw it as a step to space exploration they passed legislation to fund the project.

_____

5. _____ The first test flight occurred in 1981 various design problems surfaced.

_____

6. _____ The first operational flight happened in 1982, two communication satellites were placed in orbit.

_____

7. _____ The seventh mission was memorable, for its crew included the first U.S. female astronaut, Sally K. Ride.

_____

8. _____ The program had many successes the program was in some trouble.

_____

9. _____ The shuttle program has been lagging in its commercial plan, the military began absorbing most of the payload launches.

_____

10. _____ Despite two major accidents, the U.S. government has not given up on the space shuttle program the program is still being funded.

_____

PRACTICE 11   Correcting Run-on and Comma Splice Errors

Most of the following sentences contain run-on or comma splice errors. If you find a correct sentence, write **C** in the left-hand column. If the sentence contains a run-on or comma splice error, write either **RO** or **CS.** Then correct the error using any of the techniques you have learned. Use all methods at least once.

1. _____ The sun dominates our solar system its huge mass produces enormous gravitational force.

_____

2. _____ Electromagnetic energy radiates from the sun's surface the energy supports all life on earth.

_____

3. _____ The sun is actually quite close to the earth, stellar phenomena can be studied in great detail.

_____

4. _____ Many ancient cultures worshiped the sun, and others recognized its importance in the cycle of life.

_____

5. _____ Studying the sun has helped develop calendars solstices, equinoxes, and eclipses have also been studied for their own importance.

_____

6. _____ In 1611, Galileo used a telescope to discover dark spots on the sun's surface, Chinese astronomers reported sunspots in 200 B.C.E.

_____

7. _____ The discovery of sunspots changed science's view of the sun, for the sun finally was seen as a dynamic, evolving body.

_____

8. _____ Progress in understanding the sun has continued, new scientific instruments have allowed new advances in observation.

_____

9. _____ The coronagraph permits study of the solar corona without the assistance of an eclipse, the magnetograph measures magnetic field strength over the solar surface.

_____

10. _____ Interest in the sun has facilitated the discovery of new space instruments space telescopes and spectrographs sensitive to ultra-violet radiation revolutionized the study of the sun and outer space.

_____

PRACTICE 12   Editing to Combine Sentences with Coordinating Conjunctions

In the following paragraph, use coordinating conjunctions to reduce this eight-sentence paragraph to one containing only five sentences. Write the finished paragraph on the lines provided.

While shopping at a successful department store, customers generally

are offered products at a reduced price. Shoppers typically are offered items clearly marked with price tags. This allows customers rapidly to choose the merchandise that gives them the best value. A successful store honors its own coupons. It also accepts other department stores' advertised prices and coupons. Clearly marked prices and accepting all coupons ensure that the buyer will have a rewarding shopping experience. No matter which store it is, such policies offer shoppers an opportunity to receive the best possible price. Consumers have the convenience of shopping at one store instead of having to go to two or three.

_____

_____

_____

_____

_____

_____

_____

_____

_____

_____

PRACTICE 13   Editing to Combine Sentences with Coordinating Conjunctions

In the following paragraph, use coordinating conjunctions to reduce this eight-sentence paragraph to one containing only five sentences. Write the finished paragraph on the lines provided.

When television was invented, most people soon forgot about listening to the radio. Only the older generation continued to listen. Television, at first, was produced in black and white and had little in the way of programming. Later, television expanded its programming both day and night. Black and white gave way to color. Years later, cable television was invented.

Viewers could choose from more than 150 channels. Some people believe that television is better now than even during the 1950s, its "Golden Age."

_____

_____

_____

_____

_____

_____

_____

PRACTICE 14   Editing to Correct Run-on and Comma Splice Errors

In the following paragraph, correct any run-on or comma splice errors you find. Write the corrected paragraph on the lines provided.

Charleston and Gettysburg vary greatly in cultural attractions but both have a rich military history. Gettysburg's main attraction is based mostly on the great Civil War battle of the same name, many large monuments are located in the field where particular high points of the battle occurred. Also, a vast graveyard contains the bodies of thousands of unknown soldiers. On the other hand, Charleston possesses an equally famous Civil War monument for Fort Sumter is located at the mouth of Charleston's harbor. Tourists must ride a ferry to the island fort and there they find a five-story museum filled with national treasures. Because of their historical significance, both cities make wonderful vacation stops.

_____

_____

_____

_____

_____

_____

_____

_____

_____

_____

_____

PRACTICE 15 Editing to Correct Run-on and Comma Splice Errors

In the following paragraph, correct any run-on or comma splice errors you find. Write the corrected paragraph on the lines provided.

Aerobics are programs of physical exercise, they help people improve their level of fitness. An aerobic exercise program helps in weight reduction and it helps lower the percentage of body fat. Aerobic exercise, sometimes called *group fitness* or *group exercise*, enhances flexibility but it also increases energy levels. Aerobics has other health benefits, it helps decrease blood pressure and cholesterol levels. As always, contact a doctor before starting any exercise program.

_____

_____

_____

_____

_____

_____

_____

Visit *The Write Start* Online!

For additional practice with the materials in this chapter, go to

http://www.cengage.com/devenglish/checkett/writestartSP4e.

Chapter Self-Assessment Test

Check either True or False on the blank next to the statement.

T   F

____ ____ Coordinating conjunctions are used to connect dependent and independent clauses.

____ ____ BOYFANS are interchangeable when used between clauses.

____ ____ Always place a comma before a coordinating conjunction when combining two simple sentences.

____ ____ Run-on sentences can only be corrected by creating two separate sentences.

____ ____ Correct comma splice errors by adding a coordinating conjunction after the comma found between the two independent clauses.

____ ____ Combining sentences helps connect ideas and add sentence variety, but it does not create rhythm because it puts too much information into one sentence.

____ ____ **But** is used when the meaning in two independent clauses is contrasting.

____ ____ **Or** is used when there is a choice to be made between the meaning in two independent clauses.

____ ____ **Yet** is used when the relationship between the meaning in two independent clauses is cause and effect.

____ ____ **For** is used when adding one idea to another in two independent clauses.

____ ____ **And** is used when the first of two independent clauses is negative.

____ ____ **Nor** is used when one of the ideas in two independent clauses is a reason for the other.

____ ____ **So** is used when one of the ideas in two independent clauses is a result of the other.

Combining Independent Clauses Using the Semicolon

> **YOU NEED TO KNOW**
>
> In Chapter 3, you learned to link independent clauses (simple sentences) together to form compound sentences by using a comma with a coordinating conjunction. If you do not understand the relationship between independent clauses, simple sentences, coordinating conjunctions, and compound sentences, you should review Chapter 3.

Another method that a writer uses to combine simple sentences or independent clauses to create compound sentences is to use a **semicolon (;).** Keep in mind that a semicolon isn't a substitute for a comma; it's a substitute for a comma and a coordinating conjunction. Therefore, when using a semicolon, do not use a coordinating conjunction or a comma with it. Also, remember that the first word following the semicolon is *not* capitalized.

> **Proper Use**
>
> The anaconda is the world's largest snake; it can grow to thirty feet or more in length. (*size* is the relating idea)
>
> **Proper Use**
>
> The nurse measured the patient's blood pressure; she also took a blood sample. (*blood* is the relating idea)
>
> **Proper Use**
>
> The submarine dove to a depth of three hundred fathoms; it hovered silently at that depth for two hours. (*depth* is the relating idea)

Do not combine sentences/independent clauses with a semicolon if the ideas are not closely related.

> **Improper Use**
>
> The bear rummaged through the camp food supply; some people believe in angels. (no relating idea)
>
> **Improper Use**
>
> Japan consists of four large islands; solar panels can generate electricity. (no relating idea)
>
> **Improper Use**
>
> Sundials are practical and decorative; snorkeling is a popular vacation pastime. (no relating idea)

When there is no relating idea between two simple sentences (independent clauses), as is the case in the three preceding examples, we cannot use a semicolon to combine them. Instead, we merely separate the two sentences with a period.

> **Examples**
>
> The bear rummaged through the camp food supply. Some people believe in angels.
>
> Japan consists of four large islands. Solar panels can generate electricity.
>
> Sundials are practical and decorative. Snorkeling is a popular vacation pastime.

The semicolon is used sparingly and only to connect very closely related ideas. The semicolon can add sentence variety to your writing, but don't overuse it.

PRACTICE 1   Combining Sentences with Semicolons

The following ten simple sentences describe a medical operation. Because all the sentences deal with a common theme, we can combine some of them using semicolons. Choose those pairs of sentences that have a related idea and combine them with a semicolon. Leave the unrelated sentences as single simple sentences. Remember that the first word in the independent clause after the semicolon is not capitalized. Write your finished sentences, both those you combined and those you did not, on the lines following the list of original sentences.

The surgical team prepared the operating room for the procedure.

The surgeon dressed in a green surgical gown.

She wore a protective cap covering her hair.

Bach's *Toccata and Fugue in D Minor* was piped into the operating room during the operation.

It helped to maintain a relaxed atmosphere during the delicate procedure.

The operation was a success.

The patient experienced a quick recovery.

He was back at work in less than two weeks.

His insurance paid for the operation.

His family was happy to have him healthy again.

_____

_____

_____

_____

_____

_____

_____

_____

_____

_____

_____

_____

PRACTICE 2　　　**Writing Compound Sentences with Semicolons**

Create compound sentences by adding a semicolon and an independent clause to the independent clauses below. Be certain that the independent clause you add has a relating idea that makes connecting the two ideas appropriate.

Example: The manager trained the crew each Friday _____

The manager trained the crew each Friday; the training was important.

1. The bakery held a sale once a week _____

_____

2. The passenger passed through the metal detector _____

_____

3. The books were arranged neatly on the shelves _____

_____

4. Simone waxed the china cabinet _____

_____

5. A strange noise came from the attic _____

_____

6. A flock of geese flew over the field _____

_____

7. Ari seemed perplexed by the math problem _____

_____

8. The driver applied the car's emergency brake _____

_____

9. *Seinfeld* was a popular television comedy for many years _____

_____

10. The bells in the town hall steeple chimed every evening _____

_____

PRACTICE 3   Writing Compound Sentences with Semicolons

For each of the following topics, create a compound sentence by supplying two independent clauses combined with a semicolon. Write your finished sentences on the lines provided below the list of topics.

A favorite pet	A thoughtful gift
An exciting event	An enjoyable hobby/pastime
A memorable person	A disturbing dream
A meaningful place	A rewarding job
A fantastic meal	A fantastic vacation/trip

1. _____

_____

2. _____

_____

3. _____

_____

4. _____

_____

5. _____

_____

6. _____

_____

7. _____

_____

8. _____

_____

9. _____

_____

10. _____

_____

PRACTICE 4   Editing to Combine Sentences with Semicolons

In the following paragraph, use semicolons to reduce this nine-sentence paragraph to one containing only seven sentences. Remember, only combine sentences with a semicolon if the ideas in the two sentences are closely related. Write your paragraph on the lines below.

To potential owners, any pet with the label "exotic" signals poor health and enormous veterinarian bills. However, a cockatiel is a good choice as the family pet. Cockatiels, while exotic looking, are rather hearty and can live fifteen years or more. Most cockatiels are gray with white patches on their wings. They also have colorful crests that point straight toward the sky. A Pearl Lutino is a more exotic looking cockatiel. Its feathers are mostly yellow and white, with gray stripes running down long, elegant tail feathers. Big, perfectly round tufts that look like fuzzy peaches grow over the cockatiel's ears. Cockatiels are fairly small, usually measuring only twelve to fourteen inches and weighing only two to four ounces.

_____

_____

_____

_____

_____

_____

_____

_____

_____

_____

_____

PRACTICE 5   Editing to Combine Sentences with Semicolons

In the following paragraph, use semicolons to reduce this ten-sentence paragraph to one containing only eight sentences. Remember, only combine sentences with a semicolon if the ideas in the two sentences are closely related. Write your paragraph on the lines below.

In general, cockatiels are friendly and sociable. They love to ride around on the shoulder of their owners, as if they were being chauffeured. An occasional nip on the ear is their way of showing the chauffeur appreciation for the ride. Cockatiels like to be included in all family gatherings. The most loving and affectionate cockatiels are those that are hand fed as chicks. In addition to being affectionate, cockatiels are intelligent and amusing. They are capable of whistling tunes and learning to perform a variety of tricks. Mimicry and playful interaction are further behaviors that make these birds fascinating. Like most birds, cockatiels love to have their heads scratched behind their long crest feathers. If a family chooses a cockatiel as its pet, the rewards will be well worth the effort to train and care for the bird.

_____

_____

_____

_____

_____

_____

_____

_____

_____

_____

_____

_____

 Visit _The Write Start_ Online!

For additional practice with the materials in this chapter, go to

http://www.cengage.com/devenglish/checkett/writestartSP4e.

Chapter Self-Assessment Test

Check either True or False on the blank next to the statement.

T   F

____   ____   You cannot connect simple sentences or independent clauses with a semicolon.

____   ____   When using a semicolon, be certain the two sentences or two independent clasuses have a related idea.

____   ____   You can use a BOYFANS with a semicolon.

____   ____   The word following the semicolon is always capitalized.

Combining Independent Clauses Using the Adverbial Conjunction

In Chapter 3, you learned to combine independent clauses and simple sentences by using a comma and a coordinating conjunction; in Chapter 4, you learned to do so using just a semicolon. These techniques allow you to create sentence variety and rhythm, and to establish connections between ideas.

You can add more variety to your writing by combining independent clauses and simple sentences with the use of **adverbial conjunctions.** Adverbial conjunctions are joining words that help you move from one idea to the next by linking ideas even more forcefully.

Commonly Used Adverbial Conjunctions and Their Meanings			
Adverbial Conjunction	**Meaning**	**Adverbial Conjunction**	**Meaning**
accordingly	since, so	*however*	by contrast, in spite of
additionally	in addition	*incidentally*	by the way
also	in addition	*indeed*	in fact, undoubtedly
anyway	nevertheless, whatever	*likewise*	in the same way, similarly
besides	also, in addition	*meanwhile*	the time between events
certainly	inescapable, sure	*moreover*	in addition, more, plus
consequently	as a result of	*nevertheless*	but, despite, in spite of, still
finally	at the end	*next*	after, afterward, since
furthermore	in addition	*nonetheless*	however, nevertheless

(continued)

Adverbial Conjunction	Meaning	Adverbial Conjunction	Meaning
hence	for this reason, from now	*now*	at present, immediately
otherwise	under other circumstances	*thereafter*	from then on
similarly	as, as if, like	*therefore*	as a result, on account of
still	as before, now, yet	*thus*	as a result, in this way
then	at that time, next in time	*undoubtedly*	certainly, indeed, truly

Notice that some, but not all, adverbial conjunctions have similar meanings and can be used interchangeably. Also, notice that when using adverbial conjunctions, you must precede them with a semicolon and follow them with a comma.

> **Examples**
>
> The team practiced in the morning; furthermore, they practiced again in the evening.
>
> Aunt Louisa stopped at the bakery; meanwhile, her niece waited in the car.

PRACTICE 1   Using Adverbial Conjunctions

Add the adverbial conjunction that best expresses the appropriate relationship between the pairs of independent clauses that follow. Also, be sure to use correct punctuation. Do not use the same adverbial conjunction twice.

Examples: Sheila hit the ball; however, she was thrown out at first base.

1. The CAT scan discovered a tumor _____ it turned out to be benign.

2. Wrestling at the high school or college level is physically demanding _____ staying in shape is a necessity.

3. Jackie did not like writing essays _____ she worked hard and received an "A" in the class.

4. The dentist warned my children to floss after every meal _____ cavities and gum disease would surely develop over the next few years.

5. The vacationers didn't like the tour guide's itinerary _____ they

rented a car, bought a guide book, and went their own way.

6. The crew chief made out the weekly shift schedule _____ she

hired three evening workers.

7. The assistant unloaded the cases of soda _____ his boss settled

the account with the café's owner.

PRACTICE 2 **Writing Compound Sentences with Adverbial Conjunctions**

Add the adverbial conjunction that best expresses the appropriate relationship between the pairs of the independent clauses that follow. Also, be sure to use correct punctuation. Do not use the same adverbial conjunction twice.

Example: The painter chose yellow; <u>however,</u> the homeowner wanted beige.

1. One detective was questioning witnesses _____ her partner

called the coroner.

2. The mountain trail was curving _____ the hikers decided to

proceed.

3. The NASCAR circuit is popular in the South _____ sales of sou-

venirs there is very strong.

4. The actress won a Golden Globe Award _____ she won an

Oscar.

5. The moose charged the campers _____ the bear went after the

food.

6. The concert lasted over five hours because of encores _____ the

band left the stage for food.

7. The newlyweds could not decide on where to go for a honeymoon

_____ they bought a living room set instead.

PRACTICE 3 **Using Adverbial Conjunctions**

Read the following five independent clauses carefully. In the spaces provided, add an adverbial conjunction and an appropriately related second independent clause. Be sure that the second independent clause in each of the five resulting compound sentences clearly relates to the first and that you use the correct

gotten to know if it weren't for the volleyball team or Kiwanis club. I learned to work with others. I also am very proud of what I achieved through my activities. I learned valuable life lessons, such as forming friendships, the importance of teamwork, and pride in a job well done. Many students go into high school as shy, timid mice. They graduate as big, roaring bears. Participating in extracurricular activities helps this process take place. It gives students self-confidence which, in turn, helps them throughout their entire lives. The activities students participate in, and the knowledge they acquire, will stay with them forever.

_____

_____

_____

_____

_____

_____

_____

_____

_____

_____

_____

_____

PRACTICE 7   Editing to Combine Sentences with Adverbial Conjunctions

In the following paragraph, use adverbial conjunctions to reduce this twelve-sentence paragraph to one containing only nine sentences. Remember, use a semicolon before the conjunction and a comma afterward. Also, choose the adverbial conjunction that best describes the relationship between the sentences. Write your paragraph on the lines below.

Many of the activities I participated in during high school involved teamwork. For example, in volleyball, the team must have a plan in order to defeat the opponent. The front line players and the back line players must coordinate their movements. Defensive and offensive strategies can shift from one second to the next depending on where the ball is hit and how the other team is positioning its players. The players have to make secret signals to one another in order to act together. Another activity I was involved with in high school took us into the city to winterize houses belonging to people who couldn't afford to do it themselves. We put plastic over the windowpanes. The plastic sheets were large and difficult to hold steady in the wind. The hammers were heavy and awkward to use. It took three-person teams to finish each window. The job would have been impossible if we didn't work together. I learned how important teamwork is in everyday life.

_____

_____

_____

_____

_____

_____

_____

_____

_____

_____

_____

_____

_____

Putting It All Together

Linking two independent clauses or simple sentences by using a semicolon is the least emphatic link because it merely shows that the two ideas are related somehow.

> **Example**
>
> Glenn's favorite pastime is listening to music; he doesn't play an instrument.

Using a comma and a coordinating conjunction is a more emphatic link because the choice of BOYFANS provides a clue as to the nature of the relationship.

> **Example**
>
> Glenn's favorite pastime is listening to music, but he doesn't play an instrument.

The adverbial conjunction, however, provides the most explicit and forceful link because the choice of adverbial conjunction tells you the nature of the relationship and adds some perceived importance because of the dramatic pause.

> **Example**
>
> Glenn's favorite hobby is listening to music; however, he doesn't play an instrument.

PRACTICE 8   Combining Sentences

Combine the following pairs of independent clauses using one of the three methods you have learned in Chapters 3, 4, and 5: a semicolon, a coordinating conjunction (BOYFANS) preceded by a comma, or an adverbial conjunction preceded by a semicolon and followed by a comma. Place your choices in the spaces provided.

1. Abstract art form has little direct reference to external or perceived reality _____ it is normally synonymous with various types of twentieth-century avant-garde art.

2. The term *abstract* also refers to images that have been abstracted or derived from nature _____ the images have been considerably altered or have been simplified to their basic geometric or biomorphic forms.

3. The term *nonobjective* has been abandoned by most critics _____

now they have supplanted it with the term *abstract*.

4. Abstract expressionism appeared in the mid-twentieth century

_____ it was primarily concerned with expression through

line and color.

5. The artist was interested in expressing emotional reaction to the world

_____ objective experiences and situations were seen as less

interesting.

6. The movement was part of the organic, emotional, expressionistic approach

to art _____ it was developed to contrast with thegeometrically

structural, rationalistic approach of the cubists.

7. The roots of abstract expressionism can be found in the works of Kandinsky,

Ernst, Duchamp, Chagall, and Tanguy _____ they inspired a

blossoming of abstract expressionism among American painters in the 1950s.

8. The abstract movement centered in New York City _____ this

core of American painters was dubbed the New York School.

9. The New York School included many now-famous artists _____

Pollock, de Kooning, Kline, and Rothko were the most famous American

artists.

10. Abstract expressionism also flourished in Europe _____ the

Tachism School emphasized patches of color while the Art Informal

School rejected formal structure.

PRACTICE 9   **Combining Sentences**

Combine the following pairs of independent clauses using one of the three
methods you learned in Chapters 3, 4, and 5: a semicolon, a coordinating
conjunction (BOYFANS) preceded by a comma, or an adverbial conjunction
preceded by a semicolon and followed with a comma. Place your choices in
the spaces provided.

1. The moon is a natural satellite of the earth ＿＿＿＿＿＿ the name *moon* is sometimes applied to the satellites of other planets in the solar system.

2. The moon's diameter is about 2,160 miles ＿＿＿＿＿＿ although this is a large distance, it is only about one-fourth that of earth.

3. The moon's volume is about one-fiftieth that of earth ＿＿＿＿＿＿ the mass of the earth is 81 times greater than the mass of the moon.

4. The moon has no free water and no atmosphere ＿＿＿＿＿＿ no weather exists to change its surface topography.

5. The moon orbits the earth at an average distance of 238,000 miles ＿＿＿＿＿＿ it completes one revolution around the earth every 27 days, 7 hours, 43 minutes, and 11.5 seconds.

6. At any one time, an observer can see only 50 percent of the moon's entire surface ＿＿＿＿＿＿ an additional 9 percent can be seen around the apparent edge because of the relative motion called *libration*.

7. Libration is caused by slightly different angles of view from the earth ＿＿＿＿＿＿ different relative positions of the moon influence our "true" perception of it.

8. The moon shows progressively different phases as it moves along its orbit ＿＿＿＿＿＿ half the moon is always in sunlight, just as half the earth has day while the other half has night.

9. In the phase called the *new moon,* the face is completely in shadow ＿＿＿＿＿＿ about a week later, the moon is in first quarter, resembling a luminous half-circle.

10. Another week later, the full moon shows its fully lighted surface ＿＿＿＿＿＿ a week afterward, in its last quarter, the moon appears as a half-circle once again.

PRACTICE 10   Editing to Combine Sentences

Choose three pairs of sentences in the following paragraph and combine them by using all three of the methods you learned in Chapters 3, 4, and 5: a semicolon, a coordinating conjunction (BOYFANS) preceded by a comma, and an adverbial conjunction preceded by a semicolon and followed with a comma. Do not use the same method more than once. Write your completed paragraph on the lines provided below.

The late November clouds gathered slowly throughout the day, forming a thick, gray blanket by the time the evening sky had darkened. The winter blizzard came to the farm during the night like a stealthy coyote sneaking up on an unsuspecting hen house. In the corners of the intersecting fences, the snowflakes waltzed in circles like miniature tornadoes. They changed speed and direction depending on the wind gusts. The snow banked high against the fence posts and rails also affected the little whirlwinds of ice and snow. Rising and falling silently, the snow swirls were silhouetted against the hazy aura of the moon straining to be seen through the overcast sky. The night grew like a black tide on the ocean. The snow stopped. The air sparkled with shimmering dust-like flakes kicked by imperceptible puffs of wind. The chilled air made the snow's surface crisp and brittle. Soon, hard rubber tires would crunch the snow into stiff, well-formed patterns.

_____

_____

_____

_____

_____

_____

_____

_____

_____

_____

_____

_____

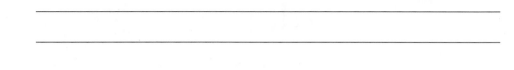

 Visit *The Write Start* Online!

For additional practice with the materials in this chapter, go to

http://www.cengage.com/devenglish/checkett/writestartSP4e.

Chapter Self-Assessment Test

Check either True or False on the blank next to the statement.

T   F

_____ _____ When combining simple sentences or independent clauses, you can use an adverbial conjunction.

_____ _____ The adverbial conjunction is preceded by a semicolon and followed by a comma.

_____ _____ The word following the comma is always capitalized.

_____ _____ The adverbial conjunction you choose should clarify the two ideas in the two simple sentences or independent clauses.

_____ _____ **Moreover** is used to clarify that one idea is caused by another idea.

_____ _____ **Additionally** is used when one idea is added to another.

_____ _____ **Therefore** is used when an idea is negative.

_____ _____ **Consequently** is used when one idea is the outcome of another idea.

_____ _____ **However** is used to show the contrast between two ideas.

6

Adding a List

So far, you have been combining independent clauses and simple sentences to add sentence variety and rhythm, and to connect related ideas. Sometimes a simple sentence or a combination of two simple sentences isn't sufficient to express your thoughts as a writer. Often, you will need to add information to clarify or expand on your ideas. Another way to add variety to your writing is to use **lists**—items in a series. Not only can lists vary your writing, they also can add necessary information to explain, clarify, or illustrate one of your ideas.

> **Example**
> Charles went to the mall to shop.

This sentence does not clarify what it was that Charles bought.

> **Example**
> Charles went to the mall and purchased a CD, a shirt, and sunglasses.
> ↑
> the list

By using a list, what Charles bought at the mall is illustrated.

A **series** can consist of single words (nouns, adjectives, verbs, adverbs) or prepositional phrases.

> **Examples**
> The pizza was topped with cheese, sausage, green onions, and mushrooms. (nouns)
> The large, powerful, and majestic lion sleeps 16 hours a day. (adjectives)
> The athlete walks, jogs, runs, and sprints during practice. (verbs)
> The sea otter swims swiftly, smoothly, and playfully. (adverbs)
> The cruise ship offers extravagant meals in the morning, in the afternoon, in the evening, and after midnight. (prepositional phrases beginning with *in* and *after*)

For definitions and examples of adjectives and adverbs, see The Writer's Resources, pages 346–349.

Punctuating and Placing the List

The list can be added at the beginning, middle, or end of the sentence.

> **Examples**
> *Beginning*: <u>Cheese, wine, and fruit</u> were served at the picnic.
> *Middle*: The hosts served <u>cheese, wine, and fruit</u> at the picnic.
> *End:* The food served at the picnic included <u>cheese, wine, and fruit.</u>

Notice the use of commas in our examples. In lists with three or more items, you need to separate each item from the other items with a comma. In lists with only two items, you do not need to use a comma. Instead, you can separate the two items with the word *and*.

> **Examples**
> *Two-item series*: The taxicab stopped <u>and</u> started. (no commas)
> *Three-or-more-item series*: The taxicab stopped, started, and sped away.

PRACTICE 1   Identifying and Punctuating Series

Underline the series in each sentence, and punctuate it correctly. If you think the sentence is correct, write a **C** in front of the sentence's number.

Example: The Super Bowl Football game <u>included four touchdown passes, three extra points failing, and a parachutist landing at midfield.</u>

1. They ordered steak potatoes and asparagus at dinner.

2. The three cats hid under the table in the closet and in the basement during the thunderstorm.

3. The weather consisted of rain and sleet.

4. King Albert Queen Lucinda and Prince Arn rode inside a golden carriage.

5. The garden consisted of tulips crocuses and jonquils during the three months of spring.

6. The groups of high school seniors corporate executives and international chefs toured Rome for three days.

7. The fog blanketed the fields in the morning during the afternoon and after dark.

8. Talent and poise are ingredients for a successful career in business.

9. The orchestra's violins cellos and violas answered the woodwinds during the second movement.

10. The trapeze artist soared over the crowd performed a loop and swung upside down.

PRACTICE 2   **Writing and Punctuating Series**

Add a list to complete each of the following incomplete sentences. Punctuate correctly.

1. _____

_____ made the workers thirsty.

2. The dolphins _____

_____

3. The hosts and their guest followed dinner _____

_____

4. The entire choir _____

_____ prior to the concert.

5. Justin's favorite rides at the amusement park were _____

_____

6. The carpenter _____

_____ to complete the project.

7. The cowboy won the rodeo by _____

_____

8. The chef prepared _____

_____ for his customers.

9. _____

_____ made the farmer successful.

10. The early morning hours are the teacher's favorite time for _____

_____

| PRACTICE 3 | Writing Sentences with Series |

Write three different sentences, each containing three or more items in a list. Place the list at the beginning of one sentence, in the middle of one sentence, and at the end of one sentence. Punctuate each sentence correctly.

1. _____

   _____

2. _____

   _____

3. _____

   _____

Parallelism in a Series

As we have seen, lists can be made up of nouns, adjectives, verbs, adverbs, and phrases. Any items work well in the list *as long as every item in the list is the same type of word or phrase*. This is known as **parallelism.**

Mixing different categories of words or phrases in the same list makes the sentence hard to read and understand.

> **Example**
> The birds are finches, under a tree, and yellow.

Yellow finches

In this example, a noun, a prepositional phrase, and an adjective have been mixed inappropriately as the items in the list. See how confusing this sentence is. It also sounds choppy. Additionally, the reader might be confused as to which item is yellow—the finch or the tree. Parallel lists read smoothly and rhythmically, and they clarify content.

Examples

At the supermarket, Sarina purchased bread, butter, and milk. (nouns)

The garden was colorful, fragrant, and beautiful. (adjectives)

Frank swims, bicycles, and runs every day for triathlon practice. (verbs)

The gymnast vaulted athletically, aggressively, and purposefully. (adverbs)

Chin looked for the passport in the dresser, on the counter, and under the newspaper. (prepositional phrases beginning with *in*, *on*, and *under*)

PRACTICE 4   Writing Lists with Parallel Items

Add a three-item list to complete each of the sentences below. Be certain that each list is parallel and achieves clear content and consistent rhythm.

Make one list each of nouns, adjectives, verbs, adverbs, and phrases.

1. My favorite music groups are _____, _____, and _____.

2. The ice-cream sundae was _____, _____, and _____.

3. When Shaunista was a teenager, she would hide her diary _____,

_____, and _____.

4. The air show audience was fascinated by the experimental airplane's

_____, _____, and _____ shape.

5. The space shuttle roared _____, _____, and _____

into the clouds over the Kennedy Space Center.

PRACTICE 5   Writing Sentences with Lists

For each of the topics listed below, write a sentence that includes a list. Be certain that each list is parallel. Make one list each of nouns, adjectives, verbs, adverbs, and phrases. Punctuate correctly.

1. Library— _____

_____

2. Weather— _____

_____

3. Car— _____

_____

4. Dating— _____

_____

5. Sky-diving— _____

_____

PRACTICE 6   Editing Series

Edit the following paragraph, combining sentences (2), (3), (4), and (5) into one sentence. Do so by reducing sentences (3), (4), and (5) to a list and adding the list to sentence (2). Remember, your finished series should exhibit parallelism. Write the paragraph on the lines below.

(1)Although most dogs are simply family pets, there is a class of dogs that earn their keep in more ways than one. (2)Working dogs serve humans daily through a variety of avenues. (3)They help blind persons. (4)They use their sense of smell to find illegal narcotics. (5)They also help ranchers control herds of livestock. (6)From the earliest recorded history, dogs have helped people survive by providing numerous services.

_____

_____

_____

_____

_____

PRACTICE 7   Editing Series

Edit the following paragraph, combining sentences (3), (4), (5), and (6) into one sentence. Do so by reducing sentences (4), (5), and (6) to a list and adding the list to sentence (3). Remember, your finished series should exhibit parallelism. Write the paragraph on the lines below.

(1)Oldies music stations play songs from the 50s, 60s, and 70s. (2)This music is a great hit with "baby boomers" and anyone else who used to listen to it. (3)These stations focus on playing music by the most popular performers. (4)They play tunes by the Beatles. (5)They play songs by Elvis. (6)They also play hits by the Supremes. (7)Even though music and the music industry have changed over the decades, stations that play oldies from the 50s, 60s, and 70s are still popular in the new millennium.

_____

_____

_____

_____

_____

_____

Using a Colon to Add Sentence Variety

To add sentence variety and to emphasize particular information, you can use a colon. A colon looks like one period above another period (:). Use a colon to do the following:

- To introduce a list
- When telling time
- For the salutation of a business letter
- To separate the title and subtitle of a book or movie

1. Use a colon after an independent clause to introduce a list.

> **Examples**
> Preparing a soufflé requires four ingredients: <u>milk, eggs, butter, and cheese.</u>
> The pharmacy technician ordered the items sold most often: <u>aspirin, gauze, bandages, and antacid.</u>

Note: Do not use a colon before a list if the list immediately follows a verb or a preposition.

Examples

The most popular condiments <u>are</u>: catsup, mustard, and mayonnaise. (incorrect: omit colon <u>after</u> verb)

You will find the cats hiding <u>under</u>: the house, the porch, the tool shed. (incorrect: omit colon <u>after</u> preposition)

It is best only to use a colon after an independent clause.

Examples

The following are the most popular condiments: <u>catsup, mustard, and mayonnaise.</u>

The cats were found in the following places: <u>under the house, under the porch, and under the tool shed.</u>

2. Use a colon when telling time.

Examples

The train arrived at 4<u>:</u>15 P.M.

My 2<u>:</u>30 P.M. doctor's appointment was changed to 5<u>:</u>00 P.M.

3. Use a colon for the salutation of a business letter.

Examples

Dear Mrs. Hilliard<u>:</u>

To Whom It May Concern<u>:</u>

Sirs<u>:</u>

4. Use a colon to separate the titles and subtitles of books or movies.

Examples

Accounting in Context<u>:</u> A Business Handbook

Writing Made Easy<u>:</u> A Plain Language Rhetoric

Washington<u>:</u> The First Leader of the Nation

Star Wars<u>:</u> Attack of the Clones

PRACTICE 8   Using Colons

Add colons to introduce lists, to tell time, and to separate titles and subtitles of books or movies in the following sentences.

1. The teacher taught using a variety of methods lecturing, using an overhead projector, and assigning in-class group projects.

2. Jerry enjoyed many activities while vacationing boating, fishing, and hiking.

3. The Concorde jetliner left Paris at 605 P.M. instead of its scheduled time of 550 P.M.

4. The librarian reshelved the book left on her desk *Retire Early How to Make Money in Real Estate Foreclosures.*

5. The two movies had different start times *Iron Man* at 440 P.M., and *The Chronicles of Narnia* at 455 P.M.

6. The office workers ate lunch in a variety of places in the employee lounge, on the roof, and out by the lake.

7. Sheila enjoyed reading the new book about food shopping *Using Coupons Free Meals for Your Family.*

8. Joaquin used three types of peppers to add color to his special salsa red, yellow, and green.

9. HOMES is a mnemonic device to help people remember the names of the five Great Lakes Huron, Ontario, Michigan, Erie, and Superior.

10. The children enjoyed the party because of the food hot dogs, hamburgers, and chips.

PRACTICE 9   Correcting Colon Errors

Correct the colon errors in the following sentences. You will have to rewrite some of the sentences to do so. Write the revised sentences on the lines provided.

1. The two falcons: found a tree, gathered twigs, and built a nest.

_____

_____

2. My bus left the station at 515, instead of 615 as written in the schedule.

_____

_____

3. The surgical team had a good reputation because: they were up on the latest techniques and had worked together for four years.

_____

_____

4. The Liberian flag is: red, white, and blue.

_____

_____

5. The movie was titled *The Lord of the Rings The Two Towers*.

_____

_____

6. The man's hidden desires turned out to be: baseball, baseball, and baseball.

_____

_____

7. The plane: could not take off: the engine wasn't powerful enough to handle the load.

_____

_____

8. The book was titled *Toward Better Scoring on the SAT An Exercise Booklet*.

_____

_____

9. Amelia was in a hurry because her date was at 700 P.M., and it was already 645 P.M.

_____

_____

10. The children's favorite schoolyard activities were: riding the merry-go-round, climbing the jungle gym, and playing hopscotch.

_____

_____

PRACTICE 10   **Writing Sentences with Colons**

Write three sentences using the colon to introduce a list, to include a time, and to illustrate a book or movie title and subtitle.

1. _____

_____

2. _____

_____

3. _____

_____

PRACTICE 11   **Editing for Colons**

Edit the following paragraph, adding colons where appropriate.

Movies are popular because of two factors actors and genres. Star-power can almost guarantee that a movie will make money. There are a handful of stars in this category Will Smith, Johnny Depp, and Nicole Kidman. If tickets for movies starring one of these actors go on sale at 200 P.M., the "Sold Out" sign usually lights up by 400 P.M. Fantasy-action movies are some of the most popular movies currently running. Some of the largest grossing movies in history belong to this genre *Star Wars The Return of the Jedi, Lord of the Rings The Fellowship of the Ring, and Harry Potter The Order of the Phoenix,* to name a few. If movie producers can combine a popular star with a popular genre, a box-office bonanza is almost a sure thing.

PRACTICE 12   **Editing for Colons**

Edit the following letter, adding colons where appropriate.

Dear Ms. Morgan

Thank you for your recent inquiry concerning what to expect here at Middletown University during your first year as a student. As you know, there are certain personal traits that will stand you in good order both at school and your future place of employment financial responsibility, time management, and cooperation. Working to help with expenses teaches the value of money and what it represents in terms of goods and services. Time management is an important skill to learn. For instance, in her best-selling business book, *Time Management Workplace Wizardry,* author Meghan Brooks suggests that you should never get out of bed later than 600 A.M. By 700 A.M. you should have your daily schedule complete. Doing this will keep you organized and focused on each task. Cooperation, of course, will help you enormously while you are attending Middletown. You will be working and interacting with a wide array of individuals administrators, staff, faculty, and other students. I hope this letter helps answer your concerns. Please do not hesitate to contact me during my office hours 300 P.M. Wednesdays and 1000 A.M. Thursdays.

Sincerely yours,

Ronald Blevins, Dean

Arts & Humanities Division

 Visit *The Write Start* Online!

For additional practice with the materials in this chapter, go to

http://www.cengage.com/devenglish/checkett/writestartSP4e.

Chapter Self-Assessment Test

Check either True or False on the blank next to the statement.

T	F	
____	____	Lists or a series of words and phrases are added to a sentence to make it longer.
____	____	In a two-item list, the word *and* plus a comma is used to separate the items.
____	____	In a three-item series, the items in the list are separated by commas. No *and* is required.
____	____	Lists can be added at the beginning, middle, or end of a sentence.
____	____	Items in a list must be parallel.
____	____	Nouns, verbs, and phrases can be mixed together to construct a series.
____	____	Use a semicolon after an independent clause to introduce a list.

_____ _____ Do not use a colon before a list if the colon immediately follows a verb or preposition.

_____ _____ Use a colon when telling time.

_____ _____ Use a comma, not a colon, in the salutation of a business letter.

_____ _____ Use a colon to separate the title and subtitle of a book or movie.

© 2010 Wadsworth, Cengage Learning

7

The Dependent Clause

In Chapter 3, you learned to link ideas using the coordinating conjunctions, *for, and, nor, but, or, yet, so,* in compound sentences. Another method to connect ideas is to use **subordinating conjunctions.** Sentences with subordinating conjunctions are called **complex sentences.**

Commonly Used Subordinating Conjunctions

after	if	when
although	since	whenever
as	though	wherever
because	unless	whether
before	until	while

Subordinating conjunctions are used to join independent clauses just as coordinating conjunctions are. However, coordinating conjunctions give the same emphasis to both clauses, whereas subordinating conjunctions de-emphasize one clause by turning it into a **dependent clause** (a process called **subordination**).

Independent versus Dependent Clauses

As you have already learned, an independent clause (a clause that can stand alone as a simple sentence) must have a subject, a verb, and complete meaning. A dependent clause also has a subject and a verb, but it does not have sufficient meaning to allow it to stand alone. It is dependent on an independent clause to complete its meaning. When using a subordinating conjunction to combine clauses, we actually start out with two independent clauses, each of which can stand on its own but is related to the other.

Example
The ship returned to port. Its propeller was broken.

The information in each of these independent clauses is considered of equal value or importance. In reality, however, the first clause is considered the more important piece of information. It is more important to know that the ship had to return to port. Why it had to return is of secondary importance.

To let the reader know which clause is of primary importance, the writer can make one of the independent clauses a dependent clause by adding a subordinating conjunction to the front of the clause.

> **Here Is the Less Important Independent Clause**
> Its propeller was broken.

Next, this independent clause is changed to a dependent clause by adding the appropriate subordinating conjunction.

> **Example**
> *Because* its propeller was broken.

Notice that this clause no longer can stand on its own because it does not have sufficient meaning. It is dependent on the independent clause for its complete meaning.

If left alone, this dependent clause would be a sentence fragment.

> **Here Is the Complete Sentence**
> The ship returned to port *because* its propeller was broken.
>
> ↑ ↑ ↑
>
> (independent clause) (subordinating conjunction) (dependent clause)

Subordination, then, is a process for making one idea of lesser value or importance than another idea. Subordination is commonly done when there are two independent clauses and the writer decides that one main idea is actually more important or needs more emphasis than the other main idea.

PRACTICE 1   Identifying Dependent Clauses

In the following sentences, underline the independent clause once, the dependent clause twice, and circle the subordinating conjunction.

Example: The crowd raced for their cars (after) the football game was over.

1. Gas prices increase during the summer because many people drive on their vacations.

2. Although the Congress consists of the House and Senate, they are distinctly different legislative bodies.

3. Golfers can play all day and night in Finland since the sun never sets.

4. The teenagers partied each day while their parents were away.

5. Before an earthquake sends tremors through the ground, some scientists believe animals can somehow sense it is going to happen.

6. The amateur hoopsters loved to travel first class as if they were a professional team.

7. Until their economy failed, the Russians were considered a world power.

8. Whether she spoke with royalty or peasants, Mother Teresa was always humble.

9. The students had a study session every Sunday evening unless there was a good concert at the student center.

10. Whenever the cartoonist finished a week's worth of strips, she rewarded herself with four cookies and a cold glass of milk.

PRACTICE 2   Using Subordinating Conjunctions

Read each of the following sentences for its meaning. Then fill in the blank space with the subordinating conjunction that best expresses the relationship between the two ideas.

1. The butcher sliced fifty pounds of roast beef each morning _____ the deli down the street sold it all during lunch.

2. _____ the blackjack player had a good hand, he pulled on his left earlobe.

3. The cruise ship passengers stayed out on deck _____ the breeze became too strong and too chilly.

4. _____ the United States purchased Alaska from the Soviet Union, it became known as "Seward's Folly."

5. His parents have to have the cracked windshield fixed _____ he can take the driver's test tomorrow.

6. _____ the ozone layer is protected, harmful radiation will cause more skin cancer.

7. _____ the bullet train gained speed, the passengers became more nervous.

8. _____ some workers sliced the lettuce from their stalks, others placed the heads into cardboard boxes.

9. The table had to be cleaned _____ the waiter let the guests sit down.

10. The pear tree lost a limb _____ the wind blew over 40 miles per hour.

Punctuating Dependent Clauses

You may have noticed in the previous practice exercises that when combining sentences with subordinating conjunctions, some of the newly created dependent clauses use a comma and others do not. This depends on whether the dependent clause precedes the independent clause or follows it.

If the dependent clause comes before the independent clause, a comma follows the dependent clause.

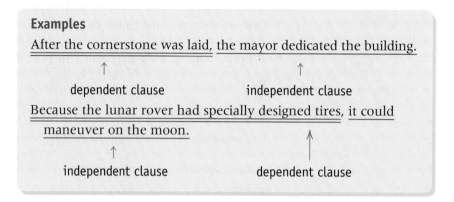

Examples

After the cornerstone was laid, the mayor dedicated the building.

    ↑   ↑

   dependent clause   independent clause

Because the lunar rover had specially designed tires, it could maneuver on the moon.

        ↑   ↑

    independent clause   dependent clause

If the dependent clause follows the independent clause, a comma is not used.

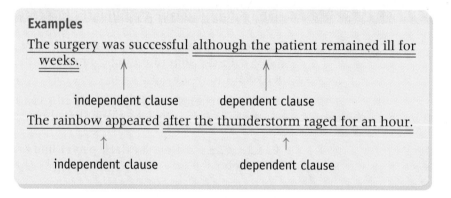

Examples

The surgery was successful although the patient remained ill for weeks.

       ↑   ↑

   independent clause   dependent clause

The rainbow appeared after the thunderstorm raged for an hour.

      ↑   ↑

   independent clause   dependent clause

PRACTICE 3   Creating Complex Sentences

Combine the following pairs of sentences to create a complex sentence. In each pair, change the first independent clause to a dependent clause by placing the appropriate subordinating conjunction in front of it. Punctuate correctly.

Example: The man at the front door was a stranger. Tajel did not let him in.

Because the man at the front door was a stranger, Tajel did not let him in.

1. She was from a desert region of Nevada. Her desire was to be a ski instructor.

_____

_____

2. Jennifer's test scores were very high. She was accepted at twelve universities.

_____

_____

3. The Oscars ceremony was completed. The stars drove off in their limousines.

_____

_____

4. The NATO peacekeeping force accomplished its goal. The fighting would cease.

_____

_____

5. The restaurant changed its menu to all Tex-Mex. Sales skyrocketed.

_____

_____

PRACTICE 4　　Creating Complex Sentences

Combine the following pairs of sentences. In each pair, change the second independent clause to a dependent clause by adding the appropriate subordinating conjunction to the front of it. Remember, do not use a comma.

Example: The wolves howled across the valley. They wanted the pack to hunt.
The wolves howled across the valley whenever they wanted the pack to hunt.

1. Winnie couldn't help diagnosing everyone in her family. She had become a doctor.

_____

_____

2. The alligator is essentially solitary. The piranha lives in schools.

_____

_____

3. The movie studio head threw an expensive party. His movies were a box office success.

_____

_____

4. Corporate headquarters never ordered extra parts. The factory produced more DVDs.

_____

_____

5. The game can never begin. The National Anthem is sung.

_____

_____

PRACTICE 5   **Writing Complex Sentences**

Using the pairs of topics below, create six complex sentences. Three of the sentences should have dependent clauses at the beginning, and the other three should end with dependent clauses. Punctuate correctly.

1. Hit/Catch— _____

_____

2. Cook/Eat— _____

_____

3. Work/Promotion— _____

_____

4. Vote/Elect— _____

_____

5. Success/Luck— _____

_____

6. Driving/Accidents— _____

_____

PRACTICE 6   **Editing to Punctuate Dependent Clauses**

Correctly punctuate the dependent clauses in the following paragraph. Remove inappropriate punctuation.

Because stress is not prejudiced it affects everyone. Every person who

has experienced stress can give it his or her own definition. Many describe it as a feeling of wanting to jump out of their skin, because they sweat and their skin becomes clammy. Some of the causes of stress are divorce, moving, or changing jobs. Although stress can be positive too much stress can cause lifelong damage. After people have a very stressful episode they often are too fatigued to work or interact with others in a productive way. Overly stressed individuals have difficulty staying focused, while they try to juggle too many responsibilities.

PRACTICE 7 Editing to Punctuate Dependent Clauses

Correctly punctuate the dependent clauses in the following paragraph. Remove inappropriate punctuation.

Because the building was so huge the hallways seemed like highways. It was another year and another new school occupied by strange faces. Although I knew there was much to look forward to getting past the blank stares and unfamiliar buildings was always the hard part. I was expected to act and perform normally, after my world had just been through months of turmoil. Believe me, climbing in and out of a U-Haul every few years is about as stressful an activity as any seventeen-year-old ever confronts. It's not something I'll be looking forward to a few years from now.

 Visit *The Write Start* Online!

For additional practice with the materials in this chapter, go to

http://www.cengage.com/devenglish/checkett/writestartSP4e.

Chapter Self-Assessment Test

Check either True or False on the blank next to the statement.

T   F

____   ____   Subordinated sentences are formed by using a subordinating conjunction to change one independent clause to a dependent clause.

_____ _____ The resulting sentence is a compound sentence.

_____ _____ When the dependent clause comes before the independent clause, you do not have to follow the dependent clause with a comma.

_____ _____ When the dependent clause follows the independent clause, a comma is placed after the independent clause.

8

Adding Information to Sentences

The Introductory Phrase

As you have seen in other chapters, there are many methods writers use to add more information to a simple sentence or independent clause. One good method for adding information or clarifying the main idea in an independent clause—as well as adding variety to your writing—is to start the sentence with an **introductory phrase.** The introductory phrase (or phrases—there can be more than one) is separated from the independent clause by a comma.

Examples

At the beginning of the tournament, the team played rather poorly.

Because of the weight loss program, Lee's cholesterol was reduced.

At the barn, the workers made a plan for harvesting all five hundred acres of wheat.

When driving across the country, Rosita always has the radio turned to the salsa station.

PRACTICE 1   Identifying Introductory Phrases

Underline the introductory phrase, or phrases, in the following sentences, and insert a comma to separate it from the main clause.

Examples: To the Navy Seals, the insurmountable obstacle was just another challenge to overcome.

On the stove in the kitchen, a small egg timer rang its warning.

1. On an African safari the tourist group saw giraffes, lions, and elephants.

2. At first I did not see the need to know CPR for my job as a lifeguard.

3. Made of thick steel the frying pan looked like it would last forever.

4. More often the traffic is heavier in the evening than in the morning.

5. To most surfers around the world the fear of shark attack is of little concern.

6. All in all it was a very profitable day selling pennants outside the stadium.

7. For the very first time in the company's history its stock price went down.

8. Being thin and tall the model easily fit into all the designer's latest gowns.

9. As worn and rundown as the town itself the old feed store was a symbol of the town's decay as a business center.

10. Whether guilty or not the defendant seemed believable when testifying.

PRACTICE 2   Identifying Introductory Phrases

Underline the introductory phrase or phrases in the following sentences, and insert a comma to separate it from the main clause.

1. After the matinee showing the tour bus left Las Vegas and headed for Reno.

2. Because of an allergic reaction the best swimmer on the team has to miss the meet.

3. On most sunny days the students gathered in the quadrangle to read and visit.

4. Inside the hull a ton of grain awaited transfer to the trucks waiting on the dock.

5. Over the mountains the highway trailed away like a giant black snake.

6. Around the dance club and near the alley five low riders gleamed hauntingly.

7. Under the bridge a homeless person had established a camp.

8. Through the looking glass in the famous story Alice found her Wonderland.

9. As lava eventually cools it turns to rock.

10. In the Galápagos Islands off of western South America Darwin made important discoveries that helped him create his theory of evolution.

Introductory Phrase Variety

The introductory phrase is used best when it contains information that helps explain or clarify the subject or the main idea in the independent clause. This information can help define the "who, what, where, when, why, and how" of the main idea.

Examples

Who   Being *Chuck Norris*, he could do his own martial arts stunts for the show.

        As *King of England*, Henry the Eighth had the power to create his own church.

What   *Snow day* after *snow day*, school was closed for an entire week.

        Large and *sturdy*, four garbage bags were used to haul out all the trash.

Where   In *India*, people use tusked elephants like we use forklift trucks.

        At the *Smithsonian Institute*, historical artifacts are on display.

When   In the *spring*, crocuses and tulips bloom even when there is still snow.

        Each *morning*, the newspaper was flung into the bushes near the porch.

Why   With *little fuel* in the tank, the barbeque grill wouldn't ignite.

        Because of the *hurricane threat*, all boats were moored in the harbor.

How   By *twisting* his body to the left, the electrician squeezed through the shaft.

        After *adjusting the carburetor*, the driver won the next heat.

PRACTICE 3   Writing Introductory Phrases

Add an introductory phrase or phrases to each independent clause in the following sentences. Punctuate correctly. In the parentheses provided after each sentence, indicate how the introductory phrase helps to explain or clarify the independent clause by writing in the appropriate label: **who, what, where, when, why,** or **how.**

Example: _____ the contestants could not answer.
<u>After the buzzer sounded</u>, the contestants could not answer. (Why)

1. _____ the plane returned to the airport.

    (   )

2. _____ fishing became a favorite pastime.

    (   )

3. _____ the clouds darkened, and the rain came pounding down on the village. (   )

4. _____ the two teams shook hands and went to the locker room. ( )

5. _____ losing to her opponent was especially painful. ( )

6. _____ Denise decided the Mediterranean cruise was much too expensive. ( )

7. _____ they needed to buy extra ice and fans. ( )

8. _____ Lonnie jumped right back up into the saddle. ( )

9. _____ three hundred geese landed on the small pond. ( )

10. _____ all three intersections were blocked by the train. ( )

Special effects, properties, and relationships that exist about and between people and events also can be clarified by using introductory phrases.

	Examples
Description	Being 6 feet 6 inches tall and weighing 260 pounds, the first-year football player was selected to be one of the starting defensive ends.
	By expanding and fluttering beautifully colored tail feathers, the peacock hopes to attract a mate.
Cause and effect	Because of the low voter turnout, the party in power retained its majority.
	Caused by too many people using major appliances, the brownouts continued throughout the night and into the next day.
Definition	Having four sides of the same length, the square is one of the basic geometric designs used in architecture.
	By crying and throwing toys, the child hoped his tantrum would force his parents to let him watch more cartoons.
Comparison	By acting rather than complaining, the newest employee was promoted before those with more seniority.

(continued)

	After the conservatives won and the liberals lost, the school board voted to accept the new budget for the upcoming fiscal year.
Process	By calculating the jet stream position and isobar readings, the meteorologist put together her forecast.
	By counting deposits against expenditures, the bank teller balanced the cash drawer.
Persuasion	With skyrocketing tuition and fees, parents should start college funds for their children before they're born!
	As the IRS is increasing its tax rate on earnings, donating to charity is becoming a more attractive method of reducing taxable income.

PRACTICE 4 — Identifying the Purpose of Introductory Phrases

In the parentheses provided after each sentence, indicate how the introductory phrase helps to explain or clarify the independent clause by writing in the appropriate label: **description, cause and effect, definition, comparison, process,** or **persuasion.** Do not write in the same label twice.

1. As interest rates on loans and credit cards climb, it would be wise to consolidate all bills into one payment to a single lending company. (   )

2. With snowcapped peaks and thick cloud cover, the Himalayas offer some of the world's most spectacular scenery. (   )

3. By using sonar and dazzling speed, dolphins hunt successfully in groups and as individuals. (   )

4. In foggy conditions or bright sunlight, driving lights have reduced the number of automobile collisions. (   )

5. Because of not recruiting younger members, the gang eventually became too old and too small to scare anyone. (   )

6. Consisting of a compartment for air and a breathing tube, the aqua lung has revolutionized undersea exploration. (   )

PRACTICE 5 — Writing Sentences with Introductory Phrases

Write five of your own sentences using an introductory phrase in front of the independent clause. Punctuate correctly. In the parentheses provided following each sentence, write in the label that best describes how the introductory phrase is helping to explain or clarify the independent clause. Use any of the labels you have studied, but don't use the same label twice.

1. _____

   _____

   _____

   (   )

2. _____

   _____

   _____

   (   )

3. _____

   _____

   _____

   (   )

4. _____

   _____

   _____

   (   )

5. _____

   _____

   _____

   (   )

PRACTICE 6   Editing to Punctuate Introductory Phrases

In the following paragraph, add appropriate punctuation to the introductory phrases.

In the movie *Schindler's List* the harshness of racism in World War II Nazi

Germany was realistically brought to the screen. Throughout the movie the idea that "the only good Jew is a dead Jew" was dramatized. During the war Nazi Germany believed that all Jews were inferior, not only to Germans, but also to most of humanity. Because of this superior attitude the only way to truly depict the violence of Nazi racism was to show the indiscriminate murder of the Jews in as realistic detail as possible. For example in one scene the Jews are herded like cattle into train cars and taken to a concentration camp where they are killed by poisonous gas before being incinerated in giant ovens. Because of the realistic interpretation many moviegoers found the movie both moving and disturbing.

PRACTICE 7   **Editing to Punctuate Introductory Phrases**

In the following paragraph, add appropriate punctuation to the introductory phrases.

After graduation from high school prospective college students are faced with the dilemma of which college to attend. All things being equal should a local or out-of-state school be considered? Of course financial concerns are always a factor in the decision. Most important should the money come from parents, loans, scholarships, grants, or some combination of all four sources? After all accumulating debt prior to graduating just adds to the pressure of finding a job afterward.

The Introductory Word

Another way to add variety and rhythm to your writing is by beginning a sentence with an **introductory word,** also called a **sentence modifier.** Although this technique is not used to combine sentences, it is important, nonetheless.

> **Examples**
> Yes, I will be going to the show.
> Well, I might buy a motorcycle instead of a car.
> Obviously, Einstein was an intelligent person by any standard.

Punctuating the Introductory Word

Notice that the introductory words in these examples are followed by a comma just as we saw in Chapter 7 when using the introductory dependent clause before the main clause and in Chapter 8 when using the introductory phrase.

When to Use Introductory Words

Introductory words are most often used to create sentence variety and rhythm, but they also can add useful information to a sentence.

Commonly Used Introductory Words

Ah	Oh
Certainly	Sure, surely
Hmmm	Typically
However	Well
Nevertheless	Yes
Nonetheless	[Names of people and pets
No	being addressed]

Use the introductory word for the following five reasons:

1. To introduce an affirmative or negative reply

> <u>Yes</u>, the team has won three games in a row.
> <u>No</u>, I don't think I will be majoring in Refuse Disposal Management.

2. To address someone by name

> <u>Lennox</u>, bring the newspaper into the dining room.
> <u>Henrietta</u>, please come to the dinner table.

3. To express surprise or wonderment

> <u>Oh</u>, what a gigantic cake!
> <u>Ah</u>, I never suspected that the butler did it!

4. To express a contrast

> <u>However</u>, the business picked up during the next quarter.
> <u>Nevertheless</u>, I will continue to support the school board's decision.

5. To express a contemplative pause

> <u>Well</u>, I was actually thinking about buying a different model of car.
>
> <u>Hmmm</u>, that doesn't sound like something that would interest me.

PRACTICE 8   Identifying and Punctuating Introductory Words

Underline the introductory word in each of the following sentences. Punctuate correctly.

1. No taking the driver's exam is not possible until Monday morning.

2. Ah that picture of the Orion Nebula is amazing.

3. Nevertheless we are spending a full week in Toronto.

4. Eugenia don't drive over the speed limit tonight.

5. Yes the mechanic says he can fix the radiator.

6. However the other team has a better pitching staff.

7. Hmmm I can't decide on sausage or pepperoni on my pizza.

8. Oh I think that news is fantastic.

9. Well I might go hang gliding if the weather conditions are good.

10. Mischa don't leave your dirty clothes on the floor.

PRACTICE 9   Identifying the Purpose of Introductory Words

Underline the introductory word in each of the following sentences. Punctuate correctly. In the parentheses following each sentence, identify one of the five reasons for using the introductory word you have learned: **affirmative or negative reply, address by name, surprise or wonderment, contrast,** or **contemplative pause.**

Example: <u>Ah,</u> that's the biggest hamburger I've ever seen! (surprise or wonderment)

1. Germaine please turn the air conditioning down.

()

2. Nevertheless the new supermarket will be built where the current children's amusement park is located. (_____)

3. No qualifying for the Olympic track team is based on how you do during the tryout meet next month. (_____)

4. Ah this apple strudel is the best I've ever eaten.
(_____)

5. Hmmm I'm not sure I want to be away from my pets that long.
(_____)

6. However the rain washed away the topsoil as well as the grass seed.
(_____)

7. Yes the German shepherd is a great guard dog.
(_____)

8. Well I might take history if it satisfies a graduation requirement.
(_____)

9. Oh the budget is already 20 percent over projected costs.
(_____)

10. Leonardo don't play with your food.
(_____)

Not all single words can be used as introductory words. For example, subordinating conjunctions (see Chapter 7) cannot be used as introductory words. These words must be part of a dependent clause and cannot beseparated from the clause by a comma.

> **Examples**
>
> **(Independent clause)** The coroner examined the body thoroughly. He released the findings to the press.
>
> **(Made into a dependent clause)** After the coroner examined the body thoroughly, he released the findings to the press.
>
> **(Incorrect use of the subordinating conjunction)** After, the coroner examined the body thoroughly, he released the findings to the press.
>
> **(Correct use of an introductory word)** Typically, the coroner examined the body before releasing the findings to the press.

PRACTICE 10 Using Introductory Words

Choose appropriate introductory words from the examples given in this chapter and place them in front of the sentences below. Do not use the same one more than once. Punctuate correctly.

_____ the law will be carried out under the watchful eye of the police.

_____ that is something I will have to think about long and hard.

_____ Manny Ramirez will hit at least one home run tonight.

_____ the nuclear reactor is functioning at 100 percent capacity.

_____ the committee will make a decision in lieu of the president's vote.

_____ go to the store and buy bread and milk.

_____ that behavior is not acceptable at any time.

_____ now that's what I call a gourmet meal.

PRACTICE 11   Writing Sentences with Introductory Words

Create sentences using the introductory words from the examples given in this chapter. Do not use the same one more than once. Punctuate correctly.

1. _____

2. _____

3. _____

4. _____

5. _____

6. _____

7. _____

8. _____

PRACTICE 12   Editing to Add Introductory Words

In the following paragraph, add introductory words to appropriate sentences. Remember, only add an introductory word to introduce an affirmative or negative reply, to address someone by name, to express surprise or wonderment, to express a contrast, or to express a contemplative pause. Be sure to punctuate correctly.

Taking on a car restoration project is a big responsibility at any age. The

pressure is on not to spend money foolishly, especially when it is hard to come by. Proper time management is important to ensure that the project is completed. Dealing with these constraints and knowing that in your hands is a piece of history can lead to stress. Most kids, at fifteen, have not acquired enough money to fund a restoration project, nor do they have an opportunity to borrow the money. By putting in long hours of strenuous work (mowing lawns or cleaning gutters) you can earn enough money to get started. The fact that your parents allow you to own an old car is an achievement in itself! Just learning the basic skills is quite an accomplishment.

PRACTICE 13   Editing to Add Introductory Words

In the following paragraph, add introductory words to appropriate sentences. Remember, only add an introductory word to introduce an affirmative or negative reply, to address someone by name, to express surprise or wonderment, to express a contrast, or to express a contemplative pause. Be sure to punctuate correctly.

Country music is more popular than ever. The music of country artists like Faith Hill, Mary Chapin Carpenter, and Garth Brooks has crossed over to the pop and soft rock audience. The steady, slow beat of traditional country ballads has given way to a more upbeat and rhythmical style that has attracted a much wider audience than ever before. As popular as country music has become, it is now becoming even more widely accepted. Country artists are beginning to make guest appearances with symphony orchestras.

Adding Interrupters to the Sentence

Simple sentences are very good for conveying simple, straightforward ideas. Sometimes, though, reading several simple sentences in a row can be dull. Variety always makes writing more interesting, and a different method of adding variety is using interrupters. Some books also call this extra information *transitional expressions,* or *parenthetical expressions,* or *parenthetical information* because it can be placed in parentheses ( ). Most often, however, interrupters are preceded and followed by commas.

Interrupters are single words, phrases, or clauses often interrupting the flow of the basic clause.

Examples of Single-Word Interrupters

The exam, however, came to an end.

The opera diva, undoubtedly, could hold a single note for a long time.

The scientists, therefore, had a different reaction to the new discovery.

Examples of Phrase Interrupters

The coach, on the other hand, was not pleased with the team's performance.

The entire town, for instance, stopped watching television for a week.

The Southern writer William Faulkner, from Mississippi, wrote "The Bear."

Notice that interrupters most often are placed between the subject and the verb of the main clause. For further discussion of clause interrupters, see The Writer's Resources, pages 392–393.

Commonly Used Interrupters

Single Words	**Phrases**
also	as a matter of fact
besides	as a result
certainly	at last
consequently	believe me
eventually	by the way
finally	for example
furthermore	for instance
however	in fact
incidentally	on the other hand
likewise	to tell the truth
meanwhile	
naturally	
nevertheless	
subsequently	
therefore	
undoubtedly	

Interrupters can be necessary or not necessary to the basic understanding of the main clause. If the interrupter is not necessary to understand the main clause, place commas around it. If the interrupter is necessary to understand the main clause, do not place commas around it.

Examples

The student, with a shocked expression, read the favorable comments on his paper. (unnecessary prepositional phrase—commas needed)

The boy with the red hair was the one riding the bike. (necessary phrase—commas not needed)

The surgeon, consequently, ordered more blood for the operation. (unnecessary single word—commas needed)

The student with the highest grades won the scholarship. (necessary prepositional phrase—commas not needed)

The boss, satisfied with employee morale, cancelled the company picnic. (unnecessary phrase—commas needed)

PRACTICE 14   Punctuating Interrupters

In the following sentences, use commas to set off the single-word interrupters from the basic idea of the sentence. Identifying the subject and the verb may help you select the interrupter.

1. World War II naturally is an event discussed to this day.

2. The United States and Japan unfortunately were both after dominance in the Far East.

3. Poor relations meanwhile developed between the two powers.

The Japanese attack on Pearl Harbor.

4. The two nations subsequently could not come to common agreement.

5. The Empire of Japan therefore attacked Pearl Harbor.

6. Although isolationist, the Congress nevertheless voted for a Declaration of War.

7. The United States consequently entered World War II on December 8, 1941.

8. The war however had begun in Europe in September of 1939.

9. The United States eventually would fight a war on two fronts: Asia and Europe.

10. After six years, the Allies finally defeated the Axis powers.

11. Today, the United States and Japan however are considered allies.

PRACTICE 15   Punctuating Interrupters

In the following sentences, use commas to set off the phrase interrupters from the basic idea of the sentence. Identifying the subject and the verb may help you select the interrupter.

1. Robert Frost for instance is one of America's most beloved poets.

2. Frost in fact was from New England.

3. The poet by the way was funny, witty, and enjoyed poking fun at himself and others.

4. His poetry on the other hand often dealt with death and alienation.

5. "Desert Places" for example is concerned with loneliness.

6. Frost as a matter of fact achieved his first success while living in England.

7. The poet as a result returned to America where his success continued.

8. Robert Frost at last had attained the status of a major poet worldwide.

PRACTICE 16   Punctuating Interrupters

After reading each of the following sentences, decide whether the interrupters are unnecessary or necessary. Punctuate correctly.

1. Our solar system the only planetary system in this part of the galaxy consists of eight major planets.

2. The eight planets commonly grouped into the inner and outer planets vary significantly in composition.

3. The inner planets Mercury, Venus, Earth, and Mars are composed primarily of rock and iron.

4. The outer planets Jupiter, Saturn, Uranus, and Neptune, are much larger and consist mainly of gas and ice.

5. Mercury not only is nearest the sun but also orbits the sun most quickly.

6. The morning star Venus is next closest to the medium-sized star.

7. Earth with a myriad of life forms is the only planet known to have abundant liquid water and oxygen.

8. Mars by the way once had water on its surface.

9. Jupiter's mass of 317 times that of Earth makes it the largest of the planets.

PRACTICE 17 Writing Sentences with Interrupters

Write a sentence for each of the following topics. From the list of commonly used interrupters, provide an appropriate interrupter in each sentence. Do not use the same word or phrase twice. Punctuate correctly.

1. School— _____

_____

2. Speeding— _____

_____

3. Voting— _____

_____

4. War— _____

_____

5. Flowers— _____

_____

6. Breakfast— _____

_____

7. Math— _____

_____

8. Cooking— _____

_____

9. Pets— _____

_____

10. Money— _____

_____

PRACTICE 18   **Writing Sentences with Interrupters**

Write a sentence for each of the following topics. From the list of commonly used interrupters, provide an appropriate interrupter in each sentence. Do not use the same word or phrase twice. Punctuate correctly.

1. Automobiles— _____

_____

2. Dating— _____

_____

3. Vitamins— _____

_____

4. Hobbies— _____

_____

5. Sports— _____

_____

6. Friends— _____

_____

7. Art— _____

_____

8. Computers— _____

_____

9. Humor — _____

_____

10. Clothes— _____

_____

PRACTICE 19 Editing to Punctuate Interrupters

In the following paragraph, place commas around any interrupter if it is unnecessary to the meaning of the main clause. If the interrupter is necessary to the meaning of the main clause, do not place commas around it.

Weight training is an excellent way to get in shape and stay in shape. However, you first need to check with your doctor and fitness expert to plan a routine that will work well for you. Proper stretching to increase flexibility should be the first activity when starting your routine. Stretching also will promote muscular development. Improved workout performance a goal you should have can be achieved with stretching, also. The best stretching according to most fitness experts starts with the muscles in the neck and works down to the ankles. After proper stretching, a ten-to-fifteen minute set of warmup exercises should be done. Only then should you begin weight training.

PRACTICE 20 Editing to Punctuate Interrupters

In the following paragraph, place commas around any interrupter if it is unnecessary to the meaning of the main clause. If the interrupter is necessary to the meaning of the main clause, do not place commas around it.

With every step as I walked down the road breaking the crust on the top of the snow my body became somewhat immune to the freezing cold. My boots caked with snow became heavier with every step, and my pants stiffened by a shellac-like frost cracked at the slightest movement. My muffler wrapped about my neck and face grew more solid as the moisture of my breath froze within its warm and insulating softness. Leaning into the wind, forcing one step after another I felt the sand-like snow piercing my face with needle-sharp harshness making my cheeks red. My eyes were forced downward since there was no way of protecting them, and I grew dependent on the tracks of others to find my way through the blinding wall of snow ahead of me.

Putting It All Together: Sentence Combining to Improve Paragraph Style

Combine the following groups of simple sentences using a combination of sentence-combining strategies (coordination, subordination, and insertion of words and phrases). Omit repeated words, phrases, and unnecessary pronouns.

These exercises are taken from paragraphs from the professional essays in the Additional Readings section at the back of this book. When you have finished combining each group of sentences, you may compare your answer to the paragraph as it was written by the original author. A sample exercise has been done for you.

> **Sample Exercise**
>
> **1.** This happened several summers ago.
> **2.** It was on one of those August evenings.
> **3.** The evenings are endless.
> **4.** The sun is hanging suspended.
> **5.** The sun is above the horizon.
> **6.** I made up my mind.
> **7.** I decided to become beautiful.
>
> **Student Paragraph**
>
> On an August evening several summers ago, I decided to become beautiful. It was one of those endless evenings when the sun was hanging suspended above the horizon.
>
> **Original Paragraph as Written by Author**
>
> Several summers ago, on one of those endless August evenings when the sun hangs suspended just above the horizon, I made up my mind to become beautiful. (Grace Suh, "The Eye of the Beholder," paragraph 1)

Notice that both paragraphs are better written than if the original sentences had been organized into a paragraph.

The professional paragraph is somewhat better organized than the student example because the most important information (the decision to become beautiful) is contained in the independent clause, and the less important information is subordinated in a series of introductory phrases and a dependent clause (Several summers ago) and (on one of those endless August evenings) and (when the sun hangs suspended just above the horizon).

In other words, it is more important to leave the readers with the idea of becoming beautiful than it is to let them know what type of evening it was.

PRACTICE 21

1. The following sentences come from the essay "The Deep Cold" by Verlyn Klinkenborg, paragraph 1. Combine each group of sentences into one sentence. Then combine these sentences into one paragraph.

1.1 Cold sounds deep.
1.2 Cold sounds like scissors.
1.3 Cold sounds like gnashing of a skater's blade.
1.4 Cold sounds like screeching.
1.5 Cold sounds like screeching as you walk across it.

2.1 The sound is like stamping feet.
2.2 The sound is stamping feet at a bus stop.
2.3 The sound is stamping feet at train stations.

3.1 The sound is muted by scarves.
3.2 The sound is muted by mufflers.
3.3 The sound is muted by scarves and mufflers pulled up over the face.
3.4 The sound is muted by scarves and mufflers pulled up around the ears.

_____

_____

_____

_____

_____

2. The following sentences are taken from "The Roommate's Death" by Jan Harold Brunvald, paragraph 5. Combine each group of sentences into one sentence. Then, combine these sentences into one paragraph.

1.1 The night was windy.
1.2 The night was especially dark.
1.3 Rain was threatening.

2.1 All went well for the girls.
2.2 The girls read stories aloud.
2.3 The girls read stories to the three little boys.
2.4 The girls were sitting for the three little boys.
2.5 The girls had no problem putting the boys to bed.
2.6 The boys were put to bed in the upstairs bedroom.

3.1 The boys were put to bed.
3.2 The girls settled down to watch television.

_____

_____

_____

_____

_____

_____

3. The following sentences are taken from "The Eye of the Beholder" by Grace Suh, paragraph 26. Combine each group of sentences into one sentence. Then, combine these sentences into one paragraph.

1.1 I bought the skincare system.
1.2 I bought the foundation.
1.3 I bought the blush.
1.4 I bought the lipliner.
1.5 I bought the lipstick.
1.6 I bought the primer.
1.7 I bought the eyeliner.
1.8 I bought the eyeshadows.
1.9 The eyeshadows came in four colors.

2.1 The stuff filled a bag.
2.2 The bag was the size of a shoe box.

3.1 There was a cost.
3.2 The cost was a lot.

4.1 Estee handed me my receipt.
4.2 She handed it to me with a flourish.

5.1 I told her, "Thank you."

_____

_____

_____

_____

_____

4. The following sentences come from the essay "Online Schools Provide New Education Options" by the Associated Press, paragraphs 7, 8, and 16. Combine each group of sentences into one sentence. Then combine these sentences into one paragraph.

1.1 Classes are held on computers.
1.2 Teachers work from a central office.
1.3 Staff work from a central office.
1.4 Students sign in from on a desktop.
1.5 Students sign in from on a laptop.

2.1 Classes are not all writing.
2.2 Classes are not all arithmetic.
2.3 The students take gym.
2.4 The students take music.
2.5 The students take piano.
2.6 The students take guitar.

3.1 Education is needed.
3.2 Technology is needed.

3.3 The marriage of education and technology is needed.
3.4 Teaching is becoming difficult.
3.5 Teaching is becoming difficult because of increasing enrollments.
3.6 Teaching is becoming difficult because of shrinking budgets.

_____

_____

_____

_____

5. The following sentences are taken from "Indistinguishable from Magic" by Robert L. Forward, paragraph 7. Combine each group of sentences into one sentence. Then, combine these sentences into one paragraph.

1.1 The first travelers to the stars will be our robot probes.
1.2 The probes will be small.
1.3 The probes won't require food.
1.4 They won't require air.
1.5 They won't require water.

2.1 The robotic probes need power supplied by the human race.
2.2 The power levels are within reach of the human race.

3.1 The first interstellar probe could be launched soon.
3.2 It could be launched at the nearest star system.
3.3 The probe could be launched in the next millennium.

_____

_____

_____

_____

 Visit _The Write Start_ Online!

For additional practice with the materials in this chapter, go to

http://www.cengage.com/devenglish/checkett/writestartSP4e.

Chapter Self-Assessment Test

A. Check either True or False on the blank next to the statement.

    T   F

____   ____   Use an introductory phrase or phrases to add information or to clarify or explain the basic idea in an independent clause.

____   ____   Introductory phrases, because they are not independent clauses, cannot explain or clarify properties about a special relationship between persons and events, such as *who*, *what*, *where*, *when*, *why*, and *how*.

____   ____   Introductory phrases, because they are so short, cannot explain or clarify properties about special relationships between persons and events, such as description, definition, cause and effect, comparison, process, and persuasion.

____   ____   The introductory phrase or phrases should be separated from the independent clause with a comma.

B. Use an introductory word at the beginning of a sentence for the following reasons:

    T   F

____   ____   To introduce an affirmative or negative reply.

____   ____   To introduce a list or series of items.

____   ____   To address someone by name.

____   ____   To express surprise or wonderment.

____   ____   To introduce constrast.

____   ____   To express hunger.

____   ____   To expresss a contemplative pause.

PART TWO

Writing Effective Paragraphs

In the preceding chapters, you have been practicing writing the basic sentence types that allow for communicating information with focus, clarity, variety, and rhythm. Sentences are good for conveying short pieces of information, but for longer, more developed ideas, a longer format such as the paragraph is necessary.

The next nine chapters in Part 2 will help you discover, understand, and write the basic paragraph. A paragraph can be a complete piece of writing by itself. However, paragraphs are usually grouped together in longer pieces of writing, for example, essays, letters, reports, research papers, and chapters in a novel or nonfiction work.

In Part 2, you will be introduced to the major elements and processes necessary to write effective paragraphs: prewriting; understanding the structure of a paragraph; creating an outline; writing first drafts; proofreading; and correcting sentence fragments, run-ons, and comma splices. You also will be introduced to the various modes (methods) of development writers use to examine topics:

- Description
- Narration
- Examples
- Classification
- Process
- Comparison and Contrast
- Definition
- Persuasion (including cause and effect)

Each mode of development is discussed in its own chapter, and you often will be assigned to write a paragraph or essay in a particular mode. However, you should keep in mind that mode techniques are usually blended in most pieces of writing. For example, the following paragraph is predominantly descriptive, but it also exhibits a blend of other modes.

> The sprawling, white and brown Tudor mansion sat like a king atop the throne-like hilltop looking down on its subjects. Unlike the mix of plain, wooden colonials and brick ranch houses surrounding it, the Tudor mansion was much more elegant and imposing. Its high arches, lead-traced windows, and fan vaults spoke to roots tracing back to Henry VIII.

The modes appear in the paragraph as follows:

Description: The phrases "sprawling, white and brown," "sat like a king atop the throne-like hilltop looking down on its subjects," "plain, wooden," "brick ranch," "elegant and imposing," and "high arches, lead-traced windows, and fan vaults" describe the three styles of houses.

Classification and *Example:* The phrases "Tudor mansion" and "colonials and brick ranch houses" categorize the houses in the area by style.

Comparison and Contrast and *Persuasion:* The paragraph compares the elegant and stately style of the Tudor mansion to the relatively plain styles of the colonial and ranch houses. The reference to King Henry VIII also supports the contrasting styles. The writer makes the case that because of its style and historical roots, the Tudor mansion is "much more elegant and imposing" than the other two styles of houses.

Definition: A topic can be defined by using one or more of the modes of development. Therefore, the Tudor mansion is defined through description, classification, example, comparison and contrast, and persuasion.

Before you begin to learn about writing paragraphs, let's examine ways to develop ideas and details that form the basis for a paragraph or other piece of writing.

ESL Prewriting Activities

There are a variety of techniques that you can use to develop specific details for writing assignments. The development of a topic is influenced by the **purpose** of the assignment, as well as the **audience.** Often, more than one method of expanding a topic or developing details is necessary for writers. The techniques of **listing, clustering, cubing,** and **cross-examining** are summarized here. You should experiment with many of these techniques (and any others suggested by your writing teachers) in order to overcome writer's block. Later, in Chapter 9, the technique of *questioning* (asking the questions *who, what, when, where, why,* or *how* of the topic) is introduced.

Listing

For this strategy, write the topic at the top of a blank sheet of paper (or at the top of your computer screen). Then quickly list any ideas that pop into your head. This is a form of free association; do not edit, correct, or revise. A list on the topic of musicianship may look like this.

Musicianship			
performance	attention	strings	practice
anxiety	phrasing	cello	technique
concerts	dynamics	violin	emotion
conductors	interpretation	flutes	control
rehearsal	crescendo	brass	tension
orchestra	audience	oboes	tone
solo	musicians	percussion	intonation

Keep writing for ten minutes to inspire more thoughts. The act of writing actually helps thinking processes for many people. Next, look at your list and see which topics are related (such as technique, control, practice, interpretation, and dynamics). After you have chosen several ideas on your list that would best develop your topic, group them in the correct order (time/space, most to least important, and so on). This last step also helps you formally outline your topic.

Clustering (Mind Mapping)

This technique is similar to listing but is less structured. Write your topic in the center of a piece of paper. Place related ideas in nearby circles, then keep connecting the circles with lines, grouping those ideas that seem to be related. Note the following diagram on the topic of violence.

After studying the diagram or map, select the cluster of ideas that best develops the topic or thesis statement you have chosen. Further clustering on these selected terms may help expand your options. Additionally, you may wish to try another method of prewriting at this point.

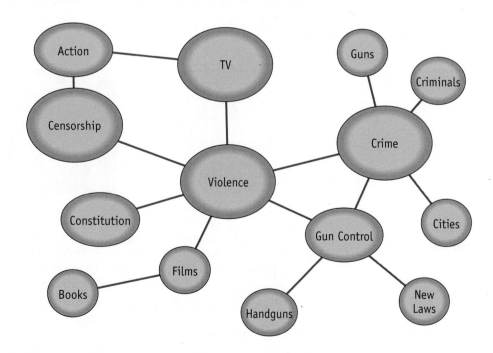

PRACTICE 1   Clustering (Mapping)

Choose one of the following topics, and write it in the center of a piece of paper. Then cluster your ideas around it.

> A favorite holiday
> The color red
> The future
> A dream
> A best/worst boss
> A hero

Cubing

Another type of brainstorming uses a cube to generate new approaches to a topic. Imagine a six-sided cube with the following questions on each side:

Describe the topic: What does the subject look like? What is the size, color, shape, texture, smell, sound, and so forth? Which details are unique?

Compare or contrast it: What is your subject like? How does it differ from similar subjects? Give details.

Free associate it: What does your subject remind you of? What further ideas do you think of?

Analyze it: What are the parts of the subject? How does each part function? How are the parts connected? What is the significance of this subject?

Argue for or against it: What are the arguments for or against your topic? What are the advantages and disadvantages?

Apply it: How can the subject be used?

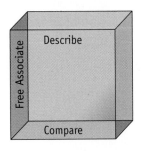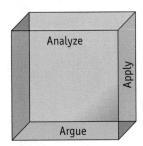

Approach your topic from each of the above six perspectives, freewriting your answers as you did with the techniques of listing or clustering and giving yourself ten to fifteen minutes to explore each idea. Do not worry about correctness at this point. Review your responses and see whether any are suited to your assignment or inspire new ideas for the writing assignment.

Cross-Examining

This approach can be used with a partner or individually. It is a variation of the questioning form that is introduced in Chapter 9. The questions can be grouped depending on either the type of essay assigned or the type of essay you would like to write. Interview yourself or your partner regarding your topic.

Definition
1. How is the topic/subject defined or explained by the dictionary or encyclopedia?
2. How do most people define the topic informally?
3. How do I define the subject?
4. What is the history, origin, or background of the topic?
5. What are some examples of the topic?

Relationship
1. What is the cause of the topic/subject?
2. To what larger group or category does the subject belong?
3. What are the values or goals of the subject?
4. What are the effects of the subject?

Comparison and Contrast
1. What is the topic/subject similar to?
2. What is the topic different from?
3. What is the subject better than?
4. What is the subject worse than?
5. What is the subject opposite to?

Testimony
1. What do people say about the topic/subject?
2. What authorities exist on this topic?
3. Has anything been written on this subject?
4. What are the important statistics?
5. Is there any further research on the topic?
6. Have I had any personal experience on this topic?

Circumstance
1. Is this subject/topic possible?
2. Is the subject impossible?
3. When has this subject happened before?
4. What might prevent it from happening?
5. Why might it happen again?
6. Who or what is associated with the topic?

Not all of these questions will apply to every topic. Choose the questions that help develop your topic most thoroughly.

Brainstorming

Brainstorming is a process by which people develop ideas, supporting examples, or new topics by tossing out ideas for general discussion. It can be done individually or as a group. However, brainstorming is most useful when a group is working on a project and the group members need to combine their ideas and experiences.

PRACTICE 2	Brainstorming

Break into groups of three or four. Choose a topic from one of the previous lists, or use a topic assigned by your instructor. The purpose of the exercise should be to find related subtopics and examples to develop the topic into a paragraph or essay. The members of the group should discuss the topic, taking turns mentioning related topics for five minutes. One member of the group should record the group's ideas.

Next, for each idea listed, each member of the group should try for five to ten minutes to think of an effective or creative example or supporting detail. The student who recorded the topics and examples can report the results to the rest of the class for comparison or general discussion.

9

The Paragraph

Using the "Listing" technique described on pages 128–129, make a list of things you associate with a graduation ceremony. Do this as free association; do not edit, correct, or revise the list. You can do that later. The object here is to write down as many ideas as you can think of.

Many of the elements in longer pieces of writing such as essays are found in the paragraph. Thus, the paragraph is a good model to use before learning to write longer pieces.

A **paragraph** is a group of sentences concerned with developing or expressing a single **topic** (one main idea). In fact, what you are reading right now is a paragraph. It is developing the concept of the paragraph. Generally, paragraphs can be as long as you want them to be, although most are usually four to fifteen sentences in length. The key to writing a good paragraph is to make it long enough to develop the topic but no longer. This paragraph is between four and fifteen sentences in length, and it is describing the elements that make up the paragraph.

There are two basic types of sentences in a paragraph: the **topic sentence** and **support sentences.** The topic sentence tells the reader what the main idea, or topic, of the paragraph is. Although there is no set place in the paragraph for the topic sentence, making the topic sentence the first sentence in the paragraph will make organizing and developing the topic easier. The topic sentence is followed by support sentences that explain, clarify, and define the topic by using specific details. Support sentences should demonstrate a variety of styles to show the relationship between the various pieces of information and to create rhythm (see Chapters 3 through 8). Exhibit 9–1 summarizes the elements and characteristics of a paragraph.

Exhibit 9–1

> 1. A topic sentence announces one main idea (the topic).
> 2. Support sentences use specific details to develop the main idea.
> 3. Sentence variety connects related ideas and adds rhythm.

Let's look at the characteristics of a basic paragraph. Specific points are illustrated in the bulleted comments following the paragraph.

> **Example Paragraph**
>
> Sophocles, the Greek dramatist, was greatly admired for his tragedies. *Oedipus* was his most famous tragedy, and Aristotle praised it as the finest example of dramatic irony. Sophocles wrote over 130 plays. Even though he was so prolific, his plays won over twenty first prizes at drama festivals.

- The first sentence is the topic sentence, and it announces the topic (Sophocles) and the **controlling idea** (which also contains the writer's attitude toward the topic: that Sophocles *was greatly admired* for his tragedies).
- The following three support sentences develop the controlling idea by (1) naming his most famous tragedy and explaining why it was praised by a famous critic; (2) giving the vast number of plays he wrote; and (3) giving the number of times his plays were rewarded.
- The sentences also exhibit variety. The first sentence contains extra information between the commas. The second sentence is coordinated with the coordinating conjunction *and*. The third sentence is a simple sentence. The fourth sentence is subordinated by using an introductory dependent clause preceding the independent clause.

The Topic Sentence

The topic sentence has two parts: the **topic/subject** and the **controlling idea.** The topic is the subject of the paragraph. The controlling idea states what the writer will be developing about the subject of the paragraph, and it contains the writer's attitude toward the subject. The controlling idea limits what you can say about the topic subject so that you don't stray to other subjects or ideas.

> **Example**
>
> In a movie, music often enhances a romantic atmosphere.

The subject is "music." The controlling idea is "often enhances a romantic atmosphere." The attitude is "often enhances."

In a paragraph with this topic sentence, the controlling idea about the music is that it is romantic. The writer cannot talk about other aspects of the movie, such as violence, comedy, production costs, advertising, or attendance figures. The controlling idea forces the writer to talk about only those features of the music that developed the romantic aspects of the movie.

Let's look at another topic sentence.

> **Example**
>
> The Marshall Plan brought economic relief to Europe.

The subject is "the Marshall Plan." The controlling idea is that it "brought economic relief to Europe." In a paragraph with this topic sentence, the writer cannot write about European art, pollution, hunting, or vegetation. The writer must focus on economic factors that became successful because of the Marshall Plan.

Topic sentences missing a controlling idea lack focus and specific direction. Without a controlling idea, the writer's attitude about the subject can be unclear.

> **Examples**
>
> Soccer is a popular high school sport. (incomplete controlling idea—*popular* is an attitude only)
>
> LeBron James is a basketball player. (no controlling idea—this is simply a statement of fact)
>
> Soccer is a popular high school sport because it is relatively inexpensive to fund. (controlling idea: *cheap funding* makes soccer popular—the attitude)
>
> LeBron James's diverse skills make him an exciting basketball player. (controlling idea: James is exciting because of *diverse skills*—*exciting* is the attitude)

PRACTICE 1	Identifying Topics and Controlling Ideas

In the following sentences, circle the topic/subject, and underline the controlling idea.

Example: (Swiss watches) are popular because of the fine craftsmanship with which they are made.

1. Mud-slinging and personal attacks turn off some people when it comes to politics.

2. Many students dislike high school because of social cliques and favoritism for some students.

3. Families can help children by being a support system for all their activities.

4. A hobby can assist people in easing the stresses of everyday life.

5. The movie was a success because of the script, the acting, and the special effects.

6. Vacation expenses can be reduced by purchasing a good travel book.

7. The depletion of the ozone layer might cause global warming and an increase in skin cancers.

8. Many current fads are driven by how the rich and famous are portrayed in the media.

9. Helping others can make almost any profession a rewarding experience.

10. Laws are effective only if they are enforced fairly and equitably.

PRACTICE 2 — Identifying Topics and Controlling Ideas

In the following sentences, circle the topic/subject, and underline the controlling idea.

1. Exercising can be more enjoyable if done in a group.

2. The fence was built to keep the coyotes away from the livestock.

3. The band played an extra hour because their fans wouldn't let them off the stage.

4. Great teamwork has made the United States' women's soccer team an international success.

5. Pizza is a best selling fast food because of the variety of toppings available.

6. Versatility and size make the laptop computer a good business tool for travelers.

7. Learning about long-term investing can help people have a happier retirement experience.

8. The Spanish Inquisition impaired scientific thought for decades.

9. Technology has as many drawbacks as it does advantages.

10. A quiet place with good lighting can help students study more effectively.

PRACTICE 3   Rewriting Poor Topic Sentences

The following sentences are inadequate as topic sentences because they lack a complete controlling idea. Turn them into topic sentences by adding a controlling idea to each.

1. The Final Four basketball tournament is exciting.

_____

_____

2. Dining out is enjoyable.

_____

_____

3. I attend college.

_____

_____

4. Live theater is dramatic.

_____

_____

5. My clothes are stylish.

_____

_____

6. I drive a Volvo.

_____

_____

7. Dr. Jonas Salk created a vaccine to combat polio.

_____

_____

8. Many new stadiums are being built with old stadium features.

_____

_____

9. Museums house many beautiful sculptures.

_____

_____

10. The final days of the Vietnam War were hectic.

_____

_____

PRACTICE 4	Writing Topic Sentences

Write topic sentences for the following subjects. Don't forget to add the controlling idea.

1. Nuclear energy _____

_____

2. Presidential elections _____

_____

3. Rock music _____

_____

4. Jogging _____

_____

5. Farming _____

_____

6. Science fiction _____

_____

7. Fight against terrorism _____

_____

8. Tornadoes _____

_____

9. Vacationing _____

_____

10. Clothes _____

_____

Support Sentences

Support sentences follow the topic sentence and develop the subject using specific examples, details, and facts. These support ideas must be consistent with the controlling idea. In other words, the controlling idea unifies the paragraph by determining the kind of support ideas you can use in the support sentences.

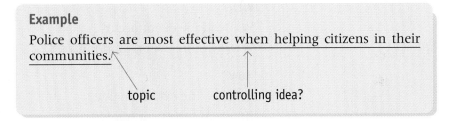

> **Example**
> Police officers are most effective when helping citizens in their communities.
>
> topic   controlling idea?

Support sentences for this topic sentence would focus on *what* police officers do to help citizens and might include such activities as

    a. finding lost/stolen property
    b. solving crimes
    c. preventing crimes

Six Important Support Questions

When writing a story, a reporter asks six questions. The answers provide the focus that allows them to select the details, facts, and examples to develop the story with specific information. The six questions are **who, what, where, when, why,** and **how.**

After you have selected or have been given the topic you are to write about, decide on the controlling idea. To do this, choose which of the following reporter's questions allows you to write about the topic with the desired focus.

For instance, suppose your topic is an *important event*. In the support sentences, you could focus on

> **Who?**
> Who started the event?
> Who attended/witnessed/participated in the event?
> Who was affected by the event?
>
> (*continued*)

What?

What was the event?

What happened before/during/after the event?

What was special about the event?

Where?

Where did the event occur?

Did the location affect the event in any way?

Did the location have historical significance?

When?

When did the event occur (A.M./P.M., day, month, year)?

Did the time frame add any special significance to the event?

Did the event coincide with a historically significant time?

Why?

Why did the event occur?

Why was the event important?

How?

How did the event happen?

How was the event funded?

How was the event advertised?

You can add your own focus to these questions if other ideas come to you. There is no need to limit yourself to the questions presented in the list.

Examples

1. Reading can help people become better educated.
2. Reading is best done in a quiet, secluded place.
3. Anyone interested in becoming a better writer should read as much as possible.

Although the topic/subject of each sentence, *reading*, is the same, the focus of the controlling idea is different. In sentence 1, the focus is on *what* reading can do for people (educate them); in sentence 2, the focus is on *where* reading is best accomplished (in a quiet, secluded place); and in sentence 3, the focus is on *who* (anyone interested in becoming a writer).

Paragraph Unity

The topic sentence in a body paragraph announces the subject of the paragraph, the attitude the writer has toward the subject, and the controlling idea by which the subject will be discussed. Therefore, all support sentences in the body paragraph should explain, clarify, and directly relate to the topic sentence. This is called *paragraph unity*. The prefix *uni-* means "as one." So, *unity* means that all the information in your body paragraph should act as "one unit" to help the reader understand what you are telling him or her about the subject.

Read the following paragraph. Does it demonstrate unity?

> Investing in the stock market can help accumulate money for retirement. Buying treasury bills directly from the federal government guarantees a small but steady dividend each year. In 1929, the stock market crashed leading to the Great Depression. John Steinbeck wrote a novel, *The Grapes of Wrath*, reflecting the terrible consequences the depression had on average families.

The answer is "no." The topic sentence states that the paragraph will explain how *investing in stocks* (the subject) *can help* (the attitude) *in accumulating money for retirement* (the controlling idea). In the paragraph above, the support sentences introduce ideas about

- Investing in treasury bills (not stocks)
- The Great Depression (a historical event not having to do with buying stocks for retirement)
- A novel written by a famous writer (the novel was not about investing in the stock market)

Although all three support sentences have something to do with investing and money and how each affects lives, they do not speak directly and specifically to the topic sentence subject. Now, look at the following paragraph. Does it display paragraph unity?

> Investing in the stock market can help accumulate money for retirement. Even though stocks go up and down over the short term, the stock market over the long term has continued to go up. Therefore, investing in stocks will make you money over your lifetime, so by the time you are ready to retire, you will have a nice "nest egg" to supplement your other retirement income, such as social security and business retirement account. The stock market has many types of investment strategies that can fit the amount of money you can invest each month.

The answer is "yes." The support sentences do explain, clarify, and directly relate to investing in stocks for retirement.

- It is important to know that the stock market has always gone up over the long term because you are going to want to accumulate money for a long time until you can retire.
- Because the stock market goes up over the long term, your stock investments will continue to accumulate funds, assuring you of a good "nest egg."
- Because all people do not have the same amount of money to invest each month, the stocks market has many investment vehicles to make certain you have stocks to invest in.

All of the sentences in the paragraph support the topic, the attitude, and the controlling idea of the topic sentence. This body paragraph demonstrates excellent paragraph unity.

Paragraph Coherence

Along with *unity*, paragraphs should demonstrate *paragraph coherence*. Just as "adhere" means for things to stick together, "cohere" means, for a paragraph, that the elements in the paragraph should "stick together." For your paragraphs to show coherence, there are five elements that you should consider:

- Logical order of events
- Transitional expressions
- Key concept repetition
- Substituting pronouns for nouns
- Parallelism

These tools are like the nuts and bolts used to connect two beams in a building's structure, or a handle of a lawn mower to the mower's deck, or the side of a computer table to its top.

Logical Order of Events

It is important that the events in your paragraphs demonstrate logical order. How you order your information helps the reader understand what you are trying to explain to the reader about the subject. There are three types of information ordering that you need to consider:

- Time order
- Space order
- Order of ideas

Time Order

It is helpful to order the ideas in your paragraphs with a sense of time. Time is important in all of our lives. We have many clocks and watches, on walls, buildings, wrists, computer monitors, and cell phones, to keep us aware of the time because the events in our lives are connected to time: when we eat breakfast, lunch, and dinner; when we work out at the gym; when we do homework; when we play with our children; when church services begin; even when it's time to sleep to take a break from worrying about time!

The following paragraph develops the ideas *chronologically* ("chronos" means "time" and "logic" refers to "order"—so "chronologically" means "time order").

> Phil had an important dinner meeting with a client at 7 P.M. At 8 A.M., Phil took his car into the dealer for repairs. After an hour's wait, the service technician explained the repairs necessary to fix the damage. By 10 A.M., Phil had talked to the service manager to get an estimate on the costs. Phil called his insurance agent at 10:30 A.M. to see if the bill was covered under his policy. Phil returned to the dealer's at 6 P.M. and picked up his car. He made it to the restaurant on time for his dinner with the client.

This paragraph demonstrates good chronological order. The topic sentence establishes the importance of an event associated with a specific time: Phil's important business meeting at 7 P.M. The time sequences "8 A.M., 9 A.M., 10 A.M., 10:30 A.M., and 6 P.M." keep the reader focused on the time frame in which the events are unfolding, and they help establish the "importance" of the time sequence of the events in Phil's life.

Space Order

Sometimes, the physical space in which the events are unfolding is important and should be emphasized. Depending on the kind of space you are describing, you can move from top to bottom, left to right, inside to outside, or any appropriate "direction." Consider the following paragraph for its space order in describing a field from a distance to close-up:

> The tall fir trees surrounded the open field. At the base of the trees, small shrubs ringed the green expanse like a floating fence. The field was dotted with blue "heal-all" flowers. On many of the flower petals, small beads of dew glistened in the morning sun. Tiny insects swam in the dew drops as if lounging in their own backyard pool.

Notice how the writer keeps you moving from the outside to the inside of the setting. You are moved from the trees, closer still to the bushes, still closer to the flowers, and even more closely to the petals, to the dew drops, and almost microscopically, to the little insects in the dew drops. It's almost like being in a movie theater at the beginning of a movie, as the director sets the scene with a long-shot and all the while moving you closer and closer to some important aspect of the scene.

Order of Ideas

If you were to explain to a friend how to save computer information on a disk, you would not explain the process with ideas given in the following order:

1. Hit the "Save as" icon on the left menu.
2. Click on the "File" icon on the top tool bar to display options.
3. Place the disk into the port on the CPU.
4. Click on the "Save in" tool bar for the drop-down menu to display.
5. Move to the lower tool bar and click on "Save."
6. Click on "3½ Floppy (A:)."
7. In the "File Name" box, type in the name of your document.

This ordering of the steps is not logical, and your friend would not be able to accomplish the task. You would be more successful in helping your friend if you ordered the ideas in the logical way they would be done.

1. Place the disk into the port on the CPU.
2. Click on the "File" icon on the top tool bar to display options.
3. Hit the "Save as" icon on the left menu.
4. Click on the "Save in" tool bar for the drop-down menu to display.
5. Click on "3½ Floppy (A:)."
6. In the "File Name" box, type in the name of your document.
7. Move to the lower tool bar and click on "Save."

This order of ideas is logical. It demonstrates a step-by-step order of events that will mean success for your friend. As a writer, it is your responsibility to order the ideas in your paragraphs for the maximum clarity in order for your reader to understand the information you are explaining about the subject.

Transitional Expressions

As you move from one idea or event in a paragraph, it is helpful to the reader if you link these ideas and events with *transitional expressions*. You may have already experienced some of these devices in other chapters where they are labeled *coordinating conjunctions, adverbial conjunctions, introductory words,* and *subordinating conjunctions.* What follows is a list of commonly used transitional expressions and how they are used:

The Relationship	The Transitional Expression
Results	as a result of . . . , consequently, therefore, thus, because
Comparison	in comparison, similarly, likewise
Contrast	in contrast, but, however, although, otherwise
Examples	for example, namely, another . . . , for instance, namely
Sequence	first . . . , second . . . , third . . . , next, then, also, finally, lastly, additionally, further more, soon

Notice in the following two paragraphs how the use of transitional expressions helps to connect the ideas to show the relationship existing between the ideas.
Without transitional expressions:

> The pilot took off from the airport in bright sunshine. The storm clouds on the horizon were thick and black. The small plane began to dip and shake. The winds from the approaching storm buffeted the small craft. The pilot struggled to keep the plane aloft. She called the airport tower for advice. She increased her speed. She headed the plane into the wind. The plane responded to the controls. She landed the plane safely at her destination. She called the tower personnel and thanked them for their help.

Notice that in this paragraph all the ideas, although related, sound separate and distinct from one another. Also, you should notice that the rhythm is choppy and has an abrupt "stop and start . . . stop and start" quality, and all the sentences either start with the word *The* or the word *She*, which does not make for good sentence variety. They are all simple sentences.
With transitional expressions:

> The pilot took off from the airport in bright sunshine; **however**, the storm clouds on the horizon were thick and black. **Soon**, the small plane began to dip and shake **because** the winds from the approaching storm buffeted the small craft, **and** the pilot struggled to keep the plane aloft. **First**, she called the airport tower for advice. **Next**, she increased her speed. **Then**, she headed the plane into the wind. **As a result**, the plane responded to the controls. **Afterwards**, she landed the plane safely at her destination. **Finally**, she called the tower personnel and thanked them for their help.

Notice how this paragraph reads with much better rhythm and how the ideas are connected to show good coherence. Each idea is connected, or linked, to the next idea by a transitional expression that helps the reader understand the information more clearly. Also notice the sentence variety in the paragraph. By using transitional expressions, your writing will be clearer and easier to understand, and the reader will be better informed.

Key Concept Repetition

In longer works, because you are expressing so many ideas, it is vital that you keep the reader focused on the topic. One technique that will help you to accomplish this task is to repeat key concepts and words. Usually, the key concepts are expressed through your nouns: people, places, and things. For instance, in a paragraph taken from a longer work, such as the one that follows, you might repeat key words and phrases to keep the reader focused on the main topic.

When trying to find a **job**, two tools are vital to the process if you hope to have any chance of success. First, complete a **resume** listing your **education**, **work history**, and **personal attributes**, such as **hobbies** and **social** and **charitable organizations** to which you belong. Along with your **resume**, write a **letter of application**. The **letter of application,** unlike the **resume**, summarizes your **education**, **work history**, **hobbies**, and **social** and **charitable organizations** and tailors them to the specific **job** for which you are applying. In this way, the **resume** and **letter of application** work together to give the prospective employer a more complete picture of you, your talents, and how they might fit with the **job** and the company.

By repeating and stressing the key words, most often nouns, the focus of the writing remains clear to the reader. However, there are times when repetition can be cumbersome and unnecessary. When this happens, the repetition can become a bit awkward. This can be overcome by replacing the key nouns with pronouns.

Substituting Pronouns for Key Nouns

Another method for achieving coherence is substituting pronouns for key nouns. The prefix *pro-* means "for," as "standing in for" or "representing." So, a *pronoun* is a word that can stand in for or represent a noun. Some commonly used pronouns are *he, she, it, you, me, him, her, us, them, we,* and *they.* [See *The Writer's Resources* for more information in regard to pronouns.]

In the following paragraph, key nouns are in bold. In the paragraph that follows, pronouns have been substituted for some of the key nouns. By doing so, the writing appears less awkward but still retains enough key noun repetition to keep the reader's focus.

The **children** attended Patricia's birthday **party**. While at the **party**, the **children** ate **cake**. The **cake** was chocolate with white icing. The **children** also ate **ice cream**. The **ice cream** was neopolitan, consisting of vanilla, chocolate, and strawberry flavors. The **children** also played **games**. The **games** included hide and seek, pin the tail of the donkey, and Twister. The **children** watched as Patricia opened her **presents**. The **children** also received a **present** for attending the **party**. The **party** was a great success. All the **children** had a wonderful time at the **party**.

Creating the Working Outline of a Paragraph

Before you begin writing, you may want to sketch out the major ideas that will appear in your paragraph. This can help you discover whether you have a topic, controlling idea, and support ideas that work together for proper development. To create a **working outline,** list your topic, controlling idea, and support ideas in a ladder-like list.

> **Example**
> Topic: Dieting
> Controlling idea: Can cause harmful effects
> Support ideas: bulimia
>   malnutrition
>   psychological problems

In this paragraph, the harmful effects of dieting are discussed. This topic is developed and supported by using bulimia, malnutrition, and psychological problems as the negative outcomes that dieting can produce. The finished paragraph might look like this:

> Dieting can cause many harmful effects. It can lead to a potentially deadly eating disorder called bulimia. This disorder is characterized by eating binges followed by self-induced vomiting or laxative abuse. Because the body is not ingesting the proper amounts of nutrients, malnutrition often occurs. Of course, physical problems are not the only negative effects caused by dieting. Stress and a poor self-image can lead to self-destructive psychological states requiring long-term medical help. The safest and most effective method to lose weight is eating balanced meals combined with a consistent exercise program.

PRACTICE 5   Creating Working Outlines

To practice creating *working outlines*, add a controlling idea for each of the subjects listed below. Then, using the reporter's six questions, list three specific details that develop the controlling idea. Try to use all six of the reporter's questions. After you are finished, you will have a list of all the basic ideas that will go into the paragraph. This is called a *working outline* because the paragraph is still unfinished.

1. The *Star Wars* movies

Controlling idea: _____

a. _____

b. _____

c. _____

2. The United Nations

Controlling idea: _____

a. _____

    b. _____

    c. _____

3. Computers

    Controlling idea: _____

    a. _____

    b. _____

    c. _____

4. Abraham Lincoln

    Controlling idea: _____

    a. _____

    b. _____

    c. _____

5. Exercising

    Controlling idea: _____

    a. _____

    b. _____

    c. _____

6. Student loans

    Controlling idea: _____

    a. _____

    b. _____

    c. _____

7. Violence

    Controlling idea: _____

    a. _____

    b. _____

    c. _____

8. Course scheduling

    Controlling idea: _____

a. _____

b. _____

c. _____

9. Recycling

Controlling idea: _____

a. _____

b. _____

c. _____

10. Vacations

Controlling idea: _____

a. _____

b. _____

c. _____

Writing the First Draft

To write your first draft of any one paragraph, combine the topic and the controlling idea listed in your working outline to create the topic sentence. Then write a sentence for each of the specific detail ideas. These will be your support sentences used to develop the topic sentence. When you match your topic sentence with your support sentences, you'll have a **first draft,** or **rough draft,** paragraph.

> **Example**
> Topic: Civil War
> Controlling idea (reporter's question—*who?*): Leaders having an impact on war.
> A. Lincoln   B. Grant   C. Lee
>
> **Rough Draft Paragraph**
> The Civil War had three great leaders. President Lincoln believed that all men should be free. General Grant enjoyed drinking whiskey and smoking cigars. General Lee symbolized the belief that an aristocratic class should govern men of unequal status.

PRACTICE 6   **Writing First Drafts**

On separate sheets of paper, using the ten examples you have created in Practice 5, turn each example into a short paragraph of four sentences.

Revising the First Draft

No one—not even professional writers—creates a perfect paragraph in the first draft. There are always some rough spots to smooth out—why else do you think the first draft is called the rough draft? To improve what you wrote in your rough draft, you must revise.

As you revise, answer these four questions:

- Is the topic/subject clear?
- Will the controlling idea develop the subject adequately?
- Do my support sentences consist of specific facts, details, and examples?
- Is there sentence variety?

Let's look at our rough draft from the previous example and ask our four revision questions.

> **Example**
>
> (A) The Civil War had three great leaders. (B) President Lincoln believed that all men should be free. (C) General Grant enjoyed drinking whiskey and smoking cigars. (D) General Lee symbolized the belief that an aristocratic class should govern men of unequal status.

1. **Is the topic/subject clear?** The topic/subject is clear: Civil War leaders.
2. **Will the controlling idea develop the subject adequately?** There is no controlling idea that clarifies how the subject will be developed. The topic sentence is simply a statement of fact.

   Revised topic sentence with controlling idea: Three great leaders embodied the ideals of the North and South during the Civil War. (Now, the controlling idea clarifies that it is the beliefs of the three leaders that will be discussed.)
3. **Do my support sentences consist of specific facts, details, and examples?** Support sentences (B) and (D) consist of details that support the controlling idea. However, sentence (C) does not. General Grant's enjoying whiskey and cigars does not explain how his beliefs symbolized the North's beliefs.

   Revised support sentence: General Grant believed that all men should determine their own destiny. (This rewrite clarifies Grant's belief and mirrors Lincoln's belief as stated in sentence [B].)
4. **Is there sentence variety?** All the sentences in the paragraph are simple sentences. Although these sentences are grammatically correct, they don't add rhythm or help to link the ideas they express.

   Revised sentences demonstrating variety: (A) Three great leaders embodied the ideals of the North and South during the Civil War. (B) While President Lincoln detested the thought of war, he believed that all men should be free. (C) General Grant shared Lincoln's belief, for he believed that all men should determine their own destiny. (D) General Lee symbolized the belief that an aristocratic class should govern men of unequal status.

> **The Final Draft**
>
> Three great leaders embodied the ideals of the North and South during the Civil War. While President Lincoln detested the thought of war, he believed that all men should be free. General Grant shared Lincoln's belief, for he believed that all men should determine their own destiny. General Lee symbolized the belief that an aristocratic class should govern men of unequal status.

In this revision, the information is presented more clearly, and the rhythm moves the reading along smoothly and quickly. This is a sign of mature, controlled writing.

PRACTICE 7   Revising First Drafts

On separate sheets of paper, revise the rough draft paragraphs you wrote in Practice 6.

Proofreading: The Final Step

After revising your rough draft into a final draft, there is still one last step you should accomplish before submitting your work.

You should always take time to make sure that your work does not have errors that will detract from its presentation. A great idea, one that professional writers use, is to have someone else read your finished writing. Sometimes, it is easier for someone else to see errors and inconsistencies than it is for the writer. Ultimately, the errors in your writing are your responsibility to find and correct. Typically, you should look for the following types of errors:

a. Sentence fragments; see Chapter 2 for a review of correcting sentence fragments.
b. Run-on sentences and comma splice sentences; see Chapter 3 for a review of correcting run-on and comma splice sentences. Use your computer's *grammarcheck* function to help you correct errors as you find them but don't rely on it entirely.
c. Spelling; use both your computer's *spellcheck* function and a dictionary to help you correct errors as you find them. Remember, *spellcheck* does not correct for meaning. If you use *lien* instead of *lean*, *spellcheck* will not correct the error because *lien* is spelled correctly even though it is not the word you meant to use.

PRACTICE 8   Correcting Sentence Fragments

Find and correct sentence fragments in the following paragraph. Neatly write your corrections in the text.

Facing the Night

I was eight years old the first time I had the biggest scare of my life. The thought of sleeping in the basement all by myself. I'll never forget that night. My brother was at the house of his best friend, and that left me in the "dungeon" all by myself. At first, I didn't think it would be that bad. Then, night came. There I was, lying in my bed in darkness. Where I could not see my hand in front of my face. Soon, could hear every sound a dark, large, haunted and gloomy house makes. As my eyes adjusted to the darkness, enough light shining through the basement window let me see all the scary monsters on the wall. Quickly, I pulled the covers over my head and started to pray for sunlight. After a few minutes I heard a noise. The covers from my head only to see my brother standing in the doorway. His best friend was sick, so he had to come home. What a relief!

PRACTICE 9   Correcting Sentence Fragments

Find and correct sentence fragments in the following paragraph. Neatly write your corrections in the text.

My Baby Brother

Nothing changed my life like the birth of my second brother. In July of 2008, my thirty-two-year-old mother; announced she was pregnant. My brother Ryan and I thrilled by the thought of a baby; however, at the time we didn't realize what actually having a new member of the family involved. Didn't know about all the crying sessions or diaper changes. Soon afterwards, the newness of the baby and things started to get back to a routine. Went back to work. Ryan began staying after school for basketball practice. As for me, my life drastically. I became my mother's full-time baby-sitter.

PRACTICE 10   Correcting Run-On Sentences

Find and correct the run-on sentence errors in the following paragraph. Neatly write your corrections in the text.

My Happiest Moment

The happiest moment of my life was the day I was married. The day started out a blustery 32 degrees. The sun was shining it looked to be a great day. First, we began decorating the hall, blowing up balloons and arranging tables my fiancé took his buddies to play a chilly round of golf. Next, the bridesmaids headed off to the beauty salon to get their hair and nails done to perfection. Time was moving very quickly there were still many projects that needed to be attended to before the wedding could begin. Finally, people began to arrive at the church they were wearing their finest dresses and suits. The ceremony was beautiful everything had fallen into place. The hardest part was over we would be heading for the reception to party away the tensions of all the hard work and worry that had gone into the planning. Before the night ended, my new husband and I made a toast we thanked each and every person for helping to make this a beautiful day that we would never forget.

PRACTICE 11 — Correcting Run-On Sentences

Find and correct the run-on sentences in the following paragraph. Neatly write your corrections in the text.

Unnatural Power

As the sky darkened and the clouds began to move in, the rain started to fall. Bursts of lightning shone across the horizon the crack of thunder pierced the air. The tentacle-like bolts of lightning struck the ground, leaving dark trenches marring the landscape. Trees were splintered and power lines were snapped. The ferocious winds were like stampeding animals so buildings were toppled like so many miniature Monopoly houses. The winds reached a treacherous ninety miles per hour the rain was just as dangerous. Small creeks swelled to overflowing so backyards and driveways carried water into the streets. The town sustained over a million dollars worth of damage yet the people began cleaning and helping each other before the storm had even abated, such is the spirit of small-town America.

PRACTICE 12   Correcting Comma Splice Errors

Find and correct the comma splice errors in the following paragraph. Neatly write your corrections in the text.

The Journey's End

It was early June, the sun was bright but not blistering on my face. The silent motion of the pedals of my bike moved me closer to my destination. It had been two months since my last visit with Bev, her usual shining face grew grim as she saw me approach. Her tone was one of concern, "Have you spoken to your mother today?" I was startled. She continued, "Your grandmother is in the hospital." I rushed home and called mother, she told me that grandmother was very ill, and I couldn't visit her without being accompanied by her. I refused to wait, I couldn't let my grandmother lay in a cold, indifferent room without being by her side, we were as close as mother and daughter.

PRACTICE 13   Correcting Comma Splice Errors

Find and correct the comma splice errors in the following paragraph. Neatly write your corrections in the text.

The Dilemma of Modern Progress

Despite senseless tragedies and horrors, well documented in history books, the twentieth century was definitely a time of continuing progression for humanity. Many wonderful advances, commonplace today, would have been beyond even the most imaginative of nineteenth-century dreamers, there was no slow down to this trend, moreover, new ideas were being developed at an ever-increasing pace at the end of the century. Although most would agree these accomplishments are desirable, many so-called time savers can have us chasing our own tails, modern technology often produces more inconvenience than convenience because of our lack of understanding of the full scope of the impact that our inventions have on us.

PRACTICE 14   Correcting Spelling Errors

Find and correct the spelling errors in the following paragraph. Neatly write your corrections in the text.

Deserted Waters

A place I find sothing is a desserted picnic area next to the river near Old Town. Standing under the roof of a small pavilion, I can look out over the dirty ruhsing water of the Mississippi River. I can hear the water craxsh as it hits the rocks with every wave. Surrounding me on the cracked concrete are half a dozen old, warpped picnic talbles. I can hear birds singing above as they guard their nests hiding in the beams. On my left stand shabby homes that once were vibrant mansions. The stairs ledding up to the front doors are missing, and the glass in the windows has been rplaced with boreds. There is a lifeless playground, grass growing over the rusting equipment, behind me. The seen may look depressing, but it is a beautifull place where I can relax.

PRACTICE 15   Correcting Spelling Errors

Find and correct the spelling errors in the following paragraph. Neatly write your corrections in the text.

The Sound of Music

How does the music we listen too broden our minds? Music an make people happy, sad, mello, or even overjoyed. The words to a song tell a story; therefore, the outcome of a great storey means a great song to the artist and listener. Music fills our lives; we hear it in doctors' offices, elevaters, and every time we turn the ignition key in our car. The music can be rock, hip-hop, soul, classicall, bluegrass, our country and wesstern. Whatever your taste, there is a style of music that will touch your heart and you soul.

The following paragraphs contain sentence fragment, run-on, comma splice, and spelling errors. Correct the errors you find. Neatly write your corrections in the text.

The Staff of Life

Bread is called "the Staff of Life" and the foodstuff is the most universal food known to man. Primiative man took centuries to discover how to identify seeds and how to grow them and adapt them to local enviroments.

Oats, barley, rye, and wheat breads are made threw the process of applying heat to a mixture of flower, grain, yeast, and water three kinds of bread were the first foods made by baking, flat bread, yeast bread, and quick bread are the three kinds, consequently, causing a surplus of food in homes. Bread sonn became a favorite food item to eat with all meals and they were a tasty and newtrisious treat.

Soon, bread production mover from the home to commercial bussiness, therefore, the amount of bread produced rose dramatically the numbers of loafs produced was staggering, it was an enormous boom. In the 1940s, newtrients and vitamens were added into commercial baking; reducing various deseases around the wrld. When bread is served in restarants, most loaves are not baked on the premises the bread is baked at a commercial bakary. With the amount of bread being eaten, is justified in beign called "the Staff of Life."

PRACTICE 17   Correcting Errors

The following paragraphs contain sentence fragment, run-on, comma splice, and spelling errors. Correct the errors you find. Neatly write your corrections in the text.

Viva Las Vegas!

The trip my family tood to Las Vegas was one of the best times of my life, the plain landed, and my family and I stepped off into the cool night air of Las Vegas the gambling capitol of the world. Our baggage was picked up first, it seemed to take forever. Then, we took a cab to the most exotic hotel casino we had ever seen. The hotel casino; a giant castle, was called the Excalibur. In the front of the hotel, was a fire-breathing dragon during the evening, its mouth blew a flame that must have been twenty feet long.

The next day, we awoke to the beautiful dessert sun. After eating a huge breakfast. My sister and I went for a swim, and took in some of the attractions like the Treasure Island Casino Ship show. Which was a virtual reality ride. We also went to Circus-Circus and watched the acrobates high above the casino floor they did have a net but it was still exciting. After a delicious dinner, we saw a show starring Bette Midler it was so funny and entertaining. It was the perfect end to a perfect day. Which I will be looking forward to taking agan some day, I just hope it is with my family again.

TOPIC BANK

The following paragraph writing assignments will suggest topics and help you practice the techniques you have learned in this chapter. Use the seven steps in the chapter review as you do your work.

As you write each paragraph, use the reporter's question in the parentheses as your focus. Remember to revise and proofread each paragraph.

1. (*Who?*) Describe a person. This can be a person you know, such as a parent, sibling, relative, friend, teacher, coworker, or a historical person with whom you are familiar. In your topic sentence, name the person, and write a controlling idea you wish to develop in the support sentences.

2. (*What?*) Describe an event. This can be an event from your own life, such as a religious ceremony, a graduation (see the "Chapter Warm-Up" photo on page 133), an operation, or a historical event with which you are

familiar. In the topic sentence, name the event, and write a controlling idea you wish to develop in the support sentences.

3. (*Where?*) Describe a location. This can be a place that you know, such as your room, house, school, workplace, or a historical location with which you are familiar. In your topic sentence, name the location, and write a controlling idea you wish to develop in the support sentences.

4. (*When?*) Describe an important time. This can be a time in your life, such as your childhood, or teenage years, or a well-known time in history with which you are familiar. In your topic sentence, name the time frame, and write a controlling idea you wish to develop in the support sentences.

5. (*Why?*) Describe why something happened. This can be something that happened to you, someone you know, or the reason something happened in history. In your topic sentence, name the reason, and write a controlling idea you wish to develop in the support sentences.

6. (*How?*) Describe how something occurs or is done. This can be something you have accomplished or were witness to or how something happened historically. In your topic sentence, name the process, and write a controlling idea you wish to develop in the support sentences.

WRITING OPPORTUNITIES

HOME You want your sister, who lives across town, to accompany you on a shopping trip to a mall. Your sister doesn't like malls. She thinks they are too boring because they all have the same shops. In one of your e-mails, you include a paragraph convincing her of why she should meet you at the brand-new mall that has just opened near your neighborhood.

SCHOOL Your Intro to Sociology professor wants you to visit a shopping mall and write one paragraph about the type of people who might be attracted by the different types of shops and services the mall offers.

WORK The owners of a shopping mall have hired the advertising agency you work for to attract customers to its newest mall. Write one paragraph of text to accompany the photograph above that will appear in a brochure advertising the grand opening of the mall

Visit *The Write Start* Online!

For additional practice with the materials in this chapter, go to

http://www.cengage.com/devenglish/checkett/writestartSP4e.

Chapter Self-Assessment Test

Check either True or False on the blank next to the statement.

T   F

____ ____ A topic sentence introduces a clear topic/subject and an essay map.

____ ____ The reporter's six questions, *who, what, where, when, why,* and *how,* are supporting details helping to establish a clear focus.

____ ____ Support sentences help to develop the topic of the paragraph.

____ ____ Only three support sentences are required to develop a topic.

____ ____ Sentence variety helps to clarify relationships and add rhythm to the paragraph.

____ ____ Revise a paragraph to achive unity.

____ ____ *Grammarcheck* and *spellcheck* are all a writer needs for proofreading.

____ ____ A few tears, creases, and smudges are acceptable in a paper's presentation.

10

Description

In Chapter 9, you learned that a topic sentence has two parts: the topic and the controlling idea. Develop a topic sentence for a paragraph describing a concert you have attended.

All paragraphs build on a topic. One way to build on a topic is by describing it in detail. Effective **description** creates images in the reader's mind by using specific details. Like a painter using color on a canvas, the writer uses words (the color) to create pictures in the reader's mind (the canvas).

Instead of merely writing

The clouds flew by overhead.

A writer using good description might write

> The billowing clouds, like delicious mounds of white mashed potatoes, floated lazily by overhead as though they hadn't a care in the world.

The specific details help develop the word-painting that describes persons, places, things, and emotions. At times, writers want their meaning to convey a feeling of sadness. At other times, they might want to evoke a feeling of happiness, or frustration, or hope, or sarcasm. Effective description adds clarity, depth, and feeling to your writing.

Types of Description

There are two types of description: **objective** and **subjective.**
Objective description relies on factual detail without much embellishment.

> **Example**
> The snowman consisted of three round balls stacked one on top of the other. It stood five feet high. Its eyes were round stones, with a carrot serving as a nose. A baseball cap sat atop its head.

From this objective description, you can picture the snowman. However, it is difficult to recognize what emotion or impression the writer wants us to feel.
In contrast, subjective description creates an easily identifiable emotion or impression.

> **Example**
> The snowman's body consisted of three plump balls of fluffy, white snow stacked like an ice-cream cone. Its eyes were made from brightly colored stones, with a squiggly, pigtail, orange carrot serving as a nose. A fuzzy, red baseball cap with a crooked bill sat cockeyed on his head.

From this subjective description, it is clear that the writer wants the snowman to evoke a funny or happy emotion. Objective description tells what the writer actually sees. Subjective description shows how the writer feels.

Dominant Impressions

The content of your descriptive writing will be clearer and more enjoyable if you focus on just one **dominant impression.** In a descriptive paragraph, each support sentence should build on the dominant, or main, impression you created in the topic sentence. Adding descriptive detail helps writers achieve these dominant impressions. Writers convey the dominant impression to the reader by a word or phrase in the topic sentence of a paragraph, then support this word or phrase throughout the paragraph by using specific detail.

> (No dominant impression) The sky was filled with dark, brooding clouds, and slivers of bright sunlight glistened toward the ground.

In this paragraph, the reader will not know the writer's intention. Is the writer trying to convey a negative or a positive mood?

> (Dominant impression) The sky was filled with dark, brooding clouds, and horrible flashes of lightning sent ugly scars across the horizon.

In this paragraph, the negative dominant impression is clear. Remember, the dominant impression is the overall feeling or emotional response that you want your reader to take away from your description. The words you choose to make your dominant impression should be specific enough to be easily understood; they should not be vague.

For example, the word *nice* has no specific meaning because it can mean almost anything. Nice can mean friendly, or pretty, or neat, or clean.

Examples

Topic sentences without dominant impressions:

Melody was a model.

It was evening in St. Louis.

The ball game was played.

The diamond necklace lay on the dresser.

Topic sentences with a dominant impression:

Melody was a glamorous model.

The evening in St. Louis was dreary.

The ball game was exciting.

The dazzling diamond necklace lay on the dresser.

Notice how much more expressive sentences are when they exhibit a dominant impression.

PRACTICE 1   Using Specific Words to Create Dominant Impressions

In the space to the right, replace the underlined, vague dominant impression word in the sentence with a more specific and descriptive word or phrase.

Example: Vague: The wedding dress was beautiful.
      Specific: The wedding dress was dazzling.

1. The haunted house was scary.   Specific: _____

2. The thick, woolen blanket felt nice.   Specific: _____

3. My Uncle Jacob is fun.   Specific: _____

4. The bowl of chili tasted hot.   Specific: _____

5. Fiona's ballet practice was good.   Specific: _____

6. The actor's performance was bad.   Specific: _____

7. The band's music was <u>loud</u>.   Specific: _____

8. The dorm room was <u>messy</u>.   Specific: _____

9. The aquarium decorations were <u>pretty</u>.   Specific: _____

10. The chocolate mousse was <u>rich</u>.   Specific: _____

Sensory Images

Description creates images. It tells the reader what a person, a place, or a thing

- Looks like
- Feels like
- Smells like
- Sounds like
- Tastes like

These **sensory images** are based on the five senses we are all familiar with: sight, touch, smell, sound, and taste. By using sensory images, writers can draw a more fully developed picture of what they are describing. Good description actually causes readers to remember similar persons, places, or things from their own experience. This personal interaction between the reader and the writing is a wonderful and powerful process.

Examples

Sight

a. Nondescriptive: The model walked down the runway wearing a dress.

b. Descriptive: The spaghetti-thin fashion model slinked down the long runway wearing a shining, cherry-red dress.

Touch

a. Nondescriptive: The new bedsheets were uncomfortable.

b. Descriptive: The new, stiff bedsheets felt like sandpaper scraping against my skin.

Smell

a. Nondescriptive: Fred's car trunk smelled awful.

b. Descriptive: Fred's car trunk smelled like a gym locker stuffed with rotten eggs.

Sound

a. Nondescriptive: The band was loud.

b. Descriptive: The band's ear-splitting punk music was loud enough to make your teeth vibrate.

Taste

a. Nondescriptive: The bread tasted old.

b. Descriptive: The bread tasted musty, like some moldy cheese I ate at my grandmother's house last year.

PRACTICE 2   **Using Sensory Images**

In the blank spaces below, rewrite the nondescriptive sentences by using various sensory images.

1. Nondescriptive: The boy's clothes didn't fit properly.

    Sight: _____

_____

2. Nondescriptive: The car was not in good shape.

    Sight: _____

_____

3. Nondescriptive: The tree bark felt rough.

    Touch: _____

_____

4. Nondescriptive: The baby's skin was soft.

    Touch: _____

_____

5. Nondescriptive: The odor of Fred's gym shoes was awful.

    Smell: _____

_____

6. Nondescriptive: The perfume smelled good.

    Smell: _____

_____

7. Nondescriptive: My younger brother was loud.

    Sound: _____

_____

8. Nondescriptive: The storm made a lot of noise.

    Sound: _____

_____

9. Nondescriptive: The breakfast pastries tasted good.

    Taste: _____

_____

10. Nondescriptive: The fancy dinner was delicious.

Taste: _____

_____

Comparisons

Another device that writers use to describe something is **comparison,** also known as **figurative language.** Comparisons to well-known or everyday objects or images provide descriptions that readers can immediately recognize. Many writers find comparison the easiest descriptive tool because comparisons allow writers to provide clear ideas to the reader by tapping into images and emotions that the reader has already experienced. The three most effective figurative language devices are

■ Simile
■ Metaphor
■ Personification

Simile

A **simile** is a comparison using either *like* or *as* to show a similarity between two different things. Notice how alike the words *simile* and *similarity* are.

> **Examples**
> My boss roars like a lion at his employees.
> The fog was like a blanket covering the city, so you couldn't see a thing.
> The runner was fast as a cheetah, and he won the race.
> The searchlight shined brightly as the sun, blocking our vision.

Metaphor

A **metaphor** is a stronger comparison between two things without using *like* or *as.* The implication is that one thing "is" the same as the other.

> **Examples**
> My boss is a lion, roaring at all his employees.
> The fog was a blanket covering the city, so you couldn't see a thing.

Personification

In **personification,** the writer gives human emotions or characteristics to animals, objects, or even ideas.

Examples

The tree howled in the wind.

Love danced in their eyes.

The bear cheated his rivals out of their food.

The house's windows winked at the passersby.

The car rested in the driveway after the long drive home.

PRACTICE 3   Using Figurative Language to Make Comparisons

In the spaces below, create comparisons between the two objects in the parentheses using the figurative language device marked in boldface.

Example: (**simile**—raindrops/ball-bearings) The raindrops sounded **like** steel ball-bearings smashing into the roof with a metallic bang!

1. (**simile**—lake/glass) _____

   _____

2. (**simile**—mansion/monster) _____

   _____

3. (**metaphor**—airplane/bird) _____

   _____

4. (**metaphor**—car/tiger) _____

   _____

5. (**personification**—wind/caring person) _____

   _____

6. (**personification**—stuffed animal/jolly person) _____

   _____

PRACTICE 4   Analyzing Descriptive Writing

The following paragraph is taken from a descriptive essay, "Halloween Havoc," by student writer Erin Nelson. The paragraph is jam-packed with expressive description that brings the special evening to life!

Read All About It . . . | To read the full essay from which this paragraph is excerpted, see page 421.

The spooky old houses come to life at night with gruesome decorations.

With grotesque carved faces, the jack-o'-lanterns give off an eerie glow.

Tombstones line the sidewalk, like a long narrow graveyard; beware of the bloody hand reaching out to grab intruders. Bats as black as the night sky fly in quick circles, darting in the air, and a black cat with razor sharp fangs crosses the path of unseen, terrified prey. The ghosts and the goblins sneak around monster-like trees, ready to snatch their next victim.

Descriptive Technique Questions

1. What is the topic?

_____

_____

2. What do you think is the dominant impression Nelson is attempting to describe?

_____

_____

3. Underline any figurative language techniques you find. How do they enhance the dominant impression?

_____

_____

_____

PRACTICE 5   Analyzing Descriptive Writing

In this paragraph from a descriptive essay, "New York—The Big Apple," by student writer Amber Barton, the cosmopolitan environs of New York City are compared to the rural area of Missouri in which she grew up.

The sights of New York City stimulate the senses; rural Missouri soothes them. From the Empire State Building to the subway system, the sights and sounds of New York City invigorate the spirit. The vision of Lady Liberty standing proudly in the East River with Ellis Island, its now silent companion, evokes pride in its visitors. The rich hills and valleys of rural Missouri are lovely, yet they pale in comparison to the stark beauty of New York skyscrapers. A traveler would have to visit more than once to be able to take in all the diverse sights New York City has to offer.

Descriptive Technique Questions

1. What is the topic?

   _____

2. What do you think is the dominant impression Barton is trying to describe?

   _____

3. Underline any figurative language techniques you find. How do they enhance the dominant impression?

   _____

   _____

| PRACTICE 6 | Analyzing Descriptive Writing |

The follow paragraph uses sensory images and figurative language to clarify and support the topic sentence. In this paragraph from the essay "Deep Cold" by Verlyn Klinkenborg, the writer uses sensory description to evoke a deep, penetrating cold that not only feels cold but sounds cold as well.

Read All About It . . .

To read the full essay from which this paragraph is excerpted, see page 416.

But the true sound of deep cold is the sound of the wind. Monday morning, on the streets of Cambridge, Massachusetts, the windchill approached fifty below zero. A stiff northwest wind rocked in the trees and snatched at cars as they idled at the curb. A rough rime had settled over that old-brick city the day before, and now the wind was sanding it smooth. It was cold of Siberian or Antarctic intensity, and I could feel a kind of claustrophobia settling in all over Boston. People went about their errands, only to cut them short instantly, turning backs to the gust and fleeing for cover.

Descriptive Technique Questions

1. What is the topic?

   _____

2. What do you think is the dominant impression Klinkenborg is attempting to describe?

   _____

3. The author uses two personifications. Identify them.

_____

_____

4. Is the tone of the paragraph more subjective or objective? Give examples of both.

_____

_____

_____

_____

_____

5. Klinkenborg uses specific nouns and adjectives to help create her images. Identify a few of them.

_____

_____

_____

PRACTICE 7　　　　**Analyzing Descriptive Writing**

The following paragraphs from Luis Rodriguez's essay, "The Ice Cream Truck," use many sensory images and figurative language devices to create a word-picture that is every bit as detailed as a fine painting. Although short, the paragraphs are packed with expressive sounds and sights. Explanations of terms in brackets are ours, not Rodriguez's.

Read All About It . . . To read the full essay from which this paragraph is excerpted, see page 417.

The Hills blistered below a haze of sun and smog. Mothers with wet strands of hair across their foreheads flung wash up to dry on weathered lines. Sweat-drenched men lay on their backs in the gravel of alleys, beneath broken-down cars propped up on cinder blocks. _Charrangas_ [a Cuban style of music with violins] and _corridos_ [a Mexican style of music] splashed out of open windows.

Suddenly from over a hill, an ice cream truck raced by with packs of children running beside it. A hurried version of "Old McDonald Had a Farm" chimed through a speaker bolted on the truck's roof. The truck stopped long enough for somebody to toss out dozens of sidewalk sundaes, tootie-fruities and half-and-half bars to the children who gathered around, thrusting up small, dirt-caked hands that blossomed open as their shrieks blended with laughter.

Then the truck's transmission gears growled as it continued up the slope, whipped around a corner and passed a few of us *vatos* [similar to "home-boys"] assembled on a field off Toll Drive. We looked over toward the echoes of the burdensome chimes, the slip and boom of the clutch and rasp of gears as the ice cream truck entered the dead-end streets and curves of Las Lomas.

Descriptive Technique Questions

1. What is the topic?

   _____

2. What do you think is the dominant impression Rodriguez is attempting to describe? Give some examples to support your answer.

   _____

   _____

   _____

   _____

3. Identify the two personifications Rodriguez uses.

   _____

   _____

4. Is the tone of the paragraphs more objective or subjective? Cite examples of both.

   _____

   _____

   _____

   _____

   _____

   _____

_____

_____

_____

A Ten-Step Process for Writing the Descriptive Paragraph

Experienced writers often follow a step-by-step process that helps them write effectively. As you develop as a writer, you will undoubtedly create your own process. In the meantime, this set of easy-to-follow guidelines will help you write an effective descriptive paragraph.

Writing the Descriptive Paragraph

1. Choose a topic. The topic should be a person, place, or thing (an idea, event, or situation).
2. Think about the topic, and choose the dominant impression (the overall feeling) you want your reader to experience.
3. Write a topic sentence with the dominant impression word included.
4. Make a list of the details you want to include in the paragraph that will support and clarify the dominant impression.
5. Put each of the details into a separate sentence.
6. Rewrite the sentences. Use sensory details and figurative language to create descriptive images.
7. Be certain that the sensory images and figurative devices support the dominant impression.
8. Proofread for punctuation errors, sentence fragments, and run-on sentences.
9. If possible, have another person read the paragraph. Ask him or her to point out any errors or unclear ideas. Rewrite if necessary.
10. Prepare your finished paragraph for presentation to your instructor.

Example of the Ten-Step Process at Work

1. Topic: A person you have observed.
2. Dominant impression: joy
3. The man was **joyful** when he learned he had the winning lotto number.
4. Details: _facial expressions_ (eyes and mouth); _mannerisms_ (hand gestures and body language); _clothing_ (style, color, accessories); _speech_ (expressions and loudness).
5. a. The man smiled and his eyes lit up.
   b. He held his arms over his head and danced all around the store.
   c. He was wearing a yellow shirt, white pants, and a gold necklace matching the three gold diamond rings on each hand.
   d. He yelled and screamed about how happy he was to be a millionaire.

First Draft of Paragraph

The man was joyful when he learned he had the winning lotto number. He smiled, and his eyes lit up. He held his arms over his head and danced around the store. He was wearing a yellow shirt, white pants, and a gold necklace matching three gold diamond rings on each hand. He yelled and screamed about how happy he was to be a millionaire.

6. Support sentence rewrites:
   a. His smile <u>flashed like a beam of light</u>, and his eyes <u>twinkled</u>.
       ↑   ↑
     (simile)   (sight)

   b. He <u>waved</u> his <u>shaking</u> arms over his head as he danced around the store
     ↑   ↑
   (sight)   (sight)
   <u>like a statue made from Jell-O</u> that had suddenly come to life.
           ↑
        (simile)

   c. He wore a <u>bright-yellow, satin</u> shirt and <u>gleaming white</u> slacks
          ↑   ↑   ↑
      (sight)   (touch)   (sight)
   accented by a <u>shining</u> gold necklace matching three <u>sparkling</u>
            ↑   ↑
      (sight)   (sight)
   diamond rings on each hand.

   d. The <u>jewelry seemed to cry out</u>, "I'm rich! I'm a millionaire!"
         ↑
   (personification)

7. Does the following list support the dominant impression of **joy**? Yes!

flashed like a beam of light	satin
twinkled	gleaming white
waved	shining
shaking	sparkling
like a statue made from Jell-O	jewelry seemed to cry out "I'm rich . . ."
bright-yellow	

8. Proofread the paragraph.
9. Have someone else read the paragraph and make comments.
10. Rewrite the paragraph.

> **Final Draft of the Paragraph**
>
> The man was joyful when he learned he had the winning lotto number. His smile flashed like a beam of light, and his eyes twinkled. He waved his shaking arms over his head as he danced around the store like a statue made from Jell-O that had suddenly come to life. He wore a bright-yellow, satin shirt and gleaming white slacks accented by a shining gold necklace matching three sparkling diamond rings on each hand. The jewelry seemed to cry out, "I'm rich! I'm a millionaire!"

Now compare this final paragraph to the original, and you can see how much more effective the final paragraph is. The dominant impression is clear, and the support sentences clearly describe the dominant impression.

PRACTICE 8   **Writing a Descriptive Paragraph**

In this exercise, you will use the step-by-step process described above. Following the ten steps, write one descriptive paragraph each for a person, place, and thing that you know very well. If you want to be adventurous, you can create a person from your own imagination. In other words, have some fun with it!

Person

Possible persons:

    a. An actor/actress
    b. An athlete
    c. An entertainer
    d. A relative
    e. A historical figure
    f. A circus performer
    g. A science fiction character
    h. A bodybuilder
    i. A movie monster
    j. A politician

1. Choose a topic: _____

2. Dominant impression: _____

3. Write a topic sentence with the dominant impression word included:

_____

_____

4. Choose three or four details that support the dominant impression:

    a. _____

    b. _____

    c. _____

    d. _____

5. Put each detail into a separate sentence:

    a. _____

_____

    b. _____

_____

    c. _____

_____

d. _____

_____

6. Rewrite the sentences creating descriptive images by using sensory details and by using figurative language techniques you have practiced.

a. _____

_____

b. _____

_____

c. _____

_____

d. _____

_____

Put these sentences into paragraph form with the topic sentence first.

_____

_____

_____

_____

_____

_____

7. Check to make sure the descriptive images support the dominant impression by making a list of the sensory details and figurative devices. Then evaluate the effectiveness of your images.

Dominant impression: _____

List of descriptive images: _____

_____

_____

_____

_____

_____

_____

8. Now proofread your paragraph, looking for punctuation errors, sentence fragments, run-on sentences, and spelling errors.

9. If possible, have another person read the paragraph. Ask him or her to point out any errors or unclear ideas. Rewrite if necessary.

10. Write your final paragraph version:

_____

_____

_____

_____

_____

_____

TOPIC BANK

Place

Using the ten steps you have practiced, write a paragraph describing one of the following places or a place you choose.

1. An amusement park	**6.** The circus
2. A restaurant	**7.** A nightclub
3. A doctor's office	**8.** A library
4. A rural setting	**9.** A grocery store
5. The zoo	**10.** A business office

Thing

Using the ten steps you have practiced, write a descriptive paragraph for a thing. (Remember, a thing can be an idea, event, or situation.)

Possible things:

11. The atmosphere at a concert (see the photo on page 159)	**16.** Christmas morning
12. A job interview	**17.** A graduation ceremony
13. A romantic date	**18.** A wedding
14. Oppression	**19.** A car wreck
15. A time of day	**20.** Freedom

WRITING OPPORTUNITIES

HOME You are traveling through the West on summer vacation with your family. You are using a video camera to record the memorable sites you see, and you've also decided to keep a journal of the sites you experience to supplement the visual images. You spot an old barn set against the backdrop of the Rockies. Write a paragraph in your journal to describe the scene you have captured with your video camera.

SCHOOL Your geography instructor has given each member of the class a picture of an old barn set against the Rocky Mountains. Your assignment is to write a paragraph describing one prominent feature of the picture, explaining how it reflects the spirit of the people who might live in the area.

WORK A mineral mining company wants to strip mine the area in the photograph above. A government committee is considering whether to comply with its request. As an employee with the Department of the Interior, you have been given the task of writing a descriptive paragraph to help your agency's director convince the committee not to vote in favor of the project.

 ## Visit *The Write Start* Online!

For additional practice with the materials in this chapter, go to

http://www.cengage.com/devenglish/checkett/writestartSP4e.

Chapter Self-Assessment Test

Check either True or False on the blank next to the statement.

T	F	
____	____	Effective description creates images by using specific details.
____	____	There are three types of description: objective, subjective, and surrealistic.
____	____	In descriptive writing, the topic is most clearly defined by creating multiple dominant impressions.
____	____	Figurative language can help create effective description through the use of simile, metaphor, and personification.
____	____	"My car is like a bullet train" is an example of a metaphor.
____	____	"The moon sneered at me from behind the dark cloud" is an example of a simile.
____	____	"The mirror was a lake" is an example of personification.
____	____	The five senses, *sight, touch, smell, sound,* and *taste,* are not useful tools for creating descriptive images.

11

Narration

CHAPTER WARM-UP

Make up answers to these *what* questions about the photograph shown here: What is the event? What happened before/during/after the event? What is special about this event? Now make up answers to these *why* questions: Why did the event take place? Why was the event important?

Writers use paragraphs to develop or express a main idea or topic. One way of doing so is through **narration.** Narration is simply the telling of a story, either to entertain or inform a reader. The stories in narrative paragraphs can be fiction (made up) or nonfiction (the retelling of an incident that actually happened). What's important, though, is that the story develops the topic of the paragraph.

The elements of a narrative paragraph are the same as those in any other type of paragraph:

■ A topic sentence announcing the subject and controlling idea
■ Support sentences using specific details to develop the subject
■ Sentence variety connecting related ideas and adding rhythm

The Point of the Story

There must be a point to every story; otherwise, no one will be interested in reading it. Therefore, every narrative paragraph you write must have a clear point or purpose. That purpose should always be to develop the topic and controlling idea of the paragraph. This might seem like an obvious and easy point to follow in a paragraph, but too many writers lose sight of it. The best way to get to the point of the story is to examine the topic sentence and see what makes it interesting to the reader. That will be the point of the story.

Exhibit 11–1 provides an example of a topic sentence for a narrative paragraph. The subject, controlling idea, and the point of the story are listed.

Example

When my mother had hip surgery, I assumed responsibility for running the household.

Subject: Running the household
Controlling idea: Assuming responsibility for running the household
Point of the story: Acting responsibly in a time of need

Exhibit 11–1

PRACTICE 1   **Identifying the Point of a Story**

In the following topic sentences, underline the subject once, the controlling idea twice, and in your own words, summarize what you think the point of the story is in the space provided.

1. I studied day and night for two weeks and passed all my exams with A grades.

   Point of the story: _____

   _____

2. I voted for the challenger even though he was behind in all the polls.

   Point of the story: _____

   _____

3. Although my first camping trip was not at all what I expected, I eventually had a good time.

   Point of the story: _____

   _____

4. I relied on my parents' advice when I bought my first car.

Point of the story: _____

_____

5. I read three fashion magazines before I went shopping for winter clothing.

Point of the story: _____

_____

PRACTICE 2 **Writing Narrative Topic Sentences**

Write your own narrative topic sentences for the topics listed below. After you have finished, underline the topic once, the controlling idea twice, and in your own words, summarize the point of your story in the space provided.

1. Topic: Driving _____

_____

Point of the story: _____

2. Topic: Working at a job _____

_____

Point of the story: _____

3. Topic: A hospital experience _____

_____

Point of the story: _____

4. Topic: Television _____

_____

Point of the story: _____

5. Topic: Video games _____

_____

Point of the story: _____

Developing the Narrative Paragraph

Once you've chosen the subject, controlling idea, and the point of the story, you must decide how to develop the subject. What details, facts, and examples will you choose to develop the story and get the point of the story across?

The easiest way to develop a subject and maintain focus is to use the reporter's six questions: *who, what, where, when, why,* and *how.* (See Chapter 9, "The Paragraph," for a broader discussion of the reporter's six questions.)

For the topic sentence example in Exhibit 11–1 presented earlier, the developing focus could be any of the following.

Examples

Who?   Who assumed responsibility for running the household? (As the topic sentence states, the writer did.)

What?   What household activities had to be done? (This might be a list of activities, such as paying bills, food shopping, cooking, cleaning, and babysitting.)

Where?   Where were the activities finished? (The household has been identified.)

When?   When were the activities completed? (The period encompassing the hospital stay and the convalescence time.)

Why?   Why did the household activities have to be assumed? (Because the mother was in the hospital.)

How?   How were the activities completed? (Did the writer use any special appliances to help out with the chores or to do the chores in a particular order each day?)

From the list above, *who, where,* and *why* are obvious and probably do not need to be developed. The important features to develop would be *what* (what activities had to be done?), *when* (how long did it take?), or *how* (how were the activities taken care of?). (For additional discussion of the importance of detail, see Chapter 10, "Description.")

Model Narrative Paragraphs

The following are examples of paragraphs developed for the topic sentence in Exhibit 11–1 using different focus questions.

1. *Focus:* **What**—all the household chores and activities that needed to be done.

When my mother had hip surgery, I assumed responsibility for running the household. First, I had to take care of a stack of bills for the month. After that, I planned a menu for the week, and I went to the supermarket to buy food. In addition to cooking daily meals, I prepared some meals in advance; afterward, I placed them in the freezer. I tried to clean part of the house each day, so I wouldn't have an overwhelming job on the weekend. Besides all of these chores, I had to take care of my younger sister and brother. Although I was very nervous at the thought of shouldering all these responsibilities, I was up to the challenge.

In this paragraph, the topic is developed using those activities that support the *what* focus question: paying bills, food shopping, cooking, cleaning, and babysitting. The list of chores is linked by the use of words and phrases that order the events: "first," "after that," and "in addition." Instead of a choppy list, the paragraph reads smoothly and rhythmically.

2. *Focus:* **When**—The period when the writer's mother was in the hospital, and the period when the mother was home recuperating but unable to help.

> When my mother had hip surgery, I assumed responsibility for running the household. The total time period for my running the house was four weeks. First, my mother had to stay in the hospital for an entire week; afterward, she came home, but she had to stay in bed for another week. Finally, when she could get out of bed, I had to be at her side to help her on short exercise walks. This lasted for two more weeks. All the while, I still had to do all the household chores by myself. After the four weeks had passed, my mother made me a special dinner, and she thanked me for being so mature in running the house. It was a proud day for both of us.

Notice that this paragraph uses "time" words and phrases to facilitate the development supporting the *when* focus question: "when," "time period," "four weeks," "entire week," "afterward," "another week," "two more weeks," "all the while," and "four weeks had passed." Also, notice the order of events is chronologically sound: The mother is in the hospital, then comes home, convalesces at home in bed, and finally, gets out of bed to exercise.

3. *Focus:* **How**—How the chores were taken care of.

> When my mother had hip surgery, I assumed responsibility for running the household. I knew that I could not take care of everything, so I enlisted some help. My brother and sister were very young, so my Aunt Jessie came every other evening to help babysit; consequently, I could do laundry and prepare some meals for the following week. My neighbor and best friend, Celeste, also helped with food shopping and yard work. After my mother came home from the hospital, there was even more to do. So every Saturday, I paid a maid service to come in and clean the house. When my mother finally was able to get up and around, we went for a walk, and she had tears in her eyes when she told me how proud she was of how I had handled all the responsibilities.

This paragraph develops the focus question *how* by describing how the chores were completed (the writer enlisted friends and relatives to help out): Aunt Jessie (babysitting), friend and neighbor Celeste (food shopping and yard work), and a maid service (housecleaning). Notice that this focus also could satisfy the *who* question. Often, one focus helps in developing ideas that are relevant to another focus.

The important aspect to remember is that each paragraph develops the same topic, yet uses information that places emphasis on a different aspect of the situation.

(ESL) Transitional Expressions: Showing Time Sequence

Because narrative paragraphs relate a story, you usually present events in the proper order. That way, the reader can stay focused on the events without being confused about when things happened. To keep track of time and show readers the correct sequence of events, you need to use **transitional expressions.**

Commonly Used Transitional Expressions in Narration		
after	first	soon
afterward	last(ly)	then
as	later	third
as soon as	meanwhile	upon
before	next	when
during	now	while
finally	second	

Exhibit 11–2

Transitional expressions are simply words and phrases that indicate when one event happened in relation to another.

PRACTICE 3   Identifying Transitional Expressions

The following paragraph is taken from a narrative essay, "Andriyivsky Descent" by student writer Oksana Taranova who emigrated to the United States from Ukraine. Underline the transitional expressions in the paragraph. Discuss how they help add rhythm and move the story from idea to idea smoothly.

> *Read All About It . . .*
>
> To read the full essay from which this paragraph is excerpted, see page 429.

The architecture of this exciting street has not been changed from when it was built in the 18th century. Historically, Andriyivsky Descent formed the shortest route between the aristocratic Upper Town and the tradesmen's Lower Town. I remember walking with my late mother through the maze of two and three-storied stone buildings, painted in a palette of lightly and richly hued colors. We would stop often to admire the splendid façades fronted with bronze doors and intricately worked bronze openwork tracery. I can still picture my mother figure outlined against Kiev's skyline dominated by St. Andrew's Cathedral at the top of the street. Designed in the 17th century by the Italian architect Bartolomeo Rastrelli, the large, domed cathedral hovers above the city like a fatherly spirit, as the sunlight reflects brilliantly off its five gold cupolas like a sunrise. It often reminds me of my mother's golden hair shiny so brightly after coming in from an afternoon of gardening in our backyard. Descending further to the lower town, we always looked into the gorgeous medieval castle, Richard Coeur de Lion (Richard

the Lion Heart). Built in the English Gothic style, the tops of the walls are

decorated with grotesque figures of gargoyles. It's impossible to forget such

dramatic architecture with its varied styles and historical significance.

PRACTICE 4 Identifying Transitional Expressions

The following paragraph is taken from a narrative essay, "Small Town Views," by student writer Matt Grant. Underline the transitional expressions. Discuss how they help add rhythm and move the story from idea to idea smoothly.

At first, the town of Sault Ste. Marie appeared large. A drive down the

main four-lane road through town revealed several restaurants, stores, and

businesses. Even though only a few streets intersected the main road, the

town seemed to sprawl before me. During my drive down Main Street, a fairly

new Wal-Mart stood out as one of the larger buildings. As soon as I passed

through town, on top of a large, grassy hill, Lake Superior State College

stood facing the divided highway that passed by town. Sitting on the hill,

the college seemed to appear larger and more majestic to cars passing by on

the highway. Finally, the Soo Locks controlled the north end of town, polic-

ing Lake Freighter traffic on the Saint Marys River. Yet, something was miss-

ing; the town was as quiet as night.

PRACTICE 5 Editing for Time Sequence

The following paragraph's topic is *how* the Spanish-American War began. The sentences are out of chronological sequence. In their current order, the ideas are not developed coherently, and the information is difficult to understand. On a separate sheet of paper, rewrite the paragraph by reordering the sentences in proper time sequence, using transitional expressions from Exhibit 11–2 to help establish the proper order, link the ideas, and add rhythm.

This savage warfare frightened Americans, but the United States did not

intervene. The Cubans reverted to destroying their land to cause the Spanish

to leave. In the year 1898, America declared war on Spain. The Spanish Army, which was commanded by General Valeriano Wyler, began capturing Cuban citizens and placing them in concentration camps. The war was an overwhelming victory for America and also for Cuba. The rebellion that arose in 1895 was the most devastating. Cubans had, for many years, attempted to overthrow Spanish rule. But, how the war actually began was the most interesting part of history. Thousands of Cubans died of disease and malnutrition.

PRACTICE 6   Planning and Writing Narrative Paragraphs

Following are six writing exercises for narrative paragraphs. Each exercise will give you the development focus (*who, what, where, when, why,* and *how*) and a topic idea on which to write. Supply a topic for each of the focus questions. Next, complete a controlling idea for the topic you have selected. Then summarize in your own words what the point of the story will be. Afterward, write a topic sentence using the elements you have created. Finally, create support sentences that develop, explain, support, and clarify the point of the story.

1. (*Who?*) Personal heroes: either people you know or persons from history

   a. Topic: _____

   b. Controlling idea: _____

   c. Point of the story: _____

   d. Topic sentence: _____

   _____

   e. Development sentences: _____

   _____

   _____

   _____

   _____

   _____

2. (*What?*) An important decision you made that affected your life

   a. Topic: _____

   b. Controlling idea: _____

   c. Point of the story: _____

d. Topic sentence: _____

_____

e. Development sentences: _____

_____

_____

_____

_____

_____

3. (*Where?*) A place that is meaningful in your life

a. Topic: _____

b. Controlling idea: _____

c. Point of the story: _____

d. Topic sentence: _____

_____

e. Development sentences: _____

_____

_____

_____

_____

_____

4. (*When?*) An important time in your life

a. Topic: _____

b. Controlling idea: _____

c. Point of the story: _____

d. Topic sentence: _____

_____

e. Development sentences: _____

_____

_____

_____

_____

_____

5. (*Why?*) Why you are looking forward to the future

    a. Topic: _____

    b. Controlling idea: _____

    c. Point of the story: _____

    d. Topic sentence: _____

    _____

    e. Development sentences: _____

    _____

    _____

    _____

    _____

    _____

6. (*How?*) How a task was completed

    a. Topic: _____

    b. Controlling idea: _____

    c. Point of the story: _____

    d. Topic sentence: _____

    _____

    e. Development sentences: _____

    _____

    _____

    _____

    _____

PRACTICE 7   Analyzing Narrative Writing

The following is a narrative paragraph taken from a chapter in a book titled *The Vanishing Hitchhiker: American Urban Legends and Their Meaning* (1981) by Jan Harold Brunvand, a folklorist and professor of English at the University of Utah. Brunvand has gathered examples of contemporary storytelling—strange, scary, funny, macabre, and embarrassing tales storytellers relate as true accounts of real-life experience. This excerpt is from an urban legend called "The Roommate's Death."

Read All About It . . .

To read the full essay from which this paragraph is excerpted, see page 422.

It was not long before the telephone rang. Linda answered the telephone, only to hear the heavy breathing of the caller on the other end. She attempted to elicit a response from the caller but he merely hung up. Thinking little of it and not wanting to panic Sharon, Linda went back to watching her television program, remarking that the caller had dialed a wrong number. Upon receiving the second call at which time the caller first engaged in a bit of heavy breathing and then instructed them to check on the children, the two girls became frightened and decided to call the operator for assistance. The operator instructed the girls to keep the caller on the line as long as possible should he call again so that she might be able to trace the call. The operator would check back with them.

Questions for Discussion

1. How does Brunvand order the events? Point out words and phrases that help the reader recognize the order of events as they occur.

_____

_____

_____

_____

_____

_____

2. What is the primary focus of the paragraph: *who, what, where, when, why,* or *how*?

_____

_____

Suggestions for Writing

1. Rewrite the paragraph using appropriate transitional expressions from Exhibit 11–2. Reread both versions. Which reads more smoothly and rhythmically?

2. Rewrite the paragraph using a different focus than the one you selected for the answer to Question 2 in "Questions for Discussion" above.

PRACTICE 8   Analyzing Narrative Writing

The following paragraph is taken from a narrative essay by Grace Suh. Suh works in academic publishing and as a poetry editor of the *Asian Pacific American Journal*. In this piece, Suh writes about her visit to a makeup counter in search of the transformation promised by the "priestesses of beauty."

Read All About It . . .
To read the full essay from which this paragraph is excerpted, see page 426.

> And so, in an unusual exertion of will, I resolved to fight back against the forces of entropy. I envisioned it as reclamation work, like scything down a lawn that has grown into meadow, or restoring a damaged fresco. For the first time in ages, I felt elated and hopeful. I nearly sprinted into the nearby Nieman Marcus. As I entered the cool, hushed, dimly lit first floor and saw the gleaming counters lined with vials of magical balm, the priestesses of beauty in their sacred smocks, and the glossy photographic icons of the goddesses themselves—Paulina, Linda, Cindy, Vendella—in a wild, reckless burst of inspiration I thought to myself, Heck, why just okay? Why not BEAUTIFUL?

Questions for Discussion

1. How does Suh order the events? Point out words and phrases that help the reader recognize the order of events as they occur.

_____

_____

_____

_____

_____

_____

2. What is the primary focus of the paragraph: *who, what, where, when, why,* or *how*?

_____

Suggestions for Writing

1. Visit a cosmetics counter at a large department store. Take notes about the products and displays that you see there. How did the advertisements and the arrangements of the products induce you to "become beautiful" by using them? Did the salespeople themselves seem to conform to a particular ideal of beauty? Write a paragraph about your findings and read it to your class. Afterward, discuss the similarities and differences between the various reports made by members of your class.

2. Write a paragraph describing a time in which you made yourself look different than you normally do (this could be for a prom, wedding, or other special occasion). Did you act differently than you normally act? Did other people treat you differently? Was the experience enjoyable or not?

TOPIC BANK

Write a narrative paragraph about one or more of the following topics or about a topic of your own choice.

1. A funny incident
2. A first date
3. An employment interview
4. An embarrassing moment
5. A tense athletic event (see the photo on page 177)
6. Your first day on a new job
7. Watching a scary movie
8. A family argument
9. Preparing for an important exam
10. Taking on a huge responsibility
11. The September 11, 2001, terrorist attacks
12. Taking a road test

WRITING OPPORTUNITIES

HOME You are looking through a family photo album when you come upon a picture of your son when he was little. The picture brings back a flood of memories. You pick up a pen and write a paragraph beneath the photograph that tells a brief story about why he was walking down the road alone.

SCHOOL The photographs taken by you and your fellow art students are going on display in the Fine Arts Building. You have been asked to choose someone else's picture and write a one-paragraph story about its subject matter. Your story will be typed on a card and affixed to the wall beneath the photo.

WORK You work for a movie studio that is going to release a new movie. The picture of the little boy on the road is going to be the advertising poster that will appear in movie theaters throughout the country. Write a one-paragraph "press release" detailing what the movie is about.

 ## Visit *The Write Start* Online!

For additional practice with the materials in this chapter, go to

http://www.cengage.com/devenglish/checkett/writestartSP4e.

Chapter Self-Assessment Test

Check either True or False on the blank next to the statement.

T   F

_____ _____ Narration is the telling of a story for the sole purpose of entertaining the reader.

_____ _____ Narrative stories only can be fiction (made up). They can never be nonfiction (the retelling of an incident that actually happened).

_____ _____ Stories do not have to have a specific point. Random ideas are enough to hold the reader's interest.

_____ _____ The six reporter's questions, *who, what, where, when, why,* and *how,* can help develop a story.

_____ _____ Transitional expressions help develop the order of events that unfold in a story.

Using Examples

Do the following prewriting activity: List all the types of vehicles you can think of that might be sold in the place shown in the photograph. Or, list items in the place you currently are employed or in a store where you frequently shop. If you need to review the listing technique, see page 128.

One of the most popular and effective methods for developing a topic is through the use of examples. The **example paragraph** can develop a topic quickly and clearly and help hold the reader's attention. Maybe you've heard a friend say, "My job is terrible." Your thought might be to question why your friend feels this way: What makes the job so terrible? What does your friend have to do that makes her feel this way? Your friend might respond with specific examples: The boss is a tyrant, working several hours after closing is a frequent demand, and the pay is low without any benefits. By recounting several examples, your friend supports and clarifies the general critical view of the job experience.

Detailed examples are used to convince, clarify, illustrate, or make concrete a general idea about the subject. For instance, the following subjects are accompanied by a list of examples that might be used to develop the subject in the paragraph.

Topic	Examples
Cars	Honda, Chrysler, VW
Wines	Bordeaux, Riesling, Merlot
Presidents	Washington, Lincoln, Truman
Houses	ranch, split-level, Tudor
Cheeses	gouda, mozzarella, cheddar

The Topic Sentence

The following is a topic sentence for an example paragraph. The subject, controlling idea, developing focus, and developing examples are given. (See Chapter 9 for clarification of the developing ideas of *who, what, where, when, why,* and *how.*)

Example

Topic sentence: President Roosevelt was a successful leader during World War II, overcoming many obstacles.

Subject: Franklin D. Roosevelt

Controlling idea: Overcoming problems

Developing focus: What

Developing examples: isolationists

Congress

illness

Finished Paragraph

President Roosevelt was a successful leader during World War II, overcoming many obstacles. For example, the American people were overwhelmingly isolationist, not wanting to go through the horrors that they remembered from World War I. Another hurdle was Congress's passing of a number of neutrality laws intended to prevent America from entering the war in Europe. Personal problems also had to be overcome. For instance, Roosevelt had to deal with poliomyelitis, a disease he had contracted in 1921. Eventually, Roosevelt's ideas won out when Congress passed his lend-lease legislation after Germany's defeat of France in 1940.

Each example helps to clarify, explain, and develop the controlling idea that President Roosevelt overcame adversity to be successful.

ESL Transitional Expressions: Introducing Examples

Transitional expressions help to connect related ideas and add rhythm to a piece of writing. In the example paragraph above, transitional expressions, such as "for example," "another example," "for instance," and "eventually," are also used to announce to the reader that an example is forthcoming. Use transitional expressions in your example paragraph so that the examples don't appear merely as a list. Examples should act in unison to develop the subject in the topic sentence.

Transitional Expressions for Example Paragraphs	
a case in point is _____	for example
another example of _____	for instance
another instance of _____	to illustrate
another illustration of _____	specifically

Exhibit 12-1

PRACTICE 1   Analyzing an Example Paragraph

The following is an example paragraph written by a student. Read the paragraph, and check to see whether it has all the elements for an example paragraph:

1. Topic sentence with controlling idea

2. A development focus

3. Three or four development examples

4. Transitional expressions

In the spaces provided after the paragraph, write in the elements that you have found.

In this paragraph from an example essay, "A Stroke of Bad Luck," Margaret Ewart relates how taking care of her father after his having a stroke affected her life.

Shortly after I started taking care of my father, I came to realize that there was never any time for myself, much less my family. I rarely ever have the time to play with my children, help my daughter with her schoolwork, or spend time with my husband. My father requires a tremendous amount of my time, which prevents me from being a mother as well as being a wife. Most of the time I feel as if I am missing out on a great deal of my children's lives due to the fact that I have become a primary care giver. I have felt like a prisoner in my own home since the stroke. I have a great fear of leaving my home in the event that he may need me. My husband tries to take me out for dinner and a movie to give me some sense of relief from all of the stress, but I always decline. I would never be able to live with myself if something were to happen to my father and I weren't at home to receive his call for help. Because I have become a recluse, our vacations are spent at home sitting by the phone. With the fear of leaving the house because of my new responsibilities, family members are reluctant to make plans with me due to the fact that I always have to decline. They began to treat me differently as well as see me as a different person.

Topic: _____

Controlling idea: _____

Development focus: _____

Development examples: _____

_____

_____

_____

Transitional expressions: _____

_____

_____

_____

PRACTICE 2   Analyzing an Example Paragraph

The following is an example paragraph written by a student. Read the paragraph, and check to see whether it has all the elements for an example paragraph.

1. Topic sentence with controlling idea

2. Development focus

3. Three or four development examples

4. Transitional expressions

In the spaces provided after the paragraph, write in the elements that you have found.

In this paragraph from an example essay, "Seaside Sensation," Lora Smith recounts how the atmosphere in a seafood restaurant captures the "seaman's life."

The atmosphere in Crabby's Crab Shack, in Cherry Grove, North Carolina, exudes the seaman's life from top to bottom and everywhere in between. For example, walking on the crunchy peanut shells strewn all over the floor simulates the creaking deck of a ship. Another example of the "sea" décor can be found on the walls, for they are lined with hunks of driftwood, fishing poles, mounted sailfish and marlin, and paintings of seascapes and sailing vessels from around the world. To see the completeness of the setting, the patrons only have to look up! Specifically, the ceiling has been hung with fishing nets interlaced with twinkling Christmas lights. When the restaurant is darkened, it's as if you are gazing up into the vast, star-filled sky as seen from the deck of a ship. At Crabby's Crab Shack, the only thing missing is the gentle rocking of the sea.

Topic: _____

Controlling idea: _____

Development focus: _____

Development examples: _____

_____

_____

_____

Transitional expressions: _____

_____

_____

_____

PRACTICE 3   Planning Example Paragraphs

For each of the following topics, choose a controlling idea and write a topic sentence. Afterward, choose a development focus (*who, what, where, when, why,* or *how*) and list three development examples. Do not use the same development focus idea more than once.

Example
Topic: <u>Bad Eating Habits</u>
Controlling idea: <u>Cause illnesses</u>
Topic sentence: <u>Poor eating habits can cause many serious illnesses.</u>
Development focus: <u>What</u>
Development examples: <u>anorexia/bulimia</u>
<u>diabetes</u>
<u>osteoporosis</u>

1. Topic: <u>Favorite Rock Groups</u>

   Controlling idea: _____

   Topic sentence: _____

   _____

   Development focus: _____

   Development examples: _____

   _____

   _____

2. Topic: <u>Vacation Locales</u>

   Controlling idea: _____

   Topic sentence: _____

   _____

   Development focus: _____

   Development examples: _____

   _____

   _____

3. Topic: <u>Video Games</u>

   Controlling idea: _____

   Topic sentence: _____

   _____

   Development focus: _____

Development examples: _____

_____

_____

4. Topic: <u>College Courses</u>

Controlling idea: _____

Topic sentence: _____

_____

Development focus: _____

Development examples: _____

_____

_____

5. Topic: <u>Job Hunting</u>

Controlling idea: _____

Topic sentence: _____

_____

Development focus: _____

Development examples: _____

_____

_____

6. Topic: <u>Studying</u>

Controlling idea: _____

Topic sentence: _____

_____

Development focus: _____

Development examples: _____

_____

_____

PRACTICE 4   Writing Example Paragraphs

Complete this exercise on separate sheets of paper. Using the topic sentences, controlling ideas, development focuses, and development examples from Practice 3, write paragraphs for each subject. Use transitional expressions from Exhibit 12–1 to announce examples and create rhythm.

Example

Subject: Bad eating habits

Controlling idea: Cause illnesses

Topic sentence: Poor eating habits can cause many serious illnesses.

Development focus: What

Development examples: anorexia/bulimia

diabetes

osteoporosis

Finished Paragraph

Poor eating habits can cause many serious illnesses. For example, because many young girls are pressured to try to emulate fashion models, their lives are threatened by becoming anorexic and bulimic. It is not only young people who are threatened by eating-related diseases; in fact, both young adults and older adults can develop diabetes. Senior citizens are not exempt from problems, either. Specifically, osteoporosis often afflicts the elderly after many years of poor eating. In order to combat these diseases, eat a well-balanced diet, and don't snack on unhealthy foods between meals.

Using One Extended Example

Sometimes, you might want to use only one very detailed example to develop the topic rather than many shorter examples. This type of longer, more detailed example is called an **extended example.**

For instance, you might want to discuss how children's television programming can help educate preschool children. Instead of discussing many different programs, you could decide to focus on one program that is particularly effective. The most successful and popular program would be a good choice because your readers have most likely heard of it and would be more willing to accept what you have to say.

Example

Sesame Street continues to help preschool children learn to enjoy learning as well as to get a head start on their education. For instance, basic math processes, such as adding and subtracting, usually are illustrated with everyday objects, such as pieces of pie and fruit, for these are objects with which the toddlers are familiar. Another instance of blending instruction into the entertainment occurs at the beginning of each broadcast. Instead

(continued)

of advertisers sponsoring the show, the shows are "sponsored" by a different number and letter of the alphabet each day. The letter and number are integrated into the many sketches that pop up throughout the program. For example, Count Count, the vampire, will count bats, spiders, and lightning bolts, always emphasizing the "sponsoring" number. Another example occurs when a spelling game emphasizes words that contain the "sponsoring" letter. By mixing educational information with entertaining characters and skits, *Sesame Street* has helped millions of young boys and girls see learning as both fun and useful.

Notice, however, that whether many examples or one example is used, the same elements are used in the paragraph:

Subject: Children's educational television
Controlling idea: Helps children enjoy learning and learn some basics
Topic sentence: *Sesame Street* continues to help preschool children learn to enjoy learning as well as to get a head start on their education.
Development focus: What
Development example: *Sesame Street*

Also notice that transitional expressions are used to announce examples and keep the number of examples from appearing as merely a list.

PRACTICE 5   Writing Extended Example Paragraphs

On separate sheets of paper, write an **extended example** paragraph for each of the following topic sentences. The controlling idea has been included. Choose a developing focus (*who, what, where, when, why,* or *how*) and a development example that will develop the subject. Do not choose the same development focus question more than once. Don't forget to use transitional expressions.

1. Fear of flying has prevented me from visiting foreign countries.

2. Success means making many sacrifices.

3. Advertisements are often very misleading.

4. Today's athletes are better than those of the past.

5. College is much more difficult than high school.

6. Being a good son/daughter requires assuming responsibilities.

PRACTICE 6   Analyzing an Example Paragraph

In this paragraph from an essay, "Online Schools Provide New Educational Options," by The Associated Press, some of the elements of education via the Internet are identified. Answer the questions following the paragraphs.

Read All About It . . . To read the full essay from which this paragraph is excerpted, see page 435.

Classes are held by computer, teachers and staff work from a central office, and students sign in from their home desktop or laptop computers. Standards for teachers ideally are the same as those of traditional schools.

It's not all reading, writing and arithmetic. In gym class over the Web, pupils keep daily logs of their exercises. They learn music theory online, then go to a designated campus for piano or guitar lessons. They fax, email or bring in art projects completed at home. Parents even dial in for an online PTA meeting.

Questions for Discussion

1. What specific examples cited in the first paragraph are the same elements you would find in a regular school?

   _____

   _____

2. In the second paragraph, what examples are identified that make online art education and PTA meetings different than in traditional education?

   _____

   _____

3. Point out where in the two paragraphs transitional expressions would have been effective.

   _____

   _____

PRACTICE 7   **Analyzing an Example Paragraph**

The following paragraph is from an essay, "Extremely Cool," by professional writer A. J. Jacobs. In the essay, Jacobs examines the over-use of the term *extreme* to describe everything from athletics to products as diverse as music and soft drinks. Answer the questions following the paragraph.

Read All About It . . . To read the full essay from which this paragraph is excerpted, see page 431.

Unlike the just-do-it enthusiasm it engenders in the sports world, *extreme* often becomes something darker in pop culture. In publishing, right on the heels of A. M. Homes' *The End of Alice,* the graphic fictional story of a pedophile, comes Poppy Brite's *Exquisite Corpse,* a novel told from a serial killer's point of view. ("People need something to kick 'em in the ass a little," says Brite.) American moviegoers will get a taste of extreme filmmaking in July with *Trainspotting,* a British ode to heroin addiction that makes *Pulp Fiction* look tame, peppered as it is with shots of flying feces and a dead baby crawling on the ceiling. "Extreme is ironic, postmodern fun with a bit of a nasty edge," says Mark Gill, president of marketing for *Trainspotting*'s distributor, Miramax. "At the end of it all, you leave having a good time."

Questions for Discussion

1. What specific examples does Jacobs use to help support his ideas about extremism?

_____

_____

_____

_____

2. Novelist Poppy Brite says that Americans need "something to kick 'em in the ass a little." Consider headline stories on television news programs and on the front pages of newspapers. Using examples, comment on Brite's assertion that Americans are not subjected to enough extreme events.

_____

_____

_____

_____

3. Name some athletic products and activities described as "extreme." How have those products and activities become, as Jacobs says, "darker in pop culture"?

_____

_____

_____

_____

_____

_____

TOPIC BANK

Write an example paragraph about one or more of the following topics, or about a topic of your own choice.

1. Buildings (function or architectural style)
2. Study habits
3. Phobias
4. Musical styles
5. Art (period, school, or medium)
6. Restaurants
7. Heroes (real or fictional)
8. Ecosystems
9. Celestial bodies
10. Signs (see the photo on page 192)

WRITING OPPORTUNITIES

HOME You have recently remarried, and the number of children in the family has doubled. Now there are four sons to add to your four daughters. To give this large and hungry new brood some breakfast variety, you travel to the nearest supermarket and make a one-paragraph inventory of the cereal possibilities, remembering that your children range in ages from five to sixteen years old, and their preferences are based on a number of different criteria: cartoon figures on the box, sugar content, numbers of colors, calories, or vitamin content.

SCHOOL Your Advertising & Marketing 205 professor wants you to go to the supermarket and write one paragraph detailing the various types of breakfast cereals and what age group you think each is targeted for, based on the information on the box.

WORK Your boss at the consumer health agency is going to appear on a television show to talk about nutrition and breakfast cereals. So that she'll have some facts to use, she wants you to write one paragraph, giving examples of a variety of breakfast cereals and pointing out their good and bad nutritional qualities.

Visit *The Write Start* **Online!**

For additional practice with the materials in this chapter, go to

http://www.cengage.com/devenglish/checkett/writestartSP4e.

Chapter Self-Assessment Test

Check either True or False on the blank next to the statement.

T	F	
_____	_____	Examples can help develop a topic quickly.
_____	_____	Transitional expressions help develop ideas, but they don't help connect specific examples.
_____	_____	Examples do not hold a reader's attention; only good action verbs do so.
_____	_____	One extended example is sometimes better than many shorter ones.

13

Classification

Put yourself in the middle of an athletic shoe store. For five minutes, write a list of every type of shoe in the store and every brand name. After you are finished, use another five minutes to list the special features of each type of shoe.

Some subjects are very complicated or contain many parts. A simple explanation or description of these subjects often is not enough for your readers to understand them fully. How, then, do you get your point across? Sometimes, you need to break a larger point into smaller points so you can explain it in your writing. **Classification** is the process of separating out smaller points from a larger concept and organizing these smaller points into easily recognized groups. These groups can be based on color, shape, kind, or any other type of category that readers will understand easily.

For instance, if you were asked to write a paragraph about the work of William Shakespeare, you could classify it into sonnets, histories, comedies, tragedies, dark comedies, and romances. Classifying his writing into smaller categories makes it easier to make a point about some aspect of his writing. Classifying can focus your writing into a specific area. For example, you could discuss his use of iambic pentameter in the sonnets as opposed to some of the plays.

Breaking Down a Topic

The same subject can be classified in a variety of ways. Whales can be classified as humpback, right, sperm, blue, sei, and pilot, among others. Food can be separated into meat, dairy, vegetables, fruits, and grains; trees into deciduous and coniferous; and music into soul, rock, alternative, jazz, classical, swing, and so on. It is important, however, to keep the units of classification of the same type.

> **Example**
> Dress slacks might be classified according to fabric: cotton, twill, wool.
>
> Adding a category of *price range* would be inappropriate. Price does not belong with fabric.

PRACTICE 1   Identifying the Item That Does Not Belong

Look at each of the following groups of items. Circle the letter of the item that does not belong with the other members of the group.

Example

Shoes

a. wingtip

b. athletic

c. blue

d. high heel

The *color* blue does not belong with the *types of shoes*.

1. Highways

a. one-lane

b. two-lane

c. tollway

d. four-lane

2. Fruit

a. apples

b. yellow

c. pears

d. grapes

3. Houses

a. split-level

b. ranch

c. colonial

d. brick

4. Money

a. lira

b. coins

c. rupee

d. yen

5. Politicians

    a. mayors

    b. senators

    c. lobbyists

    d. representatives

6. Boats

    a. yachts

    b. motorized

    c. schooners

    d. sloops

PRACTICE 2　　**Identifying the Item That Does Not Belong**

Look at each of the following groups of items. Circle the letter of the item that does not belong with the other members of the group.

1. Musicals

    a. *Phantom of the Opera*

    b. *Evita*

    c. *Cabaret*

    d. *To Kill a Mockingbird*

2. Sports

    a. tennis

    b. workout

    c. football

    d. racquetball

3. Trees

    a. elm

    b. leaves

    c. oak

    d. Douglas fir

4. Nations

    a. Russia

    b. Australia

    c. Canada

    d. California

5. Oceans

    a. Atlantic

    b. Michigan

    c. Indian

    d. Pacific

6. Medical personnel

    a. nurse

    b. surgeon

    c. anesthetist

    d. accountant

The Topic Sentence

The classification paragraph begins with a topic sentence that clearly states the subject, how the subject will be divided, and why classifying the subject is important.

> **Example**
>
> To study the geologic evolution of the Earth more easily, we can classify rocks as igneous, sedimentary, and metamorphic.
>
> *Subject:* Rocks
>
> *Categories:* Igneous, sedimentary, metamorphic
>
> *Controlling idea:* To learn about the formation of the Earth

The entire paragraph might look like this:

> To study the geologic evolution of the earth more easily, we can classify rocks as igneous, sedimentary, and metamorphic. The first type, igneous rock, is formed when a molten mass of rock (magma) from deep within the earth rises and fills in cracks close to the surface of the earth through a volcano. Magma cools rapidly and usually forms into a fine-grained, glasslike rock. Sedimentary rocks, the second category, are formed when other rocks disintegrate, and the particles from these rocks usually are carried by water into larger bodies of water where they settle on the bottom and form layers of rocks. Shale and sandstone are common sedimentary rocks. The last type, metamorphic rock, can be traced to a parent igneous or sedimentary rock and is formed through heat and pressure. For instance, the metamorphic rock slate is formed when shale is pressurized, over time, in a low-temperature environment.

- Into what categories does the writer classify the subject?
  Igneous, sedimentary, and metamorphic rocks
- What does the writer say about the first category?
  Igneous rock is formed by volcanic magma cooling near the earth's surface.
- What is said about the second category?
  Sedimentary rock is formed from the particles of other rocks.
- When classifying, using examples is an excellent method of achieving clarity. What example of a sedimentary rock does the writer use?
  Shale
- What information does the writer state about the third category?
  Metamorphic rock is formed from other rocks by heat and pressure.
- What example is given to clarify the information?
  Slate is formed from shale.

Note that the only categories of rocks discussed in the paragraph are those mentioned in the topic sentence. No new topics or subtopics were added.

(ESL) Transitional Expressions: Linking Your Classifications

In classification paragraphs, transitional expressions help link your categories together so that they don't appear simply as a list. Transitional expressions also help focus the reader's attention on the variety of categories, types, kinds, and divisions.

Transitional Expressions for Classification			
The first type	can be categorized	the first kind	the first division
The second type	can be classified	the second kind	the second division
The last type	can be divided	the next kind	the final division

| **PRACTICE 3** | **Identifying Transitional Expressions** |

List the transitional expressions you find in the example paragraph regarding types of rocks.

_____

_____

_____

| **PRACTICE 4** | **Classifying** |

Groups can be classified in more than one way. Buildings, for example, can be classified by the activity that goes on in them (medical, office, school) or by the material out of which they are constructed (brick, stucco, wood). Think of three ways to classify each of the following groups:

Example

Friends
a. to whom you can tell any secret
b. who are "fair weather"
c. who are only "social"

1. Animals

a. _____

b. _____

c. _____

2. Military personnel

a. _____

b. _____

c. _____

3. Water

a. _____

b. _____

c. _____

4. Clothing

a. _____

b. _____

c. _____

5. Fans

a. _____

b. _____

c. _____

PRACTICE 5   Writing Topic Sentences

For the following groups, separate each into similar units of classification. Afterward, write a topic sentence for each one.

Example

Group: <u>Oil paints</u>

Unit of classification: <u>Color</u>

Categories: <u>Sunset red, forest green, sky blue</u>

Topic sentence: <u>Because landscape painters want to capture nature realistically, oil paints come in a variety of colors, including sunset red, forest green, and sky blue.</u>

1. Group: Relatives

Unit of classification: _____

Categories: _____

Topic sentence: _____

_____

2. Group: Birds

Unit of classification: _____

Categories: _____

Topic sentence: _____

_____

3. Group: Restaurants

Unit of classification: _____

Categories: _____

Topic sentence: _____

_____

PRACTICE 6   Writing Classification Paragraphs

On a separate sheet of paper, write a paragraph for each of the topic sentences you have written for Practice 5. Use examples to help in classifying the groups you chose. Don't forget to use transitional phrases to connect ideas and to add rhythm.

PRACTICE 7   Analyzing a Classification Paragraph

In the following paragraph from a classification essay, "Michelangelo Madness," student writer Martin Brink takes a humorous look at tools used by homeowners. The tools are not classified by how helpful they are in making tasks easier but how they promote Murphy's Law by making any project frustrating and even dangerous.

> **Read All About It . . .**
>
> To read the full essay from which this paragraph is excerpted, see page 444.

A good rule of thumb (red and swollen by now) to follow is that any tools powered by fossil fuels—weed whackers, lawn mowers, edgers, and snow blowers—are temperamental by design. These helpful devices (a.k.a. "accidents waiting to happen") have starter cords to assist in starting the engine. According to the manual, the happy homeowner should pull the starter cord three or four times to prime the engine with gas. The manufacturer calls this activity "pre-ignition" because on the fifth pull, the engine is supposed to hum into full force. This activity should really be called "aerobic exercise" because the only thing demonstrating full force is the red-faced homeowner who is approaching unconsciousness after pulling on the starter cord fifty-seven times without so much as a puff of exhaust.

Classification Technique Questions

1. How does the writer classify power tools that use fossil fuels?

_____

_____

2. What do you think is the reaction the writer wants to get from his audience?

_____

_____

_____

_____

3. What examples does the writer give for the tools that use fossil fuels? Does this make the essay more effective? Why or why not?

_____

_____

_____

_____

4. What other examples can you think of that might fit into the category?

_____

_____

5. Does the writer use any transitional devices to connect ideas and to add rhythm? If not, would the paragraph have been more effective if the writer had done so? Where in the paragraph would you suggest using a few?

_____

_____

PRACTICE 8   Analyzing a Classification Paragraph

In the following paragraph from a classification essay, "Who Else Is Going to Do It?" student writer Nicholas Wade extols the virtues of blue-collar workers. According to Wade, these talented construction workers provide places to work and live while experiencing many dangers on the job.

Pile drivers, carpenters, and millwrights are the dedicated blue-collar

workers in the honorable field of construction. The first type of worker, the pile driver, lays the foundation for massive buildings. Unfortunately, working with heavy concrete pilings is a risky job, and many pile drivers have lost their lives performing this task. The second kind of blue-collar worker is the carpenter. They stand the walls, supply the roof, and prepare the interior. Carpenters often suffer aching joints and other early signs of aging. The last category of worker is the millwright. Millwrights install the machineryin office buildings and factories. Working with such heavy equipment is dangerous and often leads to serious injury.

Classification Technique Questions

1. What do you think is the writer's purpose in writing this paragraph?

_____

_____

_____

2. How does the writer categorize blue-collar workers? What do the categories have in common?

_____

_____

3. Can you think of other categories of blue-collar workers? Is there a dangerous aspect to their jobs?

_____

_____

4. Identify any transitional devices the writer has used. How do they add to the effectiveness of the paragraph?

_____

_____

_____

5. Does the writer's word choice support the serious tone? Point out some examples.

_____

_____

_____

PRACTICE 9   **Analyzing a Classification Paragraph**

In the following paragraph from a classification essay, "The Plot Against People," by professional writer Russell Baker, inanimate objects are classified as things that break, get lost, and malfunction—on purpose! Although short, the paragraph has many examples to support Baker's contention that inanimate objects can confound unsuspecting humans at any moment.

> *Read All About It . . .*
>
> To read the full essay from which this paragraph is excerpted, see page 442.

It is not uncommon for a pair of pliers to climb all the way from the cellar to the attic in its single-minded determination to raise its owner's blood pressure. Keys have been known to burrow three feet under mattresses. Women's purses, despite their great weight, frequently travel through six or seven rooms to find hiding space under a couch.

Classification Technique Questions

1. Personification (giving human qualities to nonhuman things) is a technique that writers use to enhance their writing. Point out some examples of personification in the paragraph. How do they enhance the tone (serious, humorous, sarcastic, ironic) of the paragraph?

_____

_____

_____

2. How does word choice support the tone of the paragraph? Give examples.

_____

_____

_____

3. What other inanimate objects can you think of, and how do they confound you?

_____

_____

4. The paragraph is short. Would the paragraph have been more effective if Baker had developed each item more fully? Explain.

_____

_____

_____

5. What do you think was Baker's purpose in writing this essay?

_____

_____

_____

_____

Suggestions for Writing

1. Using one of your answers from Question 3 in the classification technique questions above, write a paragraph about some inanimate object that confounds or frustrates you.
2. With some of your classmates, write a paragraph about an inanimate object that confounds or frustrates a group of people.

PRACTICE 10   Analyzing a Classification Paragraph

In the following paragraph from a classification essay, "Why We Carp and Harp," by professional writer Mary Ann Hogan, the author states that nagging, although seeming familiar and similar, can be classified in a variety of ways. Answer the questions following the paragraph.

Read All About It ...
To read the full essay from which this paragraph is excerpted, see page 439.

Thus, doctors can nag patients to lose their potbellies; accountants can nag timid clients to buy low; bosses can nag workers to get things done on time; special interest groups can nag the public to save the planet and send money; and the government can nag everyone to pay their taxes on time, to abstain from drink if they're pregnant, and, while they're at it, to Buy American. And when the going gets desperate, the desperate get nagging: Our recession-plagued nation, experts say, could be headed for a giant nag jag.

1. Which classifications does the author identify in the paragraph?

_____

_____

_____

2. The author states that "when the going gets desperate, the desperate get nagging." What do you think she means by this?

_____

_____

_____

3. Why is the listing of the different classifications effective?

_____

_____

_____

Suggestions for Writing

1. In her paragraph, Hogan mentions a variety of classifications. Write a paragraph classifying some of the members of your own family and how their particular brand of nagging is different from that of other family members.

2. Write a paragraph discussing how nagging affects you. Also, identify what class of nagger you are and how you think your nagging affects others.

TOPIC BANK

Write a classification paragraph about one or more of the following topics or about a topic of your own choice.

1. Fans at a sporting event
2. Bosses
3. Athletic shoes
   (see the photo on page 205)
4. Successes or failures
5. Sitcoms
6. Clothes
7. Dates you've had
8. Coworkers
9. Movies
10. Problems of a new student
   or employee

WRITING OPPORTUNITIES

HOME For your visit to your child's "Parents Day" at school, you've been asked by the teacher to talk about the various types of jobs at the company where you are employed. You decide to bring the two photographs above accompanied by a written paragraph classifying the various categories that the workers in the photographs represent.

SCHOOL Your Business 333 professor has given you an assignment to create your own manufacturing company. Your first task is to write a paragraph that identifies both the product you will be making and the types of workers necessary to make and bring your product to market.

WORK As the personnel director of your company, the president has instructed you, because of declining profits, to downsize the number of employees by 10 percent in each job classification. You decide that your first step should be to write a paragraph classifying the job categories in each of the three divisions of the company.

Visit *The Write Start* Online!

For additional practice with the materials in this chapter, go to

http://www.cengage.com/devenglish/checkett/writestartSP4e.

Chapter Self-Assessment Test

Check either True or False on the blank next to the statement.

T   F

____   ____   Large or complicated subjects can be made more manageable and easier to understand by classifying them into smaller units.

____   ____   Smaller units are often classified as *types, kinds, categories,* or *divisions.*

____   ____   It is not important to classify a group into smaller units of the same type.

____   ____   Classification paragraphs, because they will divide items into smaller units, do not have to have a topic sentence.

____   ____   A classification topic sentence clearly states the subject, how it will be divided, and why classifying the subject is important.

____   ____   In classification paragraphs, transitional expressions clarify the focus of categories, types, kinds, and divisions.

____   ____   Transitional expressions in classification paragraphs, therefore, do not connect ideas and add rhythm to the writing.

14

Process

Write a topic sentence for the process shown in the photograph or a process with which you are familiar. This could be a hobby, such as creating photo albums of important family events, or a school-related activity, such as taking an exam.

Have you ever had to explain to a friend how to perform a specific task? Perhaps you had to explain how to play a video game or how to use a certain type of equipment. Think about how you would give that explanation in writing. You would have to provide a step-by-step account. Now, consider how such an account might apply to your writing for school or work. Sometimes, you might be called on to explain how you performed a certain science experiment, how a car should be maintained, or how a meeting with a client was conducted. All of these writing situations involve a process.

Process explains the steps necessary to complete a procedure, an operation, or an event. Process is an important method when you are asked to develop ideas in areas such as science, technology, sports, medicine, and business. For example, you may be asked to explain how stars are born and how they eventually die; or you may be asked to write about the bus boycott during the civil rights movement; or you may have to give a report illustrating how to assemble a piece of machinery.

Types of Process

There are two kinds of process descriptions: **directional** and **informational.** *Directional* process explains to the reader how to do something: how to bake a cake, how to tune a car engine, or how to write a process essay. The goal of directional process is to enable readers to do something or to duplicate some process after they have followed the directions.

Informational process explains to the reader how something was made, how an event occurred, or how something works: how a treaty between two countries was finalized, how the Panama Canal was built, or how a laser is used in medical procedures. Readers are not expected to be able to actually repeat or duplicate the process explained, but they should be able to understand the process.

PRACTICE 1   **Identifying Directional and Informational Process**

In the space provided to the left, identify each topic as directional **(D)** or informational **(I).**

1. _____ How to install gas logs in a fireplace

2. _____ How Dr. Jonas Salk developed the polio vaccine

3. _____ How to balance a checkbook

4. _____ How the automobile was developed by Henry Ford

5. _____ How lightning forms

6. _____ How to sew a dress from a pattern

7. _____ How to build a brick barbecue

8. _____ How to read the stock market page

9. _____ How to begin a hobby

10. _____ How prisoners were tried during the Spanish Inquisition

---

PRACTICE 2   **Identifying Directional and Informational Process**

In the space provided to the left, identify each topic as directional **(D)** or informational **(I).**

1. _____ How to study for an exam

2. _____ How to be a friend

3. _____ How to send e-mail

4. _____ How to repair a clock

5. _____ How the War of the Roses occurred

6. _____ How to fill out a job application

7. _____ How to register to vote

8. _____ How to plan for a vacation

9. _____ How to make candied apples

10. _____ How photosynthesis works

Organizing the Process Paragraph

Both directional and informational process paragraphs are developed according to the order in which the steps of the process occur. Adhering to chronological order avoids confusion. For example, in describing how to change a tire, the instructions would not occur as suggested by the list on the left; rather, they would follow the chronological steps as listed on the right:

Poor Sequence	Chronological Sequence
1. Replace the hubcap	1. Remove the hubcap
2. Replace lug nuts and tighten	2. Unscrew and remove lug nuts
3. Replace with spare tire	3. Remove flat tire
4. Unscrew and remove lug nuts	4. Replace with spare tire
5. Remove flat tire	5. Replace lug nuts and tighten
6. Remove the hubcap	6. Replace the hubcap

PRACTICE 3   Using Chronological Order

Here are two lists of steps for process paragraphs. They are not in chronological order. Number the steps in the proper order in the spaces provided to the left. If you find any steps that should not be included, write an "X" in that space.

1. Sending an e-mail using a computer is an easy method of communication.

_____ Move the cursor to the text box and begin composing your message.

_____ Finally, click on the "Send" icon.

_____ Move your cursor to the "Subject" box, and type in a subject word or phrase.

_____ Move your cursor to the "To" box, and type the addressee's e-mail address.

_____ First, click on the "Compose Message" icon.

2. Alice became a good student through hard work and sticking to a schedule.

_____ Each evening, she studied between 7 and 10 o'clock.

_____ During class, she always took notes.

_____ She spent many hours drinking coffee in the Student Center.

_____ In the morning before class, she looked over her notes from the day before.

_____ After class each day, she did research in the library for one hour.

PRACTICE 4   Using Chronological Order

Here are two lists of steps for process paragraphs. They are not in chronological order. Number the steps in the proper order in the spaces provided to the left. If you find any steps that should not be included, write an "X" in that space.

1. How pearls are created is both a fascinating and unusual process.

_____ The particle acts as an irritant.

_____ Pearls are produced inside certain bivalve mollusks, such as oysters.

_____ A small particle, such as a grain of sand, lodges in the mollusk's soft tissue.

_____ Either spherical or irregular pearls are formed, depending on the shape of the particle.

_____ Pearl coloration varies widely, the most prized shades being white, black, rose, and cream.

_____ The irritant becomes coated with layer upon layer of lustrous nacre.

2. Although stopping smoking is difficult, it can be achieved by breaking some old habits and by establishing some new ones.

_____ Treat yourself to a thick, rich, strawberry milkshake.

_____ Instead of smoking while talking on the telephone, twirl a pencil with your fingers. Pretend it's the cigarette you normally hold when on the phone.

_____ Instead of having a cigarette the first thing in the morning, go for a brisk walk around the neighborhood.

_____ After lunch, suck on a piece of hard candy instead of having a smoke.

_____ Begin by making a list of when and where it is that you normally smoke.

_____ If all else fails, see your doctor about wearing a nicotine patch.

_____ Finally, before you go to bed, do 50 pushups and eat a piece of fruit.

_____ On the way to work, keep your mind off having a cigarette and use the CD player or iPod to learn a new language.

ESL Transitional Expressions: Connecting the Steps

Now that you have the steps of your process in the correct order, you need to connect them in your paragraph so that they follow each other chronologically. Transitional expressions are extremely helpful in connecting these steps.

Commonly Used Transitional Expressions for Process

afterward	before	initially	to begin
as	begin by	later	until
as soon as	during	meanwhile	upon
at first	finally	next	when
at last	first, second, third, etc.	now	while
at this point	following	then	

The Topic Sentence

Now that you know how to make smooth transitions between the steps of the process, you are ready to put the paragraph together. Both directional and informational paragraphs begin with a topic sentence that clearly states what the reader should be able to do or understand after reading the steps of the process and why the process is important.

Example

Great dough, a delectable sauce, and a variety of delicious toppings are the three things you need to make a gourmet pizza.

The entire paragraph might read like this:

Great dough, a delectable sauce, and a variety of delicious toppings are the three things you need to make a gourmet pizza. First, in a large bowl, pour ½ cup of warm water, 1 package

(continued)

yeast, and 1 teaspoon of sugar. Mix well, and wait about 5 to 7 minutes to allow the yeast and sugar to activate. Next, add 2 cups flour, ½ teaspoon salt, 2 tablespoons olive oil, and another ½ cup of warm water to the yeast mixture. With a fork, stir the mixture until all the water is absorbed. Now spread flour on a pastry board or table. Dust your hands with flour, and empty the dough onto the floured mixing surface. Knead the dough for about 10 minutes. Put the dough back into the bowl, drizzle some olive oil over the surface, cover with a towel, and place the bowl in a draft-free area. The dough will be ready in 45 minutes. Second, prepare the sauce. Over medium heat in a saucepan, sauté a minced clove of garlic in 2 tablespoons olive oil. Then add one 14-ounce can of crushed tomatoes, one 3-ounce can of tomato paste, and basil, parsley, oregano, salt, and pepper to taste. After this, reduce heat to low, cover, and simmer for 1 hour, stirring occasionally until sauce thickens. Third, assemble the pizza and toppings. Remove the dough from the bowl, punch it down, and spread it in a 12- to 14-inch-diameter circle on a floured surface. With a spoon, spread the sauce liberally over the dough's surface. Then add some tasty toppings, such as cooked bacon, Italian sausage, ground beef, pepperoni, shrimp, pineapple, peppers, onions, mushrooms, broccoli, cauliflower, and olives. Finally, top with shredded cheese, such as mozzarella or provolone, and bake at 475° for 15 minutes until the cheese melts. Mangia!

PRACTICE 5   Analyzing a Process Paragraph

Answer the following questions about the preceding paragraph.

1. What process does the paragraph explain?

_____

2. Is this process paragraph intended to be directional or informational?

_____

3. How many steps are there in the process? Name them.

_____

_____

4. Identify the transitional expressions in the paragraph.

_____

_____

_____

PRACTICE 6   Analyzing a Process Paragraph

In the following paragraph from a process essay, "How to be Successful at Kicking the Smoking Habit," student writer Stephanie Higgs outlines the reasons people begin smoking before tackling the daunting procedure to end the habit.

People smoke for many reasons; therefore, it is important for smokers to identify the reasons why they smoke. Analyzing the origin of the habit is the first positive step toward kicking the habit. For most people, smoking is a learned behavior; consequently, smokers tend to come from families where one or more of their parents were smokers. The majority of them are anxious people who started smoking because it seemed to provide a temporary release from current or future distress and uncertainties. Some tobacco users started smoking to be cool and to fit in with the crowd; likewise, others started smoking because they enjoyed the taste of tobacco after trying it. While others did not necessarily enjoy the act of smoking, they felt addicted to the nicotine and needed to continue to satisfy their cravings. Now, with the origin of the habit exposed, the smoker is empowered with the knowledge of why he or she smokes and each can seek out healthier alternatives to satisfying needs.

Process Technique Questions

1. What is the process that is being explained?

_____

2. Is the paragraph directional or informational?

_____

3. How many steps or reasons are discussed? What are they?

_____

_____

_____

4. Identify any transitional expressions that are used. Do they help organize the information chronologically?

_____

_____

5. What transitional expressions would be more effective, and where would you place them in the paragraph?

_____

_____

_____

PRACTICE 7　Writing an Informational Process Paragraph

On a separate sheet of paper, write an informational process paragraph for one of the informational process topics you identified in Practice 1 or Practice 2. Remember, use transitional expressions to order your steps and to connect related ideas.

PRACTICE 8　Analyzing a Process Paragraph

In the following paragraph from a process essay, "A Step-by-Step Guide to Photography," student writer Stephanie Weidemann clarifies the steps necessary to produce visually effective prints.

A photographer must set the scene, correctly develop the negative, and creatively enlarge the print to achieve a worthwhile photograph. First, using a grey card, measure the light that the camera is reading from the scene. Adjust the aperture so that the light meter is floating in the center of its scale; this insures the picture will not be under or over exposed. Next, great care must be given when developing the negative. No light must ever reach the negative during the developing process. In complete darkness, the film is loaded onto a developing reel and placed into a series of chemical liquids that develop and fix the negative. After this, the negative is enlarged. The process is achieved by first placing the negative into an enlarger, followed by shining a light through the negative onto resin coated paper. By manipulating the amount of light and time, the photographer can create a variety of special effects. The paper is then run through another series of chemical liquid baths and allowed to dry.

Process Technique Questions

1. What process is being explained in the paragraph?

   _____

2. Is the paragraph intending the process to be directional or informational?

   _____

3. How many steps are explained?

   _____

4. Identify any transitional expressions that are used. Do they help organize the information chronologically?

   _____

   _____

   _____

5. Would other transitional expressions be more effective? Which ones would you add, and where would you place them?

   _____

   _____

   _____

PRACTICE 9   Writing a Directional Process Paragraph

On a separate sheet of paper, write a directional process paragraph for one of the directional process topics you identified in either Practice 1 or Practice 2. Remember, use transitional expressions to order your steps and to connect related ideas.

PRACTICE 10   Analyzing Process Writing

In the following paragraphs from an essay, "Strive to Be Fit, Not Fanatical," Timothy Gower gives advice about a great American pastime—exercising. Although exercising is a great way to keep fit, Gower suggests that too much of a good thing may not be so good.

Read All About It ...

To read the full essay from which this paragraph is excerpted, see page 448.

Let's start with exercise. If you know that a little jogging is good for your heart, then you might assume that doing laps till you're dizzy and ready to retch would make your ticker indestructible. But you would be incorrect. A 1997 Harvard study determined that the cardiovascular benefits of an intense aerobic workout peak at about 24 minutes; pound the pavement longer if you like, but your heart won't get any stronger.

Ditto strength training. According to the gospel of the weight room, you must do a minimum of three sets of bench presses, curls, or any other strength-building exercise, to build up a muscle. But studies at the University of Florida show that's just not true; doing one set of an exercise produces more than three-quarters of the muscles you get from doing three. You gain a little less in the biceps department, maybe, but you get the heck out of that stinky, sweaty gym in one-third of the time. Sounds like a good deal to me.

Unless you are obese, forget abut dieting. (And if you are dramatically overweight, see a doctor who specializes in obesity.) Nutrition experts say crash weight-loss plans that require you to stop eating certain foods don't work; you'll lose weight, but inevitably your willpower crumbles, and the pounds return. Instead, eat a balanced meal plan that includes lots of fruit, vegetables, whole grains and an occasional splurge. Add regular exercise, and eventually you'll attain manageable, healthy weight.

Process Technique Questions

1. Is the information in the three paragraphs intended to be directional or informational?

   _____

2. How many steps in the process are described in the third paragraph?

   _____

3. In most process essays, the reader is given the steps to do or to understand. How is this process essay different?

_____

_____

4. The author does not use transitional devices to connect the steps in the processes she describes. Which transitional devices would you choose to help organize the steps in the process?

_____

_____

PRACTICE 11   **Analyzing Process Writing**

In the following paragraphs from an essay, "Conversational Ballgames," author Nancy Masterson Sakamoto discusses cultural differences between conversations in Japan and in the United States. Pay attention to how Sakamoto explains the subtle differences between the two processes that on the surface may seem similar but in actuality are completely different.

Read All About It . . .

To read the full essay from which this paragraph is excerpted, see page 445.

A Western-style conversation between two people is like a game of tennis. If I introduce a topic, a conversational ball, I expect you to hit it back. If you agree with me, I don't expect you simply to agree and do nothing more. I expect you to add something—a reason for agreeing, another example, or an elaboration to carry the idea further. But I don't expect you always to agree. I am just as happy if you question me, or challenge me, or completely disagree with me. Whether you agree or disagree, your response will return the ball to me.

And then it is my turn again. I don't serve a new ball from my original starting line. I hit your ball back again from where it has bounced. I carry your idea further, or answer your questions or objections, or challenge or question you. And so the ball goes back and forth, with each of us doing our best to give it a new twist, an original spin, or a powerful smash.

A Japanese-style conversation, however, is not at all like tennis or volleyball. It's like bowling. You wait for your turn. And you always know your place in line. It depends on such things as whether you are older or younger, a close friend or a relative stranger to the previous speaker, in a senior or junior position, and so on.

When your turn comes, you step up to the starting line with your bowling ball, and carefully bowl it. Everyone else stands back and watches politely, murmuring encouragement. Everyone waits until the ball has reached the end of the alley, and watches to see if it knocks down all the pins, or only some of them, or none of them. There is a pause, while everyone registers your score.

Process Technique Questions

1. What is the specific process the paragraphs explain?

_____

2. Is the explanation of the two different conversational processes intended to be directional or informational?

_____

3. What are the sports processes that Sakamoto uses to clarify her points about both American and Japanese conversational styles?

_____

4. Identify any transitional expressions that Sakamoto uses to help connect and organize her ideas.

_____

_____

_____

TOPIC BANK

Write a process paragraph about one or more of the following topics or about a topic of your own choice.

1. How to wash a car
2. How to plan a budget
3. How to cook a specific meal (see the photo on page 219)
4. How to repair an appliance
5. How to cut someone's hair
6. How a camera works
7. How to meet new people
8. How a bill becomes a law
9. How a bird builds a nest
10. How the war in Iraq was conducted

WRITING OPPORTUNITIES

HOME You and your spouse want to film your daughter's college graduation ceremony and the party at your home afterward. Additionally, your two youngest children want to be a part of the "crew." Write a paragraph describing the process that the four of you will follow to do a good job of filming the events.

SCHOOL The student senate at your school wants to make a short video to be shown at first-year orientation in hopes of inducing more students to become active in campus organizations. You have been chosen to direct the shoot. Write a paragraph explaining to the student senate the process that you want to follow to make the video.

WORK The chief executive officer (CEO) of a new computer software company has hired your public relations company to make a video to introduce their new product line. The CEO wants to be filmed sitting at her desk as she introduces the company and its products to the consumer. Before you and your crew arrive at the company offices, you will need her to make certain arrangements to make the shoot successful and less time-consuming. Write a paragraph to the CEO explaining the process she will need to accomplish prior to your arriving for the shoot.

 Visit *The Write Start* Online!

For additional practice with the materials in this chapter, go to

http://www.cengage.com/devenglish/checkett/writestartSP4e.

Chapter Self-Assessment Test

Check either True or False on the blank next to the statement.

T   F

____ ____   A process explains the steps necessary to complete a procedure or an operation.

____ ____   A process, however, is not used to explain an event.

____ ____   There are three kinds of process descriptions: directional, informational, and subjective.

____ ____   Directional process explains how to do something.

____ ____   Directional process allows the reader to duplicate the process.

____ ____   Informational process explains how something was made.

____ ____   Informational process explains how something works.

____ ____   Directional process explains how an event occurred.

____ ____   Informational process intends for the reader to understand the process but not duplicate it.

____ ____   Process paragraphs do not have to be arranged chronologically.

____ ____   Directional process paragraphs need a topic sentence.

____ ____   Informational process paragraphs do not need a topic sentence.

15

Comparison and Contrast

Using the cross-examining prewriting technique described on page 131, answer the questions in reference to two magazines you enjoy reading.

Often in your writing, you will need to discuss an object, idea, or item not in terms of its own features, but in terms of how it relates to another object, idea, or item. This type of writing can be a challenge because it forces you to think about each item on its own, as well as about the ways in which the items relate to one another. Are they alike? Are they different? How? Although you will often need to compare and contrast several items at one time in your writing, this chapter focuses on comparing and contrasting just two items, for the sake of simplicity.

Deciding to Compare or to Contrast

The two main tools you use in this type of writing are **comparison** and **contrast.** When you compare things, you are looking for similarities. When you contrast things, you are looking for differences. For example, consider two shirts. In comparing them, you might notice that they are both white, have collars, and have buttons. When contrasting them, you might notice that they are made of different materials, that only one has buttons on the collar, and that one is a dress shirt and the other is a casual shirt. Comparison and contrast, therefore, assists the reader in understanding one person, place, feeling, idea, or object in relation to another.

PRACTICE 1   Comparing or Contrasting

Look at the following pairs of topics. Decide whether it would be better to compare or contrast each pair.

	Compare	Contrast
1. My friends Bob and Carl	_____	_____
2. Antarctica and the Sahara Desert	_____	_____
3. Concrete and rubber	_____	_____
4. Beef and fish	_____	_____
5. Internet search engines Yahoo! and Google	_____	_____
6. Idaho and Yukon Gold potatoes	_____	_____
7. French and California wines	_____	_____
8. Nurses and doctors	_____	_____
9. Jogging and walking	_____	_____
10. Apples and oranges	_____	_____

PRACTICE 2   Comparing or Contrasting

Look at the following pairs of topics. Decide whether it would be better to compare or contrast each pair.

	Compare	Contrast
1. Board games Monopoly and Careers	_____	_____
2. Attorney and judge	_____	_____

3. Movie star and rock star _____ _____

4. Swimming in a pool or a lake _____ _____

5. Oral exam and essay exam _____ _____

6. Coin collecting and stamp collecting _____ _____

7. Canada and the United States _____ _____

8. Soccer and rugby _____ _____

9. Running shoes and walking shoes _____ _____

10. Chicago and New York style pizza _____ _____

The Topic Sentence

The comparison/contrast paragraph begins with a topic sentence that clearly states the two items being compared or contrasted and explains why comparing or contrasting them is important. Here is an example of a topic sentence for a comparison/contrast paragraph.

> When parents choose between a two-year college and a four-year college for their child, cost is often a deciding factor.

This topic sentence clearly states the two items for comparison: two-year and four-year colleges. "Cost" is the factor mentioned that indicates how the writer is going to compare the two types of colleges.

The entire paragraph might look like this:

> When parents choose between a two-year college and a four-year college for their child, cost is often a deciding factor. Tuition is a major cost when deciding on which college to attend. At a four-year college, tuition is a flat fee that can run anywhere from $8,000 to $40,000, depending on the size and selectivity of the school. The student can take from twenty-four to thirty-six credit hours per year, and the tuition charge will not vary. In addition to tuition costs, room and board adds to the expenses at the four-year college. Room and board can run from $4,000 to $15,000 per year, depending on the school's dormitory and apartment facilities. Consequently, the cost for tuition and room and board at a four-year college can run between $12,000 and $55,000. Unlike four-year colleges, two-year colleges charge by the credit hour, usually ranging from $37 to $48 per credit hour; therefore, a student taking between twenty-four and thirty-six credit hours per year will pay between $900 and $1,800 per year in tuition. Another major difference between four-year and two-year colleges is that most two-year colleges do not have dormitories.
>
> *(continued)*

They are known more as "commuter schools" because students live at home and drive to school each day. Because most families do not have to adjust their budgets for children who are going to college but still living at home as they did during high school, there is no "additional" cost for room and board. Even if parents charge room and board to their college student living at home, the charge is usually somewhat reduced, say $200 per month. This would add an additional $2,000 to the cost. Thus, the expense for a two-year college, including room and board and tuition, would be between $900 and $3,800 per year.

PRACTICE 3   Writing Compare and Contrast Topic Sentences

Compose both comparison and contrasting topic sentences for the pairs of items listed below.

Example

Topic: Two Friends

a. Julio and Angelina have very different study habits. (Contrast)

b. Aretha and Maurice have similar exercise routines. (Comparison)

1. Two Musical Groups

    a. _____

    b. _____

2. Two Restaurants

    a. _____

    b. _____

3. Two School Courses

    a. _____

    b. _____

PRACTICE 4   Writing Compare and Contrast Topic Sentences

Compose both comparison and contrasting topic sentences for the pairs of items listed below.

1. Two Vacation Spots/Resorts

    a. _____

    b. _____

2. Two Bosses

a. _____

b. _____

3. Two Types/Styles of Clothes

a. _____

b. _____

Organizing Comparisons and Contrasts

Once you know what comparisons and contrasts you are going to use, you need to organize your thoughts and decide how to present them. There are two commonly used organizational plans for comparison and contrast paragraphs: **block** and **point-by-point.** The block method presents information about one item first, then uses this information for comparison or contrast when presenting information about the second item in the second half of the paragraph. The point-by-point method presents the information about both items together, creating an ongoing series of comparisons and contrasts.

Block Method

In the preceding paragraph about two-year and four-year colleges, the block method is used. Notice that the cost elements of the four-year college are discussed in the first half of the paragraph (without mention of the two-year college). Afterward, the same cost elements concerning the two-year college are discussed in the second half of the paragraph.

The block method is illustrated in this manner:

Topic Sentence: When parents choose between a two-year college and a four-year college for their child, cost is often a deciding factor.

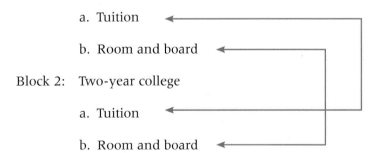

Block 1:   Four-year college

    a. Tuition

    b. Room and board

Block 2:   Two-year college

    a. Tuition

    b. Room and board

Remember, when using the block method, you discuss all the factors in the first item of comparison in the first part of the paragraph without mentioning the second item in the comparison. Then in the second half of the paragraph, discuss each point regarding the second item in the comparison, remembering to make reference to each item that was mentioned in the first half of the paragraph. This will connect the two items of the comparison so that the paragraph will not seem to be about two items that have nothing to do with one another.

Point-by-Point Method

In the point-by-point method, each point concerning each item being compared is followed by the similar point concerning the second item in the comparison. For example, in a paragraph comparing four-year and two-year colleges, as each cost element of the four-year college is mentioned, it is compared to the same cost element at the two-year college. In this way, the comparison between the elements is continually made.

The point-by-point method is illustrated in this manner:

Topic Sentence: When parents choose between a two-year college and a four-year college for their child, cost is often a deciding factor.

Point 1:   Tuition

      a. Four-year college tuition

      b. Two-year college tuition

Point 2:   Room and Board

      a. Four-year college room and board

      b. Two-year college room and board

Using the point-by-point method, the paragraph might be written like this:

> When parents choose between a two-year college and a four-year college for their child, cost is often a deciding factor. Tuition is a major cost when deciding on which college to attend. At a four-year college, tuition is a flat fee that can run anywhere from $8,000 to $40,000 per year, depending on the size and selectivity of the school. The student can take from twenty-four to thirty-six credit hours per year, and the tuition charge will not vary. However, two-year colleges charge by the credit hour, usually ranging from $37 to $48 per credit; therefore, a student taking between twenty-four to thirty-six credit hours per year will pay between $900 and $1,800 per year in tuition. In addition to tuition costs, room and board adds to the expenses at the four-year college. Room and board can run from $4,000 to $15,000 per year, depending on the school's dormitory and apartment facilities. In contrast, most two-year colleges do not have dormitories. They are known more as "commuter schools" because students live at home and drive to school each day. Because most families do not have to adjust their budgets for children who are going to college but still living at home as they did during high school, there is no "additional" cost for room and board. Even if parents charge room and board to their college student living at home, the charge is usually somewhat reduced, say $200 per month. This would add an additional $2,000 to the cost. Thus, the expense for a two-year college, including room and board and tuition, would be between $900 and $3,800 per year.

Notice that in the point-by-point method, each item in the elements to be compared is developed in the same order. It is important to keep the order consistent to avoid confusion.

ESL Transitional Expressions: Connecting Your Comparisons and Contrasts

Transitional expressions are important because they stress either comparison or contrast, depending on the type of paragraph you are writing.

Transitional Expressions Showing Comparison

again	just as
also	just like
and	like
as well as	likewise
both	neither
each	similarly
equally	similar to
furthermore	so
in addition	the same
in the same way	too

Transitional Expressions Showing Contrast

although	nevertheless
but	on the contrary
despite	on the other hand
different from	otherwise
even though	still
except for	though
however	whereas
in contrast	while
instead	yet

PRACTICE 5   Using Transitional Expressions Showing Contrast

The following paragraph is difficult to understand because of a lack of transitional expressions that stress *contrast*. On separate paper, add proper transitional expressions that show contrast. To achieve variety, do not use the same transitional expression more than once.

The United States has many historical places of interest. They are more modern than those in Mexico. The Statue of Liberty is barely a century old. The pyramids found in Tenochtitlán are at least a millennium old. Another historic place to visit in the United States is Philadelphia, where many of the events of the American Revolution occurred. It is over two hundred years old. Guanajuato, in Mexico, is historic because many events of the Mexican Revolution happened there. Walking down Guanajuato's streets is just like going back in time. The houses and roads are four and five hundred years old. Many of the houses have been ravaged by time, and the ancient roads polished shiny by the winds of time.

PRACTICE 6　Using Transitional Expressions Showing Comparison

The following paragraph is difficult to understand because of a lack of transitional expressions that stress *comparison*. On separate paper, add proper transitional expressions that show comparison. To achieve variety, do not use the same transitional expression more than once.

The occupations of cosmetologist and nurse may seem very different, but they share many common attributes. The cosmetologist makes the client's appearance better by using the proper grooming techniques. The nurse uses the latest medical procedures when treating a patient. A cosmetologist's client often feels depressed or anxious about his or her appearance. By using the coloring products appropriate to the client's complexion and age, the cosmetologist can change a person's appearance dramatically, making people feel good about themselves once again. The nurse makes the patient feel better by administering the proper medications or exercise appropriate for the patient's problem and age group. Both the cosmetologist and the nurse make the people in their care feel better about themselves.

PRACTICE 7　Analyzing a Contrast Paragraph

In the following paragraph from an essay, "'The Jury' Is In!" student writer Carol Hoxworth contrasts two novels by popular writer John Grisham. Hoxworth focuses on character development as a crucial difference between the two stories.

In *The Runaway Jury,* the character development is superb because Grisham alludes to certain aspects of the characters' personalities throughout the development of the plot. One of the strong points of this novel is being fed only enough information about them at the crucial time; therefore, a desire is created within the reader to know each character more intimately and how they will relate to the rest of the story. In contrast, *The Testament* has a glaring lack of character development from the very beginning of the novel. There is some confusion in the first few chapters as to who the main characters are. Instead of revealing the nature of each personality throughout the book, Grisham gives bland, generic, and brief descriptions of each. There also seems to be an overabundance of characters who truly are not necessary to the development and enrichment of the plot, so the desire to know the characters better and to see how the plot relates to them is not achieved.

Contrast Technique Questions

1. What is the writer contrasting in the paragraph? Is there a topic sentence that clearly states the items for contrast? If not, write one for the paragraph.

_____

_____

2. What organizational pattern does the writer use, point-by-point or block?

_____

3. How does the writer make a smooth transition to the second part of the paragraph?

_____

_____

_____

4. Does the writer use enough specific examples to develop and clarify the contrast?

_____

_____

_____

In the following paragraph from an essay, "Commercial vs. Residential Real Estate," student writer Nancy Smith compares two aspects of her job that on the surface might seem quite different but, in reality, are very similar.

Marketing costs for commercial real estate are paid for by the company; similarly, in residential real estate, costs are usually picked up by the company, as well. Like residential real estate, commercial real estate sends out thousands of flyers advertising property for lease or sale. For example, both commercial and residential agents mail advertising brochures to area residents and other agents announcing available properties. Both commercial and residential agents can work alone or share commissions with other agents when a property is sold, rented, or leased.

Comparison Technique Questions

1. What is the writer contrasting in the paragraph? Is there a topic sentence that clearly states the items for comparison? If not, write one for the paragraph.

_____

_____

_____

2. What organizational pattern does the writer use, point-by-point or block?

_____

3. How does the writer transition smoothly so that the points do not seem like merely a list of items strung together?

_____

_____

_____

4. Does the writer use enough specific examples to develop and clarify the contrast?

_____

_____

_____

PRACTICE 9   Analyzing a Contrast Paragraph

In the following paragraph from an essay, "Throughout the Years," student writer Meghan Burrows contrasts the changing aspects of her relationship with her father as she grew from a young girl into an adolescent.

When I was little, Dad often was my coach for soccer, softball, volleyball, and basketball. If not the designated coach, he would be on the sidelines helping out. We used to play catch every evening before and after dinner. Going for a ride to Wal-Mart or to the car wash was always a treat. But as I grew older, being "Daddy's Little Girl" wasn't so easy; in fact, it became a source of distance between us. Going through adolescence isn't easy for anyone, and I was no exception. The first time I remember feeling less close to my father was the day my body decided to take the plunge into womanhood. Because I felt scared and embarrassed, the last person whom I wanted to find out was my father. Needless to say, he found out. I think that was the day it came home to him that I was no longer going to be his little girl. As the next few years went by, I realized that I could make my own decisions. I could decide when to go to bed, when and what to eat, what clothes to wear, and what sports to play.

Contrast Technique Questions

1. What is the writer contrasting in the paragraph? Is there a topic sentence that clearly states the items for contrast? If not, write one for the paragraph.

   _____

   _____

   _____

   _____

2. What organizational pattern does the writer use, point-by-point or block?

   _____

3. How does the writer transition smoothly from the first part of the paragraph to the second half of the paragraph so that the contrasting points are connected?

_____

_____

_____

4. Does the writer use enough specific examples to develop and clarify the contrasts?

_____

_____

_____

_____

PRACTICE 10   Analyzing and Writing Comparison Paragraphs

In the following paragraph from an essay, "Grant and Lee: A Study in Contrasts," professional historian Bruce Catton focuses on the differences between the two great Civil War generals. However, Catton does on occasion comment on the similarities between the two leaders.

Read All About It . . . To read the full essay from which this paragraph is excerpted, see page 452.

Lastly, and perhaps greatest of all, there was the ability, at the end, to turn quickly from war to peace once the fighting was over. Out of the way these two men behaved at Appomattox came the possibility of a peace of reconciliation. It was a possibility not wholly realized, in the years to come, but which did, in the end, help the two sections to become one nation again . . . after a war whose bitterness might have seemed to make such a reunion wholly impossible. No part of either man's life became him more than the part he played in their brief meeting in the McLean house at Appomattox. Their behavior there put all succeeding generations of Americans in their debt. Two great Americans, Grant and Lee—very different, yet under everything very much alike. Their encounter at Appomattox was one of the great moments of American history.

Comparison Technique Questions

1. What is the writer comparing in the paragraph? Is there a topic sentence that clearly states the items for comparison? If not, write one for the paragraph.

_____

_____

_____

_____

2. What organizational pattern does the writer use, point-by-point or block?

_____

3. Point out transitional expressions the writer uses to connect ideas and to add rhythm. Are there any that the writer could have used to achieve smooth transitions? If so, which ones and where would they be placed for greatest effectiveness?

_____

_____

_____

4. Does the writer use enough specific examples to develop the comparison?

_____

_____

_____

Suggestions for Writing

1. Write a paragraph comparing two moral, social, economic, or political disagreements that have been or might become conflicts.

2. Write a paragraph on why the two items you chose in Question 1 are so difficult to resolve. Concentrate on explaining, not taking either side or trying to persuade the reader to adopt a particular solution.

PRACTICE 11   Analyzing and Writing Contrast Paragraphs

Read All About It . . .

To read the full essay from which this paragraph is excerpted, see page 455.

In the following paragraph from an essay, "Living on Tokyo Time," by Lynnika Butler, how the Japanese view time and how Americans view time is contrasted. Answer the questions following the paragraph.

A lot of Westerners make the glib assumption that Japanese people are

simply submissive, unoriginal, or masochistic enough to put up with such a punishing system. I don't think that's it. In Japan, time is measured in the same hours and minutes and days as anywhere else, but it is experienced as a fundamentally different phenomenon. In the West, we save time, spend time, invest time, even kill time—all of which implies that it belongs to us in the first place. We might find ourselves obliged to trade huge chunks of our time for a steady salary, but most of us resent this as something stolen from us, and we take it for granted that our spare hours are none of our teachers' or bosses' business.

Contrast Technique Questions

1. What organizational pattern does the writer use, point-by-point or block?

_____

2. Does the author use any transitional expressions to move from point to point?

_____

_____

_____

_____

3. In the first sentence of the paragraph, exactly what ideas are being contrasted?

_____

_____

TOPIC BANK

Write a comparison or contrast paragraph about one or more of the following topics or about a topic of your own choice.

1. Two pieces of art
2. Two members of your family
3. Two magazines (see the photo on page 233)
4. Your past and present position on a social or political issue
5. Two schools you have attended
6. Two bosses or two coworkers
7. A widely held belief and its real meaning
8. Two places you have lived (cities, houses, countries)
9. Two forms of government (local, state, or national)
10. Two novels

WRITING OPPORTUNITIES

HOME The community council in your town has decided to raise funds by publishing and selling a book of recipes from local townspeople. Because you are known as the best dessert maker in the community, the committee has asked you to write a paragraph comparing the variety of uses of the blueberry versus the strawberry.

SCHOOL For your final exam in Home Economics 314, you had to make one dessert using blueberries and one dessert using strawberries. Additionally, you were instructed to write a paragraph comparing the two efforts.

WORK As communications director for the National Association of Fruit Growers, your current challenge is to put together a brochure extolling the virtues of people including a variety of fruits in their daily diet. Research indicates that most people think of blueberries and strawberries as dessert fruits only. Write a paragraph that makes a case for the blueberry and the strawberry as an "anytime food," compared to apples, bananas, and oranges.

Visit *The Write Start* Online!

For additional practice with the materials in this chapter, go to

http://www.cengage.com/devenglish/checkett/writestartSP4e.

Chapter Self-Assessment Test

Check either True or False on the blank next to the statement.

T	F	
——	——	Comparison and contrast assists the reader in understanding a person, place, or object to another.
——	——	Comparison and contrast does not consider feelings and ideas.
——	——	When comparing, you look for differences.
——	——	When contrasting, you look for similarities.
——	——	There are two commonly used organizational patterns for comparison and contrast paragraphs: point-by-point and block.
——	——	In comparison and contrast paragraphs, transitional expressions are important because they stress either comparison or contrast, depending on the type of paragraph being written.
——	——	Comparison and contrast paragraphs need to begin with a topic sentence that clearly states the items being compared or contrasted.
——	——	A topic sentence in a comparison or contrast paragraph does not have to state why the comparison or contrast is important.

16

Definition

CHAPTER WARM-UP

Pick a social issue such as the one shown here and begin to define it by using the cubing method described on page 130.

Often, the writer uses words, terms, or concepts that his or her audience may not fully understand. To explain clearly what these words and terms mean is to **define** them.

For example, you might use the term *quasar*, a starlike object that emits powerful blue light and often radio waves; or you might use *griffin*, a fabulous, mythological beast with the head and wings of an eagle and the body of a lion.

Simple Definitions

Simple definitions are basic one- or two-sentence definitions, such as those you might find in a dictionary. There are three types of simple definitions:

1. **Synonym definition** supplies another simpler word that means the same thing. For example, *ubiquitous* means *everywhere*; *cacophony* means *noise*.
2. **Class definition** places a word or term in a broad group or class that readers will readily understand, then provides a specific detail that differentiates the original word or term from other members of that class. For example, a *convertible* is a *car* with a *top that goes up and down*. In this definition, *convertible* is the term being defined. It is put into a class of similar things (cars); then it is distinguished from other cars, such as sedans, because it has a top that goes up and down.
3. **Definition by negation** begins by saying what a given word or term is *not* before saying what the word or term actually is. For example: A bagel isn't just a doughnut-shaped piece of bread. It's actually a unique type of bread that's boiled before it's baked.

Definition is important because clear communication depends on clear understanding. Precise language is essential if you are to understand what someone else means. The same word can have multiple meanings, so it is essential that you define those kinds of terms for your reader.

PRACTICE 1   Using Synonym Definitions

Use a synonym definition to define each of the following terms.

Example: Chagrined: <u>To be chagrined is to be embarrassed.</u>

1. Dichotomy: _____

2. Blunder: _____

3. Literal: _____

4. Rustic: _____

5. Malevolent: _____

PRACTICE 2   Using Class Definitions

Using a class definition, define the following terms.

Example: Martini: <u>A martini is a cocktail made with gin and vermouth.</u>

1. Robin: _____

   _____

2. Banana: _____

   _____

3. Shark: _____

_____

4. Dictionary: _____

_____

5. Prude: _____

_____

PRACTICE 3	Using Definitions by Negation

For each of the following terms, write a definition by negation.

Example: Hero: <u>A hero is not just someone performing an act of bravery; it is also someone taking care of his or her daily responsibilities.</u>

1. Moral (to be): _____

_____

2. Freedom: _____

_____

3. Knowledgeable (to be): _____

_____

4. Grades: _____

_____

5. A job: _____

_____

Extended Definition

Sometimes, terms such as *self-esteem, love, free speech,* and *macroeconomics* can require much more developed definitions if they are to be fully understood. A simple, one-sentence dictionary definition may not suffice. Instead, you may need to use an entire paragraph to define such terms adequately. This longer type of definition is called an **extended definition.** Extended definition can be accomplished by means of any of the **modes of development:** description, example, comparison and contrast, process, and so forth.

To help define your term, you might

a. describe some of its parts or elements
b. explain its process

c. compare and/or contrast it to other like terms

d. give some examples

e. explain what it is not

You may use one of these modes to develop your definition, or you may use as many modes in the paragraph as you find necessary. For example, if you were writing an extended definition paragraph for the term *soul music,* you might choose one or several of the following strategies:

- Compare or contrast soul music to other kinds of music, such as blues, alternative rock, and jazz.
- State some examples of well-known soul hits.
- Describe its parts: lyrics, themes, musical motifs.

A simple definition for *soul music* might be "music relating to or characteristic of African American culture." This definition does not give the reader the full flavor of just how soul music represents a part of the American culture. An extended definition might expand on this idea:

Soul music is a combination and merging of gospel and blues, two African American musical styles. While blues praised the worldly desires of the flesh, gospel extolled the virtues of spiritualism. This opposition of themes was melded into wide-ranging and extremely diverse style, full of passion, pride, and optimism mixed with the historical emotion of pain and discrimination.

Whatever concept you are defining, use only those modes and strategies that are necessary to define the concept fully. Do not use techniques solely for the sake of variety.

The Topic Sentence of an Extended Definition

The definition paragraph begins with a topic sentence that clearly states the term(s) being defined, the mode of development that will be used to define the term(s), and why defining the term is important. Because there are many different reasons for supplying a reader with a definition and because there are many different types of terms you might want or need to define in your writing, your topic sentence must clarify why you're defining a given term. For example, are you defining

- A specialized term that is unfamiliar to most people, such as *LASIK eye surgery* or *superstring theory?*
- An abstract term that can have a variety of meanings, such as *freedom* or *indifference?*
- A concept that is often misunderstood, such as *liberalism* or *Generation X?*
- A new slang or cultural term, such as *extreme sport* or *anime?*

Here is an example of a topic sentence for a definition paragraph about being a high school freshman:

Entering new surroundings, being harassed by upperclassmen, and having four long years of school ahead of you make being a high school freshman a dreadful experience.

The entire paragraph might look like this:

> Entering new surroundings, being harassed by upperclassmen, and having four long years of school ahead of you make being a freshman a dreadful experience. Freshmen become very confused when rushed to find classes in a labyrinth of unfamiliar hallways. They act like mice attempting to find their way through a complicated maze. Additionally, harassment by upperclassmen makes running the maze even more of a challenge. Veteran students play pranks on the unsuspecting newcomers, such as asking them for elevator and hall passes. Finally, being a freshman means having four more years of headaches. Just because you are new, teachers will have little leniency in regard to the quantity of homework given and the quality of the homework returned. All three factors contribute to the realization that being a high school freshman is a dreadful existence.

In this paragraph, the term being defined is *high school freshman*, and the mode of development is by example and description, using typical events that happen to freshmen.

PRACTICE 4   Writing Definition Topic Sentences

Write a topic sentence for each of the definitions you wrote for Practice 3.

1. Moral (to be): _____

_____

2. Freedom: _____

_____

3. Knowledgeable (to be): _____

_____

4. Grades: _____

_____

5. A job: _____

_____

In the following paragraph from an essay, "My Hot Flathead," student writer Trevor Campbell defines a specific type of automobile engine not only by its design and horsepower output but through its cultural importance.

After World War II, countless GI's returned home with extra money to spend. Almost overnight, custom shops sprang up in southern California catering to the Flathead owner. The Flathead-powered Ford was cheap and plentiful, making this motor a prime candidate to customize. Within a few years, the Ford Flathead V-8 became the popular choice among custom builders; this power plant combined with a light-bodied chassis was considered a winning combination at the dragstrip. Success is often copied, a circumstance which, in turn, further established the Flathead presence.

Definition Technique Questions

1. Does this paragraph have a topic sentence that states the term to be defined? If not, how does the writer introduce the term?

_____

_____

_____

2. What is the mode of development for the paragraph?

_____

_____

_____

3. In what larger class of items would you put the Flathead-powered Ford?

_____

4. What made the Flathead engine so popular?

_____

_____

_____

PRACTICE 6   Analyzing a Definition Paragraph

In the following paragraph from an essay, "The Perfect Store," student writer Jeanette Weiland defines the perfect store in terms of pricing. According to Weiland, low price is important, but there are also other aspects of pricing that put the customer in a buying mood.

While shopping at a perfect store, customers are generally sold products at an inexpensive price. Shoppers are typically offered items that are clearly marked with price tags on each separate package. This allows customers to rapidly and easily choose the product that gives them the best buy. There aren't any reasons to look for the price on the store shelf and then have to worry about whether or not the item matches the price tag. A perfect store does not only honor its own sales coupons, but it also accepts other department store advertised prices and coupons. This gives the customers the convenience of shopping at one store instead of having to go to two or three. No matter what store they are shopping at, these pricing policies offer shoppers an opportunity to receive the best possible price.

Definition Technique Questions

1. Does this paragraph have a topic sentence stating the term to be defined? What is the mode of development?

_____

_____

2. How many different pricing policies does the writer mention?

_____

_____

_____

3. In which sentence does the writer define by negation? Point out what it is that the perfect store not only does not do, but also what it does do for its customers.

_____

_____

_____

PRACTICE 7   Analyzing and Writing Definition Paragraphs

In the following paragraph from an essay, "Discrimination Is a Virtue," professional writer Robert Keith Miller takes a deep and thoughtful look at the meaning of the often-misused word *discrimination*. Miller points out that the overuse, misuse, and misunderstanding of this word is so widespread that most people have probably never thought about its true meaning. This improper use of the term carries with it negative social consequences.

> We have a word in English which means "the ability to tell differences." That word is *discrimination*. But within the last 30 years, this word has been so frequently misused that an entire generation has grown up believing that "discrimination" means "racism." People are always proclaiming that "discrimination" is something that should be done away with. Should that ever happen, it would prove to be our undoing.

Read All About It . . . To read the full essay from which this paragraph is excerpted, see page 459.

Definition Technique Questions

1. A term's *denotation* is its direct, definite, and easily understood meaning, whereas its *connotation* is those ideas that are suggested by the word in addition to its essential meaning. In the paragraph, what is *discrimination*'s denotation and what is its connotation?

   _____

   _____

2. Miller suggests that doing away with *discrimination* would have awful consequences for all of us. What are some of the consequences you can think of?

   _____

   _____

   _____

3. Miller suggests, then, that discrimination, when properly defined, is beneficial for society. How can discrimination be a positive force?

   _____

   _____

   _____

Suggestions for Writing

1. Think of two words that you are apt to confuse, such as *lay/lie; there/their; leave/let; bring/take;* and *scratch/itch*. Check out the correct use of the words,

then write a paragraph defining them. Your topic sentence is ready-made: The two words are commonly confused.

2. Slang has become more and more a part of everyday speech, and much of it is specialized, used by a particular group. Select a slang word that you or your friends use and define it, explaining how it is both used and mis-used or misunderstood by those outside of your group.

PRACTICE 8   Analyzing Definition Paragraphs

In these paragraphs from a 1982 essay, "The Handicap of Definition," syndi-cated columnist William Raspberry defines the main reason many black chil-dren do not have good self-images and explains the impact this has on their feelings about future success. Although the famous people Raspberry men-tions may no longer be in the public eye as much as they used to be, the idea he suggests is still relevant to today's athletes and entertainers.

> **Read All About It . . .**   To read the full essay from which this paragraph is excerpted, see page 462.

Let me explain quickly what I mean. If a basketball fan says that the Boston Celtics' Larry Bird plays "black," the fan intends it—and Bird proba-bly accepts it—as a compliment. Tell pop singer Tom Jones he moves "black" and he might grin in appreciation. Say to Teena Marie or The Average White Band that they sound "black" and they'll thank you.

But name one pursuit, aside from athletics, entertainment or sexual performance in which a white practitioner will feel complimented to be told he does it "black." Tell a white reporter he writes "black" and he'll take a writing course. Tell a white lawyer he reasons "black" and he might sue you for slander.

What we have here is a tragically limited definition of blackness, and it isn't only white people who buy it.

Definition Technique Questions

1. The author, William Raspberry, is black. Does knowing this make a differ-ence in how you interpret these paragraphs? What if the author were white?

_____

2. In the paragraph in Practice 7, Miller suggests that discrimination, when properly defined, is beneficial for society. Do you think this idea applies equally to the term *black*?

_____

3. How does Raspberry build his definition of the word *black*?

_____

_____

4. If you're a black student, do you and your friends use the term *black* in the way that Raspberry suggests? If you're a non-black student, do you feel blacks use the term *black* in the way Raspberry suggests?

_____

TOPIC BANK

Write a definition paragraph about one or more of the following topics or about a topic of your own choice.

1. Success or failure
2. A political or social issue, such as animal rights or the environment (see the photo on page 249)
3. A good or bad roommate
4. A technical or medical term
5. A terrorist
6. A new form of art or music
7. A good or bad teacher, parent, friend
8. A good or bad movie, concert, party
9. Heroism or cowardice
10. A sports term

WRITING OPPORTUNITIES

HOME You want to hang a print of a surrealistic painting in your family room. You are talking about the painting's content by e-mail with your spouse, who is away on a long business trip. Your spouse is unsure about hanging the painting because the content sounds so unusual. So you send him a digital image of the painting with an accompanying paragraph defining what you think the content means.

SCHOOL Your Psych 205 professor comes into class one day and displays a slide of a surrealistic on the overhead. He directs you to write a paragraph defining what you think the artist is like by the contents of the painting. He also instructs that you can, if you like, define by negation—pointing out what you think the artist would not be like, based on the painting's contents.

WORK As a new summer tour guide at the art museum, you find out that your job will include giving brief talks about a variety of paintings. Your schedule indicates that your first stop will be a surreal painting. Write a paragraph that you will memorize to help you define surrealism for your tour group.

 Visit *The Write Start* Online!

For additional practice with the materials in this chapter, go to

http://www.cengage.com/devenglish/checkett/writestartSP4e.

Chapter Self-Assessment Test

Check either True or False on the blank next to the statement.

T F

_____ _____ Defining means the writing clearly explains the meaning of a word, term, or concept a reader might not fully understand.

_____ _____ There is more than one type of definition.

_____ _____ Synonym, class, and negation are all types of definition.

_____ _____ Using an entire paragraph or more than one paragraph is necessary for an *extended* definition.

_____ _____ Extended definitions can be accomplished by any mode of development, such as description, example, comparison and contrast, process, and so on.

_____ _____ Definition paragraphs begin with a topic sentence that clearly states the term being defined, the mode of development, and why defining the term is important.

Persuasion (Including Cause and Effect)

CHAPTER WARM-UP

Using the clustering prewriting activity described on page 130, create a map with "pollution" as the topic in the central circle. Try to extend the map outward to as many levels of circles as you can. For more ideas, use the sensory images described in Chapter 10 (page 162).

When writers use **persuasion,** they are trying to convince someone else that their point of view or belief is correct. Persuasion can be *informal, semiformal,* or *formal.* Think of informal persuasion as verbally convincing someone else of your point of view. For example, you and your friends or members of your family may try to convince each other about which college basketball team should be number one or which restaurant has the best pizza. Commercials on radio and television also are types of informal persuasion. So are public service advertisements for nonprofit organizations and most political advertisements.

Formal persuasion is usually called **argumentation.** This type of persuasion requires not only arguing for your own beliefs but also arguing directly against someone else's beliefs. Argumentation uses evidence from secondary sources (information often found in the library) that are cited by using a formal documentation process (Modern Language Association [MLA] or American Psychological Association [APA], for example). Research papers, analytical essays, and certain business reports fall into this category.

However, in this chapter, we are interested in a semiformal type of persuasion that falls somewhere in between the two mentioned above. Persuasion requires a bit more logical thought and organization than that expressed around the kitchen table in informal arguing. However, it does not have the rigid requirements that occur with the use of quotations and the accompanying documentation needed in formal argumentation.

Persuasion is one of the most common types of writing in school. Students are required to argue for and against ideas in quizzes, papers, and examinations. Therefore, learning the fundamentals of the persuasive paragraph is one of the most important skills you can learn.

Building the Persuasive Paragraph

The **topic sentence** states the writer's conclusion or point of view about a particular topic. The writer's conclusion can be for or against (pro or con) the idea concerning the topic. Therefore, the topic sentence is the key to a successful persuasive paragraph. The verbs used in a persuasive topic sentence are most often *should/should not* or *must/must not*.

Examples

The pending legislation on the right of citizens to carry concealed handguns should be defeated.

This paragraph will argue against (con) citizens having the right to carry concealed handguns.

Employers should provide day care for their employees.

This paragraph will argue for (pro) companies providing day care for the children of their employees.

Euthanasia should be legalized because of our constitutional rights of personal freedom.

This paragraph will argue for (pro) physician-assisted suicide.

Athletics should not receive more funding than academics.

This paragraph will argue against (con) sports receiving more money than academics.

PRACTICE 1   Writing Persuasive Topic Sentences

For the ten topics listed below, write either a pro (for) topic sentence or a con (against) topic sentence. Try to write five sentences pro and five con.

1. Topic: Instant replay in sports

_____

_____

2. Topic: Mandatory drug testing in schools/workplace

_____

_____

3. Topic: A federally regulated Internet

_____

_____

4. Topic: National ban on smoking

_____

_____

5. Topic: Reinstitution of the military draft

_____

_____

6. Topic: Elderly drivers

_____

_____

7. Topic: Interstate highway speed limits

_____

_____

8. Topic: Paying college athletes

_____

_____

9. Topic: National identification cards

_____

_____

10. Topic: Clubs/organizations excluding certain groups for membership on the basis of race, religion, or ethnic origin

_____

_____

PRACTICE 2   Analyzing a Persuasive Paragraph

In the following paragraph from a persuasive essay, "Nuke Nuclear Energy," student writer Danny Butler's argument is concerned with the nuclear fuel industry.

Because of waste management problems, the nuclear fuel industry must not be revived. Many researchers see nuclear energy as the source of power for the future because it can greatly lessen the consumption of other fuels. A typical nuclear reactor can produce many times more energy than plants using other materials such as fossil fuels. Although this new form of energy can help to preserve diminishing resources, it leads to a new problem of waste management. The fission of radioactive materials causes leftover wastes that can remain radioactive for many years. Waste management has already become a problem that will have to be faced by generations to come; we must decide which is more important, a new energy source, or the survival of life on Earth.

Persuasion Technique Questions

1. Identify the topic sentence. Does it clearly state whether the author is for or against the topic?

_____

_____

2. Do the support sentences support the writer's position?

_____

_____

_____

3. Point out any sentences that are simply informational and do not support the author's position.

_____

_____

| PRACTICE 3 | Analyzing a Persuasive Paragraph |

In the following paragraph from a persuasive essay, "The Recoloring of Campus Life," professional writer Shelby Steele confronts a problem and a misconception: campus racism and its cause.

Read All About It ...

To read the full essay from which this paragraph is excerpted, see page 466.

How to live with racial difference has been America's profound social problem. For the first hundred years or so following emancipation it was controlled by a legally sanctioned inequality that kept the races from each other. No longer is this the case. On campuses today, as throughout society, blacks enjoy equality under the law—a profound social advancement. No student may be kept out of a class or a dormitory or an extracurricular activity because of his or her race. But there is a paradox here: on a campus where members of all races are gathered, mixed together in the classroom as well as socially, differences are more exposed than ever. And this is where trouble starts. For members of each race—young adults coming into their own, often away from home for the first time—bring to this site of freedom, exploration, and (now, today) equality, very deep fears, anxieties, inchoate feelings of racial shame, anger, and guilt. These feelings could lie dormant in the home, in familiar neighborhoods, in simpler days of childhood. But the college campus, with its structures of interaction and adult-level competition—the big exam, the dorm, the mixer—is another matter. I think campus racism is born of the rub between racial difference and a setting, the campus itself, devoted to interaction and equality. On our campuses, such concentrated micro-societies, all that remains unresolved between blacks and whites, all the old wounds and shames that have never been addressed, present themselves for attention—and present our youth with pressures they cannot always handle.

Persuasion Technique Questions

1. What is a paradox?

_____

_____

2. What is the paradox that Steele addresses?

_____

_____

3. According to the author, where does campus racism spring from?

_____

_____

_____

The Pro/Con List

Once you have decided on the topic, it is vital that you know the major argument points on either side of the issue, regardless of whether you know which side you are going to take. For example, if the topic is nuclear energy, list as many points for either side that you can think of.

Topic: Nuclear Energy	
Pro (for) list	**Con (against) list**
Cheaper fuel costs	Radioactive waste
Less dependence on foreign oil	Causes unemployment in traditional fossil fuels industry
Creates high-tech jobs	Nuclear accidents
Saves natural resources	Nuclear weapons proliferation
Ensures strong nuclear arsenal	Theft of nuclear materials by terrorists
	Environmental pollution

Once you have listed as many points as you can think of, consider the points on both sides of the argument, and choose the side you wish to argue for. Decide which points you will use in your paragraph to support your topic.

PRACTICE 4　　Making Pro/Con Lists

Create a pro/con list for each of the following topics. Think of as many items for each list as you can.

1. Topic: Sex education should be taught in elementary school.

Pro   **Con**

_____   _____

_____   _____

_____   _____

_____   _____

_____   _____

_____   _____

2. Topic: Women should be allowed to fight as infantry soldiers.

Pro   **Con**

_____   _____

_____   _____

_____   _____

_____   _____

_____   _____

_____   _____

3. Topic: The drinking age should be reduced to eighteen years of age.

Pro   **Con**

_____   _____

_____   _____

_____   _____

_____   _____

_____   _____

_____   _____

4. Topic: English should be America's official language.

Pro   **Con**

_____   _____

_____   _____

_____   _____

_____   _____

_____   _____

5. Topic: The government should provide health insurance for all citizens.

Pro	Con
_____	_____
_____	_____
_____	_____
_____	_____
_____	_____
_____	_____

Support in Persuasion Paragraphs

Persuasion paragraphs need to demonstrate the different types of support used to convince readers. These include *answering the opposition, referring to an authority, predicting consequences, presenting facts,* and *giving examples.* Although you probably will never use all of them in one paragraph, you will use them when you write persuasively.

1. **Answering the opposition:** At times, the best way to persuade your reader is to respond to an opponent's point. This also shows your reader that you are aware of your opponent's side of the issue, not just your own.
2. **Referring to an authority:** An authority is a person or a group that is considered an expert on the subject and will give an unbiased opinion.
3. **Predicting consequences:** Predicting consequences can help your reader agree with your point of view and disagree with your opponent's.
4. **Presenting facts:** Facts are those things that actually exist or have existed, such as people, places, things, and events. A *fact* differs from an *opinion* in a quite significant way. An opinion is the way we think about, or interpret, facts. For instance, it is a fact that the United States Congress removed our currency from the gold standard in 1978. That fact cannot be argued. However, whether you think it was a good idea to remove the gold standard is your opinion, and that can be argued. Whether your *opinion*, or your opponent's *opinion*, is the more persuasive, the *fact* remains that the gold standard was removed in 1978.
5. **Giving examples:** Good examples can develop an idea quickly and clearly, and help convince your reader of your point of view. Examples also are used to clarify, illustrate, or make concrete a general idea about the subject. Therefore, be certain that your examples support your position or convincingly argue against your opponent's position.

PRACTICE 5 Distinguishing Fact from Opinion

Write an **F** for *fact* or an **O** for *opinion* in the space to the left of each item in the following list.

1. _____ There are eight known planets in our solar system.

2. _____ The Congress of the United States consists of the Senate and the House of Representatives.

3. _____ I am 6 feet tall.

4. _____ Wolves make great pets.

5. _____ Water freezes at 32 degrees Fahrenheit and 0 degrees Celsius.

6. _____ I am the greatest basketball player in my state.

7. _____ Hurricanes are more frightening than tornadoes.

8. _____ Laughter is the best medicine.

9. _____ Pastrami is better sandwich meat than ham.

10. _____ Neil Armstrong was the first man on the moon.

PRACTICE 6   Analyzing a Persuasive Paragraph

In the following paragraphs from a persuasive essay, "Indistinguishable from Magic," writer Robert L. Forward writes about interstellar space travel.

Read All About It . . .
To read the full essay from which this paragraph is excerpted, see page 469.

Scientists studying hibernating animals have found the hormone that initiates hibernation and have used the drug to induce hibernation in other animals. Whether this drug will induce hibernation in humans without causing serious side effects is unknown. Also, it is unknown whether hibernation actually increases life span, or just makes living possible when there is insufficient food. Still, there is enough biological research on suspended animation that one of these days we may use that method of keeping a crew alive long enough to carry out century-long exploration missions.

Even if these particular biological techniques do not turn into a real suspended animation capability, there is another method to carry out a slowship mission: let the people die, but allow their children to carry on. A slowship journey to the stars will send a colony of people off in a generation starship. Although only the first generation would be true volunteers, with enough thought and planning we could turn the slow-moving starship into a truly acceptable worldship, with all the amenities and few of the problems of living on earth.

Persuasion Technique Questions

1. What is the difference between hibernation and suspended animation?

_____

_____

_____

_____

_____

2. The author suggests there are two methods for sending people into interstellar space. What are they?

_____

_____

3. Identify some of the problems with hibernation as a method to accomplish interstellar travel.

_____

_____

_____

PRACTICE 7　　　**Analyzing a Persuasive Paragraph**

In the following paragraph from a persuasive essay, "Don't Give Up the Right to Carry," student writer Tim Schuette tries to persuade his audience that giving citizens the right to carry concealed guns will reduce the crime rate.

The opposition is worried that the crime rate will increase overall with a concealed weapon law. However, after passing concealed weapon laws, states have seen a decrease in crime. John Lott, who has never been a member of the National Rifle Association (NRA), is an economist at the University of Chicago. Lott examined gun laws and crime in 3,054 U.S. counties. He found that "not only did violent crime drop after states relaxed concealed weapon laws, but . . . after five years murder was down 15%, rape 9%." If Missouri residents could carry a concealed weapon, crime would likely decrease.

Persuasion Technique Questions

1. The writer does not state his attitude (pro or con) about the topic directly in a topic sentence. State in your own words what you think the author's attitude is about the topic.

_____

_____

_____

2. How convincing are the support points that the writer makes? How many of the types of support does the writer use? How convincing are the support points that the writer makes? Do quotes and statistics seem more convincing than opinion?

_____

_____

_____

Organization Patterns

Once you have made your pro/con list and have chosen the type of evidence you want to use to support your topic, you will need to organize your paragraph for an effective presentation. There is no defined pattern that a writer has to use when writing persuasively. However, several patterns logically come to mind that will organize your points into a convincing persuasive paragraph.

Pattern 1: Using only support points that argue for your point of view (only pro-list items if you are arguing for a point of view or only con-list items if you are arguing against a point of view)

Pattern 2: Stating only your opposition's support points (either pro or con) and arguing against them

Pattern 3: Alternating use of support points for your side of the argument and listing your opponent's points and arguing against them; this is a hybrid of patterns 1 and 2

Once you have chosen your organization pattern, select several points from the appropriate list or lists and write sentences for each. Arrange the sentences according to the organization pattern you have selected.

The following are three persuasive paragraph examples using the pro/con list on page 266. Each paragraph is organized according to one of the three patterns you have studied.

Pattern 1 Persuasive Paragraph: Against Nuclear Energy (Con-List Items)

<table>
<tr><td>Topic Sentence
Con Item</td><td rowspan="2">Nuclear energy should not be restored because of radioactive waste disposal problems and the possibility of a nuclear reactor accident. One of the problems with nuclear energy is waste management. Radioactive waste can remain dangerous for thousands of years; therefore, safe disposal sites must meet rigid safety standards to keep the public safe.</td></tr>
</table>

Nuclear energy should not be restored because of radioactive waste disposal problems and the possibility of a nuclear reactor accident. One of the problems with nuclear energy is waste management. Radioactive waste can remain dangerous for thousands of years; therefore, safe disposal sites must meet rigid safety standards to keep the public safe. Sites must be deep in the ground to shield the public from possible radiation exposure, and the sites must be immune to earthquake damage. Such sites are hard to find and expensive to maintain. In addition to the waste disposal problem, nuclear accidents pose a real danger to people living near nuclear reactors. In 1986, in the Ukrainian town of Chernobyl, a nuclear reactor accident put thousands at risk of radioactive poisoning. A radiation cloud spread over northern Europe and Great Britain. Thirty-one Soviet citizens died, and over 100,000 had to be evacuated from surrounding areas. The dangers involved in the long-term control and management of such a volatile substance as radioactive materials make it a very risky proposition. Until more trustworthy safeguards can be developed in both the operation and waste disposal of radioactive substances, nuclear energy should remain a thing of the past.

Margin labels: Topic Sentence, Con Item, Con Item, Conclusion, Con Item, Con Item, Example, Fact, Consequence, Conclusion, Conclusion

Pattern 2 Persuasive Paragraph: Arguing Against the Opposition (Pro-List Items)

Despite the possible benefits to society, nuclear energy should not be restored as a fuel source. Many scientists and researchers claim nuclear energy is desirable as an energy source because it creates enormous amounts of power from small resources. Although this may be true, there are other costs that outweigh the purely monetary. In 1986, in the Ukrainian town of Chernobyl, a nuclear reactor accident killed 31 Soviet citizens and caused 100,000 people to be evacuated. A radioactive cloud covered much of northern Europe and Great Britain. Military leaders in Washington, D.C. state that a nuclear energy industry will also ensure a continuous source of radioactive material necessary to maintain our nuclear weapons arsenal for the defense of the nation. However, every year there are reports of nuclear by-products missing from government inventories. Terrorist enemies of the United States could use this material to build nuclear weapons with which to threaten us. Also, the plans for building, running, and producing nuclear reactors for energy could be used to produce materials for making nuclear weapons and might be stolen and used by unfriendly nations. The potential for disaster far outweighs the potential benefits coming from a nuclear energy industry. Nuclear energy is not a safe or practical energy source.

Margin labels: Topic Sentence, Opposition/Argument, Answering Opposition, Using a Fact, Consequence, Opposition/Argument, Answering Opposition (Fact), Possible Consequence, Possible Consequence, Conclusion

Pattern 3 Persuasive Paragraph: Alternating Your Points with Arguing Against the Opposition's Points (Pro- and Con-List Items)

Despite the possible benefits to society, nuclear energy should not be restored as a fuel source. One of the problems with nuclear energy is waste management. Radioactive waste can remain dangerous for thousands of years; therefore, safe deposit sites must

Margin labels: Topic Sentence, Con Item, Con Item, Conclusion

Opposition/Argument

Answering Opposition
Using a Fact

Consequences

Opinion
Answering Opposition (Fact)

Possible Consequence
Opposition/Argument

Answering Opposition (Opinion)

Conclusion

meet rigid safety standards to keep the public safe. Sites must be deep in the ground to shield the public from possible radiation exposure, and the sites must be immune to earthquake damage. Many scientists and researchers claim nuclear energy is desirable as an energy source because it creates enormous amounts of power from small resources. Although this may be true, there are other costs that outweigh the purely monetary. In 1986, in the Ukrainian town of Chernobyl, a nuclear reactor accident killed 31 Soviet citizens and caused 100,000 people to be evacuated. A radioactive cloud covered much of northern Europe and Great Britain. Nuclear weapons proliferation is another problem if nuclear energy production is increased. Every year there are reports of nuclear by-products missing from government inventories. Terrorist enemies of the United States could use this material to build nuclear weapons with which to threaten our security. Economists like to say that increasing the nuclear energy industry will create more high-tech jobs, but the same industry will cause widespread unemployment in traditional fossil fuel industries, such as coal, oil, and gas. The potential for both disaster and a negative impact on the economy should convince lawmakers to prohibit the return of nuclear energy as a fuel source.

PRACTICE 8   Writing Persuasive Paragraphs

On separate sheets of paper, write a persuasive paragraph for three of the topics below, using a separate organization pattern for each. Write your completed draft on the lines provided.

Topics

The academic year should/should not be extended to twelve months with two weeks of vacation every three months.

Tobacco and alcohol advertising should/should not be regulated.

Young people should/should not be given college tuition money for public service just because soldiers are given tuition money for military service.

All guns should/should not be licensed and registered with the authorities.

Prayer should/should not be allowed in public schools.

Welfare recipients should/should not have to have a job to receive benefits.

Grades should/should not be abolished as the method for judging student performance.

Marijuana should/should not be legalized for medical use.

All coursework should/should not transfer to any other college in the country.

Same-sex couples should/should not be allowed legally to marry.

Persuasive Paragraph—Pattern 1

_____

_____

_____

_____

_____

_____

_____

_____

_____

Persuasive Paragraph—Pattern 2

_____

_____

_____

_____

_____

_____

_____

_____

_____

Persuasive Paragraph—Pattern 3

_____

_____

_____

_____

_____

_____

_____

_____

_____

(ESL) Transitional Expressions for Persuasion

Transitional expressions are useful in connecting related ideas and for adding rhythm to the paragraph so that it reads more smoothly.

Transitional Expressions for Persuasive Writing

Answering the Opposition and Referring to Authority	Predicting Consequences and Stating Conclusions	Facts and Examples
according to . . .	consequently	another . . .
although	in conclusion	because
nevertheless	therefore	finally
of course	thus	first
on the other hand		for
others may say . . .		last
		next
		second
		since
		third

PRACTICE 9 — Using Transitional Expressions

Rewrite the three persuasive paragraphs from Practice 8, using transitional expressions as appropriate.

Pattern 1 Rewrite

_____

_____

_____

_____

_____

_____

_____

_____

_____

Pattern 2 Rewrite

_____

_____

_____

_____

_____

_____

_____

_____

_____

Pattern 3 Rewrite

_____

_____

_____

_____

_____

_____

_____

_____

_____

_____

Persuasive Logic: Cause-and-Effect Reasoning

Often, when attempting to persuade someone about a belief or point of view you hold, you are also trying to convince them by pointing out special relationships that different things or events share. In persuasion, **cause**-and-**effect** reasoning can be a powerful tool in convincing your reader that your point of view is both logical and reasonable.

Cause-and-effect development explains the reasons behind *why* something occurs: **cause** analysis develops *why* something happens, and **effect** analysis explains *the results and consequences* stemming from the causes. These are called **causal relationships,** and they help us understand why things happen in the world around us and the possible consequences that may occur in the future.

For example, a writer might ask the question, Why did President Clinton lie to the American public? as a way of finding out the possible causes of this problem. (*Possible causes:* He didn't define his actions with Monica Lewinsky as "having sex"; he didn't want the First Lady, Hillary Rodham Clinton, to find out about his relationship with Ms. Lewinsky; he did not want to be embarrassed publicly in the press; he didn't want history to focus on this aspect of his presidency.) The writer also might ask, What will happen because President Clinton lied to the American public? as a way of figuring out the possible events stemming from the lying that might occur in the future. (*Possible effects:* He might have been impeached for "high crimes and misdemeanors"; history books might focus on this aspect of his presidency rather than his successes with domestic and foreign affairs; the Democratic Party might find it harder to get legislation passed through Congress; Democratic candidates might find it difficult to get elected or re-elected to office.)

Obviously, the search for cause-and-effect answers can be a complex undertaking. More than one explanation can be found, and often, all the answers fit. This can be helpful in achieving thorough development of the issue. In persuasion, thoroughly developing your point of view can help you persuade your reader that your side of the issue has been both logically and reasonably stated.

Causal Chains

Whether you are focusing on cause or effect, it is helpful before you begin writing to develop a **causal chain.** A causal chain demonstrates the series of events that can develop between things and can help clarify the relationships that exist between them, as well.

Example		
Causes		**Effects**
Too many unpaid bills	can lead to	increased physical tension.
Increased physical tension	can lead to	severe headaches.
Severe headaches	can lead to	nausea and loss of appetite.
Nausea and loss of appetite	can lead to	physical and mental fatigue.
Physical and mental fatigue	can lead to	health problems.

In the example above, notice how an effect can become a cause for the next effect, and so on. Things and events do not exist in a vacuum, isolated from the other things and events around them. Yes, we can focus on cause, and we can focus on effect, but for your insights to be most persuasive, it will be helpful during your argument to share with the reader the knowledge you have learned from the causal chain.

Once readers know *why* something has happened and the consequences that might occur, they are much more likely to accept your persuasive conclusions about the topic. In other words, they are clear as to why you think the way you do, and understanding an issue is often half the battle to accepting the arguer's ideas concerning the issue.

Problems to Avoid

When using cause-and-effect reasoning, do not confuse **chronological sequence** and **coincidence** with true cause-and-effect relationships.

In chronological sequence, do not assume that because one event follows another in time that the first event causes the second to occur.

Example

After I attend a movie, I read in the paper several days later that another movie star has died. Therefore, my going to the movies causes actors to die. (There are literally thousands of movie stars spanning decades of time. One movie star is likely to die on almost any day of the week, and because they are famous, their passing also is likely to be reported in newspapers. So the chances of a movie star's death being reported at about the same time as you do anything, not just attending a movie, is a likely occurrence.)

With coincidence, do not assume that because one thing occurs, it is the cause for another thing that occurs, that a cause-and-effect relationship exists between them.

Example

Every time a black cat crosses my path, something bad happens to me. (Bad things indeed may happen to you, but the proverbial "black cat," as a cause of bad luck, is a superstition that has no basis in reality. Your "bad luck" is probably due to your not being properly prepared for the events in your life or possibly just being at the wrong place at the wrong time—chance occurrence.)

(ESL) Transitional Expressions for Cause/Effect Writing

There are several transitional expressions you will find useful when writing about causes or effects.

Causes	Effects
because	as a consequence of
causes, caused by	as a result (of)

the reason . . .	consequently
since	then
	therefore

The Topic Sentence in a Cause/Effect Paragraph

After choosing your subject and figuring out some ideas using one or more of the prewriting techniques you have learned, you will need to decide whether you are going to focus on causes or effects. The topic sentence will announce your purpose to the reader, and it will clarify the paragraph's development.

Examples

Focus on Causes:
Proper nutrition, regular exercise, and a positive attitude can lead to a long, healthful life. (This paragraph will develop *proper nutrition, regular exercise, and a positive attitude* to show how each "causes" a *long, healthful life.*)

Focus on Effects:
A long, healthful life can increase earnings potential, intelligence levels, and an active retirement period. (This paragraph will develop *earnings potential, intelligence levels,* and *an active retirement period* as "effects" or "results" of a *long, healthful life.*)

PRACTICE 10   **Writing a Paragraph Focusing on Causes**

This practice will help you develop a paragraph that focuses on causes.

1. Pick one of the following topics: divorce; poor job performance; disinterest in politics.
2. List as many causes of your topic choice as you can think of.

   a. _____

   b. _____

   c. _____

   d. _____

   e. _____

3. If any of the causes in your list are merely chronological or coincidental, draw a line through them.

4. Write a topic sentence that focuses on causes.

   _____

   _____

5. Write a sentence for each of the remaining causes in your list.

_____

_____

_____

_____

_____

_____

6. On a separate sheet of paper, rewrite your sentences into paragraph form.

PRACTICE 11   Writing a Paragraph Focusing on Effects

This practice will help you develop a paragraph that focuses on effects.

1. Pick one of the following topics: drug abuse; dieting; organizational skills.

2. List as many effects of your topic choice as you can think of.

a. _____

b. _____

c. _____

d. _____

e. _____

3. If any of the effects in your list are merely chronological or coincidental, draw a line through them.

4. Write a topic sentence that focuses on effects.

_____

_____

5. Write a sentence for each of the remaining effects in your list.

_____

_____

_____

_____

_____

6. On a separate sheet of paper, rewrite your sentences into paragraph form.

TOPIC BANK

Write a paragraph about one or more of the following topics, or about a topic of your own choice.

Persuasion

1. Mandatory drug testing should/should not be allowed at schools.
2. Instant replay should/should not be used in all professional sports.
3. Controversial organizations (Communist Party, Ku Klux Klan) should/should not be allowed to advertise in campus publications.
4. National identification cards will/will not help prevent terrorism.
5. Women should/should not be allowed to be combat soldiers in the military services.
6. Affirmative action should/should not be implemented for college enrollment.
7. The legal drinking age should/should not be eighteen years of age.
8. Marijuana should/should not be legalized for medical purposes.
9. English should/should not be legally designated as the official language of the United States.
10. Health insurance should/should not be made available for all citizens of the United States.

Causes of . . .

1. drug abuse
2. the increasing high school dropout rate
3. test anxiety
4. high taxation
5. road rage
6. divorce
7. spousal abuse
8. a high teen pregnancy rate
9. low unemployment
10. high prison populations

Effects of . . .

1. prejudice
2. pollution (see the photo on page 261)
3. a school grading system
4. overprescribing antibiotics
5. high speed limits
6. high interest rates
7. international trade agreements
8. alcohol abuse
9. a tornado
10. a large corporation leaving a small town

WRITING OPPORTUNITIES

HOME The factory near your home has been releasing foul-smelling clouds of smoke for nearly three months. You have phoned City Hall on several occasions to complain, but nothing has been done. In an attempt to persuade the mayor of your city to look into the air pollution caused by the factory, write one paragraph detailing the problems associated with the factory's smokestacks.

SCHOOL Your Biology 101 professor's assignment sheet states that each student must find a potential source of pollution (air, water, or land) in the local community and write a one-paragraph report detailing the potential hazardous conditions. The report should try to persuade people in the community that action needs to take place to correct the problem. You decide to write about the fumes coming from the smokestacks at the local chemical factory just outside of town.

WORK You work for the Environmental Protection Agency (EPA). Write a one-paragraph report convincing your boss to bring action against the factory in the photograph above for violation of air pollution standards.

 Visit *The Write Start* Online!

For additional practice with the materials in this chapter, go to

http://www.cengage.com/devenglish/checkett/writestartSP4e.

Chapter Self-Assessment Test

Check either True or False on the blank next to the statement.

T	F	
____	____	Writers use persuasion to try to convince others that their point of view is correct.
____	____	The topic sentence in a persuasive paragraph states the writer's conclusion or point of view about a topic.
____	____	A fact differs from an opinion.
____	____	A fact is true.
____	____	An opinion is false.
____	____	An opinion is the way we interpret a fact.
____	____	Answering the opposition, referring to an authority, predicting consequences, facts, and examples are five types of evidence.
____	____	Cause and effect reasoning is an important tool in convincing your reader that your point of view is both logical and reasonable.
____	____	Causal analysis explains *how* something happened but not *why*.
____	____	Effect analysis explains the results and consequences stemming from causes.

PART THREE

Writing Effective Essays

Writing effective paragraphs is very useful when it comes to memos, short-answer exams, and brief writing assignments, but many business reports and longer college writing assignments require multiple paragraphs to explain many ideas.

Just as we joined sentences together to form a paragraph, we can join paragraphs together into a longer piece of writing called an *essay*.

18

The Essay

CHAPTER WARM-UP

Pair off with a classmate. Each of you should choose a favorite hobby or pastime, such as skateboarding, racquetball, movie-going, or shopping. Choose a set of questions from the cross-examining prewriting activity on page 131. Take turns interviewing each other about the hobby or pastime.

Business and academic writing often requires considerable length to express fully a variety of complex ideas. Academic writing, in particular, often demands two to three or more pages in the form of an essay.

An **essay** is a written composition made up of a number of paragraphs that develop a particular subject. Therefore, an essay can be developed using the same methods demonstrated in the preceding chapters dealing with writing single paragraphs.

Although an essay can have any number of paragraphs, we will use a five-paragraph model to introduce the basic elements of the essay.

The Five-Paragraph Essay

Almost all essays should have a **title.** The title should pique the reader's interest. It should be a catchy or dramatic phrase, usually two to six words; longer titles can become wordy and cumbersome to read. If you can't come up with something clever or dramatic, pick several of the key words from your thesis sentence and use them.

It's a good idea to wait until your essay is finished before you create the title. That way, you give yourself enough time to understand fully the point of your essay and come up with the most appropriate title.

When writing your title, do the following:

1. Capitalize the first word and all other words except articles (a, an, the) and prepositions (of, on, to, in).
2. Center the title on the page, and leave two spaces between it and the introductory paragraph.

Do not put quotation marks on either side of the title, and do not underline it.

Most essays begin with an **introductory paragraph.** Its purpose is to introduce the reader to the topic of the essay. The paragraph consists of *introductory sentences* and the *thesis sentence.*

After the introductory paragraph come the **body paragraphs.** Their purpose is to develop, support, and explain the topic idea stated in the thesis sentence. Body paragraphs consist of a *topic sentence* followed by *support sentences.*

The essay ends with a **concluding paragraph.** Its purpose is to bring the essay to a conclusion that gives the reader a sense of completeness. The most common methods for concluding an essay are emphasizing one of the following: *a call to action, a warning, a prediction,* or *an evaluation* of the important points.

The Introductory Paragraph

The purpose of the **introductory paragraph** is to introduce the reader to the topic of the essay. This can be accomplished through a series of introductory sentences followed by the thesis sentence.

The Thesis Sentence

The most important element in an essay is the **thesis sentence** because it sets the tone for the entire essay. It states what the writer is going to explain, clarify, or argue for or against about the essay's topic. Although there is no rule about which paragraph to place the thesis sentence in, it is usually placed near the end of the first paragraph. This placement makes your thesis the last element of your essay's introduction. This is important. After all, the thesis sentence is a roadmap for the entire essay, and you should want the reader to understand what your essay is about. A good thesis sentence

- announces the overall topic/subject.
- states the importance of the topic/subject (the writer's attitude toward the subject).
- can outline the organizational structure of the entire essay.
- asserts only one main idea.
- expresses the topic as an opinion that can be discussed.
- is *not* expressed as a fact.
- is *never* expressed as a question.

Examples

Preventive maintenance will help increase the resale value of your car.

Knowing you have inherited a genetic disease can help you plan for the future.

Computers have effectively reduced the cost of communications for most businesses.

PRACTICE 1   Analyzing Thesis Sentences

In the space provided after each example, explain why each thesis sentence is constructed improperly. Write **Correct** in the space if you think the example is a good thesis.

1. Is St. Louis an exciting city in which to live?

_____

2. The St. Louis Cardinals are a professional baseball team.

_____

3. Many people have different opinions on whether St. Louis is a good place to raise a family.

_____

4. St. Louis is a popular tourist city because of the nightlife and the historical sites.

_____

5. St. Louis has not fully utilized its riverfront for barge traffic; the civic leadership has not dealt effectively in revitalizing the north side of the city.

_____

6. St. Louis has a rich social, political, and cultural history.

_____

7. St. Louis is known as the "Gateway to the West."

_____

8. The Gateway Arch was a sound financial investment.

_____

9. St. Louis is strategically located in the middle of the country.

_____

10. Visitors enjoy St. Louis because of the international flavor of its restaurants.

_____

Expressing an Attitude in the Thesis Sentence

The writer's **attitude** is simply how the writer feels about the topic at hand. The verb in the thesis sentence usually starts to express the writer's attitude about the subject. For example, the verbs _are/are not, is/is not, should/should not,_ and _can/cannot_ begin to tell you how the writer feels about the subject. Perhaps the topic is good citizenship, and the writer thinks that reading a newspaper each day will make people better informed about community affairs, thus making them good citizens. The verb and the words after the verb finish expressing the writer's attitude. So the verb _will make,_ when tied to the idea of "good citizen," expresses the writer's attitude that "reading a newspaper" will make people good citizens. As a writer, your attitude expresses both why the subject is important to you and why you think the subject should be important to the reader.

> **Examples**
> In the following thesis sentences, the words that express attitude are italicized.
>
> **1.** Breakfast _is the most important_ meal of the day.
> **2.** Psycho _is a scary_ movie because of the shower scene.
> **3.** Vitamin supplements _can help_ you feel more energized.
> **4.** Vitamins _have no_ role in whether or not you feel more energized.
> **5.** Ford _makes better_ trucks than General Motors.

PRACTICE 2   **Identifying the Writer's Attitude**

Underline the words that express attitude in each of the following thesis sentences.

1. Organically grown fruits and vegetables are healthier than those chemically treated.

2. Students who study on a daily basis are more successful on exams than students who cram.

3. Hybrid fuel automobiles will help reduce America's dependence on foreign oil.

4. Metal detectors should not be installed in schools throughout the nation.

5. Warning labels on CD and DVD packaging are a violation of free speech.

6. Society during the "good old days" was not any better than today.

7. Playing violent video games can be harmful to young people's perception of reality.

8. Working at a part-time job while going to school promotes a sense of responsibility.

9. Global warming could have a negative effect on the earth's ecosystems.

10. Learning a different language helps students learn about other cultures.

The Essay Map in the Thesis Sentence

Because you are learning to write a five-paragraph essay with three body paragraphs, the three-item essay map in the thesis sentence will both organize and limit your essay's discussion of the topic. Each of the three essay map items becomes the subject of each of the three body paragraphs. The essay map automatically organizes the essay for you and limits its scope.

Examples

In the following sentences, the essay map is italicized.

1. To be safe during a tornado alert, people should *go to the basement, hide inside an interior room closet,* or *get underneath a heavy piece of furniture.*
2. *Intelligence, dedication,* and *hard work* are necessary ingredients for a successful career.
3. Because of *an excessive military budget, poor farming methods,* and *inadequate international trade strategies,* Communism was a failure in Russia.

PRACTICE 3   Analyzing the Essay Map

Read the following thesis sentences to see whether the essay map items explain, clarify, or support the writer's attitude about the topic. If the essay map does explain, clarify, or support the writer's attitude about the topic, write **correct** in the space provided. If not, indicate what is wrong.

Example: Thesis sentence: *St. Louis is an exciting city to visit because of clouds, elm trees, and cats.*

Topic: St. Louis

Attitude: An **exciting** city to visit

Why: Clouds, elm trees, cats (the three-item essay map)

Problem: The three essay map items are not exciting reasons to visit the city.

1. A vegetarian diet is healthier than one with meat because of temperature, salt, and water retention.

   _____

   _____

   _____

2. Expanding your vocabulary, learning about new places, and developing a better writing style makes reading a valuable activity.

   _____

   _____

   _____

3. Weekly household chores help children learn math, tuna salad, and opera houses.

   _____

   _____

4. Cultural awareness, civic responsibility, and volunteerism make coin collecting an interesting hobby.

   _____

   _____

   _____

5. Maintaining a successful professional sports career is difficult because of talented newcomers, the constant travel, and the aging process.

   _____

   _____

   _____

Putting It All Together

It is vital that your thesis sentence be constructed properly. Without a good thesis sentence, the essay cannot succeed. To check your thesis sentence, ask this question:

Do the **essay map items** explain or support why the writer has chosen his or her **attitude** about the **topic**?

Examples

Voting and military service are important activities for all citizens. (two topics, no essay map)

Voting is an important responsibility for all citizens. (one topic and clear attitude, no essay map)

Voting is an important responsibility for all citizens because it gives people a voice in how the government is run, removes ineffective politicians from office, and influences political decision making. (one topic, clear attitude, three-item essay map)

Many students work while going to school. (statement of fact, no attitude, no essay map)

Working while going to school can teach students valuable lessons. (one topic, clear attitude, no essay map)

Working while going to school can teach students responsibility, organizational skills, and teamwork. (one topic, clear attitude, three-item essay map)

Are regular automobile oil changes really necessary? (question—not a clear opinion, no essay map)

Regular oil changes can keep a car running better. (one topic, a clearly stated opinion, no essay map)

Regular oil changes can keep a car running more efficiently, improve gas mileage, and reduce long-term maintenance costs. (one topic, clear attitude, three-item essay map)

PRACTICE 4   Analyzing Thesis Sentences

In each of the following thesis sentences, underline the topic once, circle the attitude, and underline the essay map twice. On the line provided, indicate whether any element is missing.

1. Broccoli and oranges are good sources for vitamins.

   _____

2. Playmaking, speed, and bench-clearing brawls make ice hockey an exciting sport.

   _____

3. The Rolex is considered by many as a better wristwatch than the Breitling.

   _____

4. College students go to class, study, and write papers.

   _____

5. Laptop computers are good buys because of portability.

   _____

6. Solar power should be a governmental priority because of diminishing fossil fuels, environmental pollution, and skyrocketing costs.

_____

7. Bungee jumping is a dangerous activity.

_____

8. The St. Louis Rams, Green Bay Packers, and Pittsburgh Steelers are football teams.

_____

9. Are savings bonds better investment instruments than annuities because of interest, safety, and liquidity?

_____

10. Humor, social satire, and musicality made the Beatles popular long after their breakup as a rock group.

_____

PRACTICE 5   Rewriting Thesis Sentences

From Practice 4, rewrite those sentences that do not meet the necessary criteria for an effective thesis sentence. Number your finished sentences.

_____

_____

_____

_____

_____

_____

_____

_____

_____

_____

| PRACTICE 6 | Writing Thesis Sentences |

Write thesis sentences for the following topics. Use the criteria for writing an effective thesis sentence that you have studied.

1. A movie you have seen

_____

_____

2. A social issue you are interested in

_____

_____

3. A job you have or would like to have

_____

_____

4. A famous person you admire

_____

_____

5. A piece of artwork you like

_____

_____

Introductory Sentences

In the introductory paragraph, the thesis sentence is introduced by **introductory sentences**. The introductory sentences should catch the reader's attention and clarify your tone (humorous, serious, or satiric). Some effective techniques for introducing the thesis sentence are as follows:

■ *Shocking statistics or statements*

> One of every four babies in America is born out of wedlock. Fifty percent of teenage deaths involve alcohol. More Americans die and are injured in automobile accidents than from all diseases combined. It's time something is done about these national tragedies. (*Place thesis sentence here*)

■ *A series of questions*

> Tired of the same old political promises? Are the current politicians in Washington, D.C. not representing your concerns? Are you thinking about not voting in the upcoming elections? Maybe you simply need to find a new direction. *(Place thesis sentence here)*

■ *A common problem or misconception*

> Most people think welfare goes only to poor people living in the inner city. They believe that welfare recipients have no job and are hopelessly lazy, and that welfare recipients are poorly educated and lack skills necessary to hold a job. What you don't realize about welfare and who gets it may shock you. *(Place thesis sentence here)*

PRACTICE 7   Writing Introductory Sentences

Write introductory sentences for each of the following thesis sentences. Try to create at least three sentences that lead logically to the thesis sentence.

1. Expanding your vocabulary, learning about new places, and developing a better writing style make reading a valuable activity.

    _____

    _____

    _____

    _____

    _____

2. Solar power should be a governmental priority because of diminishing fossil fuels, environmental pollution, and skyrocketing costs.

    _____

    _____

    _____

    _____

    _____

3. Maintaining a successful professional sports career is difficult because of talented newcomers, the constant travel, and the aging process.

_____

_____

_____

_____

_____

_____

The Body Paragraphs

The **body paragraphs** get their organization from the three-item essay map located in the thesis sentence. Each topic for each body paragraph is taken from the essay map in the thesis sentence. There are two types of sentences in the body paragraph: the *topic sentence* and *support sentences.*

The Topic Sentence

The **topic sentence** tells the reader what the main idea, or topic, of the paragraph is. Although there is no set place in the paragraph for the topic sentence, making the topic sentence the first sentence in the paragraph will make organizing and developing the topic easier.

The topic sentence has two parts: the *topic/subject* and the *controlling idea.* The **topic** is the subject of the paragraph taken from the essay map in the thesis sentence. The **controlling idea** states what the writer will be developing about the subject of the paragraph. The controlling idea limits what you can say about the subject so that you don't stray to other subject areas.

Topic sentences missing a controlling idea lack focus and specific direction. Without a controlling idea, the writer's attitude about the subject can be unclear.

Examples

Soccer is a popular high school sport. (no controlling idea—popular is too ambiguous)

Michael Jordan was a popular basketball player. (no controlling idea—simply a statement of fact)

Soccer is a popular high school sport because it is relatively inexpensive to fund. (controlling idea: cheap funding makes soccer popular)

Michael Jordan's diverse skills made him an exciting basketball player. (controlling idea: Jordan is exciting because of diverse skills)

Support Sentences

Support sentences follow the topic sentence and develop the subject using specific examples, details, and facts. These support ideas must be consistent with the controlling idea. In other words, the controlling idea unifies the paragraph by determining the kind of support ideas you can use in the support sentences.

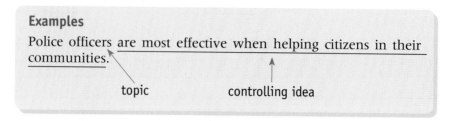

Examples

Police officers are most effective when helping citizens in their communities.

topic   controlling idea

Support sentences for this topic sentence would focus on *what* police officers do to help citizens and might include such activities as

    a. finding lost/stolen property
    b. solving crimes
    c. preventing crimes

Six Important Support Questions

When writing a story, reporters ask six questions. The answers provide the focus that allows them to select the details, facts, and examples to develop the story with specific information. The six questions are *who, what, where, when, why,* and *how.*

After you have selected or have been given the topic you are to write about, decide on the controlling idea. To do this, choose which of the following reporter's questions allows you to write about the topic with the desired focus.

For instance, suppose your topic is an important event. In the support sentences, you could focus on the following:

Who started the event?

Who attended/witnessed/participated in the event?

Who was affected by the event?

What was the event?

What happened before/during/after the event?

What was special about the event?

Where did the event occur?

Did the location affect the event in any way?

Did the location have historical significance?

When did the event occur (A.M./P.M., day, month, year)?

Did the time frame add any special significance to the event?

Did the event coincide with a historically significant time?

Why did the event occur?

Why was the event important?

How did the event happen?

How was the event funded?

How was the event advertised?

You can add your own focus to these questions if other ideas come to you. There is no need to limit yourself to the preceding list.

> **Examples**
>
> **1.** Reading can help people become better educated.
> **2.** Reading is best done in a quiet, secluded place.
> **3.** Anyone interested in becoming a better writer should read as much as possible.

Although the topic subject of each sentence, reading, is the same, the focus of the controlling idea is different. In sentence 1, the focus is on *what* reading can do for people (educate them); in sentence 2, the focus is on *where* reading is best accomplished (in a quiet, secluded place); and in sentence 3, the focus is on *who* (anyone interested in becoming a writer).

For a more developed discussion of body paragraphs and outlining, see Chapter 9.

The Concluding Paragraph

An essay should not suddenly stop after you have finished discussing the last body paragraph topic. You should leave your reader with a feeling of completion. Use the concluding paragraph to emphasize why your essay is important. The **concluding paragraph** can help convince your reader that your ideas are valid. The concluding paragraph should not introduce new points; developing new points is the function of the body paragraphs. However, the concluding paragraph should give the points you have made a dramatic purpose. Also, it is not necessary to restate the thesis sentence and essay map items at the end of your essay unless you are doing a longer paper. In a short, five-paragraph essay, the reader is not likely to forget three points.

Just as there were several introductory techniques you could use in the introductory paragraph, there also are several concluding techniques that you can use in the concluding paragraph. These include the following:

- Call to action
- Warning
- Prediction
- Evaluation

Call to Action
You are actually asking the reader to take action, to do something.

> **Example**
>
> New subdivisions are necessary to house the burgeoning population in our suburbs, but the wholesale destruction of mature trees simply to make building easier is not an acceptable construction practice. Call your local alderperson, and complain about this anti-environmental practice. It takes twenty to thirty years for a sapling to mature into a fully foliaged shade tree.

Warning
You are warning the reader that there is the possibility of something adverse happening.

Example

Buying products and services on the Internet is becoming commonplace. The amount of money being spent online is doubling every year. The main reason for the Internet's popularity for consumers is convenience. However, be careful when giving out credit card numbers on the Internet. Unauthorized use of credit cards is a growing problem for Internet shoppers. Make sure that the online business you are dealing with has a secure server for credit information. Your economic security is at stake.

Prediction

You "look into the future," so to speak, and predict outcomes stemming from the topic.

Example

The new suburban vans are becoming bigger every year. They look like off-road vehicles with glandular problems. The extra roominess inside the vans is great for large families, hauling Little League teams, and traveling with lots of luggage. But the larger vehicles are hard to handle, and their greater bumper height and extra weight cause more damage to regular-sized cars when accidents occur. Because of the proliferation of these monster-vans, insurance rates will surely rise in the near future. Suburban van manufacturers should begin to study ways to counter this potential negative impact on all drivers.

Evaluation

You summarize the importance of the overall topic.

Example

Studying plants in the Amazon rainforest has had and will continue to have many benefits for society. New drugs to combat disease are an important result of these studies. Additionally, new antibiotics are needed to replace those that bacteria have become resistant to because of overuse. Synthetic derivatives also can be developed from studying the new drugs. The Amazon rainforest is a valuable resource for all the world.

Sample Student Essay

The following is a student essay demonstrating all the elements of an effectively written essay that you have learned in this chapter. The key elements and concepts are noted in the margin and underlined in the text of the essay.

In this essay, student writer Nancy Smith relates the emotionally devastating effects of finding out that her three-year-old son has cancer, followed by the equally disturbing period of surgery and treatment.

The Ravages of Childhood Cancer

Nearly one-third of all children diagnosed as having a childhood malignancy die. This number strikes fear into the heart of any parent unfortunate enough to have to face such awful news about their child. Most everyone has been a patient in a hospital, but a grave uncertainty about leaving alive is not a common experience. Being told, "If there is a type of cancer to have, this is the kind," is of little comfort. The "C" word is frightening in any context. Diagnosis, surgery, and treatment are terrifying experiences for the family of a child having cancer.

We had taken him to Cardinal Glennon Children's Hospital for testing to find out a diagnosis. When he had not felt good over the past month, cancer was not even a remote thought in any of our minds. Apparently, it was for the doctors. Nurses tried five times before successfully finding a vein that would hold the IV tube. Derek cried out of pain and fear. I could feel myself becoming nauseous as I tried to comfort him. Next, we moved to the ultrasound room where Derek, exhausted from the IV ordeal, slept soundly. The doctor inspected the screen. Yes! There it was. A tumor the size of a quarter. Wilms tumor, otherwise known as cancer of the kidney, was Derek's diagnosis.

As the day of the surgery arrived, the family gathered at the hospital. We were told the operation to remove the tumor and infected kidney would take two to three hours. Although sedated, Derek looked at me longingly through frightened eyes. I was surrounded by my entire family, but I never felt more vulnerable. Three hours passed, then four, with no word. My hand trembled uncontrollably as I tried to sip from my coffee cup; I could not stop the tears welling in my eyes. Finally, after five hours, the surgeon entered the waiting room and told us the results. He was fairly certain they had gotten all of the tumor. If all went well, Derek would start chemotherapy and be released from the hospital in two weeks.

Derek's treatment consisted of six radiation therapy sessions and chemotherapy spread over a one and a half year period. The radiation came first—once a day for six consecutive days. The procedure only lasted a few minutes; however, thirty minutes after the session Derek would vomit every fifteen minutes for hours. His little body would convulse like a dying snake's. His little voice split the air with terrifying screams. The chemotherapy started early and lasted all day. The medicine was administered through a port-catheter in his chest. After the chemo was injected, Derek would be sick for days.

It's been five years since the operation, and there has been no sign of a tumor on his remaining kidney. The prognosis is good. Doctors and scientists still do not know all the causes of the various forms of cancer. Research is needed at all levels, so give generously to the Cancer Foundation. Someone once said that a statistic is a victim without the tears. Your continued support of cancer research will help eliminate future statistics.

PRACTICE 8   Analyzing an Essay

Sample Student Essay

In the following essay, student writer Rebecca Eisenbath revisits a horrendous time in our history—the genocide of six million people based on their race, religion, or nationality at the hands of Adolf Hitler and the Nazis before and during World War II.

First read the essay. Then answer the questions following the essay.

The Holocaust: The Ashes Remain

Most people know that World War II began in September of 1939 when Germany invaded Poland. But the year 1933 may not ring any bells; however, the event that began that year surely would: the beginning of the Holocaust. Over the next decade, six million people would be exterminated in what became euphemistically known as "the Final Solution." The Holocaust remains one of the most devastating events in human history due to its horrendous policies, number of victims, and the terrible effect it continues to have on the survivors and the people around the world.

Germany's horrendous policies led to the decision to commit genocide. Hitler and his followers believed their Aryan race was the only one that deserved to rule other "inferior" races, and they made slave laborers of those different than themselves. They blamed the Jews for their economic problems, so Reinhard Heydrich, the Chief of Reich Security, thought up the idea of mass extermination in prisoner camps. This policy came to be known as the "Final Solution." All Jews had to wear an identification badge or armband emblazoned with a yellow Star of David. They either were herded into traincars and taken to the extermination camps, or they were imprisoned in ghettos and killed by bands of SS military units.

The Holocaust also was alarming because of the numbers and types of people it claimed. The total death toll was over six million. Although they are the most written about because of the sheer numbers that were killed, the "Final Solution" did not stop with the Jews. Catholics, Poles, Czechs,

Gypsies, homosexuals, and even the mentally ill were shot, gassed, poisoned, and tortured until merciful death came.

Near the end of the war, when the Allies overran German-held countries, they liberated the concentration camps. What they found inside, emaciated prisoners, huge ovens filled with human bones, and mass graves overflowing with bodies, devastated many of the liberators. Many of these men had to undergo years of psychological treatment to deal with the horrors of the camps. The Jewish survivors were sent to Palestine after the war to try and rebuild their lives. Three years later, the State of Israel was recognized by the United Nations. The survivors of the Holocaust, although never forgetting their pain (how could they with camp numbers tattooed on their forearms?), never lost hope.

Even today, the world cannot escape what happened so many decades ago. In 1993, two museums commemorating the Holocaust were dedicated in the United States. Yet, the practice of genocide still exists as wars rage in parts of Asia, Africa, and Europe. Nations must learn from the past or, as we are seeing today, we will be doomed to repeat it. Be an advocate for peace, and let your congresspersons know how you want them to act.

Questions

1. What type of introductory technique does the writer use?

   _____

2. Write the thesis sentence on the line below.

   _____

   _____

   _____

3. Identify the topic in the thesis sentence.

   _____

4. Identify the attitude.

_____

5. What are the three essay map items?

_____

_____

6. Write the three topic sentences of the three body paragraphs on the lines below. Underline the topic in each sentence.

_____

_____

_____

_____

7. Choose the method by which the writer develops the topic in each of the body paragraphs: _who, what, where, when, why,_ or _how._

Body paragraph 1 _____

Body paragraph 2 _____

Body paragraph 3 _____

8. What technique(s) does the writer use in the concluding paragraph?

_____

_____

PRACTICE 9   **Analyzing an Essay**

Sample Student Essay

In the following essay, student writer Tim Schuette explores why exercising properly can benefit your health.

First read the essay. Then answer the questions following the essay.

Effective Exercising

Are you overweight? After cutting the grass, are you exhausted? Are you unable to keep up with your friends or your children? Would you like to feel younger? Exercising the upper body, abdominal, and leg muscles correctly is important for proper functioning.

The most important muscles to exercise in the upper body are the triceps, biceps, and pectorals. The triceps and biceps, located in the upper arm, work as a team so that your arm can flex at the elbow. Exercising only one or the other of these muscles can reduce flexibility and can facilitate injuries like "tennis elbow." When you exercise the chest, you need to use an equal amount of weight in each hand and do the exact number of repetitions so that neither right nor left pectoral muscle will dominate the other. When this happens, "pulled" muscle injuries occur more often. The upper body muscles will work freely and efficiently when exercised proportionately.

The abdominal muscles are significant because they support the entire body. Therefore, you need them to simply sit upright in a chair. The abdominals consist of eight separate muscles that must be exercised for total effectiveness. The upper and lower muscles, known as the "six pack," are located from navel to chest, and they support your body front to back. The oblique muscles are located on either side of the "six pack" and assist in supporting the body when bending left or right. If your back is constantly hurting or you simply want to lose that "spare tire," then exercising the abdominals is essential.

The three major muscles in the legs give you the ability to stand, walk, run, and jump. The rectus femoris and the semitendinous are located in the upper leg. The gastrocnemius, better known as the calf muscle, is located in the lower leg. The upper leg muscles make the leg bend at the knee, and the lower leg muscles make the foot moveable. If the muscles are worked unevenly, they can become damaged; additionally, injured or weakened leg muscles can cause shin splints and hip problems. Also, the leg muscles must be exercised properly when you are younger, so that more problems won't occur as you get older.

No single muscle works by itself; therefore, it is important to exercise all your muscles and their group partners evenly. If your muscles are worked correctly, you will lose weight, have more energy, and feel younger. A total workout only takes about thirty minutes, three times per week. Exercise regularly. Your body deserves it!

Questions

1. What type of introductory paragraph technique does the writer use?

   _____

2. Write the thesis sentence on the line below.

   _____

   _____

3. Identify the topic in the thesis sentence.

   _____

4. Identify the attitude.

   _____

5. What are the three essay map items?

   _____

   _____

   _____

6. Write the three topic sentences of the three body paragraphs on the lines below. Underline the topic in each sentence.

   _____

   _____

   _____

   _____

7. Choose the method by which the writer develops the topic in each of the body paragraphs: *who, what, where, when, why,* and *how.*

   Body paragraph 1 _____

   Body paragraph 2 _____

   Body paragraph 3 _____

8. What technique(s) does the writer use in the concluding paragraph?

_____

_____

TOPIC BANK

Write a five-paragraph essay using one of the following thesis sentences or a thesis sentence of your own.

1. Political negotiation should help solve the Israel–Palestine issue.
2. Skateboarding can be very dangerous without proper equipment (see the photo on page 287).
3. A positive attitude can help you achieve your goals.
4. Space exploration benefits mankind because of the inventions stemming from it.
5. Past performance is the best indicator of future behavior.
6. Listening to classical music can help you achieve better math scores.
7. Content warning labels on CDs are worthwhile.
8. Living in a dorm is a better way to learn good social skills than sharing an apartment.
9. Art is a waste of time unless it adds to your job skills.
10. A poor teacher is a good excuse for failing a class.

WRITING OPPORTUNITIES

HOME You convince your spouse to take you to your 25th high school reunion. It's a formal affair, strictly tuxedos and gowns. From 7 in the evening until 2 in the morning, you and your old classmates dance to the music popular the year you graduated and reminisce about the good old days at Smarmy High. When you return home, you are so excited about what you have witnessed that you decide to write about the experience and send copies to all your friends and relatives around the country. In hopes of organizing the vast amount of details in your mind and remembering your writing class from college, you decide to write a five-paragraph essay using the thesis sentence with three-item essay map.

SCHOOL You are a reporter for your school newspaper. Your editor wants a five-paragraph column detailing the major events at the year's biggest campus social activity, the Homecoming Formal Dance. You decide to make the Homecoming Queen the focus of your story.

WORK As a freelance writer, you'll take any assignment as long as the money is right or the subject interests you. For the right price, the editor of a popular national magazine, concerned with "the rich and famous," has convinced you to write a five-paragraph article about the movie industry's Academy Award ceremony. You decide that the focus of your article will be the crowds, the parade of stars, and the unfolding pageantry.

Visit *The Write Start* **Online!**

For additional practice with the materials in this chapter, go to

http://www.cengage.com/devenglish/checkett/writestartSP4e.

Chapter Self-Assessment Test

Check either True or False on the blank next to the statement.

T	F	
_____	_____	An essay consists of a number of paragraphs developing a particular topic.
_____	_____	Most essays begin with an introductory paragraph.
_____	_____	Introductory paragraphs develop several main points about the topic.
_____	_____	The thesis sentence has to be located in the introductory paragraph.
_____	_____	The thesis sentence contains only the topic of the essay.
_____	_____	Introductory sentences in the introductory paragraph draw a reader's interest by using a shocking statement or statistic, a series of questions, by stating a common problem or misconception, or any combination of them.
_____	_____	Body paragraphs develop, support, and explain the topic idea stated in the thesis.
_____	_____	Body paragraphs consist of only the support sentences.
_____	_____	The essay ends with a concluding paragraph.
_____	_____	In a short essay, it's a good idea to state the thesis sentence again.
_____	_____	The purpose of the concluding paragraph is to add new information to convince the reader that the thesis sentence was clear.
_____	_____	The most common methods for concluding the essay are to emphasize one or more of the following: a call to action, a warning, a prediction, or an evaluation of the essay's important points.

The Writer's Resources

GRAMMAR

ESL Nouns

Nouns are words that stand for people, places, or things. They can be singular or plural.

Nouns	Singular	Plural
Person	man	men
	cousin	cousins
	girl	girls
Place	cave	caves
	beach	beaches
	forest	forests
	yard	yards
	mountain	mountains
Thing	ring	rings
	computer	computers
	discussion	discussions
	truth	truths
	sport	sports
	idea	ideas
	vacation	vacations
	conversation	conversations

To **form the plural of most nouns,** you simply add an *-s* or *-es* to the end of the word. However, there are some exceptions:

1. Nouns ending in *-f* or *-fe* form the plural by adding *-ves*:

   half   halves

   knife   knives

2. Hyphenated nouns (names that are formed by joining several short words with hyphens "-") form plurals by adding *-s* or *-es* to the main word in the phrase:

   mother-in-law   mothers-in-law

   sergeant-at-arms   sergeants-at-arms

3. Some nouns form plurals in other ways, such as by changing the spelling of the plural form. These are sometimes called irregular forms of plural nouns:

   foot   feet

   child   children

   criterion   criteria

woman	women
man	men

4. Other nouns do not change at all when forming the plural. These exceptions must simply be memorized:

fish	fish
deer	deer
shrimp	shrimp

Nouns can also be classified as *proper* and *common*. **Proper nouns** are the specific names or titles of people, places, or things, and they are capitalized. **Common nouns** are general terms for people, places, or things, and they are not capitalized.

Common Nouns	Proper Nouns
singer	Sheryl Crow
beach	Corona Del Mar
magazine	*Time*
student	Julianne

PRACTICE 1   Identifying Nouns

Underline the nouns in the following sentences.

Example: The <u>family</u> travels to the <u>mountains</u> every <u>weekend</u>.

1. They pack up the family van, drive two hours, and arrive at the small cabin in Big Bear Lake.

2. The weekend is spent relaxing in the fresh air.

3. The four children spend their time hiking, skiing, swimming, or reading, depending on the season.

4. The parents try to relax as they do the yardwork, repair the cabin, and prepare meals for the children.

5. When they get home, the kids are relaxed but the parents are exhausted.

6. The next weekend the family plans a trip to the beach.

7. On Saturday morning, the van is filled with inner tubes, boogie boards, beach towels, beach chairs, and picnic baskets.

8. The drive to the beach is an hour trip through the maze of Southern California freeways.

9. Arriving at the sheltered cove, the girls throw their towels on the sand and dash down to the shore, shrieking as the cold waves splash around their ankles.

10. After spending the day swimming and resting on the shore, they gather around the fire, munching on hot dogs and s'mores.

11. As the sun sets into the fiery ocean, the group gathers its sandy belongings and staggers to the car for the gritty ride home.

PRACTICE 2   Using Nouns

Fill in the blanks with appropriate nouns. Compare your answers with those of a classmate to see how the results vary, depending on the vocabulary chosen.

The new _____ are becoming bigger every

_____. They look like _____ with

_____. The extra _____ inside the

_____ are great for _____, _____

and _____. But the larger _____ are hard to

handle, and their greater _____ and _____

make for more damage to _____ when _____

occur.

For the original paragraph, see p. 300.

Pronouns

A **pronoun** is a word that takes the place of or refers to a noun. The word or words that the pronoun refers to are known as the **antecedent(s)** of the pronoun.

> **Example**
> Fariba said that she did not understand the question. (she is the pronoun, and Fariba is its antecedent)

Pronouns can be divided into several categories. The most common categories are *personal pronouns, relative pronouns, demonstrative pronouns, indefinite pronouns,* and *reflexive pronouns.*

Personal Pronouns

Personal pronouns are those that refer to a person (*I/me, you, he/him, she/her, it, we/us,* and *they/them*). *Personal pronouns* are divided into three forms, depending on how they are used in a sentence. These forms are **subjective** (pronoun used as a subject), **objective** (pronoun used as an object), or **possessive** (the pronoun indicates possession/ownership).

Subjective Pronouns

	Singular	**Plural**
1st person	I	we
2nd person	you	you
3rd person	he, she, it	they

Objective Pronouns

	Singular	**Plural**
1st person	me	us
2nd person	you	you
3rd person	him, her, it	them

Possessive Pronouns

	Singular	**Plural**
1st person	my (mine)	our (ours)
2nd person	your (yours)	your (yours)
3rd person	his (his)	their (theirs)
	her (hers)	
	its (its)	

The following examples demonstrate the uses of these three types of personal pronouns:

I frequently listen to music when I drive. (subjective pronoun; the pronoun is used as a subject)

They enjoy decorating their home. (subjective pronoun)

Dave is starting to annoy you. (objective pronoun; the pronoun is the object of the sentence)

He gave the same gift to him. (objective pronoun)

That is my sweater. (possessive pronoun; the pronoun shows ownership or possession)

He borrowed her keys. (possessive pronoun)

The keys are hers. (possessive pronoun)

PRACTICE 1   Identifying Personal Pronouns

In the following sentences, underline subjective pronouns once, objective pronouns twice, and possessive pronouns three times. Some sentences may contain more than one type.

1. He came home from work.

2. His new car was covered with oak leaves.

3. As she walked to the water cooler, her shoe came off and slid under a desk.

4. They decided that not participating in the parade was a better decision for them.

5. It will not be as surprising to you after they explain the rules.

6. Would you like to eat at your place or ours?

7. We sold their horses for them while they were in Europe.

8. It was never my intention to buy his car for you.

9. It's never a good idea to put all of your investments into one stock.

10. I thought the best plan for you would be to go with them to the game.

PRACTICE 2   Using Personal Pronouns

Circle the correct form of personal pronoun in the following sentences.

1. The governor accepted an interview with Lisa and (he, him).

2. (She, Her) and Ellen want to be firefighters.

3. After the rehearsal, Luis and (he, him) went to the coffee shop.

4. The contractors left (their, his) tools on the desk.

5. These statistics helped (her, she) and (me, I) with our research paper.

6. That estimate seemed very expensive to my sister and (I, me).

7. Marc installed the software program, then returned it to (he, him).

8. His parent's questions caught Terrance and (we, us) by surprise.

9. It seemed as though an unresolved problem was causing difficulties between my father and (I, me).

10. The restored painting had regained (its, their) glorious colors.

Relative Pronouns
Relative pronouns are those pronouns used to introduce a qualifying or explanatory clause.

Relative Pronouns

who	Used as a subject in reference to people
whom	Used as an object in reference to people
which	Used as a subject in reference to things
that	Used as a subject in reference to people or things
whoever	Used as a subject in reference to an uncertain number of people
whichever	Used as a subject in reference to an uncertain number of things

The following examples illustrate the use of relative pronouns:

Who made the phone call? (*Who* is used as the subject)

The phone call was made by *whom*? (*Whom* is used as the object)

Which tastes better to you? (*Which* is used as a subject referring to things)

I don't like *that*! (*That* is used as the object referring to a thing)

PRACTICE 3   Using Relative Pronouns

Write the correct relative pronoun in the following sentences.

Example: The scientist <u>who</u> is studying AIDS received a grant.

1. _____ field of study has he chosen as a major?

2. For _____ did he buy this bicycle?

3. _____ wants to go to the concert may go.

4. The biology lab _____ I attend is three hours long.

5. He did not know _____ the performance had been cancelled.

6. At _____ did the clown throw the cream pie?

7. _____ will take the originals to the copy room?

8. He will marry _____ his friends approve of.

9. Give the money to _____ you choose.

10. For _____ are those gifts piled in the closet?

11. To _____ was he singing?

12. _____ would prefer skiing to snowboarding?

13. Fred chose the major _____ best suited his interests.

14. _____ has been trained in computer support technology will get the job.

15. The committee will hire _____ best fits the job description.

16. _____ is pounding on the door?

17. _____ set of problems are the most difficult?

18. Lorraine did not know _____ to ask to the backward dance.

19. The children could not decide _____ toys to take on their vacation.

20. _____ will be going to Gulf Breeze for spring break?

Demonstrative Pronouns

Demonstrative pronouns are used to point out or specify certain people, places, or things.

Demonstrative Pronouns	
Singular	**Plural**
this	these
that	those

PRACTICE 4   Using Demonstrative Pronouns

Write the correct demonstrative pronoun in the following sentences.

1. _____ book (in my hand) gives the latest statistics on the dangers of second-hand smoke.

2. He spent the afternoon staring at _____ picture across the room.

3. _____ flowers in the valley bloom only in the early fall.

4. The police found _____ puppy (in my car) on the side of the highway.

5. _____ was the most important discovery of the century.

6. _____ apples in the truck are still green.

7. Why didn't you take _____ cookies to our new neighbor?

8. _____ small tattoos are the least painful to apply.

9. His cockatiel will eat only _____ special seeds.

10. To whom do _____ keys belong?

Indefinite Pronouns

Indefinite pronouns do not refer to a specific person or thing; they refer to general or indeterminate people, places, or things.

> **Indefinite Pronouns**
> These pronouns do not refer to a specific person.
>
> **Singular**
>
> | | | | |
> |---|---|---|---|
> | everyone | someone | anyone | no one |
> | everybody | somebody | anybody | nobody |
> | everything | something | anything | nothing |
> | each | another | either | neither |
>
> **Singular or Plural**
>
> | | | |
> |---|---|---|
> | all | more | none |
> | any | most | some |
>
> **Plural**
>
> | | | | |
> |---|---|---|---|
> | both | few | many | several |

PRACTICE 5   Using Indefinite Pronouns

Write the correct indefinite pronoun in the following sentences.

1. _____ should do his or her best work for each class.

2. The rules do not apply equally to _____ in this society.

3. _____ can learn to use a computer if he or she takes the appropriate classes.

4. _____ of the new homes have a three-car garage.

5. He sold _____ of the CDs in one hour.

6. Her two children came home from school hungry, so she fixed snacks for _____ of them.

7. _____ could stop them from finishing the race!

8. Jon consulted several sources; _____ of them consistently supported limitations on handgun ownership.

9. _____ arguments are flawed.

10. _____ of the salespeople were very aggressive.

Reflexive Pronouns

The reflexive form adds *-self* or *-selves* to the pronoun and is used to indicate action performed to or on the antecedent.

Reflexive Pronouns

	Singular	**Plural**
1st person	(I) myself	(we) ourselves
2nd person	(you) yourself	(you) yourselves
3rd person	(he) himself	(they) themselves
	(she) herself	
	(it) itself	

The following examples illustrate the use of the reflexive pronoun:

> We gave *ourselves* a party to celebrate the end of the school year.
> Vinh found *himself* in an impossible situation.

The reflexive pronoun form can also be used to intensify meaning. When a reflexive pronoun is used this way it is called an **intensifier**.

> The instructor *herself* found the concepts confusing.
> Raoul *himself* had made the engine.

PRACTICE 6   Using Reflexive Pronouns

Write the correct reflexive pronoun in the following sentences.

1. Aliesha _____ was astounded at how quickly she learned the concepts.

2. My children and I painted the room _____.

3. Oksana found _____ alone in a strange city.

4. The goal is for the students to edit the essay _____.

5. Although I enjoy cooking, I cannot cook all meals by _____.

6. The computer turns _____ off after one hour.

7. Do you consider _____ exempt from the laws that apply to everyone else?

8. The cat could open the door by _____.

9. Though he hates to write in English, Kahn _____ wrote the entire research paper.

10. The professor did not consider _____ an expert on all subjects.

Pronoun-Antecedent Agreement

It is important that pronouns agree with their antecedents. For example, the singular antecedent *everyone* must be used with the singular pronouns *he* or *she*.

The following examples illustrate sentences in which pronouns agree with the antecedent:

> If *someone* works late at night, *he* or *she* may not be able to concentrate in class the next morning.
>
> or
>
> When Adam works late at night, *he* is not able to concentrate in class the next morning.
>
> *Each* ticket holder stood in line waiting for *his* or *her* refund.
>
> *Many* were angry that *their* efforts had not been rewarded.

PRACTICE 7   Pronoun-Antecedent Agreement

Fill in the blanks with the correct pronouns. Underline the antecedent of each pronoun.

Example: All <u>students</u> must do _____**their**_____ assigned reading before class.

1. Each soccer player gave _____ best effort in the World Cup match.

2. Jennifer referred to recent local social conflict in _____ history project.

3. Anyone can learn to dance if _____ has a patient instructor.

4. Someone left _____ clothes all over the locker room.

5. The managers want us to attend _____ sales meeting next week.

6. Although the average consumer wants the best price, _____ may not shop carefully enough to find one.

7. Lana and Patricia gave _____ opinions to Alicia.

8. The creative writing students turned in _____ portfolios.

9. She grows tomatoes and green beans; _____ taste best fresh from the garden.

10. _____ is going to the dance with _____ date.

PRACTICE 8   Pronoun-Antecedent Agreement

Correct any errors in pronoun reference in the sentences below. Put a **C** in the blank if the sentence has no error in pronoun reference.

Example: _____ The business has ~~their~~ problems.
                                        its

1. _____ The jury delayed their verdict.

2. _____ Mr. Billings' students are planning for its field trip to the science center.

3. _____ The crowd roared their approval as the ball dropped in Times Square.

4. _____ The group of friends has continued to share their lives over many years.

5. _____ The family did not take their annual vacation to the beach this year.

6. _____ The soccer team is at their best during challenging tournaments.

7. _____ The faculty of the college argued over their grading policies all semester.

8. _____ The musicians performed the difficult symphony as well as they could.

9. _____ Our committee changes their decision every month.

10. _____ The student council is working on an award banquet for its members.

PRACTICE 9   Pronoun-Antecedent Agreement

Write the correct pronoun in the blank, and write the antecedent of the pronoun in the column on the right.

1. The school is doing _____ best to improve   _____ student retention.

2. Each political movement has _____   _____ supporters and detractors.

3. Anyone can conquer _____ fear of   _____
   technology.

4. Many women are returning to school to achieve   _____
   _____ personal goals.

5. Each country has _____ own flag.   _____

6. The two teams recovered _____ equipment   _____
   after the game.

7. Someone left _____ keys in the empty   _____
   classroom.

8. Soap operas manipulate _____ viewers'   _____
   emotions.

9. Louisa plans to pick up _____ dry cleaning   _____
   next week.

10. When will we know the results of _____   _____
    evaluations?

PRACTICE 10 Writing Sentences with Pronoun-Antecedent Agreement

Referring to the previous practice patterns, write ten similar sentences, making sure to match each pronoun to the appropriate antecedent. Underline the pronoun and circle the antecedent.

1. _____

_____

2. _____

_____

3. _____

_____

4. _____

_____

5. _____

_____

6. _____

_____

7. _____

_____

8. _____

_____

9. _____

_____

10. _____

_____

PRACTICE 11   Editing for Pronoun Use

Edit the following paragraph to correct pronoun use. The first sentence has been done for you. The correct answer is in parentheses. Some sentences are correct. (The following paragraphs are from a student essay, "A Stroke of Bad Luck," by Margaret Ewart.)

On August 25, 1997, I received a phone call that changed the lives of ~~anyone~~ (everyone) in my family. My father had a stroke while traveling from North Carolina to Mississippi. After the detailed phone conversation about my father's condition, I realized that as a supportive and caring daughter, one needed to be at my father's side. Looking at my frail father, partially paralyzed and unable to take care of his own personal needs, I became aware that you had to take care of him throughout the rest of his life. Making the decision to become a primary care giver affected my family by the changes in a father-daughter role, and the loss of family time, which resulted in new attitudes among all family members.

PRACTICE 12   Editing for Pronoun Use

Edit the following paragraph to correct pronoun use. The first sentence has been done for you.

Shortly after I started taking care of my father, I came to realize that there was never any time for ~~me~~ (myself), much less my family. I rarely ever have the time to play with my children, help my daughter with her school work or spend time with my husband. My father requires a tremendous amount of my time, which prevents me from being a mother as well as being a wife. Most of the time I feel as if I am missing out on a great deal of mine children's lives, due to the fact that I have become a primary care giver. I have felt like a prisoner in our own home since the stroke. My husband and I have a great fear of leaving my home in the event that he may need us. My husband tries to take me out for dinner and a movie to give me some sense of relief from all of the stress, but I always decline. Due to her fear of leaving the house because of my new responsibilities, family members are reluctant to make plans with me. They have begun to treat me differently and to see me as a different person.

PRACTICE 13   Editing for Pronoun Use

Edit the following (concluding) paragraph for pronoun usage. The first sentence has been done for you.

As each day brings new obstacles and solutions, ~~you~~ (I) have overcome almost ~~anyone~~ (every one) of them. What was once a difficult situation has become part of everyday life for them. In the midst of taking care of my father, I have realized that you can't help him unless I can help oneself. I was becoming extremely exhausted trying to take care of anything, and I was losing myself. Finally, I realized that I didn't need to be around my father that much, and you could do something to better oneself. Going back to school was the first thing that came into my mind, and I said, "Why not?" So I enrolled in school. I have made a special schedule for my family, my father, my school, and most importantly, myself. Emotionally, I am the happiest that I have ever been in my life, which reflects on any member of your family.

ESL Verbs

A **verb** is a word indicating action, feeling, or being. Verbs can be divided into three classes: action verbs, linking verbs, and helping verbs (see Chapter 3). Additionally the form of the verbs can indicate the time of the action: **present, past,** or **future** (also known as **tense**). Each of these tenses has many forms that we use every day.

The most commonly used tenses are **simple present** and **simple past.**

Present Tense

> **Verbs in the Simple Present Tense**
> Sample verb: to think
>
> | | **Singular** | | **Plural** |
> |---|---|---|---|
> | 1st person | I | think | we think |
> | 2nd person | you | think | you think |
> | 3rd person | he* | | they think |
> | | she } | thinks | |
> | | it | | |
>
> *Use an *-s* or *-es* ending on the verb when the subject is *he, she,* or *it,* or the equivalent.

PRACTICE 1   Using the Present Tense

Write the present tense of the verb in parentheses in the following sentences. (This exercise is taken from a paragraph by student Jeanette Weiland.)

1. While shopping at a perfect store, customers _____ (to be) generally sold products at an inexpensive price.

2. Shoppers _____ (to be) typically _____ (to offer) items that are clearly marked with price tags on each separate package.

3. This _____ (to allow) customers to rapidly and easily choose the product that _____ (to give) them the best buy.

4. There _____ (to be, not) any reasons to look for the price on the store shelf and then have to worry about whether or not the item _____ (to match) the price tag.

5. A perfect store _____ (to do) not only honor its own sales coupons, but it also _____ (to accept) other department store advertised prices and coupons.

6. This _____ (to give) the customers the convenience of shopping at one store instead of having to go to two or three.

7. No matter what store they _____ (to shop) at, these pricing policies _____ (to offer) shoppers an opportunity to receive the best possible price.

PRACTICE 2   Using the Present Tense

Write the present tense of the verb in parentheses in the following sentences. The following paragraph is by student Amber Barton. (In some cases, the present progressive form may be used.)

1. The sights of New York City _____ (to stimulate) the senses.

2. Rural Missouri _____ (to soothe) them.

3. From the Empire State Building to the subway system, the sights and sounds of New York City _____ (to invigorate) the spirit.

4. Lady Liberty _____ (to stand) proudly in the East River with Ellis Island, its now silent companion, and _____ (to evoke) pride in its visitors.

5. The rich hills and valleys of rural Missouri _____ (to be) lovely.

6. They _____ (to pale) in comparison to the stark beauty of New York skyscrapers.

7. A traveler would _____ (to have) to visit more than once to be able to take in all the diverse sights New York City has to offer.

Past Tense
Regular Verbs
Regular verbs are those verbs that form the past tense by adding *-ed* or *-d*. The **simple past tense** is used to refer to an action that began and ended at one time period in the past.

Past Tense of Regular Verbs		
Sample verb: to dance		
	Singular	**Plural**
1st person	(I) danced	(we) danced
2nd person	(you) danced	(you) danced
3rd person	(he, she, it) danced	(they) danced

In addition to simple forms, there are other present and past verb forms. The following table illustrates the most commonly used verb tenses. Each tense expresses a specific time or duration. Students for whom English is a second language should practice the use of each tense in spoken and written English.

Common Verb Tenses
Sample verb: to talk

Tense	First Person Singular	Sample Sentence
present	I talk	I like to talk in a group.
present progressive	I am talking	I am talking on the phone now!
present perfect	I have talked	I have talked about this often.
present perfect progressive	I have been talking	I have been talking since dawn!
past	I talked	I talked to him last night.
past progressive	I was talking	I was talking about my car.
past perfect	I had talked	I had talked before I decided.
past perfect progressive	I had been talking	I had been talking before they sang.
future	I will talk	I will talk to you tomorrow.
future progressive	I will be talking	I will be talking all morning tomorrow.
future perfect	I will have talked	I will have talked enough by then.
future perfect progressive	I will have been talking	I will have been talking for three hours by the time the meeting is over.

Irregular Verbs

Many irregular verbs (more than one hundred in English) do not form the past tense by adding -ed or -d. Some verbs do not change form at all, or they form the past tense by changing the spelling of the entire word (*stem-changing verbs*). The following table lists the most commonly used irregular verbs.

An Alphabetical List of Irregular Verbs

Simple Form	Simple Past	Past Participle
arise	arose	arisen
be	was, were	been
bear	bore	borne/born
beat	beat	beaten/beat
become	became	become
begin	began	begun
bend	bent	bent
bet	bet	bet*
bid	bid	bid
bind	bound	bound
bite	bit	bitten
bleed	bled	bled

*See page 332.

Simple Form	Simple Past	Past Participle
blow	blew	blown
break	broke	broken
breed	bred	bred
bring	brought	brought
broadcast	broadcast	broadcast
build	built	built
burst	burst	burst
buy	bought	bought
cast	cast	cast
catch	caught	caught
choose	chose	chosen
cling	clung	clung
come	came	come
cost	cost	cost
creep	crept	crept
cut	cut	cut
deal	dealt	dealt
dig	dug	dug
do	did	done
draw	drew	drawn
eat	ate	eaten
fall	fell	fallen
feed	fed	fed
feel	felt	felt
fight	fought	fought
find	found	found
fit	fit	fit*
flee	fled	fled
fling	flung	flung
fly	flew	flown
forbid	forbade	forbidden
forecast	forecast	forecast
forget	forgot	forgotten
forgive	forgave	forgiven
forsake	forsook	forsaken
freeze	froze	frozen
get	got	gotten*
give	gave	given
go	went	gone
grind	ground	ground
grow	grew	grown

*See page 332.

Simple Form	Simple Past	Past Participle
hang	hung	hung
have	had	had
hear	heard	heard
hide	hid	hidden
hit	hit	hit
hold	held	held
hurt	hurt	hurt
keep	kept	kept
know	knew	known
lay	laid	laid
lead	led	led
leave	left	left
lend	lent	lent
let	let	let
lie	lay	lain
light	lit/lighted	lit/lighted
lose	lost	lost
make	made	made
mean	meant	meant
meet	met	met
mislay	mislaid	mislaid
mistake	mistook	mistaken
pay	paid	paid
put	put	put
quit	quit	quit*
read	read	read
rid	rid	rid
ride	rode	ridden
ring	rang	rung
rise	rose	risen
run	ran	run
say	said	said
see	saw	seen
seek	sought	sought
sell	sold	sold
send	sent	sent
set	set	set
shake	shook	shaken
shed	shed	shed
shine	shone/shined	shone/shined
shoot	shot	shot

*See page 332.

Simple Form	Simple Past	Past Participle
show	showed	shown/showed
shrink	shrank/shrunk	shrunk
shut	shut	shut
sing	sang	sung
sit	sat	sat
sleep	slept	slept
slide	slid	slid
slit	slit	slit
speak	spoke	spoken
speed	sped/speeded	sped/speeded
spend	spent	spent
spin	spun	spun
spit	spit/spat	spit/spat
split	split	split
spread	spread	spread
spring	sprang/sprung	sprung
stand	stood	stood
steal	stole	stolen
stick	stuck	stuck
sting	stung	stung
stink	stank/stunk	stunk
strike	strove	striven
string	struck	struck/stricken
strive	strung	strung
swear	swore	sworn
sweep	swept	swept
swim	swam	swum
swing	swung	swung
take	took	taken
teach	taught	taught
tear	tore	torn
tell	told	told
think	thought	thought
throw	threw	thrown
thrust	thrust	thrust
understand	understood	understood
undertake	undertook	undertaken
upset	upset	upset
wake	woke/waked	woke/waked
wear	wore	worn
weave	wove	woven

Simple Form	Simple Past	Past Participle
weep	wept	wept
win	won	won
wind	wound	wound
withdraw	withdrew	withdrawn
wring	wrung	wrung
write	wrote	written

*The following are some differences in verb forms between American English and British English.

American	British
bet-bet-bet	*bet-bet-bet* OR *bet-betted-betted*
fit-fit-fit	*fit-fitted-fitted*
get-got-gotten	*get-got-got*
quit-quit-quit	*quit-quitted-quitted*

American: *burn, dream, kneel, lean, leap, learn, smell, spell, spill, spoil* are usually regular: *burned, dreamed, kneeled, leaned, leaped, etc.*

British: simple past and past participle forms of these verbs can be regular but more commonly end with **-t:** *burnt, dreamt, knelt, leant, leapt, learnt, smelt, spelt, spilt, spoilt.*

Source: Azar, Betty S., *Understanding and Using English Grammar*, Volume A. 3rd edition. Englewood Cliffs, New Jersey: Prentice Hall Regents. 18–19.

Some irregular verbs do not follow the stem-changing pattern:

Irregular Verbs That Do Not Change Their Form
(All end in *-t* or *-d*)

Present Form	Past Form	Past Participle
bet	bet	bet
cost	cost	cost
cut	cut	cut
fit	fit	fit
hit	hit	hit
hurt	hurt	hurt
quit	quit	quit
spread	spread	spread

The Verb **Be**

Because the verb *be* is used so often as a helping verb, linking verb, as well as to form verb tense, it is useful to see how irregular the form is.

To Be (Infinitive Form)				
	Present Tense		**Past Tense**	
	Singular	**Plural**	**Singular**	**Plural**
1st person	I **am**	We **are**	I **was**	We **were**
2nd person	You **are**	You **are**	You were	You **were**
3rd person	He, she, it, **is**	They **are**	He, she, it **was**	They **were**

PRACTICE 3 Choosing the Correct Verb Form

Supply the past form of the past tense or the participle in the following sentences.

Example: (sing) For her recital, the soprano <u>sang</u> a variety of arias.

1. (go) Yesterday we _____ to the beach.

2. (go) All summer we have _____ to beaches on the coast.

3. (ride) We _____ the waves with boogie boards for hours in the morning.

4. (blow) The wind _____ violently all afternoon.

5. (lose) We _____ our umbrella and all of our towels.

6. (leave) We _____ the beach after searching up and down the shore for our belongings.

7. (swim) Normally, we have _____ all afternoon during a beach outing.

8. (drive) Yesterday, we _____ home, exhausted and windblown, but ready to return today.

9. (be) Why _____ you absent for three weeks?

10. (lie) The book _____ on the desk yesterday.

PRACTICE 4 Using the Past Tense of Regular and Irregular Verbs

Write the past tense of the verbs in parentheses in the following sentences, taken from a student paragraph.

1. When my mother _____ (to have) hip surgery, I _____ (to assume) responsibility for running the household.

2. I _____ (to know) that I _____ (can) not take care of everything.

3. I _____ (to enlist) some help.

4. My brother and sister _____ (to be) very young, so my Aunt Jessie _____ (to come) every other evening to help babysit.

5. Consequently, I _____ (can) do laundry and prepare some meals for the following week.

6. My neighbor and my best friend, Celeste, also _____ (to help) with food shopping and yard work.

7. After my mother _____ (to come) home from the hospital, there _____ (to be) even more to do.

8. So, every Saturday, I _____ (to pay) a maid service to come in and clean the house.

9. When my mother finally _____ (to be) able to get up and around, we _____ (to go) for a walk.

10. She _____ (to have) tears in her eyes when she _____ (to tell) me how proud she _____ (to be) of how I _____ (to have, to handle) all the responsibilities.

PRACTICE 5 — Using the Past Tense of Regular and Irregular Verbs

Convert the underlined present tense verbs to the past tense. The first sentence has been done for you. This student paragraph was from an essay written by Erin Nelson.

The spooky old houses come (came) to life at night with gruesome decorations. With grotesque carved faces, the jack-o'-lanterns give off an eerie glow. Tombstones line the sidewalk, like a long narrow graveyard; a bloody hand reaches out to grab intruders. Bats as black as the night sky fly in quick circles, darting in the air, and a black cat with razor-sharp fangs crosses the path of the unseen, terrified prey. The ghosts and the goblins sneak around monster-like trees, ready to snatch their next victim.

PRACTICE 6   Using the Past Tense of Regular and Irregular Verbs

In the following paragraphs from the same student essay, cross out all of the present tense verbs, and convert them to the past tense. The first sentence has been done for you.

The wind ~~begins~~ (began) to whip, and the branches of the trees ~~begin~~ (began) to sway like the bones of a forgotten skeleton. The fallen dead leaves whirl around like a vicious tornado. When the fog rolls in, the eyes begin to play tricks. A monster! With the fog comes the mist that makes you chilled down to the bone.

Screams echo from all directions. A witch, a vampire, and a ghost fly by; consequently, they disappear down the dark damp street. The hairy werewolf howls, and the musty old mummy moans. Next comes Freddy—with blood dripping from his razorblade fingers.

One night of the year is all it takes to get the heart pounding and the blood flowing. To be out on this night is quite a fright.

Additional Practice for Complex Verb Forms
Present Perfect/Past Perfect
How to form the present/past perfect:

Present perfect tense:	*has* or *have* + past participle of the main verb
	Has talked (singular)
	Have talked (plural)
Past perfect tense:	*had* + past participle of the main verb
	Had talked (singular and plural)

When to Use the Present/Past Perfect Tenses
The **present perfect tense** is used to describe an action that started in the past and continues to the present time. It can also be used to describe an action that has recently taken place or an action in which the exact past time is indefinite.

Julia <u>has played</u> with the symphony for five years.

This example means that Julia began playing with the orchestra five years ago and is still playing with the symphony today.

Asim has traveled to Pakistan several times recently.

This example indicates no specific time for the travel mentioned. If the specific time were to be emphasized, the simple past would have been used.

Asim traveled to Pakistan last December.

The **past perfect tense** is used to describe an action that occurred in the past before another point in time in the past or before another past activity.

Julia had played with the symphony for five years before she retired.

This example means that Julia played in the symphony for five years, and then she retired. All of this activity took place in the past.

PRACTICE 7 Using the Present and Past Perfect Tenses

In the following sentences, circle the correct form of the verb tense: past perfect, present perfect, simple past, or simple present.

1. Elena prefers to wear contact lenses; she (wore, has worn) them for several years.

2. Dane (sang, has sung) in the chorus of the musical for two years.

3. Yesterday, George (bought, has bought) a new computer.

4. Susan (was, has been) a teacher for twenty years this September.

5. The governor flew to North Dakota and (has driven, drove) miles before he reached Grand Forks.

6. The news commentator announced that the dictator (fled, has fled) the country some time in the last twenty-four hours.

7. The news commentator also reported that the dictator (fled, had fled) the country before the army arrived in the capital.

8. The year David graduated, he was given a new computer; he (planned, had planned) for this purchase for four years.

9. Insook says she (found, has found) the perfect house.

10. Insook said she (has found, had found) the perfect house before the winter weather arrived.

In the following paragraph, fill in the blanks with the correct form of the present perfect, simple present, or simple past tense.

Since Beatrice arrived in the United States from Colombia, she

_____ (to study) at this college for two years. In that time, she

_____ (to take) many courses. First, she _____ (to

study) English primarily, taking a few mathematics courses to complete her

requirements. After her English improved, she _____ (to study)

many other subjects, such as sociology, computer technology, and educa-

tion. For several months, she _____ (to tutor) many students who

are new immigrants to this country. Additionally, she _____ (to

learn) that she enjoys working with small children. Even though she

_____ (to study) to be a lawyer in Colombia, she now

_____ (to plan) to become an elementary school teacher, so that

she can continue her work with immigrant children.

Forming the Passive Voice

The **passive voice** is chosen when the actor of the sentence is not important or when the writer wishes to avoid naming the subject.

In the passive voice, the object of an active verb becomes the subject of the passive verb. The form of the verb becomes *be* **+ past participle.**

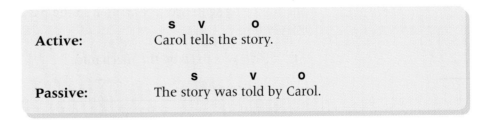

	s **v** **o**
Active:	Carol tells the story.
	s **v** **o**
Passive:	The story was told by Carol.

Use of the Active Voice Compared with the Passive Voice

In the **active voice,** the subject of the sentence does the acting (action verb/ transitive verb).

In the **passive voice,** the subject is acted upon.

Example

The students finished the project. (subject is *students;* active verb is *finished*)

The project was finished by the students. (subject is *project* [acted upon by the students]; passive verb is *was finished*)

Most writing is done in the active voice for direct, concise expression.

The following list shows the conversion of the active to the passive for the important verb tenses:

	Active	**Passive**
Present	Carol tells the story.	The story is told by Carol.
Present progressive	Carol is telling the story.	The story is being told by Carol.
Present perfect	Carol has told the story.	The story has been told by Carol.
Simple past	Carol told the story.	The story was told by Carol.
Past progressive	Carol was telling the story.	The story was being told by Carol.
Past perfect	Carol had told the story.	The story had been told by Carol.
Future	Carol will tell the story.	The story will be told by Carol.
Future progressive	Carol will be telling the story.	The story is going to be told by Carol.
Future perfect	Carol will have told the story.	The story will have been told by Carol.

Going to is often used instead of *will.*

PRACTICE 9   Writing Sentences with Active Verbs (Voice)

The following sentences are written in the passive voice. Rewrite each in the active voice.

1. The car was fixed by the mechanic.

_____

2. The wedding will be planned by his fiancée and her mother.

_____

3. The test is given by the instructor.

_____

4. The plans for the house had been created by the architect.

_____

5. The sermon was delivered by the pastor.

_____

6. His new car was polished every day, even when it rained.

_____

7. Monique's records were misplaced by the Human Resource Department.

_____

8. The diamond ring was stolen by her envious friend.

_____

9. The cello was tuned before the concert started.

_____

10. The homes in the area were overpriced before the recession.

_____

11. The child's feelings were easily hurt.

_____

PRACTICE 10   Writing Sentences with Passive Verbs (Voice)

The following sentences are written in the active voice. Rewrite each in the passive voice.

1. Josh ate the strawberry shortcake.

_____

2. Congress voted to increase Social Security payments.

_____

3. The doctors isolated the virus causing the disease.

_____

4. The youngest player won the chess tournament.

_____

5. The skiers chose the hardest, steepest run.

_____

6. He revised the report several times before presenting it to the class.

_____

7. Every night when he unloads the dishwasher, he breaks a bowl or a plate.

_____

8. The manager overpriced the new shipment of clothes.

_____

9. The new company collected the trash and recycling on Tuesday instead of Wednesday.

_____

_____

10. The family locked the door every day after they had been robbed.

_____

PRACTICE 11   Using the Correct Verb Form and Tense

Underline all the verbs in the following paragraph. Change the tense of the verb from past to present. Additional changes in the paragraph may be necessary as well.

Time stood still as I tried to reconcile in my mind what was happening in my cheery breakfast nook on that dreary Tuesday morning; a traumatic event happened there; consequently, my life has been changed forever. Before this event, I felt snug and secure in my roomy, comfortable two story home, peacefully nestled on three gently rolling acres where my loyal and intimidating German shepherds were on patrol, in a private neighborhood near suburban St. Louis. Two young men and their decision to invade my home took all of that away from me.

PRACTICE 12 Using the Correct Verb Form and Tense

In the following paragraph, supply the correct form/tense of the verb in the spaces provided. The first sentence has been done for you. Be careful to use the perfect tenses when appropriate.

Perceptions of a small town all too often <u>are</u> (to be) the same. Movie-

makers _____ (to create) the ideal vision of what a rural

American town should _____ (to look like), and society

_____ (to believe) what moviemakers create. I_____

(to live) in a large town most of my life; my experience with small towns (to

involve) _____ only driving through them on vacation. What I

_____ (to see) during my trips _____ (to give) me

the same perception as most of society. My limited views would soon

_____ (to be) expan-ded when my first experience away from home

_____ (to land) me in a small Michigan town on the U.S.-Canadian

border.

Subject-Verb Agreement

Subjects and verbs in the present tense (as well as in the past and future) should agree in number. Thus, singular subjects require verbs with singular endings, and plural subjects require verbs with plural endings. The following examples illustrate correct subject-verb agreement:

> The *woman* (singular subject) *takes* (singular verb form) a cab.
> The *men* (plural subject) *take* (plural verb form) a cab.

PRACTICE 13 Using Subject-Verb Agreement

In each of the following sentences, choose the correct form of the verb in the parentheses. First, underline the subject and decide whether it is singular or plural. Next, underline the verb form that correctly agrees with the subject.

Example: <u>He</u> always (carry, <u>carries</u>) a credit card in his wallet.

1. They (work, works) at the factory on the north side of town.

2. The group (walk, walks) in the mall every morning.

3. The senate (vote, votes) on legislation.

4. He (eat, eats) at the diner every Thursday after work.

5. The boy (run, runs) to the schoolyard to play basketball.

6. She (look, looks) like a skilled basketball player.

7. The team (eat, eats) steak and potatoes prior to each game.

8. The band (play, plays) at a local club every Friday.

9. His class (meet, meets) three times per week.

10. People (vote, votes) every four years in the presidential election.

PRACTICE 14   Using Subject-Verb Agreement

Find and correct the errors in subject-verb agreement in the following para-graph. First, underline the subject in each sentence. Next, find the verb and correct those verbs that do not agree with the subject. The first sentence has been done for you.

> The spooky old <u>houses</u> ~~comes~~ **come** to life at night with gruesome decora-tions. With grotesque carved faces, the jack-o'-lanterns gives off an eerie glow. Tombstones line the sidewalk; beware of the bloody hands, for they may grab intruders. Bats as black as the night sky flies around in the air, and a black cat with razor-sharp fangs cross the path of terrified prey. The ghosts and the goblins sneaks around monster-like trees, ready to grab their next victim with ease.

Compound Subject-Verb Agreement

In a sentence there may be more than one subject **(compound subject),** and the verb form chosen must agree in tense and number with the subjects as shown in the examples below.

If the compound subjects are connected by *and*, the verb is usually plural.

> Fredric and Elise *are* working together on the project.

However, if the compound subjects are thought of as a unit, a singular verb is used.

> Macaroni and cheese *is* a favorite dish for children.

If the compound subject is connected with the *either/or, neither/nor, not only/but also* correlative conjunctions, the verb must agree with the following rules:

If both subjects are singular, the verb is singular.

> Either Fredric or Elise *is* going to turn in the project to the boss.

If both subjects are plural, the verb is plural.

> The violins and cellos *need* to rehearse their parts with the conductor.

If one subject is singular and the other is plural, the verb agrees with the subject closest to the verb.

> My sisters or my friend plans all my formal gatherings.

PRACTICE 15 Using Subject-Verb Agreement with Compound Subject

Circle the correct verb in each sentence.

Example: During the summer, parents and children ((look), looks) forward to vacation.

1. At the high school, students and a teacher (work, works) on a project in archeology.

2. The committee and the administrators (plan, plans) the social activities for the year.

3. Both the lack of exercise and eating too much rich food (cause/causes) serious health problems.

4. Whining, begging, and nagging (indicate, indicates) a lack of problem-solving skills.

5. Television and junk food (is, are) a bad diet combination.

6. Peanut butter and jelly (is, are) his favorite sandwich.

7. His mother and father, on the other hand, often (enjoy, enjoys) going out to the show.

8. Not only children but also adults (need, needs) to be aware of the level of violence in the media.

9. My coworkers or my supervisor (are, is) going to advise me.

10. A banana or raisins (make, makes) a high-energy snack.

PRACTICE 16   Using Subject-Verb Agreement with Compound Subject

In each sentence, put two lines under the verb that agrees with the subject.

Example: The adults and children in the family often (selects, <u><u>select</u></u>) a Mexican restaurant for dinner.

1. Rice, refried beans, and corn cakes (accompany, accompanies) the serving of enchiladas.

2. Either flour tortillas or fried tortillas (come, comes) with dinner.

3. Flan, fried ice cream, or pastry (is, are) served as dessert.

4. In American restaurants, hot dogs or hamburgers (seem, seems) to be a favorite lunch.

5. French fries or, in some cases, hash browns (complement, complements) the burgers.

6. Either catsup, mustard, or both (add, adds) to the uniquely American flavor.

7. As a beverage, a soda or a shake (complete, completes) the order.

8. Neither Wendy's nor Burger King (deserve, deserves) the reputation of McDonald's.

9. Often, McDonald's, Wendy's, and Burger King (compete, competes) for business at the same intersection.

10. Enchiladas as well as burgers for dinner (have, has) been known to ruin many diets!

PRACTICE 17   Editing for Subject-Verb Agreement

Edit the following paragraph for subject-verb agreement. (The first sentence has been done for you.) Some sentences may be correct. The following paragraphs are taken from a student essay, "Nuke Nuclear Energy" by Danny Butler.

The question of nuclear energy ~~are~~ (is) a debate that has caused

protests and conflicts since its discovery. Nuclear energy have the potential

to be a remarkably effective energy source. Using the products of fission

(the splitting of atoms to create energy) military experts has used nuclear

energy for the manufacturing of defense weapons. Resources such as wood,

oil, coal, and other fossil fuels can be preserved with the use of nuclear energy to produce power. Despite the possible benefits to society, nuclear energy are extremely dangerous due to the possibility of explosion causing mass pollution, creation of nuclear weapons, and production of radioactive waste.

PRACTICE 18   Editing for Subject-Verb Agreement

Edit the following paragraph for subject-verb agreement. The first sentence has been done for you.

Several military and political leaders have suggested that nuclear energy can greatly ~~contributes~~ (contribute) to world peace by allowing for countries to have nuclear defense systems. According to this theory, when an aggressive nation launch a nuclear attack, the opposing nation will always have time to counterattack, thus creating a stalemate. Weapons of mass destruction created from nuclear energy has the potential to cause such severe damage that the entire planet could be affected. Scientists estimate that the nuclear explosions in a major nuclear war could kill 500 million people. But 4 billion more people could starve to death in the next century because of nuclear winter. Nuclear energy have the potential to cause irreversible damage to the Earth. Because this damage could possibly causes the extinction of all life, nuclear energy are not a safe and practical energy source.

PRACTICE 19   Editing for Subject-Verb Agreement

Edit the following (concluding) paragraph for subject-verb agreement. The first sentence has been done for you.

The debate over nuclear energy ~~are~~ (is) sure to be a very important topic in years to come. Standing up against using nuclear energy can possibly lead to the eventual abolishment of many nuclear weapons as well as the protection of the environment. Hopefully, we learns from our mistakes and will not repeat the tragic catastrophes of such accidents as that in Chernobyl. By finding alternate sources of energy, we can solve the nuclear energy crisis and helps to save the resources for generations to come.

(ESL) Adjectives

An **adjective** is a word that modifies (or describes) a noun or pronoun. Although adjectives usually come before the nouns they describe, they can also follow the noun (in the predicate of the sentence).

> **Examples**
> The *glistening* ocean sparkled in the sunset.
> The coffee tasted *bitter*.

Adjectives can be **objective** (describing nouns with sensory details) or **subjective** (describing concepts, feelings, ideas in more general terms). Both are useful in good writing and enhance meaning, especially in combination.

Objective Adjectives	Subjective Adjectives
glowing	beautiful
crashing	harsh
stabbing	painful
twisted	ugly
strident	annoying
tender	loving

PRACTICE 1   Using Adjectives

Complete each of the following sentences with an appropriate adjective from the list below. Use each adjective once.

beautiful	painful	young	red	large
brilliant	stuffy	rusted	broken	creative

1. The _____ star shone in the cold, night sky.

2. The actress was _____.

3. Hawks and eagles are _____ birds of prey.

4. The _____ metal on the rail of the shipwreck began to separate from the hull.

5. My dog had a _____ rash on his hind legs.

6. The loss of the championship game was very _____ after the winning season.

7. The room became warm and _____ after all the students arrived.

8. The _____ glowing sunset over the ocean was her favorite view.

9. A _____ window was the only clue to the robbery.

10. When the kitten was _____, he would bounce on the furniture.

PRACTICE 2   Identifying Adjectives

Underline the adjectives in the following passage from a student essay by Stephanie Higgs.

1. Thunderstorms the previous night had settled into a steady, rhythmic shower by daylight.

2. I was alone in the house following my predictable routine.

3. Then, I heard the scraping of the vinyl floor trim on the French door against the ceramic tiles.

4. As I rounded the corner, what I saw made fear rise in my throat like green bile forced up from the pit of my stomach.

5. As soon as I saw them, panic increased my heart rate, bringing it to ear-shattering crescendos until I thought I would go deaf or explode.

6. Incapacitating shock and disbelief bordering on denial paralyzed my entire body.

7. I stared at two masked men wielding knives, standing in my breakfast room and heading straight toward me.

8. Walking past the wall phone, in one deft move, they dropped the receiver to the floor and were right in front of me with a cold, steel blade to my throat.

9. While looking into the cold, dark eyes of the one who seemed to be in charge, I heard someone who strangely sounded like me, asking, "What are you here for?"

10. Gripped by the icy fingers of insanity, I heard myself laughing as I was pushed down onto my bedroom floor.

ESL Adverbs

An **adverb** is a word that modifies (describes) a verb or an adjective. Often adverbs end in –*ly*. Another test to identify adverbs is to ask whether it answers one of the questions *where, how,* or *when.* Adverbs describe the action of a passage; in some cases, they refer to other adverbs to intensify meaning. As with adjectives, the careful use of effective adverbs can improve the style.

Examples

Lisa stormed *angrily* up the stairs. (modifies the verb *stormed*)

He was *very* cold. (modifies the adjective *cold*)

The guests were *too* early to dinner. (modifies the adverb *early*)

Commonly Used Adverbs

happily	harshly	quietly	sadly	rudely
softly	perfectly	poorly	politely	slowly
sadly	loudly	quickly	carefully	very

PRACTICE 1   Using Adverbs

Complete each of the following sentences with an appropriate adverb from the list below. Use each adverb once.

softly	loudly	menacingly	rudely	dangerously
honestly	perfectly	poorly	swiftly	carefully

1. The bird chirped _____.

2. The intruder glared _____ at the inhabitants.

3. She sang _____ during the concert.

4. The school bus full of children rocked _____ back and forth.

5. The figure in the drawing was shaped _____.

6. _____, I did not know where I put my keys!

7. The _____ phrased melody drifted from the practice room.

8. The crowd jeered _____ at the referee when he overlooked the foul.

9. _____ planned, the ceremony dragged on for hours.

10. The students left the classroom _____, before the teacher could assign more homework.

PRACTICE 2	**Using Adverbs in a Paragraph**

Choose one sentence in the previous exercise as a topic sentence. Then write a ten-sentence descriptive/narrative paragraph using adverbs in each sentence to modify your verbs and adjectives. Do not forget that intensifiers, such as _very_, are also useful adverbs. Underline your adjectives and circle your adverbs. (See Chapters 10 and 11 for descriptive and narrative techniques.) Compare your answers with those of fellow students.

_____

_____

_____

_____

_____

_____

_____

_____

_____

_____

Conjunctions

A **conjunction** is a connecting word. There are three categories of conjunctions discussed in this text: _coordinating conjunctions_, _subordinating conjunctions_, and _adverbial conjunctions_ (also known as conjunctive adverbs).

Coordinating conjunctions (see list below) join two equal words or groups of words. See Chapters 3 and 4 for extensive instruction and practice with these conjunctions.

Coordinating Conjunctions

but   or   yet   for   and   nor   so

Examples

Gloria is sweet, _but_ she becomes angry if she is deceived.

The students brought bread, cheese, fruit, _and_ chocolate to the picnic.

Subordinating conjunctions connect a dependent clause/idea with an independent clause. See a list of the most commonly used subordinating conjunctions below. Refer to Chapter 7 for a thorough discussion of the use of these conjunctions.

Subordinating Conjunctions

after	if	when
although	since	whenever
as	though	wherever
because	unless	whether
before	until	while

Examples

Before the game was over, several members of the team were injured.
Her test scores improved *because* she had begun to get more sleep.

Adverbial conjunctions are connecting words that transition from one idea to the next or from one independent clause to another by adding emphasis or direction. See the following list for the most frequently used adverbial conjunctions. Refer to Chapters 5 and 8 for thorough discussion and practice with the use of these conjunctions.

Adverbial Conjunctions

accordingly	however	now
additionally	incidentally	otherwise
also	indeed	similarly
anyway	likewise	still
besides	meanwhile	then
certainly	moreover	thereafter
finally	nevertheless	thus
furthermore	next	undoubtedly
hence	nonetheless	

Examples

The winter days dragged in February; *additionally*, blizzards left six feet of snow on the ground.
Nevertheless, the stores began to advertise sandals and summer dresses.

Interjections

Interjections are words that express intense or sudden feelings or reactions. These words are often expressed forcefully, as in *Help!* or *Watch out!* and are followed by exclamation points if they are the entire sentence. If the words are attached to a sentence, they are followed by a comma. (See Chapter 8 regarding introductory words.)

Interjections are rarely used in formal expository writing. They are most often used in narrative or creative writing in which there is realistic dialogue.

> **Examples**
> *Wait!* You forgot your receipt!
> *Well*, now what should I do?

Clauses and Phrases

Independent and Dependent Clauses

A **clause** is a group of related words containing both a subject and a verb. There are two types of clauses: *independent clauses* and *dependent clauses*. **Independent clauses** can stand alone as a complete sentence. A **dependent clause** (or subordinate clause) begins with subordinating words/conjunctions and cannot stand alone as a sentence (see Chapter 7 for more information on dependent clauses).

> **Examples**
> We went shopping during the holidays. *Independent clause*
> (subject is *we;* verb is *went*)
> although we went shopping during the holidays *Dependent clause*
> (subordinating conjunction is *although;* subject is *we;* verb is *went*)
> Carl and Louisa were often late to class. *Independent clause*
> (subject is *Carl and Louisa;* verb is *were*)
> because Carl and Louisa were often late to class *Dependent clause*
> subordinating conjunction is *because;* subject is *Carl and Louisa;*
> (verb is *were*)

Phrases

A **phrase** is a group of related words missing a subject, verb, or both subject and verb. Phrases are used in sentences to complete thoughts or add descriptive detail; they may be restrictive or nonrestrictive (see page 411). To avoid problems with ambiguous meaning or errors in punctuation, phrases must be carefully placed next to the noun, verb, or other parts of speech to which the phrase refers.

There are several types of phrases used as modifiers in sentences: *prepositional phrases, participial phrases, gerund phrases, infinitive phrases*, and *absolute phrases*.

Prepositions and Prepositional Phrases

Prepositions connect a noun or pronoun to the rest of the sentence, often showing location or time.

Common Prepositions

about	before	despite	of	to
above	behind	down	off	toward
across	below	during	on	under
after	beneath	for	out	until
against	beside	from	over	up
along	besides	in	since	upon
among	between	into	through	with
around	beyond	like	throughout	within
at	by	near	till	without

An important element of English sentences is the prepositional phrase (**PP**). It consists of a preposition (**PREP**) and its object (**O**). The object of a preposition is a noun or pronoun.

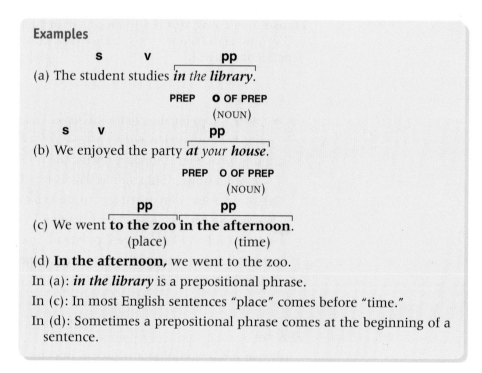

Examples

              S   V   pp

(a) The student studies *in the library*.

                                 PREP   O OF PREP
                                        (NOUN)

              S   V   pp

(b) We enjoyed the party *at your house*.

                                 PREP O OF PREP
                                       (NOUN)

                 pp   pp

(c) We went **to the zoo in the afternoon**.
             (place)   (time)

(d) **In the afternoon,** we went to the zoo.

In (a): *in the library* is a prepositional phrase.

In (c): In most English sentences "place" comes before "time."

In (d): Sometimes a prepositional phrase comes at the beginning of a sentence.

PRACTICE 1   **Identifying Prepositional Phrases**

Find the subjects (**S**), verbs (**V**), objects (**O**), and prepositional phrases (**PP**) in the following sentences. Underscore the prepositional phrases.

                  S   V   O   PP

Example: Jack put the letter in the mailbox.

1. The children walked to school.

2. Beethoven wrote nine symphonies.

3. Mary did her homework at the library.

4. Bells originated in Asia.

5. Chinese printers created the first paper money in the world.

6. The cat ran up the stairs, into the family room, and over the sofa.

7. Before spring arrives in the Midwest, there can be many bitter snowstorms in March.

8. (You) Do not come to class without your textbook, your notebook, your pen, and your homework.

9. Throughout the community, there are many individuals who would like to explore new career options.

10. He found his glasses under the sofa cushions.

PRACTICE 2   Identifying Prepositional Phrases

In the following student paragraph by Trevor Cambell, label the subjects (**S**) and verbs (**V**), and underline and label the prepositional phrases (**PP**). The first sentence has been done for you.

PP   S   PP
After World War II, countless GI's returned home with extra money to spend.

Almost overnight, custom shops sprung up in Southern California, catering to the Flathead owner. The Flathead-powered Ford was cheap and plentiful, making this motor a prime candidate to customize. Within a few years, the Ford Flathead V-8 became the popular choice among custom builders; this power plant, combined with a light-bodied chassis, was considered a winning combination at the dragstrip. Success is often copied, a circumstance which, in turn, further established the Flathead presence.

PRACTICE 3   Writing a Paragraph and Identifying Prepositional Phrases

Write a ten-sentence paragraph in the space provided. You may use a paragraph you have written for another assignment in this class. (See Chapters 9 through 17 for topics and techniques.) Analyze each sentence for subjects (**S**), verbs (**V**), and prepositional phrases (**PP**).

_____

_____

_____

_____

_____

_____

_____

_____

_____

Participial Phrases

A **participial phrase** is a group of words consisting of a participle and its completing words. All verbs have present participle and past participle forms.

> **Examples**
>
> *Staring at the blank computer screen,* Martin found himself unable to finish his essay. (present participle form)
>
> *Interrupted by the demands of her hungry two-year-old,* she could not finish reading the paper. (past participle form)
>
> *Walking down the hall,* he was hit by the door as it flew open at the end of class. (present participle form)
>
> *Bewildered by the question,* the student could not finish the test. (past participle form)

Gerund Phrases

A **gerund** is the *–ing* form of a verb that functions as a noun in the sentence. A **gerund phrase** includes a gerund and its complete words.

> **Examples**
>
> *Dancing* is her favorite activity. (*Dancing* functions as the subject of the sentence)
>
> *Writing a collection of poems* remains Sophia's secret hobby. (The gerund phrase functions as the subject of the sentence)
>
> Employees will not be paid without *completing the weekly projects.* (The gerund phrase functions as the object of the preposition *without*)

In some cases, the possessive form of a noun or pronoun precedes a gerund:

> ### Examples
> The parents were thrilled with *their son's removing all of his tattoos.*
> *Her dancing in the moonlight* amazed the children.

Infinitive Phrases

An **infinitive phrase** is a group of words consisting of *to* plus a verb and its completing words. An infinitive phrase can function as a noun, adjective, or adverb.

> ### Examples
> *To read* is the best way to study grammar. (The infinitive phrase functions as a noun, the subject of the sentence)
> Disneyland is one of the best places *to visit while on vacation.* (The infinitive phrase functions as an adjective and modifies the noun *places*)
> Her daughter was too nervous *to play the piano in front of an audience.* (The infinitive phrase functions as an adverb, modifying the adjective *nervous*)

Absolute Phrases

An **absolute phrase** is a group of words consisting of a noun or pronoun and a participle (not the regular verb form) plus any other completing words. Absolute phrases modify the entire sentence and cannot be punctuated as a complete sentence.

> ### Examples
> *Their project nearly completed,* the painters began to clean their equipment. (notice the past participle *completed* used in the phrase)
> The violinist, *her arms and shoulders aching with pain*, practiced long hours every night. (the present participle *aching* is used in this verb phrase)

PRACTICE 4   Identifying Phrases and Clauses

In the blank to the side of each group of words, write **IC** if the group is an independent clause, **DC** if the group of words is a dependent clause, and **P** if the group of words is a phrase. If the group of words is a phrase, identify the type of phrase.

Examples <u>P (prepositional)</u> under the floor.

1. _____ he was born near Los Angeles, California.

2. _____ to purchase a new car.

3. _____ until the day he died.

4. _____ even if she used the material provided.

5. _____ hidden in the loft.

6. _____ playing badminton.

7. _____ when the long winter finally ends.

8. _____ the weather being harsh and changeable.

9. _____ while she sat by the ashes of the fire.

10. _____ to complete the assignment.

PRACTICE 5   Writing Sentences with Phrases and Clauses

Convert the dependent clauses and phrases from the previous practice into complete sentences, using correct punctuation. Underline the phrase or dependent clause in the finished sentence. Label the independent clauses as correct.

1. _____

2. _____

3. _____

4. _____

5. _____

6. _____

7. _____

8. _____

9. _____

10. _____

PRACTICE 6   Identifying Phrases and Clauses

In the following paragraph from Chapter 16, "Definition," underline phrases once, identifying the type of phrase over the words, and underline the dependent clauses twice. The first sentence has been done for you.

Prep.

Soul music is a combination and merging of gospel and blues, two African

Adj.

American musical styles. While blues praised the worldly desires of the flesh, gos-

pel extolled the virtues of spiritualism. This opposition of themes was melded

into wide ranging and extremely diverse style, full of passion, pride, and opti-

mism, mixed with the historical emotionof pain and discrimination.

Misplaced and Dangling Modifiers

Misplaced modifying phrases modify the wrong word in a sentence or are placed so that it is not clear which word is being described.

Example	Incorrect:	The courier delivered the material to the vice president *in the red envelope.*
	Correct:	The courier delivered the material *in the red envelope* to the vice president.

Dangling modifying phrases do not seem to modify anything in the sentence, or they may appear to describe a word that makes no logical sense. Dangling modifiers usually occur at the beginning of the sentence. To correct the sentence, add the correct subject/verb to the phrase, **or** restructure the sentence for accurate meaning.

Example	Incorrect:	*After painting the house,* the furniture was rearranged.
	Correct:	*After painting the house*, we rearranged the furniture.

PRACTICE 7 Correcting Misplaced and Dangling Modifiers

The sentences below have misplaced or dangling modifying phrases. Underline the misplaced/dangling phrases and rewrite the sentences so that the meaning is clear and accurate.

Example: David fed the birds in his robe and slippers.

In his robe and slippers, David fed the birds.

1. The waiter swept the crumbs away from the couple on the tablecloth.

_____

_____

2. Walking down the hall, the door hit her in the face.

_____

_____

3. Working on his homework, the dog barked all evening.

_____

_____

4. The saleswoman sold the suit to the customer that needed mending.

_____

_____

5. We enjoyed the performance in the theater which we had paid twenty dollars to see.

_____

_____

6. Singing in the shower, the cat suddenly dashed across the room, and the dog began to howl.

_____

_____

7. The car is in the garage with two cartons of ice cream unlocked.

_____

_____

8. Wrapped up in a mummy costume, I enjoyed my son's preparations for Halloween.

_____

_____

9. While enjoying the family picnic, the table suddenly fell to the ground.

_____

_____

10. The teacher gave the students an essay exam which was unprepared.

_____

_____

| PRACTICE 8 | Avoiding Dangling and Misplaced Modifiers |

In this paragraph by student writer Stephanie Weidermann, combine the following sentences by converting at least one of the sentences to a phrase or clause. Be careful to avoid misplaced or dangling modifiers. When sentence combining, first cross out all repeated words and phrases after they have been stated once and change verb forms if necessary.

> **Example**   A photographer achieves a worthwhile photograph.
> The photographer sets the scene.
> He correctly develops the negative.
> He creatively enlarges the print.
>
> One correct option: (By setting the scene,) (correctly developing the negative,) and (creatively enlarging the print,) a photographer can achieve a worthwhile photograph.

1.1 First, the photographer measures the light that the camera is reading.

1.2 The light is from the scene.

1.3 The photographer uses a gray card.

_____

_____

2.1 The aperture should be adjusted.

2.2 The meter should be floating in the center of its scale.

2.3 This ensures the picture will not be under- or overexposed.

_____

_____

3.1 The film is loaded onto a developing reel.

3.2 This is done in complete darkness.

3.3 The film is placed into a series of chemical liquids.

3.4 The liquids develop and fix the negative.

_____

_____

4.1 Next, the negative is enlarged.

4.2 The enlarging process is achieved by placing the negative into an enlarger.

4.3 This is followed by shining a light through the negative onto paper.

4.4 The paper is resin coated.

_____

_____

5.1 The photographer can create a variety of special effects.

5.2 The photographer manipulates the amount of light.

5.3 The photographer manipulates the amount of time.

_____

_____

6.1 The paper is run through another series of chemical liquid baths.

6.2 The paper is finally allowed to dry.

_____

_____

Types of Sentences

There are four basic types of sentences: simple, compound, complex, and compound-complex.

The Simple Sentence

A *simple sentence* contains one independent clause. An independent clause consists of a subject, a verb (or compound subjects or verbs), and sufficient meaning to stand on its own as a complete idea. (See Chapter 2 for a detailed discussion and exercises.)

> **Examples**
> The ship sailed into port.
> A tree fell during the storm.

The Compound Sentence

Compound sentences contain two independent clauses. These independent clauses can be combined using a process called **coordination.** There are three methods of coordination: combining two independent clauses with a comma and a coordinating conjunction, combining two independent clauses with a semicolon, and combining two independent clauses with a semicolon, followed by an adverbial conjunction and comma. (See Chapters 3, 4, and 5 for a detailed discussion and exercises.)

Examples

The bird landed on the branch, **and** it warbled a beautiful song.

Satellites circle the earth; the Space Shuttle can be considered a satellite.

She intended to turn in the paper on time; **however,** her car broke down on the way to school.

The Complex Sentence

Complex sentences combine an independent clause and a dependent clause using a process called **subordination.** There are two common methods of subordination: adding a dependent clause after an independent clause, and preceding the independent clause with a dependent clause and a comma. (See Chapter 7 for a detailed discussion and exercises.) The dependent clauses are *italicized* in the examples below.

Examples

The students could not enter the building *because the smokers had created a toxic cloud of tobacco smoke in front of the door.*

If the team wins the game, the students will cheer the athletes.

The Compound-Complex Sentence

A *compound-complex* sentence combines a complete *compound sentence* with a dependent clause or a complete complex sentence.

Examples

The bird landed on the branch, and it warbled a beautiful song while the cat crouched on the ground below.

If the team wins the game, the students will first cheer the athletes and then they will head into town for pizza and hamburgers.

(ESL) Additional Practice with Sentences

Correcting Comma Splices and Run-Ons

PRACTICE 1   **Correcting Comma Splices and Run-Ons**

Correct the errors in the following sentences.

Example: Jason knocked down all the cartons, He put them out with the recycling.

1. My brother won a goldfish at the school carnival, my mother threw it away the next day when he was at school.

2. The students are very passionate about the proposed increase in tuition, they are conducting a sit-in in the administration building.

3. The final paper will be due on the last day of class students should come to see the professor if they have questions.

4. The cost of oil is going up, the public still prefers to buy large, expensive, gas-guzzling SUVs.

5. Storms, flash flooding, and hail made driving difficult the cars on the highway were speeding as though the road were clear and dry!

6. Fredrick suffered from back spasms the drugs he took made him very drowsy.

7. Although Damien was hostile at the beginning of the course, he was an enthusiastic writer at the end of the semester his final essay won the campus writing award.

8. The accountant submitted his resignation the president of the company accepted it immediately.

9. The audience at the last concert by the symphony orchestra could not refrain from coughing the conductor actually stopped the performance and waited for the coughing to cease.

10. The exotic flowers of the botanical garden provided a colorful background for the wedding ceremony, the weather, however, was cloudy and threatening.

PRACTICE 2   **Correcting Comma Splices and Run-Ons**

Correct the punctuation and any other errors in the following sentences, taken from a student essay, "Why We Carp and Harp," by Mary Ann Hogan. (Some sentences may be correct.) Then combine them into a paragraph. Include the example sentence in your paragraph.

Read All About It . . . To read the full essay from which this paragraph is excerpted, see page 439.

Example: Nagging, of course, has been around since the first cave husband refused to take out the cave garbage, but linguists, psychologists, and other scholars are just now piecing together what nagging really is, why we do it, and how to stop it before we nag each other to death.

1. Common perception holds that a nag is an unreasonably demanding wife who carps at a long-suffering husband but in truth, nagging is universal.

2. Thus, doctors can nag patients to lose their potbellies accountants can nag timid clients to buy low bosses can nag workers to get things done on time special interest groups can nag the public to save the planet and send money and the government can nag everyone to pay their taxes on time, to abstain from drink if they're pregnant, and, while they're at it, to Buy American.

3. And when the going gets desperate, the desperate get nagging.

4. Our recession-plagued nation, experts say, could be headed for a giant nag jag.

_____

_____

_____

_____

_____

_____

_____

_____

_____

_____

_____

_____

_____

Correcting Comma Splices, Run-ons, and Fragments

PRACTICE 3 | **Correcting Sentence Fragments**

In the following paragraph underline the fragments, then correct them by connecting them with correct punctuation to the surrounding sentences. See the student essay, "Halloween Havoc," by student author Erin Nelson, for the "correct" version!

Read All About It . . .

To read the full essay from which this paragraph is excerpted, see page 421.

When the wind begins to howl. Like the wolves. And the Leaves begin

to fall. The time is coming nearer to the creepiest night of the year. The

silvery moon is full; the clouds roll. Across the sky. A chill is sent down spines, and the neck hairs stand on end. What could it be? Halloween. All

Hallows Eve can be the spookiest night of the year. Because of the creepy

decorations, the chilling weather, and the scary goblins.

PRACTICE 4

In the following sentences taken from "Halloween Havoc," complete the sentence fragments with your own words.

Read All About It ...

To read the full essay from which this paragraph is excerpted, see page 421.

1. _____ with gruesome decorations.

2. Bats as black as the night sky _____.

3. The ghosts and the goblins _____ the monster-like trees, ready to grab the next victim with ease.

4. When the fog rolls in _____.

5. _____ comes the mist that makes you chilled down to the bone.

6. A witch, a vampire, and a ghost _____.

7. With blood dripping from his razorblade-like fingers _____.

8. _____ from all directions.

9. One night of the year _____.

10. With all the scary sights and the blood-curdling sounds on Halloween _____.

PRACTICE 5   Combining Sentences

Combine the following sentences from the student essay, "Virtual Violence," by Nate Kistner, using correct punctuation and a variety of sentence patterns (compound/coordinate, complex/subordinate, and compound-complex) into one paragraph with one-half the number of sentences. Avoid comma splices, run-ons, and sentence fragments. See the professional essay for the original version.

1. Americans are violent.

2. To illustrate.

3. Look back into history.

4. How did Americans acquire the "new world"?

5. Settlers did not pay Indians rent.

6. Natives were driven away by force.

7. Americans won independence.

8. Through battle not negotiation.

9. Violence has been used to settle land disputes.

10. Violence has been used to settle religious controversy.

11. Violence has been used to settle general disagreements for centuries.

_____

_____

_____

_____

_____

_____

PRACTICE 6   Sentence Combining

Combine the following sentences from the student essay, "Virtual Violence," by Nate Kistner into one paragraph as above, using a variety of sentence combining strategies, and avoiding errors in punctuation. Reduce the number of sentences by one-half! See the student essay for the original punctuation, although there is more than one way to combine sentences correctly.

1. Violence in games is quite easy to come by.

2. Violent games does not exist without demand.

3. There is the demand for such games.

4. Society would not be drawn to violent games.

5. Society is naturally prone to violence initially.

6. A Playstation, a Game Cube, a PC are choices for the consumer.

7. There are also any number of hand-held gaming systems.

8. It is difficult to blame violence on games alone.

9. There is a veritable plethora of nonviolent games.

10. There are also low-violence games.

_____

_____

_____

_____

Combining Sentences

| PRACTICE 7 | Combining Sentences |

Combine the following sentences, using correct punctuation and a variety of sentence patterns (compound/coordinate, complex/subordinate, and compound-complex) into one paragraph with one-half the number of sentences. Avoid comma splices, run-ons, and sentence fragments.

1. Being a high school freshman can be a dreadful experience.

2. Freshmen are entering new surroundings.

3. They are being harassed by upperclassmen.

4. They have four long years of school ahead of them.

5. Freshmen become very confused.

6. They rush to find classes in a labyrinth of unfamiliar hallways.

7. They act like mice attempting to find their way through a complicated maze.

8. Additionally, they are harassed by upperclassmen.

9. This makes the maze even more of a challenge.

10. Being a freshman means having four more years of headaches.

11. Because you are new, teachers will have little leniency.

12. This is in regard to the quantity of homework given and the quality of the homework returned.

13. All three factors contribute to a realization.

14. This realization is that being a high school freshman is a dreadful existence.

_____

_____

_____

_____

_____

_____

_____

_____

_____

_____

_____

_____

ESL **Preposition Combinations**

Here is a list of preposition combinations with adjectives and verbs.

> ### Preposition Combinations with Adjectives and Verbs
>
> **A** *be* absent from
> accuse of
> *be* accustomed to
> *be* acquainted with
> *be* addicted to
> *be* afraid of
> agree with
> *be* angry at, with
> *be* annoyed with
> apologize for
> apply to, for
> approve of
> argue with, about
> arrive in, at
> *be* ssociated with
> *be* aware of
>
> **B** believe in
> blame for
> *be* blessed with
> *be* bored with
>
> **C** *be* capable of
> care about, for
> *be* cluttered with
> *be* committed to
> compare to, with
> complain about
> *be* composed of
> *be* concerned about
> *be* connected to
> consist of
> *be* content with
> contribute to
> *be* convinced of
> *be* coordinated with
> count (up)on
>
> cover with
> *be* crowded with
>
> **D** decide (up)on
> *be* dedicated to
> depend (up)on
> *be* devoted to
> *be* disappointed in, with
> *be* discriminated against
> distinguish from
> *be* divorced from
> *be* done with
> dream of, about
> *be* dressed in
>
> **E** *be* engaged to
> *be* envious of
> *be* equipped with
> escape from
> excel in
> *be* excited about
> excuse for
> *be* exposed to
>
> **F** *be* faithful to
> *be* familiar with
> feel like
> fight for
> *be* filled with
> *be* finished with
> *be* fond of
> forget about
> forgive for
> *be* friendly to, with
> *be* furnished with
>
> **G** *be* grateful to, for
> *be* guilty of

H	hide from hope for	**R**	recover from *be* related to *be* relevant to rely (up)on *be* remembered for rescue from respond to *be* responsible for
I	*be* innocent of insist (up)on *be* interested in *be* involved in		
J	*be* jealous of		
K	*be* known for	**S**	*be* satisfied with *be* scared of stare at stop from subscribe to substitute for succeed in
L	*be* limited to look forward to		
M	*be* made of, from *be* married to		
O	object to *be* opposed to	**T**	take advantage of take care of *be* terrified of thank for *be* tired of, from
P	participate in *be* patient with *be* polite to pray for *be* prepared for prevent from prohibit from protect from *be* proud of provide with *be* provided with		
		U	*be* upset with *be* used to
		V	vote for
		W	*be* worried about

PRACTICE 1   Using Preposition Combinations

Fill in the blanks with the correct preposition combination. The verb has been indicated. Supply the correct form of the verb to be (if necessary) and the preposition. The first one has been done for you.

1. Shirley (be absent) <u>was absent from</u> class last week.

2. The students (be accustomed) _____ (not) _____ writing in a foreign language.

3. The exam (be composed) _____ questions from the text as well as lecture material.

4. Deirdre could not (decide) _____ which classes to take for next semester.

5. Paul and Stephanie (be devoted) _____ their daughter Lydia.

6. The family (be excited) _____ the upcoming reunion.

7. Ramon could not (forgive) _____ Teresa _____ taking his money.

8. The president will (be remembered) _____ the scandal with the intern.

9. The instructor (be satisfied) _____ the progress of her students.

10. Helen (be terrified) _____ the film *Psycho*.

■ **PRACTICE 2**   **Using Preposition Combinations**

Use the given preposition combination correctly in a sentence. Be careful with subject-verb agreement and pronoun-antecedent agreement.

Example: (be relevant to) Your comments <u>are not relevant</u> to the discussion.

1. (be acquainted with) _____

_____

2. (be aware of) _____

_____

3. (believe in) _____

_____

4. (be concerned about) _____

_____

5. (depend on) _____

_____

6. (be disappointed in) _____

_____

7. (excuse for) _____

_____

8. (be finished with) _____

_____

9. (be known for) _____

_____

10. (respond to) _____

_____

 Articles

Articles are a type of word that introduces a noun and indicates whether it is specific or countable. (The most frequently used articles are *a, an,* and *the.*)

Basic Article Usage

I. Using Articles: Generic Nouns

Ø means no article is used.

Singular Count Noun   (a) *A banana* is yellow.*

A speaker uses generic nouns to make generalizations. A generic noun represents a whole class of things; it is not a specific, real, concrete thing but rather a symbol of a whole group.

*Usually ***a/an*** is used with a singular generic count noun:
   Examples:
      *A **window** is made of glass. A **doctor** heals sick people. Parents must give **a child** love. A **box** has six sides. **An apple** can be red, green, or yellow.*

   The is sometimes used with a singular generic count noun (not a plural generic count noun, not a generic noncount noun). Generic ***"the"*** is commonly used with, in particular:
   (1) species of animals: ***The whale*** *is the largest mammal on earth.*
                              The elephant *is the largest land mammal.*
   (2) inventions: *Who invented* ***the telephone? the wheel? the refrigerator? the airplane?***
                     The computer *will play an increasingly large role in all our lives.*
   (3) musical instruments: *I'd like to learn to play* ***the piano.***
                              Do you play ***the guitar?***

Plural Count Noun   (b) Ø *Bananas* are yellow.

In (a) and (b): The speaker is talking about any banana, all bananas, bananas in general. In (c), the speaker is talking about any and all fruit, fruit in general.

Noncount Noun   (c) Ø *Fruit* is good for you.

Notice that no article (Ø) is used to make generalizations with plural count nouns and noncount nouns, as in (b) and (c).

II. Using *A* or *Some:* Indefinite Nouns

Singular Count Noun   (d) I ate *a banana.*

Indefinite nouns are actual things (not symbols), but they are not specifically identified.

Plural Count Noun   **(e)** I ate *some* bananas.

In (d): The speaker is not referring to "this banana" or "that banana" or "the banana you gave me." The speaker is simply saying that she or he ate one banana. The listener does not know nor need to know which specific banana was eaten; it was simply one banana out of that whole group of things in this world called bananas.

Noncount Noun   **(f)** I ate *some* *fruit*.

In (e) and (f): *Some* is often used with indefinite plural count nouns and indefinite noncount nouns. In addition to *some*, a speaker might use **two, a few, several, a lot of,** etc., with plural count nouns, or **a little, a lot of,** etc., with noncount nouns.

III. Using *The:* Definite Nouns

Singular Count Noun   **(g)** Thank you for ***the*** *banana*.

A noun is definite when both the speaker and the listener are thinking about the same specific thing.

Plural Count Noun   **(h)** Thank you for ***the*** *bananas*.

In (g): The speaker uses ***the*** because the listener knows which specific banana the speaker is talking about, i.e., that particular banana that the listener gave to the speaker.

Noncount Noun   **(i)** Thank you for ***the*** *fruit*.

Notice that ***the*** is used with both singular and plural count nouns and with noncount nouns.

General Guidelines for Article Usage

(a) ***The sun*** is bright today. Please hand this book to ***the teacher.*** Please open ***the door.*** Jack is in ***the kitchen.***	GUIDELINE: Use ***the*** when you know or assume that your listener is familiar with and thinking about the same specific thing or person you are talking about.
(b) Yesterday I saw *some dogs.* ***The dogs*** were chasing *a cat.* ***The cat*** was chasing *a mouse.* ***The mouse*** ran into *a hole.* ***The hole*** was very small.	GUIDELINE: Use ***the*** for the second mention of an indefinite noun*; in (b): first mention = *some dogs, a cat, a mouse, a hole* second mention = *the dogs, the cat, the mouse, the hole*
(c) INCORRECT: *The apples are my favorite fruit.* CORRECT: ***Apples*** are my favorite fruit.	GUIDELINE: Do not use ***the*** with a plural count noun (e.g., *apples*) or a noncount noun (e.g., *gold*) when you are making a generalization.
(d) INCORRECT: *The gold is a metal.* CORRECT: ***Gold*** is a metal.	
(e) INCORRECT: *I drove car.* CORRECT: I drove ***a car.*** I drove ***the car.*** I drove ***that car.*** I drove ***his car.***	GUIDELINE: Do not use a singular count noun (e.g., *car*) without: (1) an article (***a/an*** or ***the***); OR (2) ***this/that;*** OR (3) a possessive pronoun.

*****The*** is not used for the second mention of a generic noun. COMPARE:
  (1) What color is ***a banana*** (generic noun)? ***A banana*** (generic noun) is yellow.
  (2) Tom offered me ***a banana*** (indefinite noun) or an apple. I chose ***the banana*** (definite noun).

PRACTICE 1   Using Articles

In the following dialogues, determine whether the speakers would use **a/an** or **the**.

1. A: I have ___an___ idea. Let's go on ___a___ picnic Saturday.

   B: Okay.

2. A: Did you have fun at ___the___ picnic yesterday?

   B: Sure did. And you?

3. A: You'd better have _____ good reason for being late!

   B: I do.

4. A: Did you think _____ reason Jack gave for being late was believable?

   B: Not really.

5. A: Where's my blue shirt?

   B: It's in _____ washing machine. You'll have to wear _____ different shirt.

6. A: I wish we had _____ washing machine.

   B: So do I. It would make it a lot easier to do our laundry.

7. A: What happened to your bicycle? _____ front wheel is bent.

   B: I ran into _____ parked car when I swerved to avoid _____ big pothole in the street.

   A: Did you damage _____ car?

   B: A little.

   A: What did you do?

   B: I left _____ note for _____ owner of _____ car.

   A: What did you write on _____ note?

   B: My name and address. I also wrote _____ apology.

8. A: Can you repair my car for me?

   B: What's wrong with it?

   A: _____ radiator has _____ leak, and one of _____ windshield wipers doesn't work.

   B: Can you show me where _____ leak is?

9. A: Have you seen my boots?

B: They're in _____ closet in _____ front hallway.

| PRACTICE 2 | Using Articles |

Complete the sentences with **a/an**, **the**, or Ø. (Ø means no article.)

1. ___Ø___ beef is a kind of ___Ø___ meat.

2. ___The___ beef we had for dinner last night was excellent.

3. Jack is wearing _____ straw hat today.

4. Jack likes to wear _____ hats.

5. _____ hat is _____ article of clothing.

6. _____ hats are _____ articles of clothing.

7. _____ brown hat on that hook over there belongs to Mark.

8. Everyone has _____ problems in _____ life.

9. My grandfather had _____ long life.

10. That book is about _____ life of Helen Keller.

11. Tommy wants to be _____ engineer when he grows up.

12. The Brooklyn Bridge was designed by _____ engineer.

13. John Roebling is _____ name of _____ engineer who designed the

Brooklyn Bridge. He died in 1869 from _____ infection. He died before

_____ bridge was completed.

14. _____ people wear _____ jewelry to make themselves more attractive.

15. _____ jewelry Diana is wearing today is beautiful.

16. Mary is wearing _____ beautiful ring today. It is made of _____ gold

and rubies. _____ gold in her ring was mined in Canada. _____ rubies

came from Burma.

17. One of the first things you need to do when you move to _____ new

city is to find _____ place to live. Most _____ newspapers carry _____

advertisements (called "want ads") for _____ apartments that are for rent. If you find _____ ad for _____ furnished apartment, _____ apartment will probably contain _____ stove and _____ refrigerator. It will also probably have _____ furniture such as _____ beds, _____ tables, _____ chairs, and maybe _____ sofa.

18. My wife and I have recently moved to this city. Since we're going to be here for only _____ short time, we're renting _____ furnished apartment. We decided that we didn't want to bring our own furniture with us. _____ apartment is in _____ good location, but that's about the only good thing I can say about it. Only one burner on _____ stove works. _____ refrigerator is noisy, and _____ refrigerator door won't stay closed unless we tape it shut. _____ bed sags in the middle and creaks. All of the rest of _____ furniture is old and decrepit too. Nevertheless, we're still enjoying living in this city. We may have to look for _____ another apartment, however.

CAPITALIZATION AND NUMBERS

Capitalization

1. Capitalize proper nouns, the names of people, places, and specific products.

> Fredric Chopin
> Sacramento, California
> German class
> Fords

2. Capitalize the days of the week, names of months, and the titles of holidays.

> Saturday, August 28
> Friday the 13th
> Christmas holiday

3. Capitalize the first word of every sentence.

> The dog, cat, and birds all began to bark, growl, and chirp at once.

PRACTICE 1 Correcting Capitalization

Correct the capitalization errors in the following sentences.

1. Every friday, the sociology class met in the eisenhower library.

2. The rent-a-car company used fords, chevrolets, and buicks.

3. Julie's birthday fell on saturday, august 14.

4. ludwig van beethoven wrote nine symphonies.

5. In chicago, the sears tower is the tallest skyscraper.

6. The vice president of international business, incorporated slashed the budget.

7. Next summer, we hope to camp at yellowstone national park.

8. The lincoln memorial and jefferson memorial are impressive historic sites in washington, d. c.

9. The categories for general education courses are communication, mathematics, social science, and humanities.

10. Angelina is from bulgaria, but she has lived in the united states for two years.

PRACTICE 2   Correcting Capitalization

Correct the errors in capitalization in the following paragraph.

many scientists and researchers claim nuclear energy is desirable as an energy source because it creates enormous amounts of power from small resources. while this may be true, there are other costs that outweigh the purely monetary. in 1986, in the ukrainian town of chernobyl, a nuclear reactor accident killed 31 soviet citizens and caused 100,000 people to be evacuated. a radioactive cloud covered much of northern europe and great britain. nuclear weapons proliferation is another problem if nuclear energy production is increased. every year there are reports of nuclear by-products missing from government inventories. enemies of the united states could use this material to build nuclear weapons with which to threaten our security.

Numbers

1. Numbers (instead of words) should be used for dates, street addresses, page numbers, telephone numbers, and time stated in terms of A.M. and P.M. (words are used with the phrase "o'clock").

> August 29, 2003
> 321 Walnut St.
> page 34
> 12:00 A.M.
> 922–8000

2. Use numbers for figures above 100 (although some authorities tell us to spell out numbers that can be expressed in one or two words).

> 1,000 pages to be completed
> Twenty-four hours
> $20,000 or twenty thousand dollars

3. Use numbers in a short passage in which several numbers are used.

> On the initial placement test, Julia scored 75, Celia scored 60, and Luis scored 85.

4. Never begin a sentence with a number.

> 25 students filled the course. (Incorrect)
> Twenty-five students filled the course. (Correct)

PRACTICE 1   Correcting Number Errors

Correct the number errors in the following sentences.

1. 45 truck drivers participated in the salary dispute talks.

2. Meldrick lives at forty-two seventy-two Main Street.

3. The contestant won thirty-seven dollars playing the lottery.

4. Tickets for the tour cost eight dollars.

5. The program began at ten-thirty, Eastern Standard Time.

6. We should meet for lunch at 1:00 o'clock; the restaurant will be too crowded at 12:00 o'clock.

7. 750 students dressed in caps and gowns stood nervously in line, waiting to enter the auditorium.

8. Lisa crept into the house, through the family room window, at two-thirty A.M.

9. Oil was discovered on his ranch in the nineteen fifties.

10. 260,000 ancient Chinese artifacts were packed into the crates.

PRACTICE 2   Correcting Number Errors

Correct any errors with numbers in the following paragraph.

The Yukon Territory is located in northwestern Canada. The vast area (one hundred and eighty six thousand, three hundred square miles) is bordered by Alaska and British Columbia. Its mineral wealth and scenicvistas are 2 of its main attractions. Forests cover about forty percent of the total land area. A subarctic climate prevails with severe winters and hotsummers, and the annual precipitation ranges from nine to thirteen inches.

ADDITIONAL PUNCTUATION RULES

Basic rules of punctuation and sentence structure are covered in Chapters 3–8, where periods, semicolons, commas, question marks, and exclamation points are discussed.

The Apostrophe

The **apostrophe** is used to indicate contractions or possession/ownership.

1. Some words can be combined, usually in informal writing, by using an apostrophe. This is a contraction.

> *Isn't* this strange? (is + not)
> We *couldn't* drive any farther. (could + not)

2. Add an apostrophe plus *s* to a noun to indicate possession.

> *Anna's* papers were left in the office.

3. To a plural noun ending in *s*, add only an apostrophe to indicate possession.

> *Parents'* advice often is ignored.

4. For some words, an apostrophe plus *s* should be added to a singular word ending in *s*. This is most often true for a proper name.

> The *Billings's* recipe book

5. Apostrophe plus *s* can be used to form the plurals of figures, letters, and words being treated as words in isolation. (It is also acceptable to leave out this apostrophe.)

> Many students are not satisfied with C's.
> The 1970's were confusing years.
> Don't use so many "okay's" when you speak.

PRACTICE 1   Correcting Apostrophe Errors

Correct any apostrophe errors in the following sentences. (Some sentences may be correct.)

1. The Smiths in this society are very difficult to track down individually.

2. December 31, 1999, was a very exciting New Year's Eve!

3. Whose your favorite football team?

4. Your right!

5. If she wasnt on time, she shouldve been.

PRACTICE 2   Correcting Apostrophe Errors

Correct the apostrophe errors in the following sentences.

1. Whats his name?

2. The 1960s brought about changes in many institutions in our society.

3. In your essays, change the *a lots* to words such as *many* or *several*.

4. When you change batteries, align the +*s* and −*s* correctly.

5. Its not correct to omit necessary apostrophes.

6. Students questions are usually not frivolous.

7. The mans shoes were made of leather.

8. Mr. Lewis donation to the walkathon was very generous.

9. The families plans for a joint vacation were put on hold.

10. George and Shirleys relationship is very unpredictable.

PRACTICE 3   Correcting Apostrophe Errors

Correct the apostrophe errors in the following sentences. (Some sentences may be correct.)

1. The boss plan was to intimidate his employees.

2. The months work was destroyed by a computer virus.

3. Luis frequently asked his father-in-laws advice.

4. The ladies raincoats dripped in the hall closet.

5. The sisters reunion in San Antonio was a fantastic success.

6. The minivan is theirs; the Porsche is yours.

7. The suns rays began to filter through the clouds.

8. The shirts for the boys were destroyed in the washing machine.

9. Louisa is suffering from the terrible twos.

10. The students spirits improved after their papers were returned.

Quotation Marks

1. Use **quotation marks** to set apart written words or the spoken words indialogue.

> 'My mother wrote, "We will be traveling in our mobile home."
> Jung said, "I need to change my grammar text."

2. Periods and commas are placed inside the quotation marks, whereas semi-colons and colons are placed outside the quotation marks. If the quoted material is a question, place the question mark inside the quotation marks. However, if the quoted material is part of a longer sentence that asks a question, put the question mark outside the quotation marks.

> "Do the bats fly at night?" he asked.
> Did I hear you ask, "Do the bats fly at night?"
> He politely remarked, "I would like tea"; however, his wife asked for coffee.
> In his short story "Hills Like White Elephants," the male character makes several references to a "simple operation" as a solution to an inconvenient pregnancy, as a way to convince his girlfriend that the operation posed no risk, and as a way to keep his life uncomplicated.

3. Use quotation marks to set apart titles of essays (except for the title of your own essay on your title page), articles in magazines, short stories, short poems, songs, and chapter headings.

> The class discussed "My Life on the Streets" for two days.
> "Music of the Night" is her favorite song in *Phantom of the Opera*.
> The poem "Fire and Ice" by Frost illustrates two types of anger and destruction.
> "Letters from a Birmingham Jail" is an essay that effectively illustrates argumentation.

4. Quotation marks or italics can be used to set apart a word, phrase, or letter being discussed.

> Do not follow the conjunction "although" with a comma.
> Descriptive words such as "brilliant," "glowing," and "illuminating" support the dominant impression of "light."

5. Uncommon names/nicknames and words used in irony or sarcasm should be surrounded by quotation marks.

> "Buzz" McCarthy prefers to shave his head.
> His crime of adultery almost made him "public enemy number one."

6. Single quotation marks should be used to indicate a quotation within a quotation.

> Tasha said, "My favorite song is 'Layla' performed by Eric Clapton."

PRACTICE 1 — Using Quotation Marks

Wherever necessary, add quotation marks to the following sentences. Put a **C** in front of any correct sentence.

_____ **1.** Two of the best short stories in our anthology are Hills Like White Elephants by Hemingway and Chrysanthemums by Steinbeck.

_____ **2.** The new sign reads Please Do NOT Park on the Driveway!

_____ **3.** Brillig and slithy toves are portmanteau words created by Lewis Carroll.

_____ **4.** The superintendent reported, Most students in the city have improved their test scores .

_____ **5.** The *St. Louis Post Dispatch* carries a hysterical column entitled Your Serve in the food section.

_____ **6.** At the end of the visit, the doctor stated firmly, Cut back on the caffeine and get more exercise!

_____ **7.** The Fox Theater is performing *Annie Get Your Gun* this fall.

_____ **8.** Spring is the most beautiful time of the year in the Midwest! she exclaimed.

_____ **9.** The songs on The White Album by the Beatles are still quite popular.

_____ **10.** Please compare the short stories Yellow Wallpaper by Gilman and Story of an Hour by Chopin for your final essay in the Gender Communication unit.

PRACTICE 2   Using Quotation Marks

Add quotation marks as necessary in the following sentences, taken from a student essay on a poem by Robert Frost. Also correct the quotation marks and italics/underlining in the Works Cited material at the end of the exercise.

1. In Robert Frost's poem After Apple-Picking, the analogy between a person's life and the seasons is well paralleled.

2. The problem is whether to attach to the After of the title a finality (death) or a shorter pause that has at its core a continuation.

3. According to Alvan Ryan, Few of Frost's protagonists are passive victims, nor do they escape into a romantic dream world; we see them at a moment of crisis . . . (136).

4. In the first two lines, the two-pointed ladder's sticking through a tree/ Toward heaven still (1–2) could be seen as an affirmation of something joyously attained after hard work is finished.

5. Additionally, note that the woodchuck in the poem is only hibernating; He will awaken from this form of death in the spring to resume life.

6. As Lawrance Thompson writes, Most of the Puritans were more bold than talented in their attempts to prove that art is concerned with directing the individual to apprehension; that art is therefore a means to knowledge and truth . . . (32).

7. The frustration and weariness sets in because of the emotional letdown occurring when the farmer realizes that the original goal of picking the ten thousand fruit (30) was not possible.

8. The lines, No matter if not bruised or spiked with stubble,/ went surely to the cider-apple heap/ As of not worth (34–36) indicate that the fruit of our life's work will often be discarded, despite how good and noble our intentions may have been.

9. But the farmer says, I am done with apple-picking now (6).

10. It is important to note that the line ends with the word now, not forever.

Works Cited

Ryan, Alvan S. Frost and Emerson: Voice and Vision. <u>Critical Essays on</u> <u>Robert Frost</u>. Ed. Phillip Gerber. Boston: G.K. Hall, 1982. 124–37.

Thompson, Lawrance. Robert Frost's Theory of Poetry. <u>Robert Frost: A</u> <u>Collection of Critical Essays</u>. Ed. James Cox. Englewood Cliffs: Prentice-Hall, 1962. 16–35.

■ PRACTICE 3	Correcting Apostrophe and Quotation Mark Errors

Correct the apostrophe and quotation mark errors in the following sentences.

1. My Uncle Silas wrote, I'll be in St. Louis on Wednesday evening.

2. Marks car was left in the parking lot overnight.

3. The winning dragster was driven by Bud The Snake Collins.

4. The Joness prize heifer won the Blue Ribbon at the county fair.

5. The short story Mrs. Garland's Garden appeared in *Horticulture* magazine.

6. Studying all night for the exam is not what I wanted to do.

7. Slang expressions, such as dissed and way cool, should not be used informal writing.

8. The 1960s saw the rise of hippies and the counterculture in American society.

9. Marva said, My favorite saying is P. T. Barnum's Never Give a Sucker an Even Break.

10. Lawyers legal advice is usually based on case law.

■ PRACTICE 4	Using Correct Punctuation

Add the correct punctuation to the following student paragraph (taken from a student essay, "Don't Give Up the Right to Carry" by Tim Schuette).

proposition b will allow people twenty-one or older, who have never

been convicted of a felony, the ability to carry a concealed weapon if they

pass a background check and 12-hour handgun safety course people opposed

to proposition b believe criminals will have easier access to weapons. the

danger for police officers will greatly increase. people will misuse the guns therefore the crime rate will increase vote yes for proposition b because criminals already have guns police support concealed weapons and the crime rate will decrease.

Parentheses

1. **Parentheses** are used to set off specific details giving additional information, explanations, or qualifications of the main idea in a sentence. This would include words, dates, or statements.

> Many students name famous athletes as heroes (Albert Pujois, Alex Rodriguez, and Maurice Green, for example).
>
> *Tom Sawyer* (1876) is one of Mark Twain's most enduring works.

2. Notice that the period for the sentence is placed outside the closing parenthesis when the enclosed information occurs at the end of the sentence and is not a complete sentence itself. If the enclosed information is a complete sentence, the period is placed inside the closing parenthesis.

PRACTICE 1   Using Parentheses

Insert parentheses when necessary in the following sentences. The first item has been done for you.

1. Three new students (Marta, Eric, and Elena) were admitted to the class.

2. The rich desserts Bavarian chocolate cake, chocolate cream pie, and peach melba were added to the menu.

3. Johann Sebastian Bach 1685–1750 is the featured composer for tonight's concert.

4. The appendix pp. 300–385 provides additional exercises for the text.

5. They thought she died from the "joy that kills" Chopin 344.

6. Women were restricted by the social role required of wives in the Victorian period 1837–1901.

7. The media television, magazines, newspapers, radio, and the Internet play a crucial role in each election.

8. The four brothers Thomas, Robert, Steven, and John Corey have grown up with one sister Amy.

9. His explanation of the "silent phase" see page 646 in language learning is very helpful for new teachers.

10. Wolfgang Amadeus Mozart 1756–1791 composed many favorite piano concertos.

PRACTICE 2   **Using Parentheses**

Insert parentheses when necessary in the following sentences.

1. In *definition* the rhetorical mode that explains or clarifies meaning the strategies of narration, description, and comparison/contrast can all be used.

2. So many cities in Europe Rome, for example are too rich in artifacts and history to be appreciated on a one-day tour.

3. Many students suffer from "test-taking anxiety" a condition that is much like "performance anxiety" for musicians.

4. Jane Austen's two most well-known novels *Pride and Prejudice* and *Sense and Sensibility* have both been made into successful films.

5. He plans to major in herpetology the study of snakes.

6. The following is an analysis of the Robert Frost poem "After Apple-Picking," from his book of poems *North of Boston* 1914.

7. The paper also cites outside sources and uses MLA documentation format see Chapter 16 in your text.

8. Denotative language the use of words in their accepted, dictionary-defined sense is complemented by connotative language the use of words that have or develop associations and implications apart from their explicit sense.

9. Thus, the heart represents love "She has given her heart to her partner", empathy "he has a lot of heart", or courage "She has the heart of a lion"—this is also a metaphor.

10. In this poem, are people or things animals, etc. portrayed as good or evil or indifferent?

Brackets

1. **Brackets** are used in quoted material to set apart editorial explanations.

> The tenor sang "Angel of Music" [original version sung by Michael Crawford] for his encore.

2. Brackets are also used to indicate editorial corrections to quoted material. The word *sic* (which means "thus") placed next to an error in quoted material means that the mistake appeared in the original text and that it is not the writer's error.

> The dean wrote, "All faculty must teach sumer [sic] school."

PRACTICE 1   Using Brackets

Insert brackets where necessary in the following sentences.

1. In his instructions, the professor made the following explanation: "Each answer will be wort sic 25 points."

2. According to Davidson, "He the Irish hero Cuchulain became horrible, many shaped, strange, and unrecognizable" (84).

3. The Vice President for Instruction wrote the following memo: "All faculty must fellow sic the graduates into the stadium."

4. According to Public Citizen, a watchdog group that does not accept corporate or government support, "Using trade flow data to calculate job loss under NAFTA North American Free Trade Agreement yields net job destruction numbers in the hundreds of thousands" ("Talking Points").

5. "The hypothesis of a killer instinct," according to a commentator summarizing a recent conference on the anthropology of war, is "not so much wrong as irrevelant sic."

6. Lori Wallach, director of Public Citizen's Global Trade Watch, stated in a Senate Commerce Committee meeting, "Thus, even if Congress opposes permanent normal trade relations with China, U.S. exporters would obtain the potential benefits China must provide other nations if it enters the WTO World Trade Organization while retaining the effective U.S. trade enforcement mechanisms forbidden under the WTO, such as Section 301" ("Testimony").

PRACTICE 2   Using Parentheses and Brackets

Add parentheses and brackets where appropriate in the following sentences.

1. World War II 1939–1945 was divided into two main theaters of conflict.

2. The historian wrote, "Napoleon was exiled to the Island of Elbi sic."

3. Many famous presidents Washington, Lincoln, and Roosevelt are quoted in speeches by political candidates.

4. The coach said, "The Fighting Irish Notre Dame will be a tough opponent next week."

5. The student wrote "I threw the paper on the grownd sic yesterday."

6. Brian analyzed the performance of the concerto by Dvorak as performed by Rostropovich.

7. The President stated, "She the Vice-President described the financial crisis."

8. The erratic weather rain, wind, and sudden snow storms in Missouri makes it difficult to plan outdoor activities.

9. The reporter wrote, "The sailors were innured sic in the explosion."

10. These popular shoes Reebok, Adidas, and Naturalizer were available in a variety of sizes.

The Dash

1. The dash is used to set apart parenthetical information that needs more emphasis than would be indicated by parentheses.

> Irina's new teacher—a dynamic sociology teacher—helped her to understand American society.

2. Use a dash before a statement that expands on or summarizes the preceding statement (this could also include ironic or humorous comments).

> He studied for the exam for two days—then fell asleep before he finished!

PRACTICE 1   Using the Dash

Add dashes to the following sentences.

1. Alexis Jordan and I do not believe this is an exaggeration is a genius.

2. She is running I think in the 10K race.

3. Anna-Lee and Jake have traveled to every state I am not kidding!

4. Marjo and Marc met Gayle and Larry in Denver, Colorado, for vacation luckily they all like mountains!

5. He turned in the financial report and I know this is true before the deadline.

6. Brenda indicated in fact she insisted that the patient see a specialist.

7. Sergei arrived so we were told an hour ago.

8. Every morning so he says Andrew runs 3 miles.

9. Is dinner if you can call it that ready?

10. Never and I mean never open an attachment on e-mail!

PRACTICE 2   Using the Dash

Add dashes to the following sentences.

1. The caretakers of society mothers, teachers, nurses are devalued in modern society.

2. There is only one way to do this his way so we are forced to agree.

3. If you eat a heavy dinner as you usually do when we eat at a restaurant you will be unable to sleep later!

4. Oksana the only Russian student in the class prefers to study poetry.

5. Please try to remember although you never do to take the phone with you when you take the car.

6. When Grandpa the best storyteller at the family gatherings begins to talk about life on the farm, even the grandchildren listen.

7. A first date as you well know can be a tense experience.

8. Television the bane of modern existence can hypnotize an entire family.

9. Although the emphasis of the class was composition skills prewriting, drafting, and revising the class took time every week to debate current events.

10. The elephant and the gorilla two of the most powerful animals in the jungle are also vegetarian!

The Hyphen

1. Hyphens are used to join descriptive adjectives before a noun.

> a well-written play
> a forty-year-old woman

2. Do not use a hyphen when the descriptive phrase includes an adverb that ends in –*ly*.

> a quickly changed opinion
> a beautifully designed home

3. Check the dictionary for compound words that always require a hyphen.

> compound numbers (twenty-five, fifty-six)
> good-for-nothing
> father-in-law (mother-in-law, and so on)
> President-elect

4. Some words with prefixes use a hyphen; check your dictionary if you are unsure.

> ex-husband
> non-English-speaking
> All-American

5. Use a hyphen to separate syllables at the end of a line. Do not divide a one-syllable word.

> Do not forget to review dependent clauses and subordinate con-
> junctions.

PRACTICE 1   Using Hyphens

Add hyphens where needed in the following sentences. The first sentence is done for you.

1. My brother-in-law will leave for Florida next week.

2. The seventeen year old driver was nervous on the highway.

3. The old violin was a very well constructed instrument.

4. The scientist prefers up to date results.

5. She stared into the blue green water.

6. When the cleaners arrived at the house, they did not know how to dis arm the security system.

7. Every year his tax forms were rapidly completed; then, he waited to see if he would be audited.

8. Hal's ex wife never saw him again.

9. At age forty nine, her mother discovered that she really wanted to be a gardener rather than a nurse.

10. Even though it was not a particularly well written essay, the concepts were unusual.

PRACTICE 2   Identifying Hyphen Errors

Indicate whether hyphens are used correctly in the words below. Write **C** for correct and **I** for incorrect.

1. all-inclusive   _____

2. re-dress (dress again)   _____

3. brilliantly-stated   _____

4. pre-1950   _____

5. re-dress (set right)   _____

6. anti-gun control   _____

7. night-shift   _____

8. badly-shaken   _____

9. cedar-shingles   _____

10. kilowatt-hours   _____

Underlining or Italics

1. The titles of books, magazines, journals, movies, works of art, television programs, CDs, plays, ships, airplanes, and trains should be underlined.

The Sun Also Rises
Good Housekeeping
The New York Times
The Last Supper
Tapestry
Buffy the Vampire Slayer
Queen Mary

2. There are some exceptions to this rule: the Bible, titles of legal documents (including the U.S. Constitution), and the title of your own essay on your title page.

3. Also, underlining is equivalent to or a symbol for *italics*, which may be used instead of underlining.

PRACTICE 1 Using Underlining and Italics

In the following Works Cited entries, correct the underlining/italics when necessary and add quotation marks when appropriate. The first item has been done for you.

1. Davidson, Hilda Ellis. Myths and Symbols in Pagan Europe: Early Scandinavian and Celtic Religions. Syracuse, NY: Syracuse UP, 1988.

2. Fox, Robin. Fatal Attraction: War and Human Nature. The National Interest Winter 1992/93: 11–20.

3. Grossman, Lt. Col. Dave. On Killing: The Psychological Cost of Learning to Kill in War and Society. Boston: Little, Brown, 1995.

4. McCauley, Clark. Conference Overview. The Anthropology of War. Ed. Jonathan Haas. Cambridge: Cambridge UP, 1990. 1–25.

5. Metraux, Alfred. Warfare, Cannibalism and Human Trophies. Handbook of South American Indians. Ed. Julian H. Steward. Vol. 5. New York: Cooper Square, 1963. 383–409.

6. Mitchell, Timothy. Colonizing Egypt. Berkeley: U of California P, 1991.

7. Sagan, Eli. Cannibalism: Human Aggression and Cultural Form. New York: Harper & Row, 1974.

8. Stoessinger, John G. Why Nations Go to War. New York: St. Martin's, 1993.

9. Sun Tzu. The Art of War. Trans. Samuel B. Griffith. London: Oxford UP, 1971.

10. Van Creveld, Martin. The Transformation of War. New York: Free Press, 1991.

| PRACTICE 2 | Using the Dash, Hyphen, and Underlining |

Add dashes, hyphens, and underlining where needed in the following sentences. Some sentences may be correct.

1. The fifteen year old cat sat on top of the television most of the day and night.

2. In the event of a nuclear accident, it is important to listen for broadcasts about emergency procedures.

3. Jack Nicklaus the greatest golfer of all times is also a successful golf course designer.

4. Singer Bob Dylan wrote a novel titled Tarantula.

5. Her son in law always dropped by on Saturday to mow the lawn.

6. Sela baked four dozen cookies for her younger sister's camping trip then it rained!

7. Dawson's Creek was a very popular television program for younger adults.

8. Jim Thorpe was the first All American of Native American extraction.

9. The long jump winner at the Senior Olympics was seventy two years old.

10. Jose's new wrestling coach a woman competed for four years at Dellwood College.

Interrupters: Restrictive and Nonrestrictive Clauses and Phrases (Modifiers)

1. Sentences may be interrupted by clauses or phrases that clarify or provide additional meaning. These clauses usually begin with the relative pronouns *who, whom, which,* or *that*. These are also known as **restrictive and nonrestrictive clauses/phrases.**

> They did not know the man *who was speaking.*
> Their dog, *which was barking all night,* annoyed the neighbors.

2. **Restrictive clauses** are essential to identify nouns or to complete the meaning of the sentence. These clauses simply follow the nouns or ideas they are modifying. No commas are used to set off restrictive clauses.

clause
In the line, the young woman *who was wearing a red bandana and hoop earrings* needed a ticket. (This relative clause is essential to identify which woman needed a ticket)

phrase
The film *showing at the Rialto* is very provocative. (This descriptive phrase is necessary to identify which film/theater is under discussion)

3. **Nonrestrictive clauses/phrases** are not essential to complete the meaning of the sentence. You can remove them from the sentence, and the basic meaning of the sentence will remain clear. Because they are nonessential, these phrases or clauses are always set off by commas.

clause
Linda and Burt, *who just returned from Alaska,* would go on another vacation tomorrow. (This relative clause is not essential because it just adds interesting details to the sentence; without it, the meaning of the sentence is still clear)

phrase
The cockatiels, *chirping loudly to the music of the nearby television,* should live for up to twenty years. (This verb phrase is nonessential, supplying interesting details but not essential information)

4. Most clauses beginning with *that* are not set off with commas.

Where is the report *that he left on the the desk this morning*?

PRACTICE 1   Punctuate Restrictive and Nonrestrictive Clauses and Phrases

Punctuate the phrases or clauses in the following sentences correctly, putting commas only around nonessential phrases and clauses. Some sentences may be correct.

1. A person who insists on piling papers on any available space can be difficult to live with.

2. Mrs. Collins who once dreamed of being an anthropologist now works at the local bookstore.

3. The Alamo the site of the famous battle is a popular tourist attraction in San Antonio.

4. Calculus 101 which is required for many majors is a very demanding course for most college freshmen.

5. He reminds me of my son who always enjoys a spirited discussion of film. (The answer differs, depending on the number of sons!)

6. Asim who took Composition 102 last semester passed the course easily even though English is not his first language.

7. The storm racing up the eastern seaboard threatened South Carolina with dangerous winds.

8. The class nodding and yawning woke up quickly when the teacher announced a pop-quiz.

9. Fariba who is from Iran enjoyed meeting Svetlana who is from Bulgaria.

10. Pet dogs that run away at any opportunity should be fenced.

PRACTICE 2 Punctuating Restrictive and Nonrestrictive Clauses and Phrases

Create a sentence including the phrase or clause given. Determine whether the phrase or clause is restrictive or nonrestrictive in your sentence; then punctuate the sentence correctly. The first sentence has been done for you.

1. who ran up the stairs

   The young man who ran up the stairs had just finished his final exam.

2. crying in the corner

   _____

3. which he had not known

   _____

4. that he detested

   _____

5. singing in the shower

   _____

6. wearing a purple coat

   _____

7. which creaked and moaned

   _____

8. who remained silent

   _____

9. howling in the dark

_____

10. a difficult problem

_____

PRACTICE 3   **Punctuating Restrictive and Nonrestrictive Clauses and Phrases**

Combine the following sentences, inserting phrases and clauses when necessary and punctuating correctly. Omit any repeated words or phrases. The first group of sentences has been done for you.

1.1 Being a freshman can be a dreadful experience.

1.2 Freshmen are entering new surroundings.

1.3 Freshmen are harassed by upperclassmen.

1.4 Freshmen have four long years ahead of them.

_____

_____

_____

2.1 The new suburban vans are becoming bigger every year.

2.2 The vans look like off-road vehicles with glandular problems.

_____

_____

3.1 There is extra roominess inside the vans.

3.2 The roominess is great for large families.

3.3 The roominess is great for hauling Little League teams.

3.4 The roominess is great for traveling with lots of luggage.

_____

_____

_____

4.1 However, the larger vehicles are hard to handle.

4.2 Their greater bumper height makes extra weight.

4.3 The extra weight makes for more damage to regular-sized cars.

4.4 The damage results when accidents occur.

_____

_____

_____

5.1 These monster-vans are proliferating.

5.2 This proliferation will surely cause insurance rates to rise.

5.3 The rates will rise in the near future.

_____

_____

_____

6.1 Higher insurance rates will affect all drivers.

6.2 The impact will be negative.

6.3 Suburban minivan manufacturers should begin to study ways to counteract this problem.

_____

_____

_____

(ESL) WORDS AND MEANING

Commonly Misspelled Words

The following is a list of words that are difficult to spell:

across	grammar	possible
address	height	prefer
answer	illegal	prejudice
argument	immediately	privilege
athlete	important	probably
beginning	integration	psychology
behavior	intelligent	pursue
calendar	interest	reference
career	interfere	rhythm
conscience	jewelry	ridiculous
crowded	judgment	separate
definite	knowledge	similar
describe	maintain	since
desperate	mathematics	speech
different	meant	strength
disappoint	necessary	success
disapprove	nervous	surprise
doesn't	occasion	taught
eighth	opinion	temperature
environment	optimist	thorough
embarrass	particular	thought
exaggerate	perform	tired
familiar	perhaps	until
finally	personnel	weight
government	possess	written

PRACTICE 1   Identifying Correctly Spelled Words

Circle the correctly spelled word in each of the following pairs.

1. arguement   argument

2. seperate   separate

3. judgment   judgement

4. privelege   privilege

5. writen   written

6. jewelery   jewelry

7. sucess   success

8. desparate   desperate

9. occasion   ocasion

10. embarass   embarrass

PRACTICE 2 Identifying Correctly Spelled Words

Circle the correctly spelled word in each of the following pairs.

1. weight   wieght
2. untill   until
3. thought   thot
4. thorough   thorugh
5. rhithem   rhythm

6. preform   perform
7. mathmatics   mathematics
8. grammer   grammar
9. goverment   government
10. optimist   optomist

PRACTICE 3 Correcting Misspelled Words

Cross out any misspelled words and rewrite them correctly.

1. He ansered the questions about his odd behaviour.

2. David wants to pursu a carer in computer science.

3. The student struggled with a troubled consience.

4. Don't exagerate your hieght by wearing those ridiculus shoes!

5. Grammer and spelling problems make the writer look uneducated.

6. The children disaproved when their parents began to dance.

7. He had a suprising knowledge of mathmatics.

8. On one occasion, Beth's opinon was paticulary essential.

9. The rhithem of Maya Angelou's speech enhances the beauty of her poetry.

10. He was so tird he thot that the weiht of his eyelids was overwhelming.

Words That Sound Alike

Many words in English are pronounced alike but are spelled very differently. These words need special study or memorization. The following list includes word pairs that pose problems for all writers.

Words aural/oral	Definition	Example
aural	having to do with hearing	The doctor said that he needs testing for *aural* skills.

Words	Definition	Example
oral	having to do with speech/the mouth	He had to give an *oral* presentation.
buy/by		
buy (verb)	to purchase	They *buy* shoes whenever there is a sale.
by (preposition)	past; near; not later than	The dog sits *by* the door.
capital/capitol		
capital (adjective)	fatal; major	The class debated *capital* punishment.
		The college is making *capital* improvements.
capital (noun)	money; leading city	He invested his *capital* in the stock market.
		Sacramento is the *capital* of California.
capitol (noun)	a legislative building	The *capitol* building in Washington D.C. is often visited by tourists.
complement/compliment		
complement (noun)	something that adds to or completes	The drapery *complements* the furniture.
compliment (verb)	to express praise or admiration	He rarely gives *compliments*.
passed/past		
passed (verb)	to move ahead	The jeep *passed* the car on the highway.
past (noun)	time before present	The *past* haunted him.
past (preposition)	beyond	The boys ran *past* the graveyard.
past (adjective)	not current	The storms were dangerous this *past* year.
plain/plane		
plain (adjective)	clear; ordinary	The letter lay on the table in *plain* sight.
plain (noun)	flat land with few trees	Early settlers lived in sod homes on the *plains*.
plane	flat/level surface; aircraft; degree of development	As part of her geometry assignment, she was told to plot a line through a *plane*.
		He was afraid of *planes*. They talk on different *planes*.
presence/presents		
presence	being present; a person's way of behavior	Her *presence* calmed the child.
		The president has a hypnotic *presence*.

Words	Definition	Example
Presents	gifts	Piles of *presents* were stacked under the Christmas tree.

principal/principle

principal (adjective)	main; most important	The *principal* idea is truth. The *principal* violinist led the orchestra.
principal (noun)	the head administrator of a public elementary or high school; amount of money	The *principal* is rarely popular. The *principal* earns interest in the account.
principle (noun)	a comprehensive and fundamental law, doctrine; a primary source; an ingredient that exhibits or imports a characteristic quality	Faith is a complex *principle*.

rain/reign/rein

rain	water falling to earth from clouds	The *rain* ended the drought.
reign	the time a king or queen rules	The *reign* of Queen Elizabeth II of England has been controversial.
rein	a strap attached to the bridle, used by the rider to control a horse	The young rider grabbed the *reins* in fear.

sight/site/cite

sight	ability to see; a view	Her *sight* was excellent. The pep assembly was a confusing *sight*.
site	a location	They visited the *site* of their new home.
cite	to quote as an expert in research	Always *cite* any outside sources used in your writing.

to/too/two

to (preposition)	toward a given direction	The students ran *to* class.
too (adverb)	very; also	The sale was *too* tempting. My friend bought a dress and shoes, *too*.
two	the number 2	He needs *two* cups of coffee in the morning.

waist/waste

waist	the middle of the body and the part of clothing that covers this area	The *waist* of the suit fits too snugly.

Words	Definition	Example
waste (verb)	careless use	Don't *waste* your time in class.
waste (noun)	objects/concepts that are not used and discarded	Often, *waste* can be recycled.

weather/whether

weather (noun)	conditions of the atmosphere	The *weather* in the Midwest changes hourly.
whether (conjunction)	if this were the case	He does not know *whether* or not he will pass.

whole/hole

whole	all; complete	She read the *whole* novel in one day.
hole	an opening	The mouse came through the *hole* in the wall.

write/right/rite

write	to convey ideas using words; to create	The students will *write* several essays.
right	correct	She enjoys being *right*!
	conforming to morality, justice, or law	We all know the *right* thing to do.
	close to a conservative position	The president's position is shifting to the *right*.
rite	ritual; repeated ceremonial action	Getting a driver's license at age sixteen is a *rite* of passage for teenagers in our society.

PRACTICE 1   Frequently Confused Words

Underline the correct sound-alike word in the parentheses for the sentence's meaning.

1. The students were nervous because this was their first (aural/oral) exam.

2. The (capital/capitol) of Missouri is Jefferson City.

3. The school's (principle/principal) left for a week to attend an educational seminar.

4. The guests brought many (presents/presence) to the baby shower.

5. The dessert was rather (plane/plain) for such a fancy party.

6. The taxi drove (past/passed) the address where it was supposed to have stopped.

7. (To/Too) many travelers often cause congestion at airports over Thanks-giving.

8. The belt was too small for my (waist/waste).

9. The game would begin (whether/weather) or not all the team members arrived on time.

10. Because his mother was watching, Jeremy ate the (whole/hole) plate of spinach.

PRACTICE 2   Frequently Confused Words

Underline the correct sound-alike words in the following sentences.

1. We should (buy/by) a new car before the old one falls completely apart.

2. His uncle cannot accept a (compliment/complement).

3. Students need to learn how to (site/cite) sources used in research.

4. Linda leads the horse while holding the (reins/reigns).

5. Natalie is a dramatic (presents/presence) when she enters a room.

6. Getting a driver's license is a (right/rite) of passage in the United States.

7. She jogs (two/to) miles before work every day.

8. James is the (principal/principle) cellist of the local symphony orchestra.

9. The young couple does not have much (capital/capitol) to invest.

10. The runner (passed/past) the walkers on the track.

PRACTICE 3   Frequently Confused Words

Write a sentence using each of the following words correctly.

1. aural: _____

2. oral: _____

3. compliment: _____

4. complement: _____

5. passed: _____

6. past: _____

7. plain: _____

8. plane: _____

9. rain: _____

10. reign: _____

11. rein: _____

12. too: _____

13. two: _____

14. to: _____

15. weather: _____

16. whether: _____

17. whole: _____

18. hole: _____

19. write: _____

20. right: _____

21. rite: _____

Contractions That Sound Like Other Words

Another category of words that sound alike but are spelled differently are **contractions**. The following words are often punctuated/spelled incorrectly.

Contractions it's/its	Definition	Example
it's	contraction: it is	*It's* going to rain.
its	belonging to it	*Its* wings were broken.
they're/their/there		
they're	contraction: they are	*They're* ready for any adventure.
their	belonging to them	*Their* pets run their home.
there	at that place	The library is over *there*, not here.
we're/were/where		
we're	contraction: we are	*We're* going to the beach for vacation.
were	verb/past tense of *are*	We *were* ready for a week.
where	in which location?	*Where* is the map?

Contractions	Definition	Example
who's/whose		
who's	contraction: who is	*Who's* going to the party?
whose	belonging to whom?	*Whose* socks are on the sofa?
you're/your		
you're	contraction: you are	*You're* in the way.
your	belonging to you	*Your* gift is in the mail.

PRACTICE 1 Contractions That Sound Like Other Words

Underline the correct word in the parentheses for the meaning of the sentence.

1. (You're/Your) package was sent yesterday by overnight mail.

2. (It's/Its) in (they're/their/there) best interest to listen to the supervisor.

3. Do you know (whose/who's) socks these are?

4. I forgot where (were/we're) going this afternoon.

5. (Whose/Who's) going to the ice cream shop after dinner?

6. Are you certain that (you're/your) ready to take the driving test?

7. (Their/There/They're) is a trail that (their/there/they're) supposed to walk.

8. Exactly (we're/were/where) did you think the restaurant was located?

9. (It's/Its) engine overheated in the hot, arid Nevada desert.

10. The leaves (we're/were/where) turning colors as autumn approached.

PRACTICE 2 Contractions

Underline the correct word in the parentheses.

1. (Your/You're) luck is about to change.

2. He isn't sure (whose/who's) book is under the desk.

3. (Where/Were) did you expect to find happiness?

4. Getting from here to (their/there) is not as easy as it seems.

5. The cat howled for (it's/its) dinner every night at five o'clock.

6. (Were/Where) (your/you're) notes on the computer?

7. (Who's/Whose) leaving early for the concert?

8. (There/They're) are no tickets left!

9. We (were/where) going to camp out overnight to get good seats.

10. (It's/Its) not a good idea to wait until the last minute to start an essay.

Words That Sound or Look Almost Alike

The following words may not be spelled exactly alike. However, they sound alike and are often confused.

Words	Definition	Example
accept/except		
accept (verb)	to acknowledge as true;	She *accepted* his explanation.
	to receive	They *accepted* the wedding gifts.
except	other than	All of the assignments *except* one were easy.
advice/advise		
advice (noun)	wise suggestions about solutions to a problem	He never listens to *advice*.
advise (verb)	to make suggestions; to give advice	The counselor *advises* the confused freshmen.
affect/effect		
affect (verb)	to influence	The weather will *affect* your mood.
effect (noun)	end product; result	The *effect* of the accident was obvious for years.
breath/breathe		
breath (noun)	air inhaled or exhaled by living creatures	The swimmer held his *breath*.
breathe (verb)	to exhale or inhale	The cat *breathes* silently.
choose/chose		
choose (verb, present tense)	pick/select	They could not *choose* a restaurant.
chose (past tense)	picked/selected	They *chose* to order pizza.
conscience/conscious		
conscience	thought process acknowledging right and wrong	He has no *conscience*.
conscious	aware of being/ existence; thinking	The students were not *conscious* after lunch.

Words	Definition	Example
council/consul/counsel		
council (noun)	group that meets/ plans/governs	The city *council* meets each month.
consul (noun)	government official in foreign service	The German *consul* met with the President.
counsel (verb)	to advise	The department chair *counseled* the frustrated student.
desert/dessert		
desert (noun)	dry, barren land	The sunsets on the *desert* are spectacular.
desert (verb)	to leave alone/abandon	His friends *deserted* him.
dessert (noun)	last dish of a meal; often sweet	They decided to avoid sweet, fat *desserts*.
diner/dinner		
diner (noun)	a long, narrow type of restaurant with counters and booths; a person who is eating	At the *diner*, they have an old juke box. The *diners* enjoy listening to oldies from the juke box.
dinner	the large, important meal of the day (mid-day or evening)	The fried chicken is for *dinner*.
emigrate/immigrate		
emigrate	to leave a country	They *emigrated* from China.
immigrate	to enter a new country	*Immigration* is very complex.
farther/further		
farther (physically)	greater distance	The sprinter ran *farther* than he had to.
further	to advance an ideal/ goal/cause; greater distance (mentally)	The protesters *further* the cause of equality. Most arguments can be *further* developed.
loose/lose		
loose	not tight	*Loose*-fitting clothing has been in style recently.
lose (verb)	to misplace; to be unable to find; to fail to win	I always *lose* my earrings. He *lost* the tennis match.
personal/personnel		
personal	pertaining to the individual; private concerns	*Personal* information should remain confidential.
personnel	employees	*Personnel* should be aware of their benefits.

Words	Definition	Example
quiet/quit/quite		
quiet	little noise; peaceful	The class is too *quiet*.
quit	to stop suddenly, to give up	The employee *quit* suddenly.
quite	definitely	You were *quite* right.
special/especially		
special (adjective)	unique	Their anniversary was a *special* event.
especially (adverb)	even more; very	Final exams can be *especially* difficult.
than/then		
than	word to make comparison	Sale prices are better *than* original prices.
then	at that time	First they studied; *then* they took the exam.
thorough/though		
thorough	detailed, complete, accurate	Social attitudes changed after several *thorough* studies were made.
though (conjunction)	despite	*Though* the trees are changing colors, the temperature is warm.
through/threw		
through	in one side and out the other	The ball crashed *through* the window.
threw (verb)	to throw/past tense	The president *threw* the first pitch.

© 2010 Wadsworth, Cengage Learning

PRACTICE 1   Words That Sound or Look Almost Alike

Underline the correct word in parentheses for the meaning of the sentence.

1. After the race, the swimmer was short of (breathe/breath).

2. The county (council/consul/counsel) met shortly after the disaster occurred.

3. The members of the symphony orchestra ate (diner/dinner) at the (diner/ dinner).

4. I need to (loose/lose) weight before my next physical exam.

5. Shanika ran (further/farther) than her brother Latrelle.

6. The Surf Shop clerk didn't (except/accept) the shipment of dogsleds.

7. The library was (quiet/quit/quite) (quiet/quit/quite).

8. The officer's talk about drugs had quite an (affect/effect) on the seventh-grade class.

9. The (personal/personnel) office's task was to evaluate all employees.

10. In the (desert/dessert), nuts and dates often are eaten for (desert/dessert).

| PRACTICE 2 | **Words That Sound or Look Almost Alike** |

Write a sentence for each of the following words, demonstrating the difference in meaning from similar words.

1. accept: _____

2. except: _____

3. advice: _____

4. advise: _____

5. conscience: _____

6. conscious: _____

7. loose: _____

8. lose: _____

9. thorough: _____

10. though: _____

Confusing Verbs That Sound Alike: Lie/Lay; Rise/Raise; Sit/Set

These six verbs are often confused. To understand how to use them correctly, it is important to understand the difference between *reflexive verbs* that *do not* take an object (the verb needs no noun to complete the meaning of the sentence) and *transitive verbs* that *do* take an object. *Lie, rise,* and *sit* are reflexive; *lay, raise,* and *set* are transitive.

Lie, Rise, Sit

Meaning	Present	Present Participle	Past	Past Participle
lie (to rest or recline)	lie	lying	lay	has/have lain
rise (to move upward)	rise	rising	rose	has/have risen

Meaning	Present	Present Participle	Past	Past Participle
sit (to move body into sitting position)	sit	sitting	sat	has/have sat

The family dog loves *to lie* by the front door.

The bread dough *rises* well on the warm kitchen counter.

She *sits* in front of a computer for eight hours every day.

Reflexive verbs are often followed by a prepositional phrase, not a stand-alone noun.

Lay, Raise, Set

Meaning	Present	Present Participle	Past	Past Participle
lay (to put an object down)	lay	laying	laid	has/have laid
raise (to lift or move something up)	raise	raising	raised	has/have raised
set (to carefully place something)	set	setting	set	has/have set

She *lay* the flowers carefully on the table.

Please *raise* the window shades.

She *sets* a lovely table.

The object (underlined) is necessary to complete the meaning of these sentences.

PRACTICE 1   Using Lie/Lay, Rise/Raise, Sit/Set

Fill in the blanks with the correct form of the above verbs.

1. The book has _____ (lie/lay) out in the rain all day.

2. Steam is _____ (raise/rise) from the hot pavement.

3. He _____ (lie/lay) the knife carefully on the counter.

4. _____ (sit/set) the boxes down before you hurt yourself!

5. She felt ill suddenly, so she is _____ (lie/lay) down in the guest room.

6. He had to move because the landlord _____ (raise/rise) the rent.

7. Don't _____ (sit/set) on those chairs!

8. His clothes are _____ (lay/lie) all over the room.

9. _____ (Rise/Raise) in unison, the students left the classroom.

10. They are _____ (sit/set) the chairs in the park for the picnic.

PRACTICE 2   Using Lie/Lay, Rise/Raise, Sit/Set

Write your own sentences, using each verb correctly.

1. Lie/Lay

_____

_____

2. Rise/Raise

_____

_____

3. Sit/Set

_____

_____

PRACTICE 3   Using Lie/Lay, Rise/Raise, Sit/Set

Determine whether the verbs are used correctly in the following sentences. Change those that are incorrect.

1. He is lying about his curfew.

2. You do not have to rise your hand at the dinner table!

3. She spent the day laying on the sand or sitting by the shore.

4. Set the table, and set up straight!

5. At the end of the paintball tournament, the losing team raised a white flag.

6. Tatyana has set in the front row all semester because she lost her glasses.

7. Her empty purse lay on the desk all day yesterday.

8. The moon is rising slowly this evening.

9. The vase had been sit on the table.

10. You have lain on your bed all afternoon!

Two- and Three-Word Verb Phrases

These phrases are often difficult for nonnative speakers. Many of them are idiomatic expressions, and they need to be studied or memorized.

> **Phrasal Verbs (Two-Word and Three-Word Verbs)**
>
> The term *phrasal verb* refers to a verb and preposition that together have a special meaning. For example, **put + off** means "postpone." Sometimes a phrasal verb consists of three parts. For example, **put + up + with** means "tolerate." Phrasal verbs are also called *two-word verbs* or *three-word verbs*.
>
> | | |
> |---|---|
> | **Separable Phrasal Verbs** | A phrasal verb may be either *separable* or *nonseparable*. |
> | (a) **I *handed* my paper *in*** yesterday. | |
> | (b) **I *handed in* my paper** yesterday. | With a separable phrasal verb, a noun may come either between the verb and the preposition or after the preposition, as in (a) and (b). |
> | (c) **I *handed it in*** yesterday. *(INCORRECT: I handed in it yesterday.)* | A pronoun comes between the verb and the preposition if the phrasal verb is separable, as in (c). |
> | **Nonseparable Phrasal Verbs** | With a nonseparable phrasal verb, a noun or pronoun must follow the preposition, as in (d) and (e). |
> | (d) **I *ran into* an old friend** yesterday. **I *ran into* her** yesterday. *(INCORRECT: I ran an old friend into.)* | |
> | (e) *(INCORRECT: I ran her into yesterday.)* | |

Phrasal verbs are especially common in information English. Below is a list of common phrasal verbs and their usual meanings. This list contains only those phrasal verbs used in the exercises in the text. The phrasal verbs marked with an asterisk (*) are nonseparable.

A	ask out	*ask someone to go on a date*
B	bring about, bring on	*cause*
	bring up	*(1) rear children; (2) mention or introduce a topic*
C	call back	*return a telephone call*
	call in	*ask to come to an official place for a specific purpose*
	call off	*cancel*
	*call on	*(1) ask to speak in class; (2) visit*
	call up	*call on the telephone*
	*catch up (with)	*reach the same position or level*

---

*Indicates a nonseparable phrasal verb.

	*check in, check into	register at a hotel
	*check into	investigate
	check out	(1) take a book from the library; (2) investigate
	*check out (of)	leave a hotel
	cheer up	make (someone) feel happier
	clean up	make clean and orderly
	*come across	meet by chance
	cross out	draw a line through
	cut out	stop an annoying activity
D	do over	do again
	*drop by, drop in (on)	visit informally
	drop off	leave something/someone at a place
	drop out (of)	stop going to school, to a class, to a club, etc.
F	figure out	find the answer by reasoning
	fill out	write the completions of a questionnaire or official form
	find out	discover information
G	*get along (with)	exist satisfactorily
	get back (from)	(1) return from a place; (2) receive again
	*get in, get into	(1) enter a car; (2) arrive
	*get off	leave an airplane, a bus, a train, a subway, a bicycle
	*get on	enter an airplane, a bus, a train, a subway, a bicycle
	*get out of	(1) leave a car; (2) avoid work or an unpleasant activity
	*get over	recover from an illness
	*get through	finish
	*get up	arise from bed, a chair
	give back	return an item to someone
	give up	stop trying
	*go over	review or check carefully
	*grow up (in)	become an adult
H	hand in	submit an assignment
	hang up	(1) conclude a telephone conversation; (2) put clothes on a hanger or a hook
	have on	wear
K	keep out (of)	not enter
	*keep up (with)	stay at the same position or level
	kick out (of)	force (someone) to leave

*Indicates a nonseparable phrasal verb.

L   *look after .... *take care of*

    *look into .... *investigate*

    *look out (for) .... *be careful*

    look over .... *review or check carefully*

    look up .... *look for information in a reference book*

M   make up .... (1) *invent;* (2) *do past work*

N   name after, name for ...... *give a baby the name of someone else*

P   *pass away .... *die*

    pass out .... (1) *distribute;* (2) *lose consciousness*

    pick out .... *select*

    pick up .... (1) *go to get someone (e.g., in a car);* (2) *take in one's hand*

    point out .... *call attention to*

    put away .... *remove to a proper place*

    put back .... *return to original place*

    put off .... *postpone*

    put on .... *put clothes on one's body*

    put out .... *extinguish a cigarette or cigar*

    *put up with .... *tolerate*

R   *run into, *run across .... *meet by chance*

    *run out (of) .... *finish a supply of something*

S   *show up .... *appear, come*

    shut off .... *stop a machine, light, faucet*

T   *take after .... *resemble*

    take off .... (1) *remove clothing;* (2) *leave on a trip*

    take out .... (1) *take someone on a date;* (2) *remove*

    take over .... *take control*

    take up .... *begin a new activity or topic*

    tear down .... *demolish; reduce to nothing*

    tear up .... *tear into many little pieces*

    think over .... *consider carefully*

    throw away, throw out ... *discard; get rid of*

    throw up .... *vomit; regurgitate food*

    try on .... *put on clothing to see if it fits*

    turn down .... *decrease volume or intensity*

    turn in .... (1) *submit an assignment;* (2) *go to bed*

    turn off .... *stop a machine, light, faucet*

    turn on .... *begin a machine, light, faucet*

    turn out .... *extinguish a light*

    turn up .... *increase volume or intensity*

*Indicates a nonseparable phrasal verb.

| PRACTICE 1 | Using Two- and Three-Word Phrases |

For each sentence, choose a verb phrase from the previous list. Write it correctly in the sentence.

1. I cannot _____ the answer to the physics problem.

2. Don't _____ Grandmother without calling first.

3. _____ the facts before you make accusations.

4. After Luis stopped attending classes, he was _____ school.

5. James Rojas III was _____ his father and grandfather.

6. Don't forget to _____ the kids from soccer practice.

7. He _____ her note to destroy the evidence.

8. _____ your plans to drop out of school; you may regret your decision.

9. _____ the volume on your television! I think the phone is ringing.

10. Please _____ your homework on the assigned date!

Readings

DESCRIPTION

DEEP COLD*

Verlyn Klinkenborg

In this essay, the author recounts some of his experiences living and working on small farms. Pay close attention to the number of sensory images the author creates to get the reader to do more than just "see" the elements but to "feel" them as well.

Pre-reading exercise: Meaning comes primarily from words. Before reading the essay, look up the definitions of the following words appearing in the text. The numbers in parentheses refer to the paragraph number in the essay.

audible (1)	paradox (3)
brood (3)	reservoirs (3)
clapboard (3)	rime (2)
claustrophobia (2)	superstitiously (3)
gnashing (1)	trepidation (3)

1   If deep cold made a sound, it would be the scissoring and gnashing of a skater's blades against hard gray ice, or the screeching the snow sets up when you walk across it in the blue light of afternoon. The sound might be the stamping of feet at bus stops and train stations, or the way the almost perfect clarity of the audible world on the icy day is muted by scarves and mufflers pulled up over the face and around the ears.

2   But the true sound of deep cold is the sound of the wind. Monday morning, on the streets of Cambridge Massachusetts, the wind chill approached fifty below zero. A stiff northwest wind rocked in the trees and snatched at cars as they idled at the curb. A rough rime had settled over the old-brick city the day before, and now the wind was sanding it smooth. It was cold of Siberian or Antarctic intensity, and I could feel a kind of claustrophobia settling in all over Boston. People went about their errands, only to cut them short instantly, turning backs to the gust and fleeing for cover.

3   It has been just slightly milder in New York. Furnace repairmen and oil-truck drivers are working on the memory of two hours' sleep. Swans in the smaller reservoirs brood on the ice, and in the swamps that line the railroad tracks in Dutchess Country, you can see how the current was moving when the cold snap brought it to a halt. The soil in windblown fields looks—and is—iron hard. It's all a paradox, a cold that feels absolutely rigid yet which nonetheless seeps through ill-fitting windows, between clapboards, and along uninsulated pipe chases. People listen superstitiously to the sounds in their heating ducts, to the banging of the radiators, afraid of silence. They turn the key in their cars with trepidation. It's an old world this cold week.

---

*Excerpt from "Deep Cold" from *The Rural Life* by Verlyn Klinkenborg. Copyright © 2003 by Verlyn Klinkenborg. By permission of Little, Brown and Company, Inc.

Descriptive Technique Questions

1. Why is the paradox in paragraph 3 effective in supporting the author's idea that the cold is not just a temperature but an invading force?

2. How many sensory images does the author use to help create the cold atmosphere being described?

3. Is the essay more subjective or objective? Point out some examples to support your conclusion.

Suggestions for Writing

1. Write an objective descriptive paragraph about one of the four seasons.

2. Now, rewrite the same descriptive paragraph subjectively.

THE ICE CREAM TRUCK*

Luis J. Rodriguez

> In this essay taken from Rodriguez' *Always Running,* the author, a former Los Angeles gang member, describes people, places, and things, and paints an intimate and tactile portrait of an environment and its population in "ruin." Pay attention to how the random act of violence that occurs during the story doesn't seem shocking or unexpected; rather, it is an almost natural consequence of the poverty-stricken surroundings. Because of its liberal use of colloquial speech and slang, this essay is not a typical model for college essay writing. It is used here to emphasize the power of descriptive creativity and personal expression.

Pre-reading exercise: Meaning comes primarily from words. Before you start to read, use a dictionary to look up the definitions for the following words appearing in the essay. The numbers in the parentheses refer to the paragraph number of the essay.

burdensome (3)	hovered (37)
chimed (2)	litany (8)
cinder (1)	protruding (10)
clod (13)	rasp (3)
crevice (37)	ricocheted (32)
embankment (38)	spittle (15)

See the Glossary at the end of the essay for a translation of the words marked with an asterisk (*).

---

*Luis J. Rodriguez, "The Ice Cream Truck." From *Always Running—La Vida Loca, Gang Days in L.A.* by Luis J. Rodriguez. (Curbstone Press, 1993). Reprinted with permission of Curbstone Press. Distributed by Consortium.

"You cholos* *have great stories about climbing fences."*

—*a barrio boxing coach*

1　The Hills blistered below a haze of sun and smog. Mothers with wet strands of hair across their foreheads flung wash up to dry on weathered lines. Sweat-drenched men lay on their backs in the gravel of alleys, beneath broken-down cars propped up on cinder blocks. *Charrangas** and *corridos** splashed out of open windows.

2　Suddenly from over a hill, an ice cream truck raced by with packs of children running beside it. A hurried version of "Old McDonald Had a Farm" chimed through a speaker bolted on the truck's roof. The truck stopped long enough for somebody to toss out dozens of sidewalk sundaes, tootie-fruities and half-and-half bars to the children who gathered around, thrusting up small, dirt-caked hands that blossomed open as their shrieks blended with laughter.

3　Then the truck's transmission gears growled as it continued up the slope, whipped around a corner and passed a few of us *vatos** assembled on a field off Toll Drive. We looked over toward the echoes of the burdensome chimes, the slip and boom of the clutch and rasp of gears as the ice cream truck entered the dead-end streets and curves of Las Lomas.

4　"*Orale, ése, ¿qué está pasando?"** a dude named Little Man asked while passing a bottle of Tokay wine to Clavo.

5　"It's Toots and the *gaba*, you know, Axel," Clavo replied. "They just stole an ice cream truck on Portrero Grande Drive."

6　"*¡Qué cábula!*" Little Man said. "They sure is crazy."

7　We continued to talk and drink until the day melted into night.

8　Little Man and one of the López brothers, Fernie, all Tribe, were there in the field with me and my *camaradas* Clavo, Chicharrón, and Wilo. The four of us were so often together that the list of our names became a litany. We spray-painted our *placas** on the walls, followed by *AT* for Animal Tribe or *SSG* for South San Gabriel.

9　Everyone called me Chin because of my protruding jawbone. I had it tattooed on my ankle.

10　We sat around a small roasting pit Chicharrón made from branches and newspaper. Around us were ruins, remains of a home which had been condemned and later ravaged by fire. We assembled inside the old cement foundation with its scattered sections of brick and concrete walls splattered with markings and soot with rusted reinforcing bars protruding from stone blocks.

11　We furnished the lot with beat-up couches and discarded sofas. Somebody hung plastic from a remaining cinder-block wall to a low branch so homeboys could sleep there—and miss most of any rain—when there was nowhere else to go. It was really a vacant lot but we called all such lots "the fields."

12　Even as we talked, there was Noodles, a wino and old *tecato,** crashed out on the sofa.

13　"Get up Noodles, time for some *refin*,*" Chicharrón exclaimed as he placed stolen hot dogs and buns on the fire. Wilo threw a dirt clod at the sofa and Noodles mumbled some incoherent words.

14　"*Orale,* leave the *vato* alone, *ése*,*" Little Man said.

15　But Noodles got up, spittle dripping from his mouth.

16　"Hey *ése*, Noodles is awake, and man is he pissed," Wilo said.

17　"How can you tell?" Chicharrón asked.

18　"When he moves fast and you can't understand what he's saying, then he's pissed," Wilo answered. "When he moves slow and you still can't understand what he's saying, he's all right."

19　Noodles staggered toward us, his arms flailing, as if boxing—huffing, puffing, and dropping mucus from his nose.

20   "Get the hell out of here, *pinche**," Wilo said as he stood up and pushed the wino aside.

21   "You thinks youse are tuss dues . . . you ain't so tuss," Noodles said, throwing sloppy left hooks and uppercuts into the air.

22   Wilo placed his hand over Noodles' head, whose wiry body looked like a strand from a dirty mop. Wilo was also thin and slippery. The rest of us laughed and laughed at the two *flaquillos** goofing around.

23   "Ah leave the *vato* alone, homeboy," Clavo suggested. "Let's break out another bottle."

24   As we cooked, shared wine and told stories of *jainas** and the little conquests, of fights for honor, homeys and the 'hood, a gray Mercury sedan with its headlights turned off crept up the road. Wilo was the closest up the slope to the street. He looked over at the Mercury, then frowned.

25   "Anybody recognize the *ranfla**"? Wilo inquired.

26   "*Chalo*," Chicharrón responded. "It looks too funky to be gangbangers."

27   "Unless that's what they want it to look like."

28   Wilo moved up the slope from the field, followed by Clavo, Chicharrón, and Little Man. Fernie stayed back with Noodles and me. Wilo and Clavo were the first ones to hit the street as the Mercury delayed a turn around a curve.

29   Clavo moved to one side of the Mercury, its occupants covered in darkness. He stretched out his arms and yelled out: "Here stand The Animal Tribe—*¡y qué!**

30   The Mercury stopped. A shadow stepped out of a bashed-in side door, a sawed-off shotgun in his hands. Another shadow pushed an automatic rifle out the side window.

31   "Sangra Diablos! *¡Qué rifa!**" the dude with the shotgun yelled out. Then a blast snapped at the night air.

32   Wilo and Chicharrón fell back down the slope. Automatic gunfire followed them as they rolled in the dirt. The bullets skimmed off tree branches, knocked over trash cans and ricocheted off walls, Wilo ended up face-down; Chicharrón landed on his butt. Noodles knelt behind the sofa, whimpering. The cracking sounds stopped. The Mercury sped off, its tires throwing up dirt and pebble behind it.

33   I could see the car speeding down another hill. I ran up the slope, slipping and sliding toward the road. On the street, Little Man kneeled over Clavo, who lay sprawled on the ground and trembling. Half of Clavo's face was shot full of pellets, countless black, streaming round holes; his eye dripping into the dirt.

34   Wilo and the others climbed up and rushed up to Little Man. Fernie began jumping up and down like he had been jolted with lightning, letting out *gritos**. I kept looking at Clavo's face, thinking something stupid like how he was such a dummy, always taking chances, all the time being "the dude." Then I squatted on the ground, closed my eyelid and let a tear stream down the side of my face.

35   Windows flung upwards. Doors were pushed aside. People bolted out of their homes. Mothers cursed in Spanish from behind weather-beaten picket fences.

36   As Clavo was taken to the hospital, Fernie talked about getting all the Tribe together, about meeting later that night, about guns and warfare and "*ya estuvo*"—that's it. A war, fought for generations between Lomas and Sangra, flared up again.

37   Later, as I walked down the hills on the way back home, sirens tore across the sky and a sheriff's helicopter hovered nearby, beaming a spotlight across shacks and brush, over every hole and crevice of the neighborhood.

38   I mounted a fence which wound around a dirt embankment, hoping to get out of the helicopter's sights. I looked over the other side and there overturned at the bottom of the gully, to be ravaged by scavengers for parts, to be another barrio monument, lay an ice cream truck.

Glossary

chale (expression) something akin to "Aww, man!"

charranga lively Latin music

cholos gangbangers; homeboys

corridos Mexican ballads usually accompanied by guitar

flaquillos skinny ones

gaba (gabacho) gringo

gritos shouts or yells

jainas young women; chicks

"Orale, ése, ¿qué . . ." "Hey, you, what's happening?"

pinche kitchen boy

placa graffiti: badge of honor; name or nickname (personal); gang name or symbol

¡Qué cábula! "They sure are crazy!"

ranfla car

refin unpaid for; stolen

"Sangra Diablos! . . ." "The Bloods are devils!"

tecato addict (usually heroin)

vato (bato) simpleton; hombre of low esteem

". . .—¡y qué!" "So there!"

Descriptive Technique Questions

1. Is the essay more objective or subjective? Point out examples to support your choice.

2. Rodriguez uses many Spanish words and phrases. How do they add to the descriptive quality of the essay?

3. How does the ice cream truck come to represent the barrio Rodriguez describes in the essay?

4. Point out some figurative language devices (simile, metaphor, personification) Rodriguez uses in the essay. How do they effectively support the author's description of the barrio and its inhabitants?

Suggestions for Writing

1. Write a paragraph about a group of people and their environment that is familiar to you. Use several figurative language devices to help describe them and their relationships.

2. Do the people you know use slang or other specialized language? Write a paragraph using slang or terms (even from a different language) that help describe the people and their culture.

HALLOWEEN HAVOC

Erin Nelson (student)

In the following descriptive essay, student writer Erin Nelson creates a spooky night of Halloween fun, filled with all the traditional images of ghosts and goblins that have scared and excited children through the ages. Pay particular attention to the author's use of figurative language devices (e.g., personification and simile) to create vivid images and sensory emotion.

Pre-reading exercise: Meaning comes primarily from words. Before reading the essay, look up the definitions of the following words that appear in the text. The numbers in parentheses refer to the paragraph number of the essay.

briskly (1)	musty (4)
curdle (5)	prey (2)
grotesque (2)	vicious (3)
gruesome (2)	

1   When the wind begins to howl like the wolves and the leaves begin to fall, the time is coming nearer to the creepiest night of the year. The silvery moon is full; the clouds briskly roll across the black sky. A chill is sent down spines, and the neck hairs stand on end. What could it be? Halloween? All Hallows Eve can be the spookiest night of the year because of the creepy decorations, the chilling weather, and the scary goblins.

2   The spooky old houses come to life at night with gruesome decorations. With grotesque carved faces, the jack-o-lanterns give off an eerie glow. The tombstones line the sidewalk; beware of the bloody hands, for they may grab intruders. Bats as black as the night sky fly around in the air, and a black cat with razor-sharp fangs crosses the path of terrified prey. The ghosts and the goblins sneak around the monster-like trees, ready to grab the next victim with ease.

3   The wind begins to whip, and the branches of the trees begin to sway like the bones of a forgotten skeleton. The fallen dead leaves whirl around like a vicious tornado. When the fog rolls in, the eyes begin to play tricks. A monster! With the fog comes the mist that makes you chilled down to the bone.

4   Screams echo from all directions. A witch, a vampire, and a ghost fly by; consequently, they disappear down the dark, damp street. The hairy werewolf howls, and the musty old mummy moans. Look out! Here comes Freddy—with blood dripping from his razorblade fingers. He's going to get you!

5   One night of the year is all it takes to get the heart pounding and the blood flowing. To be out on this night is quite a fright, so beware of the boogie man. With all the scary sights and the blood-curdling sounds on Halloween, a flashlight will come in handy. Happy Halloween!

Descriptive Technique Questions

1. Alliteration is the repetition of the same sounds (e.g., consonants: the willowy, whipping wind; or vowels: as loose as a goose or a moose), usually done to support or help create a particular mood. Point out examples of alliteration in the essay using both consonants and vowels, and explain how they help support or create a mood.

2. Brief writing doesn't have to mean underdeveloped writing. All of the paragraphs in this essay are short. However, the author packs each paragraph with vivid descriptions. Point out single words, phrases, similes, metaphors, and sensory images that help create distinct moods quickly and fully.

3. The author refers to "Freddy" in paragraph 4 but does not explain who he is. Is an explanation necessary? Did you know to whom the author is referring? Explain how making such a reference might hurt an essay.

Suggestions for Writing

1. In her light-hearted essay, Erin Nelson describes Halloween as spooky. Write a paragraph describing a holiday that evokes one particular emotion for you.

2. Choose one of the body paragraphs in Nelson's essay and rewrite it, choosing a feeling other than spooky. Remember to use figurative language and sensory images to create and support the feeling you have chosen.

NARRATION

THE ROOMMATE'S DEATH*

Jan Harold Brunvand

> In his essay, "The Roommate's Death," Jan Harold Brunvand relates one of a series of stories he calls "urban legends" because they have found their most popular and long-lived run in America and because, like all legends, they have been passed on from one person to another as having really occurred. The one telling the story usually states that he or she knew the person involved or that it was someone whom a close friend or family member had known. As Brunvand unveils the story and makes comments about it, see whether you can recognize any larger contemporary fears held by society that might be captured by the specific incidents in the story.

Pre-reading exercise: Meaning comes primarily from words. Before reading the essay, look up the definitions of the following words that appear in the

---

text. The numbers in parentheses refer to the paragraph number of the essay.

adornments (12)	plausible (3)
assailant (1)	refuge (1)
commission (1)	resolve (12)
elicit (7)	variants (10)
generalization (12)	venture (13)
motifs (4)	

1 Another especially popular example of the American adolescent shocker story is the widely known legend of "The Roommate's Death." It shares several themes with other urban legends. As in "The Killer in the Backseat" and "The Babysitter and the Man Upstairs," it is usually a lone woman in the story who is threatened—or thinks she is—by a strange man. As in "The Hook" and "The Boyfriend's Death," the assailant is often said to be an escaped criminal or a maniac. Finally, as in the latter legend, the actual commission of the crime is never described; only the resulting mutilated corpse is. The scratching sounds outside the girl's place of refuge are an additional element of suspense. Here is a version told by a University of Kansas student in 1965 set in Corbin Hall, a freshman women's dormitory there:

2 These two girls in Corbin had stayed late over Christmas vacation. One of them had to wait for a later train, and the other wanted to go to a fraternity party given that night of vacation. The dorm assistant was in her room— sacked out. They waited and waited for the intercom, and then they heard this knocking and knocking outside in front of the dorm. So the girl thought it was her date and she went down. But she didn't come back and she didn't come back. So real late that night this other girl heard a scratching and gasping down the hall. She couldn't lock the door, so she locked herself in the closet. In the morning she let herself out and her roommate had had her throat cut, and if the other girl had opened the door earlier, she [the dead roommate] would have been saved.

3 At all the campuses where the story is told, the reasons for the girls' remaining alone in the dorm vary, but they are always realistic and plausible. The girls' homes may be too far away for them to visit during vacation, such as in Hawaii or a foreign country. In some cases they wanted to avoid a campus meeting or other obligation. What separates the two roommates may be either that one goes out for food, or to answer the door, or to use the rest room. The girl who is left behind may hear the scratching noise either at her room door or at the closet door, if she hides there. Sometimes her hair turns white or gray overnight from the shock of the experience (an old folk motif). The implication in the story is that some maniac is after her (as is suspected about the pursuer in "The Killer in the Backseat"); but the truth is that her own roommate needs help, and she might have supplied it had she only acted more decisively when the noises were first heard. Usually some special emphasis is put on the victim's fingernails, scratched to bloody stumps by her desperate efforts to signal for help.

4 A story told by a California teenager, remembered from about 1964, seems to combine motifs of "The Babysitter and the Man Upstairs" with "The Roommate's Death." The text is unusually detailed with names and the circumstances of the crime:

5 Linda accepted a babysitting job for a wealthy family who lived in a two-story home up in the hills for whom she had never babysat before. Linda was

rather hesitant as the house was rather isolated and so she asked a girlfriend, Sharon, to go along with her, promising Sharon half of the babysitting fee she would earn. Sharon accepted Linda's offer and the two girls went up to the big two-story house.

6   The night was an especially dark and windy one and rain was threatening. All went well for the girls as they read stories aloud to the three little boys they were sitting for and they had no problem putting the boys to bed in the upstairs part of the house. When this was done, the girls settled down to watching television.

7   It was not long before the telephone rang. Linda answered the telephone, only to hear the heavy breathing of the caller on the other end. She attemped to elicit a response from the caller but he merely hung up. Thinking little of it and not wanting to panic Sharon, Linda went back to watching her television program, remarking that the caller had dialed a wrong number. Upon receiving the second call at which time the caller first engaged in a bit of heavy breathing and then instructed them to check on the children, the two girls became frightened and decided to call the operator for assistance. The operator instructed the girls to keep the caller on the line as long as possible should he call again so that she might be able to trace the call. The operator would check back with them.

8   The two girls then decided between themselves that one should stay downstairs to answer the phone. It was Sharon who volunteered to go upstairs. Shortly, the telephone rang again and Linda did as the operator had instruced her. Within a few minutes, the operator called back telling Linda to leave the house immediately with her friend because she had traced the calls to the upstairs phone.

9   Linda immediately hung up the telephone and proceeded to run to the stairway to call Sharon. She then heard a thumping sound coming from the stairway and when she approached the stairs she saw her friend dragging herself down the stairs by her chin, all of her limbs severed from her body. The three boys also lay dead upstairs in their beds.

10   Once again, the Indiana University Folklore Archive has provided the best published report on variants of "The Roommate's Death," Linda Dégh's summary of thirty-one texts and several subtypes and related plots collected since 1961. The most significant feature, according to her report, is the frequent appearance of a male rescuer at the end of the story. In one version, for example, two girls are left behind alone in the dorm by their roommate when she goes downstairs for food; they hear noises, and so stay in their room all night without opening the door. Finally the mailman comes around the next morning, and they call him from the window:

11   The mailman came in the front door and went up the stairs, and told the girls to stay in their room, that everything was all right but that they were to stay in their rooms [sic]. But the girls didn't listen to him cause he had said it was all right, so they came out into the hall. When they opened the door, they saw their girlfriend on the floor with a hatchet in her head.

In other Indiana texts the helpful male is a handyman, a milkman, or the brother of one of the roommates.

12   According to folklorist Beverly Crane, the male-female characters are only one pair of a series of significant opposites, which also includes home and away, intellectual versus emotional behavior, life and death, and several

others. A male is needed to resolve the female's uncertainty—motivated by her emotional fear—about how to act in a new situation. Another male has mutilated and killed her roommate with a blow to her head, "the one part of the body with which women are not supposed to compete." The girls, Crane suggested, are doubly out of place in the beginning, having left the haven of home to engage in intellectual pursuits, and having remained alone in the campus dormitory instead of rejoining the family on a holiday. Ironically, the injured girl must use her fingernails, intended to be long, lovely, feminine adornments, in order to scratch for help. But because her roommate fails to investigate the sound, the victim dies, her once pretty nails now bloody stumps. Crane concluded this ingenious interpretation with these generalizations:

13   The points of value implicit in this narrative are then twofold. If women wish to depend on traditional attitudes and responses they had best stay in a place where these attitudes and responses are best able to protect them. If, however, women do choose to venture into the realm of equality with men, they must become less dependent, more self-sufficient, more confident in their own abilities, and, above all, more willing to assume responsibility for themselves and others.

14   One might not expect to find women's liberation messages embedded in the spooky stories told by teenagers, but Beverly Crane's case is plausible and well argued. Furthermore, it is not at all unusual to find up-to-date social commentary in other modern folklore—witness the many religious and sexual jokes and legends circulated by people who would not openly criticize a church or the traditional social mores. Folklore does not just purvey the old codes of morality and behavior; it can also absorb newer ideas. What needs to be done to analyze this is to collect what Alan Dundes calls "oral-literary criticism," the informants' own comments about their lore. How clearly would the girls who tell these stories perceive—or even accept—the messages extrapolated by scholars? And a related question: Have any stories with clear liberationist themes replaced older ones cautioning young women to stay home, be good, and—next best—be careful, and call a man if they need help?

Narrative Technique Questions

1. Narrative storytelling is most effective when the tale appears realistic (that it really happened)—not made up or too fantastic to have actually happened. Pick one of the stories that Brunvald relates and point out elements that convinced you that the stories are based on real events.

2. What do you think of Beverly Crane's interpretation of the "Roommate's Death"? Are her ideas about feminist themes convincing?

Suggestions for Writing

1. Think of a horror story that scared you. Write a paragraph explaining what elements of the story had the greatest effect on you.

2. By yourself or in a group, create your own "urban legend." Write a narrative paragraph detailing the action.

THE EYE OF THE BEHOLDER*

Grace Suh

> In "The Eye of the Beholder," Grace Suh recounts a visit she made to a cosmetics counter for a facial makeover guaranteed by the "priestesses of beauty." However, after the process is complete, Suh does not like what she sees. Pay particular attention to the difference between "Estée's" idea of beauty and that eventually expressed by the author.

Pre-reading exercise: Meaning comes primarily from words. Before reading the essay, look up the definitions of the following words that appear in the text. The numbers in parentheses refer to the paragraph number of the essay.

astringent (9)	imperious (6)
bourgeois (3)	reclamation (5)
emulsifier (9)	renounce (3)
entropy (5)	reverie (11)
epiphanous (4)	scythe (5)
icons (5)	stark (2)

1   Several summers ago, on one of those endless August evenings when the sun hangs suspended just above the horizon, I made up my mind to become beautiful.

2   It happened as I walked by one of those mirrored glass-clad office towers, and caught a glimpse of my reflection out of the corner of my eye. The glass on this particular building was green, which might have accounted for the sickly tone of my complexion, but there was no explaining away the limp, ragged hair, the dark circles under my eyes, the facial blemishes, the shapeless, wrinkled clothes. The overall effect—the whole being greater than the sum of its parts—was one of stark ugliness.

3   I'd come home from college having renounced bourgeois suburban values, like hygiene and grooming. Now, home for the summer, I washed my hair and changed clothes only when I felt like it, and spent most of my time sitting on the lawn eating mini rice cakes and Snickers and reading dogeared back issues of *National Geographic*.

4   But that painfully epiphanous day, standing there on the hot sidewalk, I suddenly understood what my mother had been gently hinting these past months: I was no longer just plain, no longer merely unattractive. No, I had broken the Unsightliness Barrier. I was now UGLY, and aggressively so.

5   And so, in an unusual exertion of will, I resolved to fight back against the forces of entropy. I envisioned it as reclamation work, like scything down a lawn that has grown into meadow, or restoring a damaged fresco. For the first time in ages, I felt elated and hopeful. I nearly sprinted into the nearby Nieman Marcus. As I entered the cool, hushed, dimly lit first floor and saw the gleaming counters lined with vials of magical balm, the priestesses of beauty in their sacred smocks, and the glossy photographic icons of the goddesses themselves—Paulina, Linda, Cindy, Vendella—in a wild, reckless burst of inspiration I thought to myself, Heck, why just okay? Why not BEAUTIFUL?

6   At the Estée Lauder counter, I spied a polished, middle-aged woman whom I hoped might be less imperious than the aloof amazons at the Chanel counter.

7   "Could I help you?" the woman (I thought of her as "Estée") asked.

8   "Yes," I blurted. "I look terrible. I need a complete makeover—skin, face, everything."

9   After a wordless scrutiny of my face, she motioned me to sit down and began. She cleansed my skin with a bright blue mud masque and clear, tingling astringent and then applied a film of moisturizer, working extra amounts into the rough patches. Under the soft pressure of her fingers, I began to relax. From my perch, I happily took in the dizzying, colorful swirl of beautiful women and products all around me. I breathed in the billows of perfume that wafted through the air. I whispered the names of products under my breath like a healing mantra: cooling eye gel, gentle exfoliant, nighttime neck area reenergizer, moisture recharging intensifier, ultra-hydrating complex, emulsifying immunage. I felt immersed in femininity, intoxicated by beauty.

10   I was flooded with gratitude at the patience and determination with which Estée toiled away at my face, painting on swaths of lip gloss, blush, and foundation. She was not working in vain, I vowed, as I sucked in my cheeks on her command. I would buy all these products. I would use them every day. I studied her gleaming, polished features—her lacquered nails, the glittering mosaic of her eyeshadow, the complex red shimmer of her mouth, her flawless, dewy skin—and tried to imagine myself as impeccably groomed as she.

11   Estée's voice interrupted my reverie, telling me to blot my lips. I stuck the tissue into my mouth and clamped down, watching myself in the mirror. My skin was a blankly even shade of pale, my cheeks and lips glaringly bright in contrast. My face had a strange plastic sheen, like a mannequin's. I grimaced as Estée applied the second lipstick coat: Was this right? Didn't I look kind of—fake? But she smiled back at me, clearly pleased with her work. I was ashamed of myself: Well, what did I expect? It wasn't like she had anything great to start with.

12   "Now," she announced. "Time for the biggie—Eyes."

13   "Oh. Well, actually, I want to look good and everything, but, I mean, I'm sure you could tell, I'm not really into a complicated beauty routine . . . " My voice faded into a faint giggle.

14   "So?" Estée snapped.

15   "Sooo . . . " I tried again, "I've never really used eye makeup, except, you know, for a little mascara sometimes, and I don't really feel comfortable———."

16   Estée was firm. "Well, the fact is that the eyes are the windows of the face. They're the focal point. An eye routine doesn't have to be complicated, but it's important to emphasize the eyes with some color, or they'll look washed out."

17   I certainly didn't want that. I leaned back again in my chair and closed my eyes.

18   Estée explained as she went: "I'm covering your lids with this champagne color. It's a real versatile base, 'cause it goes with almost any other color you put on top of it." I felt the velvety pad of the applicator sweep over my lids in a soothing rhythm.

19   "Now, being an Oriental, you don't have a lid fold, so I'm going to draw one with this charcoal shadow. Then, I fill in below the line with a lighter charcoal color with a bit of blue in it—frosted midnight—and then above it, on the outsides of your lids, I'm going to apply this plum color. There. Hold on a minute . . . Okay. Open up."

20   I stared at the face in the mirror, at my eyes. The drawn-on fold and dark, heavy shadows distorted and reproportioned my whole face. Not one of the

features in the mirror was recognizable, not the waxy white skin or the redrawn crimson lips or the sharp, deep cheekbones, and especially, not the eyes. I felt negated; I had been blotted out and another face drawn in my place. I looked up at Estée, and in that moment I hated her. "I look terrible," I said.

21   Her back stiffened. "What do you mean?" she demanded.

22   "Hideous. I don't even look human. Look at my eyes. You can't even see me!" My voice was hoarse.

23   She looked. After a moment, she straightened up again, "Well, I'll admit, the eye shadow doesn't look great." She began to put away the pencils and brushes, "But at least now you have an eyelid."

24   I told myself that she was a pathetic, middle-aged woman with a boring job and a meaningless life. I had my whole life ahead of me. All she had was the newest Richard Chamberlain miniseries.

25   But it didn't matter. The fact of the matter was that she was pretty, and I was not. Her blue eyes were recessed in an intricate pattern of folds and hollows. Mine bulged out.

26   I bought the skincare system and the foundation and the blush and the lip liner pencil and the lipstick and the primer and the eyeliner and the eyeshadows—all four colors. The stuff filled a bag the size of a shoebox. It cost a lot. Estée handed me my receipt with a flourish, and I told her, "Thank you."

27   In the mezzanine level washroom, I set my bag down on the counter and scrubbed my face with water and slimy pink soap from the dispenser. I splashed my face with cold water until it felt tight, and dried my raw skin with brown paper towels that scratched.

28   As the sun sank into the Chicago skyline, I boarded the Burlington Northern Commuter for home and found a seat in the corner. I set the shopping bag down beside me, and heaped its gilt boxes and frosted glass bottles into my lap. Looking out the window, I saw that night had fallen. Instead of trees and backyard fences I saw my profile—the same reflection, I realized, that I'd seen hours ago in the side of the green glass office building. I did have eyelids, of course. Just not a fold. I wasn't pretty. But I was familiar and comforting. I was myself.

29   The next stop was mine. I arranged the things carefully back in the rectangular bag, large bottles of toner and moisturizer first, then the short cylinders of masque and scrub and powder, small bottles of foundation and primer, the little logs of pencils and lipstick, then the flat boxed compacts of blush and eyeshadow. The packages fit around each other cleverly, like pieces in a puzzle. The conductor called out, "Fairview Avenue," and I stood up. Hurrying down the aisle, I looked back once at the neatly packed bag on the seat behind me, and jumped out just as the doors were closing shut.

Narrative Technique Questions

1. What are the factors that influence Suh to seek out a facial "makeover"?

2. At what point in the story does Suh realize that what she is doing is not going to solve the problem she thought she was correcting?

3. What does Suh finally realize about herself, and how do her final thoughts relate to the essay's title?

Suggestions for Writing

1. Write a paragraph about some part of your looks that you would like to change or a change that you had contemplated but decided not to complete.

2. Write a paragraph about how you think the culture influences people to want to change their appearance. Explore how this can be a negative or positive experience.

ANDRIYIVSKY DESCENT

Oksana Taranova (student)

In the following narrative essay, student writer Oksana Taranova, an émigré from Russia, recounts an experience in Kiev that became imprinted on her memory. Pay attention to how the elements of the story build in intensity as she becomes more emotional as the narration unfolds.

Pre-reading exercise: Meaning comes primarily from words. Before reading the essay, look up the definitions of the following words appearing in the text. The numbers in parentheses refer to the paragraph number of the essay.

aristocratic (2)	gargoyles (2)
cupolas (2)	immerse (1)
declaim (3)	panorama (1)
eminent (3)	tracery (2)
façades (2)	

1   I was thinking the other day, trying to remember the last time I enjoyed drinking coffee from a real porcelain cup while slowly turning the pages of a magazine in an open café in the early morning or late afternoon. I've become tired looking at modern buildings and skyscrapers consisting of the same boring glass and concrete. I've become bored looking at endless rows of parking lots jammed with cars and SUVs. And, I suppose just like you, I've become emotionally drained at the thought of another day surrounded by vista-less and drab surroundings. I need to immerse my soul in an architectural ocean, but the one I am thinking of is, indeed, across an ocean. Although I cannot visit the splendor of the city of my youth, I can travel there in times of need by merely closing my eyes. On such occasions, I can envision the magnificent architecture, fascinating art galleries, and breathtaking panoramas of the Dnieper River on a visit to the Andriyivsky Descent, the most fantastic street in Kiev.

2   The architecture of this exciting street has not been changed from when it was built in the 18th century. Historically, Andriyivsky Descent formed the shortest route between the aristocratic Upper Town and the tradesmen's Lower Town. I remember walking with my late mother through the maze of two and three-storied stone buildings, painted in a palette of lightly and richly hued colors. We would stop often to admire the splendid façades fronted with

bronze doors and intricately worked bronze openwork tracery. I can still picture my mother figure outlined against Kiev's skyline dominated by St. Andrew's Cathedral at the top of the street. Designed in the 17th century by the Italian architect Bartolomeo Rastrelli, the large, domed cathedral hovers above the city like a fatherly spirit, as the sunlight reflects brilliantly off its five gold cupolas like a sunrise. It often reminds me of my mother's golden hair shiny so brightly after coming in from an afternoon of gardening in our backyard. Descending further to the lower town, we always looked into the gorgeous medieval castle, Richard Coeur de Lion (Richard the Lion Heart). Built in the English Gothic style, the tops of the walls are decorated with grotesque figures of gargoyles. It's impossible to forget such dramatic architecture with its varied styles and historical significance.

3   Andriyivsky Descent is often called Kiev's Montmartré, a reference to the famous area in Paris where artists paint and sell their creations. The Descent is the heart and soul of Kiev's artistic community, where musicians, poets, and painters rent apartments an studios. Early on spring, summer, and autumn mornings, the street transforms into a vibrant, open-air market of colors and sounds; while musicians "play" and poets "say," artists hang their works on the walls of houses and arrange their sculptures on the green lawns. My mother and I would often mingle with the hundreds of tourists looking for the finest in Ukrainian crafts and arts. The steep, winding, stone street is a traditional locale for outdoor festivals and concerts. We were never surprised at the spontaneous clapping and cheering as each poet read aloud their latest work, or, as my mother often reviewed them with a mischievous smile: masterpieces of ambiguity!

4   A spectacular view is enjoyed at any point along the Descent. However, to the right of the Richard Castle is a steep, twisting flight of black, iron steps leading to a platform which provides an incredible panorama of the Dnieper River and its six bridges. The river is like an unbelievable expanse of crystal glittering in the sun. The sky is normally a deep, azure blue dotted with fluffy, white clouds reflected on the mirrored surface of the river. Visitors, my mother and I included, returned to the platform often to sip a hot coffee or cocoa while a soft breeze rose from the Dnieper and gently lifted our senses. You begin to feel as if gravity itself is being released, allowing you to float above the spectacular sight below. My mother often felt as if she were a bird soaring in the heavens, her heart beating with passion; she suddenly realized what paradise must look like.

5   Andriyivsky Descent is an exciting locale to visit. If you are looking for a vacation to stimulate your senses and your soul, a visit to Kiev in the Ukraine will satisfy your hunger. For me, it is like oil on a canvas. I keep it in the museum in my mind. In that way, even though I miss my mother every day, I can visit the Andriyivsky Descent and with her on my arm, we descend towards the Dnieper, letting the sights and sights envelope us like a warm, comforting breeze. Live to pursue your dreams. They will give you life's greatest rewards and life's greatest adventures.

Narrative Technique Questions

1. What were the two significant elements in the author's life that prompted her to write about Andriyivsky Descent?

2. How does the author make the essay a narrative story rather than merely a travelogue?

3. Identify the similes the author uses in the essay. How do they make you respond emotionally to the author's story?

Suggestions for Writing

1. Think of a place that has special meaning for you. Write a narrative paragraph incorporating those elements having the greatest affect on you.

2. Write a narrative paragraph about a place you have never visited. Explain why you think it would have special meaning for you.

EXAMPLE

EXTREMELY COOL*

A. J. Jacobs

> A. J. Jacobs penned "Extremely Cool" in 1996 for *Entertainment Weekly*. As a writer and journalist, the author is concerned about the overuse and misuse of the term *extreme*. Even though the article was written in the last century (!), the term is still used today in phrases ranging from "extreme" sports to "extreme" deodorant.

Pre-reading exercise: Meaning comes primarily from words. Before reading the essay, look up the definitions of the following words that appear in the text. The numbers in parentheses refer to the paragraph number of the essay.

coup (1)   nihilistic (14)
divulges (1)   semantic (4)
hoary (15)   unction (4)
infantile (18)   zeitgeist (7)

DUSTBIN OF HISTORY AND CULTURE

Barry Goldwater: A politician from Arizona who ran as the Republican candidate—and obviously lost—against Lyndon B. Johnson in 1964. He also wrote *Conscience of a Conservative* and *The Conscience of a Country*.

Che Guevara: (1928–1967) A guerilla leader and revolutionary, Guevara believed that revolution was the solution for Latin America's social and economic problems. He played an important role in Fidel Castro's rise to power, serving as Cuba's minister of industry from 1961–65. He was captured and shot by the Bolivian army on October 9, 1967.

Quentin Tarantino: Writer and director of *Reservoir Dogs, Pulp Fiction,* and other films.

Charles Manson: Convicted mass murderer and cult leader of the 1960s responsible for the death of actress Sharon Tate, among others. He remains in prison.

Lenny Bruce: Controversial comedian of the 1950s and 1960s, known for lewd humor and language which might seem tame today. Bruce went to jail for his brand of comedy, but he broke ground for comedians who followed.

---

*A. J. Jacobs, "Extremely Cool," *Entertainment Weekly*, 1996. Reprinted by permission of the author.

1   Perhaps you've seen this commercial: A twentysomething bald dude emits a glass shattering "Aaaaarrggh!" Heavy guitar riffs pummel your eardrums. A water-skier—on bare feet, no less—makes a death-defying leap off a monster ramp. What ultra-funky, Gen-X product are they peddling now? The latest Soundgarden album, perhaps? A new flavor of Fruitopia? Nope, this ad is pitching . . . a long-distance phone service from the NYNEX company. And here's the real marketing coup: The service is called Xtreme Dialing. Yes, folks, we have a winner! The suites at NYNEX, the Northeastern Baby Bell, have strrrrretched the word extreme to its most ludicrous form in pop culture thus far. But you can hardly blame them. As good capitalists, they're duty-bound to exploit the concept du jour; and for those who've spent the past year in a biosphere watching Blockbuster videos, extreme is just that (Xtreme Dialing, by the way, has something to do with collect calls; we're still not clear.)

2   In its purest sense, something extreme should be dangerous, shock inducing, and envelope pushing. But pure or not, extreme is everywhere. On ESPN, you can watch extreme sports—a buffet of bone-crunching competitions ranging from bungee jumping to mountain biking. In *Twister,* you can root for the Extreme, Bill Paxton's ballsy tornado chaser. In *New York* magazine, you'll spot a close contender for NYNEX's crown: recipes for Extreme Lemonade (just add pineapple juice!).

3   Still, *extreme* is more than just this week's happenin' term. A survey of today's pop culture indicates we may have entered the Age of Extreme. From Alanis Morissette's revenge ballads to Dennis Rodman's feather boa, from a website about exploding heads to Jim Carrey's martian facial contortion, moderation has finally met its match.

4   It's difficult to pinpoint when things started getting extreme. As with many bygone trendy words (see *wicked* and *bad*), *extreme* began its semantic life on the wrong side of the tracks. Traditionally, you avoided things extreme—think extreme poverty, extreme measures, or extreme unction. At the 1964 Republican National Convention, Barry Goldwater tried to give the word a makeover. "Extremism in the defense of liberty is no vice," he intoned. No dice. Goldwater lost the election to Lyndon B. Johnson by, uh, an extreme margin.

5   The true reform of the word began in the late '70s, when a pack of suicidal skiers, some sporting Day-Glo outfits and Mohawks, decided it might be fun to helicopter onto remote mountains and jump off 80-foot cliffs. Calling themselves extreme skiers, they had a snappy motto: "You fall, you die!" Extreme skiing gave birth to an entire genre of gonzo sports such as sky surfing, skateboard jumping, and the ugliest offshoot, Extreme Fighting, a bloody Cro-Magnon version of boxing that airs on pay per view.

6   These Che Guevaras of sports, covered with tattoos and scabs, fueled a fast-growing multimillion-dollar business (in 1995, 2.3 million snow-boarders swarmed the slopes, up 92 percent from three years before). ESPN took note. The sports channel last year created the Extreme Games, a kind of weeklong athletic Lollapalooza that grabbed such good ratings the channel is now holding this in-your-face Olympics yearly instead of biannually, as originally planned. "We're a nation of thrill seekers," says Frank Farley, former president for the American Psychological Association and a recreational sports expert. "It's in tune with what we are."

7   Well, it's certainly in tune with what Madison Avenue craves. Fast, flashy, and oh so visual, extreme sports reel in that all-important Gen-X consumer. "They are an advertiser's wet dream," says Steven Daly, coauthor of *alt. culture,* a book cataloging the '90s zeitgeist. "They're modern, contemporary, colorful, adventurous."

8   In 1993, Mountain Dew touched off the extreme-ad stampede with spots featuring cliff-jumping bikers; since then, the yellow fizz has become the fifth

best-selling soft drink. This summer, Mountain Dew, along with such companies as MTV and Burton Snowboards, will sponsor the Extreme Network, a bizarre summer contest that equips half a million teens with low-cost beepers so they can receive messages from the likes of Evel Knievel and extreme–dial in for prizes. A torrent of other companies, from Kellogg's to Acura, have jumped on the bandwagon, packing their ads with hyperkinetic warriors. (See Tony the Tiger rock climbing. *Major concussions are greeeeeat!*)

9   From extreme sports, the word spread far and wide. Marketers on the World Wide Web, for instance, have started extreme clubs, 'zines, and the *Extreme Résumé Drop,* which automatically sends out your CV to 200 firms of your choice. Oh, the rush! As Randall Rothenberg, former *New York Times* Advertising columnist, says: "*Extreme* is to 1996 what *new and improved* was to 1963." And it's an apt comparison. Just as the latter catchphrase captured the wide-eyed optimism of the Kennedy era, extreme seems to suit our current culture.

10   More specifically, our popular culture. There isn't a corner of entertainment that doesn't have some high-decibel example of extremism. Just try *Pacific Blue,* the USA Network's *Baywatch* rip-off, an hour of buff dudes doing flips on their mountain bike. MTV has *Singled Out,* an extreme version of *The Love Connection,* in which Jenny McCarthy shouts down hapless frat boys. And the birth of the Net has allowed everyone with a modem to indulge his most extreme compulsions, whether they be lust for Wilma Flintstone or a dweebish obsession with *Dr. Who.*

11   Then there are the extreme personalities that dot the landscape: Rodman dyes his hair the color of Tang, divulges gritty details about his sex life, and dynamites our traditional idea of how an athlete ought to strut his stuff. Quentin Tarantino lets loose with a platoon's worth of bullets in one over-the-top movie after another. And no doubt Courtney Love's mascara-smeared mug will one day appear next to the word *extreme* in your Funk & Wagnall's.

12   Perhaps we've thought of these various characters as odd or fresh, or maybe just incredibly annoying. But with the concept of extreme as a prism, these stars snap into focus: We embrace them not just for their talent but also because their attitude gives us the same adrenaline-fueled rush as extreme sports—sans helmet. They're the pop equivalent of street lugers: slightly dangerous, one step beyond.

13   Granted, boundary-busting entertainment is hardly a new idea. Just ask your parents, even your grandparents. It's traveled under pseudonyms such as *hip* or *cool,* showing up on Lenny Bruce's cursing lips and in Elvis' '70s excesses. Still, in today's pop culture, not only is there more of it, but the bar has been raised: The extreme has become more extreme than ever.

14   And more nihilistic, too. Unlike the just-do-it enthusiasm it engenders in the sports world, extreme often becomes something darker in pop culture. In publishing, right on the heels of A. M. Homes' *The End of Alice,* the graphic fictional story of a pedophile, comes Poppy Brite's *Exquisite Corpse,* a novel told from a serial killer's point of view. ("People need something to kick 'em in the ass a little," says Brite.) American moviegoers will get a taste of extreme filmmaking in July with *Trainspotting,* a British ode to heroin addiction that makes *Pulp Fiction* look tame, peppered as it is with shots of flying feces and a dead baby crawling on the ceiling. "Extreme is ironic, postmodern fun with a bit of a nasty edge," says Mark Gill, president of marketing for *Trainspotting's* distributor, Miramax. "At the end of it all you leave having a good time."

15   In music, traditionally the most extreme medium, the Wonder bread Hootie & the Blowfish fad seems to have abated for the moment (their second album isn't breaking sales records). Filling their spot, Lollapalooza '96 band Psychotica waxes psychotic (the lead singer often appears in the buff on stage), Marilyn Manson conjures up images of Charles Manson, and the surviving members of the hoary extremist band the Sex Pistols are touring again.

16   Even Broadway, home to Velveeta productions such as *Cats* and genteel revivals like *The King and I,* has gone gaga for *Rent,* a cheddar-sharp tale of junkies and AIDS in New York's East Village. "We're not going to settle for the quiet puppet shows of yore," says Michael Marsden, a culture watcher and author. "The idea is to continually stun people. Entertainments that will survive are exaggerated ones that appeal to the senses in the fullest possible way."

17   If we are in the midst of an Extreme Invasion, what's driving it? Ask around and you'll get some appropriately extreme theories. Eric Perlman, the director of nine documentaries on extreme skiing, blames it on society's lack of a good war. "Men have a genetic and psychological need for speed, a need for danger," says Perlman. "And as the number of battles diminishes in the atomic age, we need a place to express them ourselves."

18   Or maybe it's about the plight of those deprived white folks. "All they have is a sort of soft culture," theorizes *alt. culture*'s Daly. "Like that episode of *Friends* where Chandler and Joey got these La-Z-Boy recliners and reverted to this infantile state of neediness. If we take that as a symbol of white male culture, extreme sports are one way to feel real again, to get back your physicality."

19   Perhaps. But the most common theory lays the blame on that reliable old scapegoat: *kids today*. The thing is, kids today *are* different. Having been spoon-fed so many hours of Buzz Bin-intensity stimuli with minimal human contact, they like their entertainment fast, and they like it alone. "Extreme sports are done individually," says *Adweek* editor at large Barbara Lippert. "It's for the generation that likes to be by themselves and wired to the Net all night."

20   Of course, the very success of the word *extreme* spells its doom among the hipnoscenti. "It used to mean the total commitment of a samurai warrior," sighs director Perlman. "Now it's drink with two types of fruit juice." (Yes, but one of them's pineapple!)

21   Today some extreme athletes are opting for other adjectives, calling their passion aggressive skiing or alternative sports. Even such a thoroughly mainstream outlet as ESPN has already shed the word: This year, the Extreme Games has been changed to the X Games.

Example Technique Questions

1. In paragraph 4, point out examples of how the use of the term *extreme* differs from its use today.

2. Although young people use the term *extreme* as a word of their own generation, point out examples of corporations using the term for their own benefit in advertising and marketing campaigns.

3. Some athletes and corporations have stopped using *extreme* to define their activities. What term has replaced *extreme,* according to the author?

Suggestions for Writing

1. Write a paragraph giving examples of extreme activities you enjoy watching or participating in. Discuss the qualities influencing its appeal for you.

2. Write a paragraph about an extreme athlete you admire. Discuss the qualities that are appealing for you.

ONLINE SCHOOLS PROVIDE NEW EDUCATION OPTIONS

Adapted from Associated Press

> In this essay, adapted from an Associated Press article, online education and its increasing popularity as an education delivery system are discussed. Pay particular attention to the variety of examples used in the article to explain and support the topic.

Pre-reading exercise: Meaning comes primarily from words. Before reading the essay, look up the definitions of the following words appearing in the text. The numbers in parentheses refer to the paragraph number of the essay.

anthropologist (10)   designated (8)
attentive (16)   hyperactivity (9)
cyberspace (4)   skeptical (4)
deficit (9)

1   A generation growing up on the Internet may now get its formal education there—from new schools offering kindergarten through 12th grade online.

2   Backers of education technology say the Internet can help children isolated from traditional schoolhouses by distance or disabilities or benefit children already schooled at home by their parents.

3   "Education is what America cares about the most, and technology is what we do best," said former Education Secretary William Bennett, introducing a new online school Thursday. The for-profit school, K12, begins enrollment next fall in kindergarten through second grade and promises eventually to offer lessons in all grades from math and science to arts and sex education. Costs would range from $25 for skill tests to about $2,000 for full lessons plans and software for a year.

4   As a past critic of education technology, Bennett once gave schools' efforts to increase use of computers in teaching an "F−." Yet he is joining companies and school districts willing, even eager, to sail into uncharted cyberspace despite skeptical child development experts and the spiraling business failure rate in the dot-com world.

5   There's no exact count of public and private elementary and secondary schools that have followed the lead of Web-based colleges; the nonprofit, Orlando-based Florida Online High School has offered online course since 1997 for grades 9 to 12 nationwide. Public charter schools from California to Pennsylvania teach children online. At the state-funded Valley Pathways online school based in Palmer, Alaska, roughly 300 students take one to six courses a semester on the Web.

6   "We wouldn't do it if we didn't think it could produce an equal education—or better," said Pathways teacher Kathi Baldwin. "I know my students online and in detail. They tell you things in writing they would never tell you fact-to-face."

7   Classes are held by computer, teachers and staff work from a central office, and students sign in from their home desktop or laptop computers. Standards for teachers ideally are the same as those of traditional schools.

8   It's not all reading, writing and arithmetic. In gym class over the Web, pupils keep daily logs of their exercises. They learn music theory online, then go to a designated campus for piano or guitar lessons. They fax, email or bring in art projects completed at home. Parents even dial in for an online PTA meeting.

9   Linda Deafenbaugh said online schooling has filled a void for her son, a third-grader with attention deficit/hyperactivity disorder. Each morning, despite his behavioral disorder, Douglas Meikle, 8, signs on to the Western Pennsylvania Cyber Charter School and downloads his reading, science and math assignments himself. He completes the lessons, working with online teachers, including a special-education expert, to keep him focused.

10   "He definitely had a bad school experience, to the point teachers were not letting him in the door of the classrooms," said Deafenaugh, a cultural anthropologist who works for the federal government. "Not only was his social life falling apart, but his academics were, too."

11   Douglas, who stays home with his father in Pittsburgh, socializes with other children at after-school sessions, sporting events and church groups, she said.

12   The going has been bumpy for some online schools. Teachers have to keep up student interest with interactive lessons, guard against student cheating and do without body language or verbal cues to tell them whether students understand lectures.

13   And in October, a 15-year-old in an online charter school in California hacked into the system and racked up $18,000 in damage, knocking the school offline for two days and destroying homework assignments, lesson plans and attendance records.

14   "There simply is not enough research," said William Rukeyser, coordinator of the nonprofit Woodland, California-based Learning in the Real World. "Too often, people say 'Let's spend the money and maybe the wisdom will miraculously transfer from the computer to the child.'"

15   Schools spent more than $5 billion on education technology last years, and a congressional panel concluded last week that 70 percent of America's classrooms are connected to the Web.

16   But the marriage of education and technology is needed, say educators who believe teaching is becoming more difficult in today's environment. Growing enrollments and shrinking budgets are leaving less room for one-on-one, hands-on learning at the side of an attentive teacher.

17   "We shouldn't be stuck with one model," Bennett said.

Example Technique Questions

1. Identify the examples of types of online classes mentioned in the article.

2. Identify two examples of statements made by education professionals in the article. Are they helpful in your understanding of what the article is trying to explain?

Suggestions for Writing

1. Write a paragraph using two or three examples of why you think online education promotes learning.

2. Write a paragraph using two or three examples explaining the qualifications both students and teachers should have before using online education.

BENEFITS OF A LARGE CORPORATION

Shelly Nanney (student)

In the following example essay, student writer Shelly Nanney writes about the positive aspects of working for a large corporation. She has worked at both a large corporation and a small business, but she uses many specific examples to explain her preference for the larger business.

Pre-reading exercise: Meaning comes primarily from words. Before reading the essay, look up the definitions of the following words appearing in the text. The numbers in parentheses refer to the paragraph number of the essay.

assigning (4)	median (1)
denote (1)	reinforce (2)
enhance (3)	restorative (2)
facet (5)	supplement (1)

1   In a time of great economic stress, many employees are looking for jobs with benefits to supplement salaries. Many states have high unemployment rates with large corporations downsizing in order to decrease expenses. The Census Bureau reports the median household income has been on the decline for many years. Most people in the country are employed by small businesses, and working for a small business usually denotes little benefits. This being said, working for a large corporation can be rewarding because of excellent health, finance, and education benefits.

2   Large corporations primarily provide healthcare through an HMO in which the employee can select the plan best meeting their personal and family needs. Coverage may become effective as early as 30 days after initial employment. Other healthcare plans, such as dental, vision, and prescription drugs most often are added assets. Dental plans include coverage for diagnostic, preventative, restorative and orthodontic services; moreover, these benefits greatly increase the bottom line on a paycheck because the corporation negotiates lower rates because of the increased number of employees in the plan. Diagnostic and preventative dental care will save thousands of dollars for the employee over a lifetime. Skyrocketing prescription drug costs reinforces the need for a prescription drug plan. A plan with a flat co-payment as small as $7-25 dollars per prescription is extremely cost saving.

3   Building financial security is a very important aspect of life for all workers. A major corporation offers various financial aids in the form of a secure pension plan, such as a 401(k) savings plan, and additional benefits such as financial planning and legal services. For instance, a good pension plan guarantees retirement years can be spend without substantial worry as to the source of monthly income. In addition to a pension plan, a 401(k) savings plan will enhance an employee's financial portfolio. Also, employers often will match employee contributions up to a certain percentage. Financial planning accomplished through a knowledgeable source is critical in today's up-and-down market; planning should begin early on in any career, and corporations

will often assist employees through this complex process. Another service having connections to financial aspect of life is legal assistance. A legal service plan with access to professional financial advisor and attorneys is an invaluable service. A good financial planner can mean the difference between a comfortable or stressful retirement and having to secure post-retirement employment to make ends meet. The golden years should include travelling and relaxing with the extended family on a regular basis, and corporate assistance throughout an employee's career can help realize these rewards.

4   Moving up the corporate ladder is a goal for most employees. Over the length of a career, education is the best method for achieving such successes. A large corporation provides educational assistance in numerous forms. For example, "on-the-job" training is a principle source. Executives help educate employees by assigning them small jobs. As the importance of the jobs increase, the employee will become more competent and will be rewarded with raises and promotions. Often, however, new skills need to be learned as work becomes more complicated. Corporations, in this increasingly high-tech world, now offer web-based training because learning at home can be very convenient and less cost-prohibitive than training at the home office. At home learning means that the employee can log onto their computer anytime day or night to complete assignments. Corporate tuition assistance and textbook subsidies are two of the many educational benefits provided by the company. The rising cost of college fees can add an enormous debt to any employee's budget, so corporate assistance can be invaluable. Such help assists both the employee and the employer over the long haul.

5   Evaluating a job offer should be done with great consideration. Beware: the salary is only one part of a complicated and multi-faceted proposal. Don't merely contemplate money needed for immediate bills. Consider medium- and long-term financial and educational needs and goals. Many types of benefits, if available, add tremendous weight to the decision.

Example Technique Questions

1. Corporations are often portrayed as uncaring about employees and only interested in making profits. Did the examples in the essay convince you otherwise?

2. What specific examples does the author use to convince the reader that corporations do care about employees?

Suggestions for Writing

1. Write a paragraph about another aspect of working for a large corporation that might help employees. Use two or three examples to support and explain your idea.

2. Write a paragraph using examples that argue against working for a large corporation. Use personal examples if you wish.

CLASSIFICATION

WHY WE CARP AND HARP*

Mary Ann Hogan

> In this essay, which originally appeared in the *Los Angeles Times,* writer Mary Ann Hogan confronts the issue of why people nag. In doing so, she also places naggers into distinct categories.

Pre-reading exercise: Meaning comes primarily from words. Before reading the essay, look up the definitions of the following words that appear in the text. The numbers in parentheses refer to the paragraph number of the essay.

crescendo (1)	recession (3)
paradox (13)	status quo (9)
procrastinators (5)	timbre (1)
purveyor (8)	toxic (4)

1   Bring those dishes down from your room! Put those scissors away. . . . I told you not to smoke in the kitchen and you shouldn't be smoking anyway! Take your feet off the table! Why do I have to tell you again and again! . . .? The hills are alive with the sound of nagging—the gnawing, crescendoing timbre of people getting in each other's face. Parents nag children, wives nag husbands, husbands nag wives, friends nag friends . . . "*Use* your fork . . . *Stop* spending money like water . . . *Can't* you be ready on time? . . . *Act* like an adult. . . ." Nagging, of course, has been around since the first cave husband refused to take out the cave garbage. But linguists, psychologists, and other scholars are just now piecing together what nagging really is, why we do it, and how to stop it before we nag each other to death.

2   Common perception holds that a nag is an unreasonably demanding wife who carps at a long-suffering husband. But in truth, nagging is universal. It happens in romances, in families, in businesses, in society—wherever people gather and one person wants another to do something he or she doesn't want to do. "It's a virus. You pick it up through kissing, shaking hands and standing in crowded rooms with people who have perfect children, wonderful husbands and sterilized homes," says humor columnist Erma Bombeck, whose family members nag her as artfully as she nags them. "It makes you feel good—like you're getting something done. Most of us want perfection in this world," she adds.

3   Thus, doctors can nag patients to lose their potbellies; accountants can nag timid clients to buy low; bosses can nag workers to get things done on time; special interest groups can nag the public to save the planet and send money; and the government can nag everyone to pay their taxes on time,

---

*Mary Ann Hogan, "Why We Carp and Harp." First appeared in the *Los Angeles Times,* March 10, 1992. Reprinted by permission of the author.

to abstain from drink if they're pregnant, and, while they're at it, to Buy American. And when the going gets desperate, the desperate get nagging: Our recession-plagued nation, experts say, could be headed for a giant nag jag.

4   "When people are generally dissatisfied, they tend to harp at other people more," says Bernard Zilbergeld, a Bay Area psychologist. Naggers tend to fall into four categories—friendly, professional, social, and domestic—that range from the socially acceptable to the toxic.

5   The Friendly Ones are proud of their art. "My sisters call me a nag, but that's not necessarily a bad thing," says Bari Brenner, a 44-year-old Castro Valley resident who describes herself as "a third-generation nag" with a low tolerance for procrastinators. "I get things done. The truth is I'm organized, they're not. I can see the big *picture*. They can't. We're going on a trip to England. 'Did you call the travel agent?' 'No.' 'Well, *call* the travel agent . . . book the hotel . . . call *now*!' It's the same thing at work. Nagging can be a means to an end."

6   Professional Nags—people who do it for a living—have to disguise what they do to get what they want. "I have to nag all the time—but you have to be careful about using the word *nag*," says Ruth Holton, a lobbyist for Common Cause, the good-government advocacy group. "I have to ask [legislators] for the same thing over and over again, year in, year out. But if they perceive what you're doing as nagging, they'll say, 'I've heard this 100 times before,' and they'll shut down. There's a fine line between artful persistence and being perceived as a nag."

7   Social nags don't see themselves as naggers. The U.S. Surgeon General's office peppers us with health warnings and calls it education. Environmentalists harp on people to recycle and save the rain forest, all in the name of the Greater Good. "One person's nagger is another person trying to save the world," says Arthur Asa Berger, a popular culture critic at San Francisco State University.

8   Then, somewhere beyond the limits of social convention, lies the dangerous world of the good old-fashioned Domestic Nag. Observers of the human condition, from the Roman poets to the purveyors of prime-time TV, have mined domestic nagging's quirkiness for laughs. But behavioral experts say that's where nagging can run amok. At best, domestic nagging is irritating. In Neil Simon's *The Odd Couple*, Felix wanted Oscar to clean up his act. Oscar liked being a slob, Felix nagged, nothing changed, and Felix finally moved out. At its worst, domestic nagging is murderous. In England last May, a 44-year-old businessman strangled his wife after 15 years of her nagging finally made him snap. In January, a judge ruled that the wife's verbal abuse justifiably provoked him and gave the husband an 18-month suspended sentence.

9   What causes this dynamic of domestic demolition? At the root of nagging, behavioralists say, lies a battle for control. It begins with a legitimate request: "I need you to hear me . . . to be with me . . . to be around, to do things like take out the garbage." But the person being asked doesn't want to change and sees the request as a threat to his or her control of the status quo. So the request is ignored.

10   "From the nagger's point of view, the naggee isn't listening," says Andrew Christensen, a UCLA psychology professor who has studied nagging for four years. "From there, it escalates. The further you withdraw, the more I nag. The naggee's point of view is, 'If I don't respond, maybe you'll shut up.'" The original request gets lost in the power struggle. The nagging takes on a life of its own. The desperate refrain of "Take out the garbage" can

stand for a whole universe of complaints, from "You never do anything around here" to "I hate your stupid brown shoes!" "Sometimes I go through the house saying, 'Dammit, close the cupboards! Don't leave the towels on the floor! What's so hard about moving a vacuum cleaner across the hall. . . .' Bang! Bang! Bang! The list goes on," says a 40-year-old Mill Valley mother of two schoolchildren. "It's like the tape is stuck on replay and nobody's listening."

11   UCLA's Christensen calls it the "demand-withdraw pattern." In 60 percent of the couples he's studied, women were in the demanding, or nagging, role. In 30 percent of the cases, men were the demanders. In 10 percent, the roles were equal. "It may be that, traditionally, women have been more interested in closeness and sharing feelings, and men have been more interested in privacy," he says.

12   The scenario of the man coming home from work and the woman spending the day with the kids feeds the gender stereotype of the female nag. "He wants to sit in front of the TV, she's primed to have an empathetic listener," Christensen says. "The reverse is true with sex. There, men tend to be in the nagging role. Either way, one feels abandoned, neglected, and deprived, the other feels intruded upon. It's a stalemate."

13   Communications experts say there is a way to end the nagging. Both people have the power to stop. What it takes is earnest willingness to step out of the ritual. The naggee could say: "You keep bringing up the issue of the garbage. I'd like to sit down and talk about it." But the gesture would have to be heartfelt, not an exercise in lip service. The nagger could write a note instead of carping. "People tend to react differently to written communication," says Zilbergeld. In either case, the effect is paradoxical: When the nagger stops, it leaves room for the naggee to act. When the naggee listens, there's nothing to nag about.

14   And if it doesn't stop? "It gets more and more robotic," says Gahan Wilson, the *New Yorker* magazine artist who explored the fate of the Nag Eternal in a recent cartoon. "We spend much of our lives on automatic pilot."

Classification Technique Questions

1. According to the author, what is the real goal or objective of the nagger?

2. What are Hogan's classification categories that the naggers fall into?

3. Research suggests that women tend to nag more than men. What reasons do psychologists give for this?

Suggestions for Writing

1. Write a paragraph about someone you know who is a nagger. What category does he or she fall into and why?

2. Are you a nagger? Discuss what category you place yourself into and why.

THE PLOT AGAINST PEOPLE*

Russell Baker

In "The Plot Against People," Russell Baker takes a humorous look at the frustrating relationship that often exists between people and inanimate objects. Pay particular attention to how Baker divides the various objects into distinct categories as he classifies them.

Pre-reading exercise: Meaning comes primarily from words. Before reading the essay, look up the definitions of the following words that appear in the text. The numbers in parentheses refer to the paragraph number of the essay.

conciliatory (12)	inanimate (1)	plausible (7)
constitutes (11)	incapable (6)	utterly (15)
cunning (3)	invariable (10)	virtually (9)
idle (3)	locomotion (7)	

1   Inanimate objects are classified into three major categories—those that don't work, those that break down and those that get lost.

2   The goal of all inanimate objects is to resist man and ultimately to defeat him, and the three major classifications are based on the method each object uses to achieve its purpose. As a general rule, any object capable of breaking down at the moment when it is most needed will do so. The automobile is typical of the category.

3   With the cunning typical of its breed, the automobile never breaks down while entering a filling station with a large staff of idle mechanics. It waits until it reaches a downtown intersection in the middle of the rush hour, or until it is fully loaded with family and luggage on the Ohio Turnpike.

4   Thus it creates maximum misery, inconvenience, frustration and irritability among its human cargo, thereby reducing its owner's life span.

5   Washing machines, garbage disposals, lawn mowers, light bulbs, automatic laundry dryers, water pipes, furnaces, electrical fuses, television tubes, hose nozzles, tape recorders, slide projectors—all are in league with the automobile to take their turn at breaking down whenever life threatens to flow smoothly for their human enemies.

6   Many inanimate objects, of course, find it extremely difficult to break down. Pliers, for example, and gloves and keys are almost totally incapable of breaking down. Therefore, they have had to evolve a different technique for resisting man.

7   They get lost. Science has still not solved the mystery of how they do it, and no man has ever caught one of them in the act of getting lost. The most plausible theory is that they have developed a secret method of locomotion which they are able to conceal the instant a human eye falls upon them.

8   It is not uncommon for a pair of pliers to climb all the way from the cellar to the attic in its single-minded determination to raise its owner's blood pressure. Keys have been known to burrow three feet under mattresses. Women's purses, despite their great weight, frequently travel through six or seven rooms to find hiding space under a couch.

---

9   Scientists have been struck by the fact that things that break down virtu-ally never get lost, while things that get lost hardly ever break down.

10   A furnace, for example, will invariably break down at the depth of the first winter cold wave, but it will never get lost. A woman's purse, which after all does have some inherent capacity for breaking down, hardly ever does; it almost invariably chooses to get lost.

11   Some persons believe this constitutes evidence that inanimate objects are not entirely hostile to man, and that a negotiated peace is possible. After all, they point out, a furnace could infuriate a man even more thoroughly by get-ting lost than by breaking down, just as a glove could upset him far more by breaking down than by getting lost.

12   Not everyone agrees, however, that this indicates a conciliatory attitude among inanimate objects. Many say it merely proves that furnaces, gloves and pliers are incredibly stupid.

13   The third class of objects—those that don't work—is the most curious of all. These include such objects as barometers, car clocks, cigarette lighters, flashlights, and toy train locomotives. It is inaccurate, of course, to say that they never work. They work once, usually for the first few hours after being brought home, and then quit. Thereafter, they never work again.

14   In fact, it is widely assumed that they are built for the purpose of not working. Some people have reached advanced ages without ever seeing some of these objects—barometers, for example—in working order.

15   Science is utterly baffled by the entire category. There are many theories about it. The most interesting holds that the things that don't work have attained the highest state possible for an inanimate object, the state to which things that break down and things that get lost can still only aspire.

16   They have truly defeated man by conditioning him never to expect any-thing of them, and in return they have given man the only peace he receives from inanimate society. He does not expect his barometer to work, his elec-tric locomotive to run, his cigarette lighter to light or his flashlight to illumi-nate, and when they don't, it does not raise his blood pressure.

17   He cannot attain that peace with furnaces and keys and cars and women's purses as long as he demands that they work for their keep.

Classification Technique Questions

1. According to the author, what is the goal of all inanimate objects?

2. What are Baker's classification categories? You can group them by para-graphs 3–6, 7–12, and 13–16.

3. In the concluding paragraphs, 15–17, Baker suggests that these inanimate objects have defeated both science and humanity. How does this add to the overall tone of the essay?

Suggestions for Writing

1. Write a paragraph about an inanimate object in your life that has caused you problems.

2. Select an inanimate object that "science" has touted as having the ability to save you time and effort in your life. Explain how it had the opposite effect.

MICHELANGELO MADNESS

Martin Brink (student)

> In the following essay by student writer Martin Brink, tools that are supposed to help humans are classified by their design and by how they actually frustrate us. Pay attention to the examples the author uses; for the most part, they are activities that most people have, unfortunately, experienced.

Pre-reading exercise: Meaning comes primarily from words. Before reading the essay, look up the definitions of the following words that appear in the text. The numbers in parentheses refer to the paragraph number of the essay.

averted (1)	evoke (1)
cloaks (4)	gizmo (1)
contraption (1)	indispensable (5)
cunning (4)	primal (5)
ensue (1)	tedious (3)

1   Since the dawn of man, humanity has striven to enhance the quality of life by inventing and employing gadgets and gizmos to reduce time and labor in everyday chores. Man, consequently, also created maintenance mayhem because of a dependency on machines, not only in the work place, but also at home. The contraptions are truly wonderful when fully functional, but when failing as a result of Murphy's law, frustration and anger ensue. Stress can be averted by avoiding the use of three types of home maintenance tools that are unreliable, counterproductive, and evoke health hazards to the operator.

2   A good rule of thumb (red and swollen by now) to follow is that any tools powered by fossil fuels—weed whackers, lawn mowers, edgers, and snow blowers—are temperamental by design. These helpful devices (a.k.a. "accidents waiting to happen") have starter cords to assist in starting the engine. According to the manual, the happy homeowner should pull the starter cord three or four times to prime the engine with gas. The manufacturer calls this activity "pre-ignition" because on the fifth pull, the engine is supposed to hum into full force. This activity should really be called "aerobic exercise" because the only thing demonstrating full force is the red-faced homeowner who is approaching unconsciousness after pulling on the starter cord fifty-seven times without so much as a puff of exhaust.

3   Believe it or not, science has created tools that are actually counterproductive. One such tool comes to mind: "The Wagner Power Roller Machine." This machine is supposed to save time when applying paint to walls; consequently, anything within ten feet of the operator is painted, too. Apart from dripping paint on everything, cleaning the machine is a tedious and time-consuming task, greater than the job of painting itself.

4   Basic instinct is all that is needed to realize the danger involved with chain saws and 35-foot extension ladders especially when used together. But none are more cunning and unsuspected as a hammer, the most widely used tool. Its simplistic design cloaks its true destructive force; anyone who is experienced in the application of this hand tool knows of the potential hazards or pain of a smashed thumb.

5 Over the years, man's tireless refinement of machines has only made life more complicated. Despite the frustration of mechanical failures and injuries caused by these devices, mankind still finds them indispensable. Humans are enslaved by the notion that bigger is better, faster is fabulous; therefore, the smell of two-cycle exhaust in the morning is addicting. Satisfying primal instincts to mulch, cut, and conquer, machines are embedded in our minds.

Classification Technique Questions

1. The author does not define Murphy's law. Why not? If you don't know what Murphy's law is, can you figure out what it might mean from the essay? Point out some examples that support your definition of Murphy's law.

2. What is the essay's tone: serious, humorous, sarcastic, or angry? Point out some examples to support your answer.

3. Personification is giving human qualities to inanimate objects. Can you find some examples in the essay? How do they support the tone of the essay you identified in question 2?

4. How many categories does the author use to classify tools? Can you think of some other tools that would fit into the categories in the essay?

Suggestions for Writing

1. Write a paragraph about an appliance or electronic device that was supposed to make your life easier but, in reality, often had the opposite effect.

2. The computer is an amazing invention. There is hardly an aspect of life that it has not touched. Write a paragraph about how different types of computers or computer programs have helped or hurt life as we know it. Your tone can be serious, sarcastic, ironic, or humorous.

PROCESS

CONVERSATIONAL BALLGAMES*

Nancy Masterson Sakamoto

> Nancy Masterson Sakamoto lived in Japan with her artist/Buddhist priest husband for over twenty years. In this essay, the author discusses the processes involved in the conversational styles of Japanese and Americans. Notice that her specific comments about the two different styles also apply to the differences between the two cultures in general.

*Nancy Masterson Sakamoto, "Conversational Ballgames" from *Polite Fictions*. Tokyo: Kinseido, Ltd., 1982. © 1982 by Nancy Masterson Sakamoto. Reprinted by permission of the author.

Pre-reading exercise: Meaning comes primarily from words. Before you start to read, use a dictionary to look up the definitions for the following words appearing in the essay. The numbers in parentheses refer to the paragraph number of the essay.

belatedly (18)	instinctively (18)
converse (20)	murmuring (10)
customarily (19)	refer (15)
elaboration (4)	register (verb) (10)
etiquette (22)	unconsciously (3)
indispensable (20)	vigorous (6)

1   After I was married and had lived in Japan for a while, my Japanese gradually improved to the point where I could take part in simple conversations with my husband and his friends and family. And I began to notice that often, when I joined in, the others would look startled, and the conversational topic would come to a halt. After this happened several times, it became clear to me that I was doing something wrong. But for a long time, I didn't know what it was.

2   Finally, after listening carefully to many Japanese conversations, I discovered what my problem was. Even though I was speaking Japanese, I was handling the conversation in a western way.

3   Japanese-style conversations develop quite differently from western-style conversations. And the difference isn't only in the languages. I realized that just as I kept trying to hold western-style conversations even when I was speaking Japanese, so my English students kept trying to hold Japanese-style conversations even when they were speaking English. We were unconsciously playing entirely different conversational ballgames.

4   A western-style conversation between two people is like a game of tennis. If I introduce a topic, a conversational ball, I expect you to hit it back. If you agree with me, I don't expect you simply to agree and do nothing more. I expect you to add something, a reason for agreeing, another example, or an elaboration to carry the idea further. But I don't expect you always to agree. I am just as happy if you question me, or challenge me, or completely disagree with me. Whether you agree or disagree, your response will return the ball to me.

5   And then it is my turn again. I don't serve a new ball from my original starting line. I hit your ball back again from where it has bounced. I carry your idea further, or answer your questions or objections, or challenge or question you. And so the ball goes back and forth, with each of us doing our best to give it a new twist, and original spin, or a powerful smash.

6   And the more vigorous the action, the more interesting and exciting the game. Of course, if one of us gets angry, it spoils the conversation, just as it spoils a tennis game. But getting excited is not all the same as getting angry. After all, we are not trying to hit each other. We are trying to hit the ball. So long as we attack only each other's opinions, and do not attack each other personally, we don't expect anyone to get hurt. A good conversation is supposed to be interesting and exciting.

7   If there are more than two people in the conversation, then it is like doubles in tennis, or like volleyball. There's no waiting in line. Whoever is nearest and quickest hits the ball, and if you step back, someone else will hit it. No one stops the game to give you a turn. You're responsible for taking your own turn.

8   But whether it's two players or a group, everyone does his best to keep the ball going, and no one person has the ball for very long.

9   A Japanese-style conversation, however, is not at all like tennis or volleyball. It's like bowling. You wait for your turn. And you always know your

place in line. It depends on such things as whether you are older or younger, a close friend or a relative stranger to the previous speaker, in a senior or junior position, and so on.

10 When your turn comes, you step up to the starting line with your bowling ball, and carefully bowl it. Everyone else stands back and watches politely, murmuring encouragement. Everyone waits until the ball has reached the end of the alley, and watches to see if it knocks down all the pins, or only some of them, or none of them. There is a pause, while everyone registers your score.

11 Then, after everyone is sure that you have completely finished your turn, the next person in line steps up to the same starting line, with a different ball. He doesn't return your ball, and he does not begin from where your ball stopped. There is no back and forth at all. All the balls run parallel. And there is always a suitable pause between turns. There is no rush, no excitement, no scramble for the ball.

12 No wonder everyone looked startled when I took part in Japanese conversations. I paid no attention to whose turn it was, and kept snatching the ball halfway down the alley and throwing it back to the bowler. Of course the conversation died. I was playing the wrong game.

13 This explains why it is almost impossible to get a western-style conversation or discussion going with English students in Japan. I used to think that the problem was their lack of English language ability. But I finally came to realize that the biggest problem is that they, too, are playing the wrong game.

14 Whenever I serve a volleyball, everyone just stands back and watches it fall, with occasional murmurs of encouragement. No one hits it back. Everyone waits until I call on someone to take a turn. And when that person speaks, he doesn't hit my ball back. He serves a new ball. Again, everyone just watches it fall.

15 So I call on someone else. This person does not refer to what the previous speaker has said. He also serves a new ball. Nobody seems to have paid any attention to what anyone else has said. Everyone begins again from the same starting line, and all the balls run parallel. There is never any back and forth. Everyone is trying to bowl with a volleyball.

16 And if I try a simpler conversation, with only two of us, then the other person tries to bowl with my tennis ball. No wonder foreign English teachers in Japan get discouraged.

17 Now that you know about the difference in the conversational ballgames, you may think that all your troubles are over. But if you have been trained all your life to play one game, it is no simple matter to switch to another, even if you know the rules. Knowing the rules is not at all the same thing as playing the game.

18 Even now, during a conversation in Japanese I will notice a startled reaction, and belatedly realize that once again I have rudely interrupted by instinctively trying to hit back the other person's bowling ball. It is no easier for me to "just listen" during a conversation than it is for my Japanese students to "just relax" when speaking with foreigners. Now I can truly sympathize with how hard they must find it to try to carry on a western-style conversation.

19 If I have not yet learned to do conversational bowling in Japanese, at least I have figured out one thing that puzzled me for a long time. After his first trip to America, my husband complained that Americans asked him so many questions and made him talk so much at the dinner table that he never had a chance to eat. When I asked him why he couldn't talk and eat at the same time, he said that Japanese do not customarily think that dinner, especially on fairly formal occasions, is a suitable time for extended conversation.

20 Since westerners think that conversation is an indispensable part of dining, and indeed would consider it impolite not to converse with one's dinner partner, I found this Japanese custom rather strange. Still, I could accept it as a cultural difference even though I didn't really understand it. But

when my husband added, in explanation, that Japanese consider it extremely rude to talk with one's mouth full, I got confused. Taking with one's mouth full is certainly not an American custom. We think it very rude, too. Yet we still manage to talk a lot and eat at the same time. How do we do it?

21   For a long time, I couldn't explain it, and it bothered me. But after I discovered the conversational ballgames, I finally found the answer. Of course! In a western-style conversation, you hit the ball, and while someone else is hitting it back, you take a bite, chew, and swallow. Then you hit the ball again, and then eat some more. The more people there are in the conversation, the more chances you have to eat. But even with only two of you talking, you still have plenty of chances to eat.

22   Maybe that's why polite conversation at the dinner table has never been a traditional part of Japanese etiquette. Your turn to talk would last so long without interruption that you'd never get a chance to eat.

Process Technique Questions

1. Is the essay intended to be informational or directional?

2. What sports does the author use to discuss the processes of western and Japanese conversation?

3. Do you think the comparisons make the process more understandable? Use examples to support your answer.

4. Identify some transitional expressions that help connect the various steps in the processes the author discusses.

Suggestions for Writing

1. Write a paragraph about a process that is different for you than for someone else. This could involve a sport, a cultural event, or an everyday occurrence.

2. Write a paragraph discussing how processes can help or hinder how we get along with others, either as individuals or as groups.

STRIVE TO BE FIT, NOT FANATICAL*

Timothy Gower

In his essay, "Strive to Be Fit, Not Fanatical," columnist Timothy Gower writes about men's health in relation to exercise. Two pertinent questions he raises are, Is exercise important? and, For maintaining good health, how much exercise does a male have to do? The author writes regularly on men's health issues, so he has done extensive research on the subject.

Pre-reading exercise: Meaning comes primarily from words. Before reading the essay, look up the definitions of the following words that appear in the text. The numbers in parentheses refer to the paragraph number in the essay.

aerobic (6)	obese (8)
blasé (9)	orb (10)
chromosomes (13)	protoplasm (4)
malarkey (5)	unabashedly (2)

1   I know what you're thinking. Who's this clown? Another fitness Nazi with a word processor who's going to scold and call me a girly-man if I don't do 150 chin-ups before breakfast? Or maybe he's one of those camera-hogging doctors who's always turning up on TV news shows, insisting that if I eat one more bacon cheeseburger my body will be declared a biohazard?

2   Nope. I'm just a reporter whose beat for much of the last decade has been health and medicine, with a particular focus on the care and feeding of the male animal. My interest is unabashedly personal: I just turned 38 and have begun to notice a few chinks in the armor. Chances are you have, too.

3   And if you're reading this column, maybe you've also picked up your share of health books and magazines that are targeted at men. Me, too, and you know what I've noticed? Some contain a lot of valuable information, but they all seem to have two things in common: 1) they avoid using big words, and 2) they take the old "no pain, no gain" philosophy very seriously. All that talk about "getting ripped" and "feeling the burn"—ouch!

4   Of course, "no pain, no gain" is hardly a new idea. Many men grew up hearing it from coaches who insisted that if you didn't collapse in a puddle of protoplasm at the end of practice, then you obviously weren't hustling. We've been led to believe that working out isn't supposed to be fun; it's supposed to leave your muscles aching and stomach rolling. Is it any wonder that only about one in five U.S. men exercises regularly?

5   The thing is, getting enough exercise and eating right aren't as hard as you might think. The idea that it takes long, grueling workouts to get in shape is malarkey. Believe it or not, more isn't always better when it comes to exercise. And if you're tired of diets that leave you with a fridge full of icky cabbage soup, then tuck in your napkin: Healthy eating doesn't have to bum out your palate.

6   Let's start with exercise. If you know that a little jogging is good for your heart, then you might assume that doing laps till you're dizzy and ready to retch would make your ticket indestructible. But you would be incorrect. A 1997 Harvard study determined that the cardiovascular benefits of an intense aerobic workout peak at about 24 minutes; pound the pavement longer if you like, but your heart won't get any stronger.

7   Ditto for strength training. According to the gospel of the weight room, you must do a minimum of three sets of bench presses, curls, or any other strength-building exercise, to build up a muscle. But studies at the University of Florida show that's just not true; doing one set of an exercise produces more than three-quarters of the muscles you get from doing three. You gain a little less in the biceps department maybe, but you get the heck out of that stinky, sweaty gym in one-third of the time. Sounds like a good deal to me.

8   Unless you are obese, forget about dieting. (And if you are dramatically overweight, see a doctor who specializes in obesity.) Nutrition experts say

crash weight-loss plans that require you to stop eating certain foods don't work; you'll lose weight, but inevitably your willpower crumbles, and the pounds return. Instead, eat a balanced meal plan that includes lots of fruit, vegetables, whole grains and an occasional splurge. Add regular exercise, and eventually you'll attain a manageable, healthy weight.

9   Bottom line: Modest lifestyle changes can make a huge difference. Consider the evidence. Exhibit A: me. In high school my classmates gave me the nickname "Blaze." At first, I thought they were mispronouncing "blasé," but it turns out they were poking fun at me for being a slow and easily winded runner. During forced-jogging sessions in gym class, I'd bring up the rear, gasping like I was born sucking a Camel. Though I managed to weasel my way on to a few sports teams, few people mistook me for an athlete.

10   In the two decades that followed, I wasn't much of a Healthy Man. I'd go running occasionally, but only if it was getting close to 11 p.m. and the liquor stores were closing. Then, a few years ago, I began to notice a pale, flabby orb forming where my flat stomach used to be. it had to go; I started jogging for half an hour every other day and have never looked back.

11   Last winter I injured my back and went to the hospital. As a nurse took my heart rate, she suddenly arched her eyebrows.

12   "Are you an athlete?" she asked. It turns out my resting heart rate was 56 beats per minute. The average guy's heart rate is about 70, but with regular aerobic training, the cardiovascular system becomes more efficient, and the heart doesn't have to work as hard.

13   I lay back on the exam table and thought of that lonely teenager, huffing and puffing behind the pack during gym class, and how I could totally humiliate him in a race today. See ya, Blaze! If I can become a Healthy Man, anyone with the right chromosomes can, too.

Process Technique Questions

1. Is the essay intended to be informational or directional?

2. Who is the author's intended audience? In your opinion, would the information in the essay interest the target audience?

3. How many different weight-loss programs does the author discuss?

4. What conclusion does the author reach about exercising and dieting?

Suggestions for Writing

1. Write a paragraph about a process that is different for you than for someone else. This could involve a sport, a cultural event, or an everyday occurrence.

2. Write a paragraph discussing how processes can help or hinder how we get along with others, either as individuals or as groups.

HOW TO BECOME A SUCCESSFUL STUDENT

Aaron Breite (student)

In this essay, student writer Aaron Breite explains the steps necessary to achieve more success as a student. The process should help students no matter what college or university they attend.

Pre-reading exercise: Meaning comes primarily from words. Before reading the essay, look up the definitions of the following words that appear in the text. The numbers in parentheses refer to the paragraph number of the essay.

adhering (1)   software (4)
determine (5)   solution (2)
enhancement (4)   strenuous (1)
response (3)

1   Colleges and universities can be strenuous places to learn; however, many students think it is easy because they can schedule their own class times to allow for breaks between classes, and they can work in study groups. Yet, each semester, thousands of students flunk out of colleges and universities all across the country. How can a student be assured of doing well in college? No matter the school, a student can be successful by adhering to the following steps: first, schedule time for homework and studying; second, pay attention in class; and third, ask for assistance in the Tutoring Center.

2   First, a student should schedule time to do homework or studying. The next step is to get a daily planner, costing about five or six dollars, so scheduling times is easier. Then, in the planner, write down the subject for that day, and then write the time it will take to study for those subjects. It is wise to schedule time after class to review notes, so that the information in the class becomes more familiar when studying later at night. Now, schedule some free time, perhaps 15–30 minutes, in between studying for a study break. It's important to keep your mind fresh as you move from subject to subject. After the study break, the student can come back to difficult problems. After scheduling homework, make time for studying at least two or three days in advance of upcoming tests. This gives the brain enough time to gather and differentiate information.

3   The second step is to pay attention in class. Paying attention is the main key in being a successful student. By paying attention, a good student will take notes and ask questions. When taking notes, write questions you have in the margins. When the teacher asks if anyone has any questions, it is time to ask any questions you might have about the material. After the questions are asked, the instructor's responses need to be written down as well. Before leaving the classroom, check the board to see if the instructor has written down any new assignments.

4   Finally, the last step is getting help from the Tutoring Center. The Tutoring Center provides tutors who help with writing skills, note taking, test taking, and study skills. In addition, students can use a wide variety of methods to study with, such as video tapes, workbooks, and computer software. The tutors give suggestions to the student on how to write papers but are not there to write the paper for the student. Many students have achieved success at college due to the help received in the Tutoring Center. The atmosphere is

friendly and the tutors are willing to work one-on-one with students. Those not taking advantage of the Tutoring Center are missing a great opportunity to enhance their academic skills. Lastly, students need to realize that visiting the Tutoring Center on a regular basis will hasten their success.

5   When trying to better their educational experience, students need a well-defined pattern of behavior to facilitate the process. There are many challenges and distractions on college campuses to derail even the most serious student. So, it is well to remember that the effort put into the work will determine the grade. And, good grades are an important measurement of success.

Process Technique Questions

1. Is the essay intended to be informational or directional?

2. In paragraph 2, although the author contends that "taking a break" is a necessary step in the process, he doesn't go into detail. Why do you think he doesn't? Discuss why you think taking a break from doing homework is important.

3. Identify some of the transitional expressions that help connect the various steps in the process.

Suggestions for Writing

1. Write a paragraph discussing a process you think is important in becoming a good student.

2. Write a paragraph discussing a process a favorite teacher used to help you learn a particular skill or piece of information.

COMPARISON AND CONTRAST

GRANT AND LEE: A STUDY IN CONTRASTS*

Bruce Catton

> In this essay, "Grant and Lee: A Study in Contrasts," Catton contrasts the two great American Civil War military leaders. However, while he recounts the basic differences between the two men, he also is making commentary on the significance the two men had in shaping the two sides embroiled in the conflict. By doing so, Catton makes understandable the reasons why the Union and the Confederacy came to war.

---

*Bruce Catton, "Grant and Lee: A Study in Contrasts" from *The American Story*, Earl Schneck Miers, editor. Capitol Historical Society. Reprinted by permission of the United States Capitol Society.

Pre-reading exercise: Meaning comes primarily from words. Before reading the essay, look up the definitions of the following words that appear in the text. The numbers in parentheses refer to the paragraph number of the essay.

aspiration (13)	indomitable (14)
burgeoning (12)	obeisance (7)
diametrically (12)	sinewy (7)
fidelity (14)	tenacity (11)
implicit (8)	

1   When Ulysses S. Grant and Robert E. Lee met in the parlor of a modest house at Appomattox Court House, Virginia, on April 9, 1865, to work out the terms for the surrender of Lee's Army of Northern Virginia, a great chapter in American life came to a close, and a great new chapter began.

2   These men were bringing the Civil War to its virtual finish. To be sure, other armies had yet to surrender, and for a few days the fugitive Confederate government would struggle desperately and vainly, trying to find some way to go on living now that its chief support was gone. But in effect it was all over when Grant and Lee signed the papers. And the little room where they wrote out the terms was the scene of one of the most poignant, dramatic contrasts in American history.

3   They were two strong men these oddly different generals, and they represented the strengths of two conflicting currents that, through them, had come into final collision.

4   Back of Robert E. Lee was the notion that the old aristocratic concept might somehow survive and be dominant in American life.

5   Lee was tidewater Virginia, and in his background were family, culture, and tradition . . . the age of chivalry transplanted to a New World which was making its own legends and its own myths. He embodied a way of life that had come down through the age of knighthood and the English country squire. America was a land that was beginning all over again, dedicated to nothing much more complicated than the rather hazy belief that all men had equal rights and should have an equal chance in the world. In such a land Lee stood for the feeling that it was somehow of advantage to human society to have a pronounced inequality in the social structure. There should be a leisure class, backed by ownership of land; in turn, society itself should be keyed to the land as the chief source of wealth and influence. It would bring forth (according to this ideal) a class of men with a strong sense of obligation to the community; men who lived not to gain advantage for themselves, but to meet the solemn obligations which had been laid on them by the very fact that they were privileged. From them the country would get its leadership; to them it could look for the higher values—of thought, of conduct, or personal deportment—to give it strength and virtue.

6   Lee embodied the noblest element of this aristocratic ideal. Through him, the landed nobility justified itself. For four years, the Southern states had fought a desperate war to uphold the ideals for which Lee stood. In the end, it almost seemed as if the Confederacy fought for Lee; as if he himself was the Confederacy . . . the best thing that the way of life for which the Confederacy stood could ever have to offer. He had passed into legend before Appomattox. Thousands of tired, underfed, poorly clothed Confederate soldiers, long since past the simple enthusiasm of the early days of the struggle, somehow considered Lee the symbol of everything for which they had been willing to die. But they could not quite put this feeling into words. If the Lost Cause, sanctified by so much heroism and so many deaths, had a living justification, its justification was General Lee.

7 　　Grant, the son of a tanner on the Western frontier, was everything Lee was not. He had come up the hard way and embodied nothing in particular except the eternal toughness and sinewy fiber of the men who grew up beyond the mountains. He was one of a body of men who owned reverence and obeisance to no one, who were self-reliant to a fault, who cared hardly anything for the past but who had a sharp eye for the future.

8 　　These frontier men were the precise opposites of the tidewater aristocrats. Back of them, in the great surge that had taken people over the Alleghenies and into the opening Western country, there was a deep, implicit dissatisfaction with a past that had settled into grooves. They stood for democracy, not from any reasoned conclusion about the proper ordering of human society, but simply because they had grown up in the middle of democracy and knew how it worked. Their society might have privileges, but they would be privileges each man had won for himself. Forms and patterns meant nothing. No man was born to anything, except perhaps to a chance to show how far he could rise. Life was competition.

9 　　Yet along with this feeling had come a deep sense of belonging to a national community. The Westerner who developed a farm, opened a shop, or set up in business as a trader could hope to prosper only as his own community prospered—and his community ran from the Atlantic to the Pacific and from Canada down to Mexico. If the land was settled, with towns and highways and accessible markets, he could better himself. He saw his fate in terms of the nation's own destiny. As its horizons expanded, so did his. He had, in other words, an acute dollars-and-cents stake in the continued growth and development of his country.

10 　　And that, perhaps, is where the contrast between Grant and Lee becomes most striking. The Virginia aristocrat, inevitably, saw himself in relation to his own region. He lived in a static society which could endure almost anything except change. Instinctively, his first loyalty would go to the locality in which that society existed. He would fight to the limit of endurance to defend it, because in defending it he was defending everything that gave his own life its deepest meaning.

11 　　The Westerner, on the other hand, would fight with an equal tenacity for the broader concept of society. He fought so because everything he lived by was tied to growth, expansion, and a constantly widening horizon. What he lived by would survive or fall with the nation itself. He could not possibly stand by unmoved in the face of an attempt to destroy the Union. He would combat it with everything he had, because he could only see it as an effort to cut the ground out from under his feet.

12 　　So Grant and Lee were in complete contrast, representing two diametrically opposed elements in American life. Grant was the modern man emerging; beyond him, ready to come on the stage, was the great age of steel and machinery, of crowded cities and a restless burgeoning vitality. Lee might have ridden down from the old age of chivalry, lance in hand, silken banner fluttering over his head. Each man was the perfect champion of his cause, drawing both his strengths and his weaknesses from the people he led.

13 　　Yet it was not all contrast, after all. Different as they were—in background, in personality, in underlying aspiration—these two great soldiers had much in common. Under everything else, they were marvelous fighters. Furthermore, their fighting qualities were really very much alike.

14 　　Each man had, to begin with, the great virtue of utter tenacity and fidelity. Grant fought his way down the Mississippi Valley in spite of acute personal discouragement and profound military handicaps. Lee hung on in the trenches at Petersburg after hope itself had died. In each man there was an indomitable quality . . . the born fighter's refusal to give up as long as he can still remain on his feet and lift his two fists.

15   Daring and resourcefulness they had, too: the ability to think faster and move faster than the enemy. These were the qualities which gave Lee the dazzling campaigns of Second Manassas and Chancellorsville and won Vicksburg for Grant.

16   Lastly, and perhaps greatest of all, there was the ability, at the end, to turn quickly from war to peace once the fighting was over. Out of the way these two men behaved at Appomattox came the possibility of a peace of reconciliation. It was a possibility not wholly realized, in the years to come, but which did, in the end, help the two sections to become one nation again . . . after a war whose bitterness might have seemed to make such a reunion wholly impossible. No part of either man's life became him more than the part he played in their brief meeting in the McLean house at Appomattox. Their behavior there put all succeeding generations of Americans in their debt. Two great Americans, Grant and Lee—very different, yet under everything very much alike. Their encounter at Appomattox was one of the great moments of American history.

Comparison and Contrast Technique Questions

1. Catton calls both Grant and Lee symbols of their respective sides. Point out some of the differences between the two men.

2. Beginning with paragraph 13, Catton changes his mode of development of Grant and Lee. Point out the similarities the two leaders share.

3. Catton has two paragraphs (paragraphs 3 and 4) consisting of only one sentence each. Do you find these effective or not? Explain.

Suggestions for Writing

1. Select two of today's world leaders, and write a paragraph either comparing or contrasting them.

2. Using yourself and someone you know or two other people you know, write a paragraph describing how the differences between these people actually make their relationship better, not worse.

LIVING ON TOKYO TIME*

Lynnika Butler

In this essay, the author, who taught English in Japanese schools for five years, compares how the Japanese view time as opposed to Western culture. Her work as an interpreter and in the area of international relations also allowed her to experience a multitude of other area of Japanese life that focused on the importance of time.

*Excerpt from "Living on Tokyo Time" by Lynnika Butler from the *UTNE Reader*, January/February 2003. Reprinted by permission of the author.

Pre-reading exercise: Meaning comes primarily from words. Before reading the essay, look up the definitions of the following words appearing in the text. The numbers in parentheses refer to the paragraph number of the essay.

communal (4)   masochistic (3)
glib (3)   phenomenon (3)
hedonistic (1)   submissive (3)
implies (3)   unique (5)

1   It's fair to say than Japanese people are unbelievably busy. Working 10 hours a day, and often coming in on days off, they rarely take a vacation of more than three or four days. A straight week is a hedonistic luxury. Students have less than a month for summer vacation, and even then they have all kinds of assignments to do.

2   Watching people live like this, with almost no time for themselves, makes an American like me wonder why more of them don't throw themselves under subways trains. But I seem to have far more anxiety about free time than my Japanese friends do—even though, compared to them, I have much more of it. Why doesn't this cradle-to-grave, manic scheduling bother them?

3   A lot of Westerners make the glib assumption that Japanese people are simply submissive, unoriginal, or masochistic enough to put up with such a punishing system. I don't think that's it. In Japan, time is measured in the same hours and minutes and days as anywhere else, but it is experienced as a fundamentally different phenomenon. In the West, we save time, spend time, invest time, even kill time—all of which implies that it belongs to us in the first place. We might find ourselves obliged to trade huge chunks of our time for a steady salary, but most of us resent this as something stolen from us, and we take it for granted that our spare hours are none of our teachers' or bosses' business.

4   The Japanese grow up with a sense of time as a communal resource, like the company motor pool. If you get permission, you can borrow a little for your own use, but the main priority is to serve the institution—in this case, society as a whole. Club activities, overtime, drinks with the boss, and invitations to the boring weddings of people you hardly know are not seen as intruding on your free time—they are the *shikata ga nai* (nothing you can do about it) duties that turn the wheels of society. "Free" time (*hima*) is something that only comes into existence when these obligations have all been fulfilled. This is nicely borne out by an expression my boss uses whenever he leaves work a little early: *chotto hima morau* ("I'm going to receive a little free time").

5   Though I can't pretend I like living on a Japanese schedule, I try hard not to make judgments. *Oku ga fukai*—things are more complicated than they appear. The Japanese sacrifice their private time to society, but in return they get national health insurance, a wonderful train system, sushi, the two thousand temples of Kyoto, and traditional culture so rich that every back-water village seems to have it own unique festivals, seasonal dishes, legends, and even dialect. All of which are invaluable social goods that I would not trade for a lifetime of free hours.

Compare and Contrast Technique Questions

1. Point out several of the obvious differences between how the Japanese view time and how the West views time.

2. The author states that the Japanese are "busy." Does this, in effect, imply that those in the West are not? How does this make you feel about the effectiveness of the author's essay?

Suggestions for Writing

1. Write a paragraph comparing how you and someone you know use time.

2. Now, write a paragraph contrasting how you and another person you know use time.

THE FAMILY SEDAN VERSUS DAD'S SPORTS CAR

Yvonne Olson (student)

> To hot rod or not to hot rod—that is the question! In this essay, student writer Yvonne Olson takes the reader for a ride in the four-door, wire-rimmed family dilemma. Along the drive, she outlines both her and her parents' concerns.

Pre-reading exercise: Meaning comes primarily from words. Before reading the essay, look up the definitions of the following words that appear in the text. The numbers in parentheses refer to the paragraph number in the essay.

adrenaline (5)	fishtails (2)
distract (3)	premium (4)
diverted (3)	primary (1)
envious (2)	

1   There are two cars in my garage at home—one is a fun car, and one is a practical family car. The fun car is a shiny, white 1993 Corvette, and the practical car is a 1996 Dodge Intrepid. Of course, I would like to be the primary driver of the Corvette, but my parents think that the logical choice for me is the Intrepid. That was fine with me for a long time until the family car went in the repair shop, and my parents had to let me drive the Corvette to school. After one day, I was hooked. Corvette fever seeped in, and I have tried to persuade my parents ever since to let me drive the car all the time. While I see no reason why I cannot drive a Corvette at my age, my parents have many objections about safety, practicality, and the cost of me driving the sports car.

2   One reason my parents want me to drive the family car is that they feel it is safer. With over 325 horsepower under the hood of the Corvette, they think that I will be tempted to speed and try to race all of the cars around me. My mother has visions of tires smoking, fishtailing, and the car spinning out of control, causing a massive car pileup on the highway. Since the Intrepid is a family car, my parents feel that I will not try to outrun cars, and that no one will challenge me to a race. The Corvette does attract a great deal of attention from young males, and they often try to race me after a stoplight turns green. With the Intrepid, I stay unnoticed and just go my way. Of course, part of the thrill of driving the Corvette is the attention that I get from envious males. Even though it is fun to get all this attention, sometimes this attention can be bad. A year ago, my mother and I were held up at gunpoint by a teenage male demanding us to give him the car keys. Luckily nothing happened to us

except the aggravation of having our car taken from us. This is just another reason for my parents to worry about me when I go places in the Corvette. This fear does bother me sometimes, yet it has taught me to be extra cautious of my surroundings. They fear that this could happen again, but that the next time I won't get away unharmed. Yet another reason my parents worry greatly when I drive the Corvette is the way it handles in bad weather. Since the Intrepid handles fine in the rain and has no problems with a few inches of snow, my mom and dad point out that the Corvette easily fishtails when the roads are wet, and that it is impossible to drive in snow. This is an inconvenience; however, I prefer to stay at home when the weather is too bad for driving anyway.

3   Besides all the danger of driving my dream car, my parents also point out how impractical a Corvette is for me. Since the Corvette has only two seats, there is only room for one passenger. That is fine with me since I won't have to worry about friends asking me to pick them up and drive them all over town. Nothing bothers me more than friends asking me to pick up this person or that person. On the other hand, the Intrepid is a five-passenger vehicle, which allows me to drive with more passengers. Because my friends easily distract me, being able to transport more passengers is not always a good thing. When people are carrying on conversations in the car, my attention is easily diverted from the road. My passenger seat is already taken up with a baby car seat, which makes it almost impossible to transport anyone except my daughter. My parents think that the Corvette is inconvenient because I cannot fit a stroller into the tiny hatchback. Though this is true, I find it easier to carry my daughter than to go through the hassle of getting out a stroller. My mother and father think that these inconveniences will make me want to drive the Intrepid; however, they are wrong.

4   When all else fails to convince me to be happy with the Intrepid, my parents tell me that the expenses of driving a Corvette are too much for a teenager to pay for. The cost of insuring me on the Corvette, versus the Intrepid, is something they do not even want to consider since high-risk insurance is three times more expensive. Although the insurance is more expensive, I have kept the cost down by having no speeding tickets, by having no accidents, and by keeping my grade-point average high. There is also the cost of the gasoline to consider. The Corvette uses premium unleaded while the Intrepid uses less expensive regular gas. My parents offer to pay for gas in the Intrepid, but I will gladly pay for the more expensive gas for the opportunity to drive my dream car. They often tell me that I cannot expect to own a car like this at my age because the maintenance is too costly. Four tires alone on the Corvette cost about $1,200 while the set for the Intrepid is around $400. I do not drive as much as my parents, which allows the tires to last longer, and this is another expense that can be kept low. My mom and dad argue that the Corvette needs frequent repairs although the Intrepid has been in the repair shop more than one time. I agree that Corvette maintenance is expensive, but most cars do need repairs often.

5   Even though I hear all these arguments over and over again, they have little effect on my opinion. My parents, especially my dad, are just jealous of the fact that I have so much fun driving the Corvette. I am a teenage girl; therefore, I must have a sporty car that turns young guys' heads. Safety, practicality, and cost are important, but I have Corvette fever, and I will have to wait until it passes. There is nothing like the feeling of getting behind the wheel of that white dream machine and hearing the engine roar while driving a tad bit over the speed limit. Adrenaline rushes through my body every time my foot presses on the gas peddle because I know that my car is probably

faster than most of the cars around me. Only one thing can spoil my fun, and that is the sight of a Viper or a Porsche!

Comparison and Contrast Technique Questions

1. Is this a comparison or a contrast essay?

2. Depending on how you answered question 1, point out similarities or differences between the Intrepid and the Corvette.

3. How do Yvonne Olson's reasons for wanting to drive the Corvette differ from her parents' reasons for not wanting her to drive the Corvette?

Suggestions for Writing

1. Write a paragraph discussing how you and your parents once had differences about an issue.

2. Write a paragraph discussing the similar attitudes that you and your parents held in regard to an issue.

DEFINITION

DISCRIMINATION IS A VIRTUE*

Robert Keith Miller

In this essay, "Discrimination Is a Virtue," Miller defines *discrimination* in a very unconventional manner. Miller states that the term's true meaning is often misused and misunderstood. Pay particular attention to his use of *denotative* meaning (the conventional, literal meaning) and *connotative* meaning (the meanings evoked or suggested beyond a word's essential meaning).

Pre-reading exercise: Meaning comes primarily from words. Before reading the essay, look up the definitions of the following words that appear in the text. The numbers in parentheses refer to the paragraph number of the essay.

arbitrary (14)	irony (9)	radically (11)
euphemistically (12)	notion (7)	realm (2)
hypocrites (3)	obsessed (7)	

*Robert Keith Miller, "Discrimination Is a Virtue" from *Newsweek*, July 21, 1980. Reprinted by permission of the author.

1   When I was a child, my grandmother used to tell me a story about a king who had three daughters and decided to test their love. He asked each of them "How much do you love me?" The first replied that she loved him as much as all the diamonds and pearls in the world. The second said that she loved him more than life itself. The third replied "I love you as fresh meat loves salt."

2   This answer enraged the king; he was convinced that his youngest daughter was making fun of him. So he banished her from his realm and left all of his property to her elder sisters.

3   As the story unfolded it became clear, even to a 6-year-old, that the king had made a terrible mistake. The two older girls were hypocrites, and as soon as they had profited from their father's generosity, they began to treat him very badly. A wiser man would have realized that the youngest daughter was the truest. Without attempting to flatter, she said, in effect, "We go together naturally; we are a perfect team."

4   Years later, when I came to read Shakespeare, I realized that my grandmother's story was loosely based upon the story of King Lear, who put his daughters to a similar test and did not know how to judge the results. Attempting to save the king from the consequences of his foolishness, a loyal friend pleads, "Come sir, arise, away! I'll teach you differences." Unfortunately, the lesson comes too late. Because Lear could not tell the difference between true love and false, he loses his kingdom and eventually his life.

5   We have a word in English which means "the ability to tell differences." That word is *discrimination*. But within the last 30 years, this word has been so frequently misused that an entire generation has grown up believing that "discrimination" means "racism." People are always proclaiming that "discrimination" is something that should be done away with. Should that ever happen, it would prove to be our undoing.

6   Discrimination means discernment; it means the ability to perceive the truth, to use good judgment and to profit accordingly. The *Oxford English Dictionary* traces this understanding of the word back to 1648 and demonstrates that for the next 300 years, "discrimination" was a virtue, not a vice. Thus, when a character in a nineteenth-century novel makes a happy marriage, Dickens has another character remark, "It does credit to your discrimination that you should have found such a very excellent young woman."

7   Of course, "the ability to tell differences" assumes that differences exist, and this is unsettling for a culture obsessed with the notion of equality. The contemporary belief that discrimination is a vice stems from the compound *discriminate against*. What we need to remember, however, is that some things deserve to be judged harshly: we should not leave our kingdoms to the selfish and the wicked.

8   Discrimination is wrong only when someone or something is discriminated against because of prejudice. But to use the word in this sense, as so many people do, is to destroy its true meaning. If you discriminate against something because of general preconceptions rather than particular insights, then you are not discriminating—bias has clouded the clarity of vision which discrimination demands.

9   One of the great ironies of American life is that we manage to discriminate in the practical decisions of daily life, but usually fail to discriminate when we make public policies. Most people are very discriminating when it comes to buying a car, for example, because they realize that cars have differences. Similarly, an increasing number of people have learned to discriminate in what they eat. Some foods are better than others—and indiscriminate eating can undermine one's health.

10   Yet in public affairs, good judgment is depressingly rare. In many areas which involve the common good, we see a failure to tell differences.

11   Consider, for example, some of the thinking behind modern education. On the one hand, there is a refreshing realization that there are differences among children, and some children—be they gifted or handicapped—require special education. On the other hand, we are politically unable to accept the consequences of this perception. The trend in recent years has been to group together students of radically different ability. We call this process "mainstreaming," and it strikes me as a characteristically American response to the discovery of differences: we try to pretend that differences do not matter.

12   Similarly, we try to pretend that there is little difference between the sane and the insane. A fashionable line of argument has it that "everybody is a little mad" and that few mental patients deserve long-term hospitalization. As a consequence of such reasoning, thousands of seriously ill men and women have been evicted from their hospital beds and returned to what is euphemistically called "the community"—which often means being left to sleep on city streets, where confused and helpless people now live out of paper bags as the direct result of our refusal to discriminate.

13   Or to choose a final example from a different area: how many recent elections reflect thoughtful consideration of the genuine differences among candidates? Benumbed by television commercials that market aspiring officeholders as if they were a new brand of toothpaste or hair spray, too many Americans vote with only a fuzzy understanding of the issues in question. Like Lear, we seem too eager to leave the responsibility of government to others and too ready to trust those who tell us whatever we want to hear.

14   So as we look around us, we should recognize that "discrimination" is a virtue which we desperately need. We must try to avoid making unfair and arbitrary distinctions, but we must not go to the other extreme and pretend that there are no distinctions to be made. The ability to make intelligent judgments is essential both for the success of one's personal life and for the functioning of society as a whole. Let us be open-minded by all means, but not so open-minded that our brains fall out.

Definition Technique Questions

1. How does Miller define *discrimination*? How does he say most other people define it? What problems does this cause in various areas of society?

2. How does the personal story at the beginning of the essay help you understand what Miller is saying about the problems that misunderstanding terms can cause?

3. What is "one of the great ironies of American life" (paragraphs 9–13)? How does this affect American culture?

Suggestions for Writing

1. Select two words that you commonly confuse, and write a paragraph clarifying their definitions. Has confusing the words ever caused you any problems?

2. Write a paragraph about words you and your friends use that could be misunderstood by adults. Would most of the misunderstandings be innocent, or might some of the misunderstandings cause problems?

THE HANDICAP OF DEFINITION*

William Raspberry

> In this essay, syndicated columnist William Raspberry discusses the many definitions of the word *black* and how those definitions negatively affect young black children. Pay attention to how the author extends and broadens the definition through a variety of examples that distinguish between "positive" and "negative" meanings.

Pre-reading exercise: Meaning comes primarily from words. Before you start to read, look up the definitions of the following words appearing in the essay. The numbers in parentheses refer to the paragraph number of the essay.

academia (6)	elocution (10)	perverted (13)
array (6)	inculcated (13)	prowess (13)
concede (12)	innate (11)	quintessentially (9)
deprivation (1)	myth (9)	scrimping (5)

1   I know all about bad schools, mean politicians, economic deprivation and racism. Still, it occurs to me that one of the heaviest burdens black Americans—and black children in particular—have to bear is the handicap of definition: the question of what it means to be black.

2   Let me explain quickly what I mean. If a basketball fan says that the Boston Celtics' Larry Bird [3-time NBA MVP and 12-time NBA All-Star] plays "black," the fan intends it—and Bird probably accepts it—as a compliment. Tell pop singer Tom Jones [still a fixture in Las Vegas] he moves "black" and he might grin in appreciation. Say to Teena Marie [for over two decades she recorded for Motown] or the Average White Band that they sound "black" and they'll thank you.

3   But name one pursuit, aside from athletics, entertainment or sexual performance in which a white practitioner will feel complimented to be told he does it "black." Tell a white broadcaster he talks "black," and he'll sign up for diction lessons. Tell a white reporter he writes "black" and he'll take a writing course. Tell a white lawyer he reasons "black" and he might sue you for slander.

4   What we have here is a tragically limited definition of blackness, and it isn't only white people who buy it.

5   Think of all the ways black children can put one another down with charges of "whiteness." For many of these children, hard study and hard work are "white." Trying to please a teacher might be criticized as acting "white." Speaking correct English is "white." Scrimping today in the interest of tomorrow's goals is "white." Educational toys and games are "white."

6   An incredible array of habits and attitudes that are conducive to success in business, in academia, in the nonentertainment professions are likely to be thought of as somehow "white." Even economic success, unless it involves such "black" undertakings as numbers banking, is defined as "white."

7   And the results are devastating. I wouldn't deny that blacks often are better entertainers and athletes. My point is the harm that comes from too narrow a definition of what is black.

8   One reason black youngsters tend to do better at basketball, for instance, is that they assume they can learn to do it well, and so they practice constantly to prove themselves right.

9   Wouldn't it be wonderful if we could infect black children with the notion that excellence in math is "black" rather than white, or possibly Chinese? Wouldn't it be of enormous value if we could create the myth that morality, strong families, determination, courage and love of learning are traits brought by slaves from Mother Africa and therefore quintessentially black?

10   There is no doubt in my mind that most black youngsters could develop their mathematical reasoning, their elocution and their attitudes the way they develop their jump shots and their dance steps: by the combination of sustained, enthusiastic practice and the unquestioned belief that they can do it.

11   In one sense, what I am talking about is the importance of developing positive ethnic traditions. Maybe Jews have an innate talent for communication; maybe the Chinese are born with a gift for mathematical reasoning; maybe blacks are naturally blessed with athletic grace. I doubt it. What is at work, I suspect, is assumption, inculcated early in their lives, that this is a thing our people do well.

12   Unfortunately, many of the things about which blacks make this assumption are things that do not contribute to their career success—except for that handful of the truly gifted who can make it as entertainers and athletes. And many of the things we concede to whites are the things that are essential to economic security.

13   So it is with a number of assumptions black youngsters make about what it is to be a "man": physical aggressiveness, sexual prowess, the refusal to submit to authority. The prisons are full of people who, by this perverted definition, are unmistakably men.

14   But the real problem is not so much that the things defined as "black" are negative. The problem is that the definition is much too narrow.

15   Somehow, we have to make our children understand that they are intelligent, competent people, capable of doing whatever they put their minds to and making it in the American mainstream, not just in a black subculture.

16   What we seem to be doing, instead, is raising up yet another generation of young blacks who will be failures—by definition.

Definition Technique Questions

1. Some of the examples in the essay might seem out of date, but what about Raspberry's thesis? Do you agree with it or not? Is it still a valid topic for discussion?

2. How would you define the term *black*? Try to develop a definition in one or two sentences.

3. Does it make any difference that Raspberry is a black man? What if he were white? How would that affect your perception of the article?

Suggestions for Writing

1. What label is attached to you or your peer group? Are you labeled a soccer mom; a slacker; a Generation X-er, Y-er, Z-er; a suit; a rocker; a geek; or a homeboy? Write a paragraph defining the label most associated with you or your peer group. Comment on whether you think the definition is accurate.

2. What ethnic heritage do you claim? Are you Hispanic American, Ukrainian American, Thai American, African American, or some other "American"? Write a paragraph defining your cultural label. You can develop your definition by including such elements as food, music, dance, art, rituals, religion, etc.

WHAT IS SUCCESS?

Hannah Glascock (student)

In this essay, student writer Hannah Glascock defines what it means to be a success. However, she also expands the definition beyond the traditional concept of dramatic accomplishment.

Pre-reading exercise: Meaning comes primarily from words. Before reading the essay, look up the definitions of the following words that appear in the text. The numbers in parentheses refer to the paragraph numbers of the essay.

accomplishment (3)   determination (1)
aspect (4)   realistic (4)
concept (1)

1   Success is a part of life that makes it worthwhile. Any situation faced either ends in success or failure. The emotions and feelings that occur by success are rarely produced by any other outcome. Success cannot be taken away, and it seldom is simply handed right to a person. It is something that is earned through hard work and determination. Many people would rather master a situation which makes them feel good about themselves and whatever they have accomplished. Success is a concept based on accomplishments, victory, and the achievement of set goals.

2   What exactly is an accomplishment? When a situation works out the way it is planned, that is considered an accomplishment. Many people in the world are labeled successful. They have worked very hard to reach their dreams; therefore, they are comfortable with their lives and what they have gained from their successes. The President of the United States, for example, is successful; he is the leader of the Free World and has to make many important decisions. Becoming President was not just handed to him; he first needed to be successful and set goals to achieve, and then he did whatever he could to reach them. It is a huge accomplishment to be elected the President, but everyone else in the world has the opportunity to be successful in one endeavor or another. To be a parent and raise children is an accomplishment of major proportions. When they mature, start their own families, and are happy with themselves, then the parents have accomplished what they started when they decided to have children.

3   Achieving a victory and being the best that you can be is another type of success. For example, athletes live for a victory and work hard to be the best at what they do. Once they reach the win, they feel successful, which is a better feeling than finishing in second place. A prime example is Tiger Woods

because he has won many major golf tournaments against the best golfers in the world and being voted "Player of the Year" many times. Because of his success, he has been able to fund the Tiger Woods Foundation which helps children all over the world. Young people all over the world look up to him as a role model, not just because of his success as an athlete, but also because he is a good, caring, generous, human being.

4   Setting and reaching goals is another path to success. Everyone in the world, no matter their situation in life, dreams. Everyone wonders if they will make it to college, find the right fob, or save enough money for a house. The key to reaching dreams is to set goals. If a person wants to reach their dreams badly enough they will do what it takes to accomplish their goals. The goals should be written down and placed so they can be seen every day, so the goals are never far from the mind's eye. For example, if your dream is to go to college, then hard work and studying each day should be the immediate goals. Another important step in goal-setting is to make sure the goals are realistic. If the goals are set too high and are unable to be reached, then the interest and motivation could be lost, and the dream never realized. As long as goals are set to help support determination instead of sabotage it, the goals can be reached.

5   Goal-setting is just an easier method to reach dreams and fulfill expectations. So many dreams are eventually tossed aside because of poor planning and unreasonable expectations. But challenges make life interesting. Although not everyone can be as successful as a president or a star athlete, even the everyman can achieve importance and self-worth through accomplishing goals. With such a plan, victory should not escape our grasp.

Definition Technique Questions

1. In how many ways does the author define *accomplishment*?

2. How do Tiger Woods's accomplishments, defining him as a personal success, extend beyond that definition?

3. What does the author point out as the greatest danger to achieving success?

Suggestions for Writing

1. Write a paragraph clarifying your definition of success.

2. Write a paragraph outlining what has stopped you from being successful at some endeavor in the past.

PERSUASION

THE RECOLORING OF CAMPUS LIFE*

Shelby Steele

> The following is a selection from "The Recoloring of Campus Life," an essay from a collection entitled *The Content of Our Character* by Shelby Steele. The author, an African American and Hoover Institute Fellow, often takes conservative positions on issues, drawing the ire and fire of the more liberal African American community.

Pre-reading exercise: Meaning comes primarily from words. Before reading the essay, look up the definitions of the following words that appear in the text. The numbers in parentheses refer to the paragraph number of the essay.

appease (5)	paradox (2)
archetypal (1)	parity (7)
capitalization (5)	presumption (9)
inchoate (2)	volatile (3)

1   I have long believed that the trouble between the races is seldom what it appears to be. It was not hard to see after my first talks with students that racial tension on campus is a problem that misrepresents itself. It has the same look, the archetypal pattern, of America's timeless racial conflict—white racism and black protest. And I think part of our concern over it comes from the fact that it has the feel of a relapse, illness gone and come again. But if we are seeing the same symptoms, I don't believe we are dealing with the same illness. For one thing, I think racial tension on campus is more the result of racial equality than inequality.

2   How to live with racial difference has been America's profound social problem. For the first hundred years or so following emancipation it was controlled by a legally sanctioned inequality that kept the races from each other. No longer is this the case. On campuses today, as throughout society, blacks enjoy equality under the law—a profound social advancement. No student may be kept out of a class or a dormitory or an extracurricular activity because of his or her race. But there is a paradox here: on a campus where members of all races are gathered, mixed together in the classroom as well as socially, differences are more exposed than ever. And this is where the trouble starts. For members of each race—young adults coming into their own, often away from home for the first time—bring to this site of freedom, exploration, and (now, today) equality, very deep fears, anxieties, inchoate feelings of racial shame, anger, and guilt. These feelings could lie dormant in the home, in familiar neighborhoods, in simpler days of childhood. But the college campus, with its structures of interaction and adult-level competition—the big exam, the dorm, the mixer—is another matter. I think campus racism is born of the rub between racial difference and a setting, the campus itself, devoted to interaction and equality. On our campuses, such concentrated micro-societies, all that remains

unresolved between blacks and whites, all the old wounds and shames that have never been addressed, present themselves for attention—and present our youth with pressures they cannot always handle.

3   I have mentioned one paradox: racial fears and anxieties among blacks and whites, bubbling up in an era of racial equality under the law, in settings that are among the freest and fairest in society. But there is another, related paradox, stemming from the notion of—and practice of—affirmative action. Under the provisions of the Equal Employment Opportunity Act of 1972, all state governments and institutions (including universities) were forced to initiate plans to increase the proportion of minority and women employees and, in the case of universities, of students too. Affirmative action plans that establish racial quotas were ruled unconstitutional more than ten years ago in *University of California v. Bakke,* but such plans are still thought by some to secretly exist, and lawsuits having to do with alleged quotas are still very much with us. But quotas are only the most controversial aspect of affirmative action; the principal of affirmative action is reflected in various university programs aimed at redressing and overcoming past patterns of discrimination. Of course, to be conscious of past patterns of discrimination—the fact, say, that public schools in the black inner cities are more crowded and employ fewer top-notch teachers than a white suburban public school, and that this is a factor in student performance—is only reasonable. But in doing this we also call attention quite obviously to difference: in the case of blacks and whites, racial difference. What has emerged on campus in recent years—as a result of the new equality and of affirmative action and, in a sense, as a result of progress—is a *politics of difference,* a troubling, volatile politics in which each group justifies itself, its sense of worth, and its pursuit of power, through difference alone. . . .

4   The politics of difference sets up a struggle for innocence among all groups. When difference is the currency of power, each group must fight for the innocence that entitles it to power. To gain this innocence, blacks sting whites with guilt, remind them of their racial past, accuse them of new and more subtle forms of racism. One way whites retrieve their innocence is to discredit blacks and deny their difficulties, for in this denial is the denial of their own guilt. To blacks this denial looks like racism, a racism that feeds black innocence and encourages them to throw more guilt at whites. And so the cycle continues. The politics of difference leads each group to pick at the vulnerabilities of the other.

5   Men and women who run universities—whites mostly—participate in the politics of difference because they handle their guilt differently than do many of their students. They don't deny it, but still they don't want to *feel* it. And to avoid this feeling of guilt they have tended to go along with whatever blacks put on the table rather than work with them to assess their real needs. University administrators have too often been afraid of guilt and have relied on negotiation and capitulation more to appease their own guilt than to help blacks and other minorities. Administrators would never give white students a racial theme dorm where they could be "more comfortable with people of their own kind," yet more and more universities are doing this for black students, thus fostering a kind of voluntary segregation. To avoid the anxieties of integrated situations, blacks ask for theme dorms; to avoid guilt, white administrators give theme dorms.

6   When everyone is on the run from their anxieties about race, race relations on campus can be reduced to the negotiation of avoidances. A pattern of demand and concession develops in which both sides use the other to escape themselves. Black studies departments, black deans of student affairs, black counseling programs, Afro houses, black theme dorms, black homecoming dances and graduation ceremonies—black students and white administrators have slowly engineered a machinery of separatism that, in the name of sacred difference, redraws the ugly lines of segregation.

7   Black students have not sufficiently helped themselves, and universities, despite all their concessions, have not really done much for blacks. If both faced their anxieties, I think they would see the same thing: academic parity with all other groups should be the overriding mission of black students, and it should also be the first goal that universities have for their black students. Blacks can only *know* they are as good as others when they are, in fact, as good—when their grades are higher and their dropout rate lower. Nothing under the sun will substitute for this, and no amount of concessions will bring it about.

8   Universities can never be free of guilt until they truly help black students, which means leading and challenging them rather than negotiating and capitulating. It means inspiring them to achieve academic parity, nothing less, and helping them to see their own weaknesses as their greatest challenge. It also means dismantling the machinery of separatism, breaking the link between difference and power, and skewing the formula for entitlement away from race and gender and back to constitutional rights.

9   As for the young white students who have rediscovered swastikas and the word "nigger," I think that they suffer from an exaggerated sense of their own innocence, as if they were incapable of evil and beyond the reach of guilt. But it is also true that the politics of difference creates an environment that threatens their innocence and makes them defensive. White students are not invited to the negotiating table from which they see blacks and others walk away with concessions. The presumption is that they do not deserve to be there because they are white. So they can only be defensive, and the less mature among them will be aggressive. Guerrilla activity will ensue. Of course this is wrong, but it is also a reflection of an environment where difference carries power and where whites have the wrong "difference."

10   I think universities should emphasize commonality as a higher value than "diversity" and "pluralism"—buzzwords for the politics of difference. Difference that does not rest on a clearly delineated foundation of commonality is not only inaccessible to those who are not part of the ethnic or racial group, but also antagonistic to them. Difference can enrich only the common ground.

11   Integration has become an abstract term today, having to do with little more than numbers and racial balances. But it once stood for a high and admirable set of values. It made difference second to commonality, and it asked members of all races to face whatever fears they inspired in each other. I doubt the word will have a new vogue, but the values, under whatever name, are worth working for.

Persuasion Technique Questions

1. What is Steele's thesis?

2. What evidence does Steele use to support his thesis?

3. Why is Steele's thesis a paradox?

4. Discuss why you agree or disagree with the author's thesis.

Suggestions for Writing

1. Write a paragraph about the racial atmosphere at your school. Discuss whether or not Steele's thesis accurately depicts conditions at your school.

2. Write a paragraph agreeing or disagreeing with Steele's assertion that "racial difference has been America's profound social problem." If you disagree, discuss what you think America's most profound social problem is.

INDISTINGUISHABLE FROM MAGIC*

Robert L. Forward

> In this essay, "Indistinguishable from Magic," physicist Robert L. Forward confronts the problem of manned spaceships traveling to the stars. Notice that although space travel is a highly technical subject, the author refrains from using overly technical language in an attempt to make the concepts easier for the layperson to understand.

Pre-reading exercise: Meaning comes primarily from words. Before reading the essay, look up the definitions of the following words that appear in the text. The numbers in parentheses refer to the paragraph number of the essay.

amenities (7)	initiates (8)
benevolent (2)	interstellar (6)
evoked (2)	millennium (7)
folly (2)	speed of light (6)

1   It was only a few centuries ago that the human race realized those bright lights in the night sky were suns, like our Sun. We then realized that those other suns probably had worlds orbiting around them, some possibly like our world. Since that time, one of the dreams of the human race has been to visit those other worlds in ships that travel between the stars. But as we began to realize the immensity of the distances that separate our star from the other stars, we began to despair of ever building a starship using the puny technology that the human race controls.

2   Science fiction writers, in an attempt to get their storybook heroes to the stars before the readers got bored, evoked starships with faster-than-light drives, space warps, and other forms of future technology that were indistinguishable from magic. At the same time, the general public evoked fantasy starships in the form of flying saucers flown to the Earth *from* other stars. These starships were propelled by antigravity or magnetism, and were piloted by benevolent little green men who would save the world from its folly.

3   If little green men can cross the great gulf, can we?

4   Yes. It is difficult to go to the stars, but it is not impossible. The stars are far away, and the speed of light limits us to a slow crawl along the starlanes. To travel to the stars will take years of time, gigawatts of power, kilograms of energy, and billions (if not trillions) of dollars. Yet it can be done—if we wish to. And if we decide to go, what kind of starships can we build?

5   It turns out that there are many types of starships possible, each using a different technology. There are some starships that we can build now. For these technologies we know the basic physical principles and have demonstrated the ability to achieve the desired reactions on a laboratory scale. All that is needed is the application of large amounts of money, material, and manpower. There are also some promising starship designs that use future technology that is barely distinguishable from magic. Here we know the basic physical principles, but we have not yet controlled the future technology in the laboratory. Once we have turned that future technology from magic into reality, we can then proceed with starship designs based on those technologies.

*Robert L. Forward, "Indistinguishable Magic" excerpted from *Indistinguishable Magic*. Baen Books, copyright © 1995. Reprinted by permission of Baen Books.

6   No matter how fast we can make a starship go, we must resign ourselves to the fact that interstellar travel will always take a long time. Even if we had a starship that traveled at the speed of light, it would take over 4.3 years to travel to the nearest star system, then another 4.3 years before a message (or the starship) returns. We don't have speed-of-light starships yet, and won't for a long time.

7   The first travelers to the stars will be our robotic probes. They will be small and won't require all the amenities like food, air, and water that humans seem to find necessary. The power levels to send the first squadron of robotic probes out to the stars are within the present reach of the human race. if we wanted to, we could have the first interstellar probe on the way to the nearest star system early in the next millennium.[1]

8   Scientists studying hibernating animals have found the hormone that initiates hibernation and have used the drug to induce hibernation in other animals. Whether this drug will induce hibernation in humans without causing serious side effects is unknown. Also, it is unknown whether hibernation actually increases lifespan, or just makes living possible when there is insufficient food. Still, there is enough biological research on suspended animation that one of these days we may use that method of keeping a crew alive long enough to carry out century-long exploration missions.

9   Even if these particular biological techniques do not turn into a real suspended animation capability, there is another method to carry out a slowship mission: let the people die, but allow their children to carry on. A slowship journey to the stars will send a colony of people off in a generation starship. Although only the first generation would be true volunteers, with enough thought and planning we could turn the slow-moving starship into a truly acceptable worldship, with all the amenities and few of the problems of living on Earth.

10   The important thing to realize is that our present technology can take us to the stars. To be sure, our first robotic interstellar probes will be slow, will consume a lot of power and money, and will return small amounts of data.

11   It is difficult to go to the stars. But it is not impossible. There are not one, but many, many future technologies, all under intense development for other purposes, that, if suitably modified and redirected, can give the human race a magic starship that will take us to the stars.

12   And go we will.

Persuasion Technique Questions

1. According to the author, who will be the first travelers to the stars?

2. What two problems does the author state are the main hurdles for interstellar travel?

3. How have science fiction writers promoted the idea that interstellar travel is possible?

Suggestions for Writing

1. Write a paragraph about a product you would like to see invented in the future.

2. Write a paragraph either agreeing or disagreeing with Forward's position, "And go we will [to the stars]."

---

[1] [*Indistinguishable from Magic* was published in 1995, so we are already in the "next" millennium.]

UNCONDITIONAL SUPPORT

Beth Glenn (student)

THE FAMILY COLLECTIVE

Denise Hillis (student)

> In this set of essays, student writers Beth Glenn and Denise Hillis take opposite sides in a debate as to whether families should give unconditional support to adult children during times of need. Glenn takes the affirmative or pro position, and Hillis supports the negative or con position.

Unconditional Support

Pre-reading exercise: Meaning comes primarily from words. Before reading the essay, look up the definitions of the following words that appear in the text. The numbers in parentheses refer to the paragraph number in the essay.

adjust (3)   extraordinary (1)
circumstances (2)   moreover (3)
evident (3)   numerous (1)

1 What happens when people suddenly lose their jobs? Where do they go, and to whom can they turn? How will they support themselves? With the economy continuing to worsen, even those currently employed have to ask themselves such questions. On some occasions, the suddenly jobless find that moving back home is their best, and sometimes only, recourse. Parents should give unconditional support to adult children needing to return home because children always need to have a sense of family, to learn to overcome challenges, and to have help meeting sudden financial demands.

2 Despite the fact that eighteen-year-olds are considered adults, they still need a sense of family. When children turn eighteen, often, parents make them pay rent. Consequently, the sense of having a family turns to the sense of having a landlord. Children should not have to feel that way; children should know what home is, and they should know that they can always come back. A family can provide not only shelter but also a shoulder to lean on. When children are home, they should always feel loved. Although children often have friends, a family will be there through thick and thin; therefore, they can understand any circumstance that life may bring; thus, a sense of family can provide both physical and emotional support.

3 Often, young adults think that they have life figured out; however, life will bring challenges that they will have to learn to overcome. For instance, if a divorce occurs or a job is lost, a move back to the family home may have to happen. Consequently, the returning child will have to learn to adjust to new surroundings and, hopefully, this will help them learn to adapt and move on more quickly. Although such a learning process can be difficult, acceptance to

these challenges will have to be made deep within the child's heart and mind as they become stronger.

4   Moving back home will provide an excellent opportunity for temporary financial support. A young adult can never be fully prepared when they lose their job; consequently, it can be a difficult and challenging time. Parents, by allowing the child to come home, will be able to help their offspring with food and shelter while they look for employment. Moving back home also will give the youngster time to heal from what is most likely their first job loss. After a divorce, moving back home to be with a loving family can help fill the void of loneliness. Parents need to let their child move back home because everyone faces challenges at some point, and everyone needs help dealing with them.

5   When parents decide to have children, those children will be theirs forever. Therefore, parents should provide unconditional support for the children, no matter what the age. Parents need to welcome their children home with open arms because people will make mistakes in life. However, with the support of parents, those mistakes can be easier to conquer.

The Family Collective

Pre-reading exercise: Meaning comes primarily from words. Before reading the essay, look up the definitions of the following words that appear in the text. The numbers in parentheses refer to the paragraph number in the essay.

breach (3)	perseverant (1)
census (1)	precludes (1)
dilemma (2)	regressive (1)
disservice (2)	sabotage (3)
equitably (4)	sympathetic (2)
expenditures (4)	virtually (4)

1   Failed marriages, job loss, and the high cost of housing are only a few reasons why children are moving back in with their parents. The number of adults ages 25 and over living with their parents was 3.7 million according to the 1970 census. That number has risen to approximately 8.5 million in 1995. It is projected to reach 12 to 15 million by 2010. This move is in a regressive direction, and does not look good. Children should not move back in with their parents because it precludes a perseverant attitude, puts a strain on family relationships, and adds to household duties.

2   The opposite of persistence is quitting; quitting is not a character quality that a parent hopes their children master. Some say it may become necessary, due to circumstances, for children to move back with their parents. They argue that the purpose of a family is to be supportive during a time of crisis. Yet, a parent can be supportive in many ways that are more productive than sharing their home. Parents can assist their children emotionally, financially, and practically in other more positive ways. They can gather information about jobs, run errands, lend a sympathetic ear, offer advice or even babysit. A parent should express confidence in the ability of their child to resolve a dilemma. Bailing them out of a bad situation should not be an option. Parents can do their children a disservice when they offer them an easy way out.

3   A serious breach in personal relationships can be a direct result of parents and children living together. Some expect living with family will provide

"quality time" together. However, this expectation can sabotage the relationship. Parents and children often have time schedules that clash; consequently, there is disappointment and misunderstanding on both sides. Also, parents usually have a set of household rules, and children can resent the restrictions placed on them. Still, according to some experts, children would help with the household chores and maintenance. Nevertheless, parents are usually set in their ways of doing jobs around the house in a specified manner at a specific time. They are not always appreciative of a job that is not done to their standards. Also, mixed degrees of tolerance for a messy house will cause strife.

4   Children have every intention of sharing domestic responsibility when they move back home, but it is very easy for a parent to fall back into a "taking care of the kids" mentality. It is difficult for children, when they return to live in their parent's home, to exercise any authority in simple matters such as what they eat, when they eat, or how they eat. A situation is set that is ripe for making a grown child dependent and resentful. Furthermore, financial problems become a substantial hurdle. Sudden increases in the number of people living in a household always increase expenditures. It is virtually impossible to equitably divide expenses when the children have little or no income. Financial friction is a quick way to split family ties.

5   In the end, it is far better for parents to complete the job of raising children by not making them dependent as they become older. Parents would do well to remember their goal is to equip their children with the skills and confidence to become self-sufficient. Although leaving the nest can be arduous, the result will be a stronger, multi-family unit.

Persuasion Technique Questions

1. Do you agree with Glenn's assertion that children, no matter what their age, need a sense of family? What reasons does she give to support her opinion? Are they different or similar to your own?

2. Do you agree with Hillis's position that "moving back home" is out of the question?

3. Hillis is not against the family helping a child in need. In what ways does she state the family can support children in trouble?

4. Glenn states that the parents' responsibility for the children is unconditional and should last forever. This position seems extreme because, unlike Hillis's position, there are no exceptions. Do you agree or disagree with Glenn?

Suggestions for Writing

1. If you agree with Glenn's position, write a paragraph disagreeing with her.

2. If you agree with Hillis's position, write a paragraph disagreeing with her.

Note: Answers are not included for practice materials in which answers will vary.

Chapter 2

PRACTICE 1

1. airliner
3. lights
5. air traffic controller
7. Passengers
9. Signs

PRACTICE 2

2. It
4. Adler and Sullivan Company
6. philosophy
8. carport
10. Frank Lloyd Wright

PRACTICE 3

1. Yukon Territory
3. wealth; vistas
5. plateaus
7. Forests
9. climate

PRACTICE 6

2. The carton of oranges floated in the water.
4. Between the two hills, the houses are made from cedar logs.
6. During the week and on the weekend, homework is a constant activity.
8. Over the river and through the woods, the wolf raced to Grandmother's house.
10. Three of the guitarists are alternative musicians.

PRACTICE 7

1. In a presidential election, the challenger has to choose a running mate.
3. At the beginning of the process, many candidates are considered.
5. After the elimination of some candidates, a short list is assembled.
7. Without the interview process, the final choice cannot be made.
9. By the end of the process, the challenger can make a clear choice for the party.

PRACTICE 8

2. The rocking motion of the plane was somewhat disturbing.
4. Outside the cabin, the stars shone like small fireflies in the dark.
6. In most cases, smaller children slept on their parents' laps.
8. After the flight landed, the passengers walked to the baggage carousel.
10. During the trip to the hotel, their bags were carried on the top of the bus.

PRACTICE 9

1. As a young child, he learned the proper mechanics of the swing.
3. The youngster progressed rapidly as a golfer.

5. Without hesitation, Woods won three straight Amateur championships.
7. He regularly launched 300-yard drives on the longer holes.
9. Tiger stunned the golfing world with his outstanding and exciting play.

PRACTICE 10

2. She opened the letter on the kitchen table.
4. She unfolded the piece of paper.
6. Tears of happiness flowed from her eyes.
8. After calming down, Marjorie called her mother and father on the phone.
10. She had won round trip tickets for four to London.

PRACTICE 11

1. Most people participate in outdoor activities.
3. Another skis in the mountains of Colorado.
5. A group from Vermont searches for rare birds in the deep forests.
7. Missourians ride bikes on the scenic Katy Trail.
9. Others leap from bridges with bungee cords attached to their ankles.

PRACTICE 13

2. The foyer looked buffed and polished from floor to ceiling.
4. People in the audience seemed nervous.
6. The symphony orchestra sounded confident and well-rehearsed.
8. The music remained controlled throughout the evening.
10. At the concert's end, the applause became louder with each bow.

PRACTICE 14

1. My life was not wonderful.
3. My family said I looked depressed.
5. Even food smelled dull and tasteless.
7. I felt disassociated from my true self.
9. I turned to a counselor for help.

PRACTICE 16

2. However, exercising must be done on a regular basis.
4. On the other hand, exercising too much may be detrimental to your health.
6. Lifting weights should be accompanied by an aerobic exercise.
8. Mental health also will be stimulated by physical exercise.
10. Regular exercising would lower health-related costs nationally.

PRACTICE 17

1. How do you start a hobby?
3. Then, you should ask your friends and neighbors what hobbies they have.
5. Budgeting may help you narrow your choices.
7. This could put you in touch with other enthusiasts interested in the same hobby as you.

9. (Being a member) of a club also might get you discounts on materials and publications.

PRACTICE 19

2. danced
   dances
   will dance
4. played
   plays
   will play

PRACTICE 20

1. cornered
   corners
   will corner
3. consumed
   consumes
   will consume
5. camped
   camps
   will camp

PRACTICE 21

2. coordinated
   coordinates
   will coordinate
4. juggled
   juggles
   will juggle

PRACTICE 24

1. The child's ears and nose (looked) just like its mother's.
3. Jupiter, Mars, and Venus (are) planets in our solar system.
5. The antique sofa, the art deco clock, and the abstract painting (were sold) at auction.
7. The slithery snake, the prickly hedgehog, and the colorful parrot (are) the most popular animals at the children's zoo.
9. *Hamlet* and *Macbeth* (are) two of Shakespeare's most famous plays.

PRACTICE 25

2. Brad Pitt, George Clooney, and Julia Roberts (are) popular movie stars.
4. The lawn mower, the edger, and the cultivator (sat) unused in the garage.
6. Either you or I (will have to make) dinner for the Cub Scouts.
8. In the middle of the night, snoring, cat calls, and crying infants (can reduce) sleep.
10. Nike, Adidas, and Reebok (are) best-selling athletic shoes.

PRACTICE 26

1. The horse trotted and galloped around the track.
3. The audience laughed and cried at the actor's performance.
5. The motel room was clean and smelled of lilacs and roses.
7. In New York City, skateboarders ride on subways and skate in parking garages.
9. The legislature argued and voted on fifty-three bills this current session.

PRACTICE 27

2. In the auditorium, students clapped their hands and stomped their feet.
4. The old fire engine jiggled and rattled down the cobblestone street.
6. After the huge meal, the diners moaned and groaned.

8. Seabirds fly, dive, swim, and float while searching for food.
10. The dancers twirled and leaped in time with the music.

Chapter 3

PRACTICE 1

1. Jawan hit the ball, but Christie caught the ball.
3. Pang ran quickly to third base, yet Chinua tagged him out.
5. Tom singled four times, and Angie hit two home runs.
7. Joe caused three errors, so the other team scored five runs.

PRACTICE 2

2. , so
4. , for
6. , yet

PRACTICE 10

Sentence corrections will vary.
1. CS
3. C
5. RO
7. C
9. CS

PRACTICE 11

Sentence corrections will vary.
2. RO
4. C
6. CS
8. CS
10. RO

Chapter 4

PRACTICE 1

The surgical team prepared the operating room for the procedure.

The surgeon dressed in a green surgical gown; she wore a protective cap covering her hair.

Bach's *Toccata and Fugue in D Minor* was piped into the operating room during the operation; it helped to maintain a relaxed atmosphere during the delicate procedure.

The operation was a success.

The patient experienced a quick recovery; he was back at work in less than two weeks.

His insurance paid for the operation.

His family was happy to have him healthy again.

Chapter 6

PRACTICE 1

1. They ordered steak, potatoes, and asparagus at dinner.
3. C
5. The garden consisted of tulips, crocuses, and jonquils during the three months of spring.
7. The fog blanketed the fields in the morning, during the afternoon, and after dark.
9. The orchestra's violins, cellos, and violas answered the woodwinds during the second movement.

PRACTICE 8

2. Jerry enjoyed many activities while vacationing: boating, fishing, and hiking.
4. The librarian reshelved the book left on her desk: *Retire Early: How to Make Money in Real Estate Foreclosures*.
6. The office workers ate lunch in a variety of places: in the employee lounge, on the roof, and out by the lake.
8. Joaquin used three types of peppers to add color to his special salsa: red, yellow, and green.
10. The children enjoyed the party because of the food: hot dogs, hamburgers, and chips.

PRACTICE 9

1. The two falcons found a tree, gathered twigs, and built a nest.
3. The surgical team had a good reputation because they were up on the latest techniques and had worked together for four years.
5. The movie was titled *The Lord of the Rings: The Two Towers*.
7. The plane could not take off; the engine wasn't powerful enough to handle the load.
9. Amelia was in a hurry because her date was at 7:00 P.M., and it was already 6:45 P.M.

PRACTICE 11

Movies are popular because of two factors: actors and genres. Star-power can almost guarantee that a movie will make money. There are a handful of stars in this category: Will Smith, Johnny Depp, and Nicole Kidman. If tickets for movies starring one of these actors go on sale at 2:00 P.M., the "Sold Out" sign usually lights up by 4:00 P.M. Fantasy-action movies are some of the most popular movies currently running. Some of the largest grossing movies in history belong to this genre: *Star Wars: The Return of the Jedi, Lord of the Rings: The Fellowship of the Ring*, and *Harry Potter: The Sorceror's Stone*, to name a few. If movie producers can combine a popular star with a popular genre, a box-office bonanza is almost a sure thing.

PRACTICE 12

Dear Ms. Morgan:
Thank you for your recent inquiry concerning what to expect here at Middletown University during your first year as a student. As you know, there are certain personal traits that will stand you in good order both at school and your future place of employment: financial responsibility, time management, and cooperation. Working to help with expenses teaches the value of money and what it represents in terms of goods and services. Time management is an important skill to learn. For instance, in her best selling business book, *Time Management: Workplace Wizardry*, author Meghan Brooks suggests that you should never get out of bed later than 6:00 A.M. By 7:00 A.M. you should have your daily schedule complete. Doing this will keep you organized and focused on each task. Cooperation, of course, will help you enormously while you are attending Middletown. You will be working and interacting with a wide array of individuals: administrators, staff, faculty, and other students. I hope this letter helps answer your concerns. Please do not hesitate to contact me during my office hours: 3:00 P.M. Wednesdays and 10:00 A.M. Thursdays.
Sincerely yours,
Ronald Blevins, Dean
Arts & Humanities Division

Chapter 7

PRACTICE 1

1. Gas prices increase during the summer (because) many people drive on their vacations.
3. Golfers can play all day and night in Finland (since) the sun never sets.
5. (Before) an earthquake sends tremors through the ground, some scientists believe animals can somehow sense it is going to happen.
7. (Until) their economy failed, the Russians were considered a world power.
9. The students had a study session every Sunday evening (unless) there was a good concert at the student center.

Chapter 8

PRACTICE 1

2. At first, I did not see the need to know CPR for my job as a lifeguard.
4. More often, the traffic is heavier in the evening than in the morning.
6. All in all, it was a very profitable day selling pennants outside the stadium.
8. Being thin and tall, the model easily fit into all the designer's latest gowns.
10. Whether guilty or not, the defendant seemed believable when testifying.

PRACTICE 2

1. After the matinee showing, the tour bus left Las Vegas and headed for Reno.
3. On most sunny days, the students gathered in the quadrangle to read and visit.
5. Over the mountains, the highway trailed away like a giant black snake.
7. Under the bridge, a homeless person had established a camp.
9. As lava eventually cools, it turns to rock.

PRACTICE 4

2. description
4. comparison
6. definition

PRACTICE 8

1. No, taking the driver's exam is not possible until Monday morning.
3. Nevertheless, we are spending a full week in Toronto.
5. Yes, the mechanic says he can fix the radiator.
7. Hmmm, I can't decide on sausage or pepperoni on my pizza.
9. Well, I might go hang gliding if the weather conditions are good.

PRACTICE 9

2. Nevertheless,   (contrast)
4. Ah,   (surprise or wonderment)
6. However,   (contrast)
8. Well,   (contemplative pause)
10. Leonardo,   (address by name)

PRACTICE 14

1. World War II, naturally, is an event discussed to this day.
3. Poor relations, meanwhile, developed between the two powers.
5. The Empire of Japan, therefore, attacked Pearl Harbor.
7. The United States, consequently, entered World War II on December 8, 1941.

9. The United States, eventually, would fight a war on two fronts: Asia and Europe.

11. Today, the United States and Japan, however, are considered allies.

PRACTICE 15

2. Frost, in fact, was from New England.

4. His poetry, on the other hand, often dealt with death and alienation.

6. Frost, as a matter of fact, achieved his first success while living in England.

8. Robert Frost, at last, had attained the status of a major poet worldwide.

PRACTICE 16

1. Our solar system, the only planetary system in this part of the galaxy, consists of eight major planets.

3. The inner planets, Mercury, Venus, Earth, and Mars, are composed primarily of rock and iron.

5. Mercury not only is nearest the sun but also orbits the sun most quickly. (No commas needed)

7. Earth, with a myriad of life forms, is the only planet known to have abundant liquid water and oxygen.

9. Jupiter's mass of 317 times that of Earth makes it the largest of the planets. (No commas needed)

Chapter 9

PRACTICE 1

1. (Mud-slinging and personal attacks) turn off some people when it comes to politics.

3. (Families) can help children by being a support system for all their activities.

5. The (movie) was a success because of the script, the acting, and the special effects.

7. The (depletion) of the ozone layer might cause global warming and an increase in skin cancers.

9. (Helping others) can make almost any profession a rewarding experience.

PRACTICE 2

2. The (fence) was built to keep the coyotes away from the livestock.

4. Great teamwork has made the (United States' women's soccer team) an international success.

6. Versatility and size make the (laptop computer) a good business tool for travelers.

8. The (Spanish Inquisition) impaired scientific thought for decades.

10. A (quiet place) with good lighting can help students study more effectively.

PRACTICE 14

soothing
deserted
rushing
crash
warped
tables
leading
replaced
boards
scene
beautiful

PRACTICE 15

to
broaden
can
mellow
story
elevators
classical
or
western
your

Chapter 10

PRACTICE 4

1. Halloween—stated in the title, not in the paragraph.

3. Similes add descriptive images that support the "scary" dominant impression. The trees are also personified because they can "snatch their next victim."

PRACTICE 5

2. Excitement

PRACTICE 6

1. The sound of deep cold.

3. "A stiff northwest wind rocked in the trees and snatched at cars . . ." and ". . . the wind was sanding it smooth."

5. "deep cold," "the sound of the wind," "windchill," fifty below zero," "stiff northwest wind," "rough rime," "Siberian," "Antarctic, "intensity," and "gust."

PRACTICE 7

3. The ice cream truck.

5. In ¶ 3, "Then the truck's transmission gears growled," and "the echoes of the burdensome chimes."

Chapter 11

PRACTICE 7

1. The writer uses telephone calls to order the events. There are two phone calls, and a third is inferred. The first call is introduced in the first sentence: "It was not long before the telephone rang." The second call is introduced in sentence 5: "Upon receiving the second call. . . ." And the third call is inferred by the operator in the last sentence: "The operator would check back with them."

PRACTICE 8

1. The writer orders the events chronologically as they occur: first, the writer resolves to do something about her looks; second, how she feels about the project; third, she sprints to the department store; fourth, she goes to the cosmetics counter; and last, her decision to broaden her original desire to go for BEAUTIFUL, rather than just attractive.

Chapter 12

PRACTICE 6

2. The students can fax or email their art project to school, and the parents participate in PTA meetings online.

PRACTICE 7

1. A. M. Homes' *The End of Alice*, the graphic fictional story of a pedophile; Poppy Brite's *Exquisite Corpse*, a novel told

from a serial killer's point of view; *Trainspotting*, a British ode to heroin addiction; *Pulp Fiction*; peppered with shots of flying feces and a dead baby crawling on the ceiling.

3. If the class has a difficult time coming up with some ideas, you might suggest the higher-priced "extreme" athletic clothing promoted by the various professional sports and how young people have actually been robbed and killed for the apparel.

Chapter 13

PRACTICE 1

2. b
4. b
6. b

PRACTICE 2

1. d
3. b
5. b

PRACTICE 3

2. "The second category" (sentence 4)

PRACTICE 7

1. They all have "starter cords."
3. Weed whackers, lawn mowers, edgers, and snow blowers. Yes, because many people probably own at least one of these machines, so they have personal knowledge of and experience with them.
5. No, the writer does not use transitional expressions. Other answers will vary.

PRACTICE 8

2. Pile drivers, carpenters, and millwrights. All their jobs are dangerous.
4. "The first type" (sentence 2); "The second kind" (sentence 4); "The last category" (sentence 7). They organize the three types of workers chronologically. This organization helps the reader remain focused on the categories.

PRACTICE 9

1. "Pliers . . . climb" with "single-minded determination"; "Keys . . . burrow"; "Women's purses . . . travel . . . to find hiding space." The tone is humorous. It's as though the objects are planning to do these things to annoy us.
3. Answers will vary.
5. To entertain by giving us humorous situations that we can identify with because we have all most likely experienced such exasperating activities.

PRACTICE 10

2. Although answers will vary, one possibility is that in desperate situations, to keep some semblance of "control," people begin to nag others to do what they think will keep them in control.

Chapter 14

PRACTICE 1

1. D
3. D
5. I
7. D
9. I

PRACTICE 2

2. I
4. D
6. D

8. I
10. I

PRACTICE 3

1. 4, 5, 3, 2, 1

PRACTICE 4

2. X, 5, 2, 4, 1, 7, 6, 3

PRACTICE 5

1. How to make a pizza.
3. Three steps: making the dough, making the sauce, assembling the pizza and toppings.

PRACTICE 6

2. Informational
4. "first . . . step" (sentence 2); "while" (sentence 6); "now" (sentence 7)

PRACTICE 8

1. Producing a photograph from a negative.
3. Three: setting the scene, developing the negative, and enlarging the print.
5. Answers will vary.

PRACTICE 10

2. Two
4. Answers will vary.

PRACTICE 11

1. Conversation
3. Tennis and bowling

Chapter 15

PRACTICE 1

Answers may vary, but the following are the most popular approaches.

2. Contrast
4. Contrast
6. Compare
8. Contrast
10. Contrast

PRACTICE 2

1. Compare
3. Compare
5. Contrast
7. Contrast
9. Compare

PRACTICE 7

2. Point-by-point
4. Although the author talks about "character," in general terms, no specific characters are offered as examples.

PRACTICE 8

1. Who pays for the commercial and residential real estate marketing costs—the company or the agent? Yes, the first sentence.
3. By using transitional expressions: "similarly" (sentence 1); "like" (sentence 2).

PRACTICE 9

2. Block
4. Yes, the author mentions activities when she was a girl, such as sports and driving with her father to Wal-Mart, and she mentions the things she did on her own as an adolescent, such as deciding when to go to bed, what to wear, and what to eat.

PRACTICE 10

1. Ulysses S. Grant and Robert E. Lee, the two military commanders for the North and South during the Civil War. Yes, although Grant and Lee are not specifically mentioned. It might have been a more effective topic sentence, had the author done so.
3. "again" (sentence 3); "very different" (sentence 5); "very much alike" (sentence 5). Yes. Answers will vary.

PRACTICE 11

1. Point-by-Point.
3. That most Japanese are submissive, unoriginal, or masochistic [stated] while most American are not [not directly stated]

Chapter 16

PRACTICE 1

2. To blunder is to make a mistake.
4. *Rustic* means relating to the rural or country life or people.

PRACTICE 2

1. A robin is a bird having a red breast and gray and black upper plumage.
3. A shark is a marine carnivorous fish having a cartilage skeleton and scratchy skin.
5. A prude is a person who is excessively concerned with appearing proper, modest, or righteous.

PRACTICE 5

2. Informational process: World War II soldiers returning home. Description: The engine was cheap, plentiful, a popular choice, easy to customize, and a winning combination when coupled to a light-bodied chassis.
4. It was cheap, plentiful, easy to customize, and powerful.

PRACTICE 6

1. Yes, the perfect store. Process—how the customer is sold merchandise and how the customer can evaluate merchandise by price.
3. Sentence 5. It not only honors its own coupons and advertised prices, but it does so for its competitors' coupons and advertised prices as well.

Chapter 17

PRACTICE 2

2. The writer uses the first sentences to state the opposition's point of view. Then he uses the next two sentences to refute the opposition's position by introducing the negative aspects of nuclear waste material.

PRACTICE 3

1. A seemingly contradictory statement that may be true.
3. Between social differences and the campus setting. The campus, by law, cannot discriminate. So the unresolved problems are brought onto the campus, where they conflict with an environment of equality.

PRACTICE 5

2. F
4. O
6. O
8. O
10. F

PRACTICE 6

1. Hibernation is a long, deep sleep occurring during periods of sustained cold weather, and the hibernating animal uses stored body fat for sustenance. Suspended animation, on the other hand, refers to a state where life processes in the body are lowered to a state akin to death, and oxygen is replaced in the blood by carbon dioxide (asphyxia).
3. (1) Scientists do not know whether hibernation would work with humans; (2) they don't know what the side effects would be; (3) they don't know whether hibernation increases life spans.

Chapter 18

PRACTICE 1

1. Not a good thesis because it is in the form of a question.
3. Not a good thesis because the writer's position is not clear.
5. Not a good thesis because it asserts two main ideas.
7. Not a good thesis because it is a statement of fact.
9. Not a good thesis because it does not clearly define the topic.

PRACTICE 2

2. are more successful
4. should not be installed
6. was not any better
8. promotes
10. helps

PRACTICE 3

1. Salt and water retention may be related as unhealthy aspects of eating meat versus vegetables, but temperature is not a viable reason supporting a vegetarian diet.
3. These three essay map items do not support why household chores help children in any way.
5. Correct.

PRACTICE 4

2. Playmaking, speed, and bench-clearing brawls make ice hockey an exciting sport.
4. College students go to class, study, and write papers. (No attitude.)
6. Solar power should be a governmental priority because of diminishing fossil fuels, environmental pollution, and skyrocketing costs.
8. The St. Louis Rams, Green Bay Packers, and Pittsburgh Steelers are football teams. (No attitude.)
10. Humor, social satire, and musicality made the Beatles popular long after their breakup as a rock group.

PRACTICE 8

1. A shocking statistic: Over six million people were exterminated.
3. The Holocaust.
5. Horrendous policies; numbers of victims, and the terrible effects it continues to have on the survivors.
7. Body Paragraph #1: What the horrendous policies led to. Body Paragraph #2: Who was affected by the Holocaust. Body Paragraph #3: How the liberators and survivors were affected.

PRACTICE 9

2. Exercising the upper body, abdominal muscles, and leg muscles correctly is important for proper functioning.
4. Is important
6. The most important muscles to exercise in the upper body are the triceps, biceps, and pectorals. The abdominal muscles are significant because they support the entire body. The three major muscles in the legs give you the ability to stand, walk, run and jump.
8. Call to action: It is important to exercise. Prediction: If you exercise properly, you will lose weight, have more energy, and feel younger.

Absolute phrase: A group of words consisting of a noun or pronoun and a *participle* (not the regular verb form), plus any other completing words. Absolute phrases modify the entire sentence and cannot be punctuated as a complete sentence.

Action verb: A verb that states what a subject does (in the past, present, or future tense).

Active voice: A verb form in which the subject of the sentence does the acting (using action verb/transitive verb).

Adjective: A word that modifies (or describes) a noun or pronoun. Adjectives come before the nouns they describe; they can also follow the noun. Adjectives can be objective (describing nouns with sensory details) or subjective (describing concepts, feelings, or ideas in more general terms). Both are useful in good writing and enhance meaning, especially in combination.

Adverb: A word that modifies (describes) a verb or an adjective. Often adverbs end in *–ly.* Another test to identify adverbs is to ask whether it answers one of the questions *where, how,* or *when.* Adverbs describe the action of a passage; in some cases, they refer to other adverbs to intensify meaning.

Adverbial conjunction: A word that often follows a semicolon to explain how or in what way the two clauses joined by the semicolon are logically related; often called a *transitional word.*

Antecedent: The noun (or words) to which a pronoun refers in a sentence. (See *Pronoun.*)

Apostrophe: The apostrophe is used to indicate contractions or possession/ownership.

Appositive: A word or phrase that renames the word or phrase preceding it. Appositive words or phrases are often called *noun phrases.*

Article: A type of word that introduces a noun and indicates whether the noun is specific or countable. Frequently used articles are *a, an, the.*

Body: The central section of a paragraph or essay that explains the topic sentence of the paragraph or the thesis statement of the essay.

Brackets: Punctuation marks [ ] used in quoted material to set apart editorial explanations.

Brainstorming: A form of freewriting in which the writer lists thoughts freely, at random.

Chronological order: An organization system for events according to how they occur in order of time. This order is used most often in narratives, process analysis, and cause-effect essays.

Classification: An organization system that divides the subject matter into categories determined by one criterion or basis for grouping.

Clause: A group of related words containing both a subject and a verb. There are two types of clauses: *independent clauses* and *dependent clauses. Independent clauses* can stand alone as a complete sentence. A *dependent clause* (or subordinate clause) begins with subordinating words/conjunctions and cannot stand alone as a sentence (see Chapter 7 for more information on dependent clauses).

Clustering: A type of pre-writing in which the writer explores and organizes thoughts in a chart that begins with putting the main topic in a circle in the center of the page, then connecting related ideas (in smaller circles) with lines (branches).

Coherence: A quality in which the relationship between ideas is clear throughout a paragraph or essay.

Colon: A punctuation mark [:] that is most often used to show that a list is following a complete introductory sentence.

Comma: A punctuation mark [,] used for separating ideas, independent clauses, and items in a list, and for enclosing descriptive phrases.

Comma splice: A sentence containing two independent clauses incorrectly joined by a comma.

Comparison-contrast: An organization system showing similarities and differences between two or more subjects/topics. The organization can be blocked by topic or point by point by criteria.

Complex sentence: A sentence that contains an independent clause and a dependent clause.

Compound verb (predicate): A predicate (the part of the sentence containing the verb) containing two or more verbs.

Compound sentence: A sentence consisting of two or more independent clauses.

Compound subject: A subject consisting of two or more nouns and/or pronouns joined by a coordinating conjunction.

Conclusion: The last sentence of a paragraph or the last paragraph of an essay, which ties together the preceding ideas and smoothly ends the work.

Conjunction: A joining word or phrase. (See *Coordinating conjunction, Adverbial conjunction,* and *Subordinating conjunction.*)

Coordinating conjunction: A word that joins grammatically equal structures. There are seven of these conjunctions: *but, or, yet, for, and, nor, so (BOYFANS).*

Coordination: Joining of two or more grammatically equal structures, most often with a coordinating conjunction or a semicolon.

Countable nouns: Nouns that can be either singular or plural.

Criterion: The method used to classify things (basis for grouping, evaluating, comparing, and contrasting).

Dangling modifier: A descriptive phrase or clause that does not modify (describe) any word or phrase in a sentence.

Dash: Punctuation mark [—] used to set apart parenthetical information that needs more emphasis than would be indicated by parentheses.

Definition: An organization system that explains the meaning of a term or concept using a variety of strategies (examples, contrast, description, etc.).

Demonstrative pronouns: The demonstrative pronouns (*this, that, these,* and *those*) are used to point out or specify certain people, places, or things.

Dependent clause: A group of words with a subject and verb but one that cannot stand alone and must be joined to an independent clause to complete its meaning. Most dependent clauses begin with subordinating conjunctions or relative pronouns.

Direct object: The word or words (usually nouns or pronouns) following and receiving the action of an action verb, or following a preposition.

Editing: One of the final steps in the writing process during which the writer checks over the draft of the essay for misspelled words, grammatical errors, missing words, and other errors.

Essay: An organized written work on a topic in a series of paragraphs, including an *introduction*, which attracts the reader's attention and states the *thesis* of the essay; *body* paragraphs, which present the supporting points of the thesis and develop them with facts, details, and examples; and a *conclusion*, which summarizes the ideas and coherently ends the work.

Exemplification: The use of examples to clarify or illustrate a topic.

Expository writing (exposition): Informative writing, the primary purpose of which is to explain a concept.

Fact: A statement that can be proven to be true.

Fragment: An incomplete sentence because it (1) is missing a subject, a verb, or both; (2) the verb is incomplete; or (3) it is a dependent clause that is not attached to an independent clause.

Freewriting: Writing that is used to explore the author's ideas without concern for grammar, spelling, or organization.

Gerund: The *–ing* form of a verb that functions as a noun in the sentence.

Gerund phrase: A gerund phrase includes a gerund and its completing words.

Helping verb: The part of the verb before the main verb, conveying the most important information about tense or mood of the verb (examples are forms of *have, be, do, will,* etc.).

Hyphen: A punctuation mark [-] used to join descriptive adjectives before a noun, to join compound words and prefixes, or to separate syllables at the end of a line.

Indefinite pronouns: These pronouns do not refer to a specific person; they refer to general or indeterminate people, places, or things. Examples are *everyone, everybody, someone, somebody, everything, something, nothing, anyone,* etc.

Independent clause: A clause that can stand alone as a sentence and contains a complete subject and verb.

Indirect object: A noun or pronoun following a verb that is receiving a direct object.

Infinitive phrase: A group of words consisting of *to* plus a verb and its completing words. An infinitive phrase can function as a noun, adjective, or adverb.

Interrupters: Sentences may be interrupted by clauses or phrases that clarify or provide additional meaning. These clauses usually begin with the relative pronouns *who, whom, which,* or *that.* See also *Restrictive clause* and *Nonrestrictive clause.*

Irregular verbs: Many irregular verbs (more than 100 in English) do not form the past tense by adding *–ed* or *–d.* Some verbs do not change form at all, or they form the past tense by changing the spelling of the entire word ("stem-changing verbs").

Linking verb: A verb that does not express action but links the subject to the word or words that describe the subject. The most common linking verbs are forms of the verb *to be.*

Main verb: The last word in a verb phrase, usually conveying the action of the sentence.

Metaphor: A way to describe a topic in terms of another concept (e.g., love is *a rose*).

Modifier: A word or group of words that functions as an adjective or adverb (providing description).

Narration: A story, typically told in chronological order, that usually builds to a climax, then resolves.

Nonrestrictive clause: A clause that is not essential to complete the meaning of the sentence. If a nonrestrictive clause is removed from the sentence, the basic meaning of the sentence will remain clear. Because it is nonessential, commas always set off this type of clause.

Noun clause: A clause functioning as a noun, usually beginning with *a, the, what, where, why,* or *when.*

Nouns: Words that stand for people, places, or things. They can be singular or plural.

Object: A word or words (usually nouns or pronouns) following action verbs or following words formed from verbs (*–ing* words, past participles, and infinitives); prepositions; or direct objects/indirect objects.

Paragraph: A group of sentences that discuss/develop a topic.

Parallel construction (parallelism): The repetition of the same grammatical structure for coherence or emphasis.

Paraphrase: The writers restatement of ideas in his or her own words and sentence structure (not directly quoting another author's words).

Parentheses: Punctuation marks [( )] used to set off specific details giving additional information, explanations, or qualifications of the main idea in a sentence. This would include words, dates, or statements.

Participle: A verb form ending in *–ed* or *–ing,* used as an adjective or used with helping verbs to form present perfect or past perfect forms.

Participial phrase: A group of words (verb phrase) consisting of a participle and its completing words that can function as an adjective or adjective phrase. Participles are also used with helping verbs to clarify tense or voice. All verbs have present participle and past participle forms.

Passive voice: A verb form chosen when the actor of the sentence is not important or when the writer wishes to avoid naming the subject. In the passive voice, the object of an active verb becomes the subject of the passive verb. The form of the verb becomes *be* + past participle.

Past continuous (progressive) tense: A verb tense showing an action in progress in the past, formed from helping verbs *was/were* and adding *–ing* to the verb form.

Past perfect tense: A verb tense used to describe a past action or event occurring prior to a later time in the past. The past perfect is formed from *had* + the verb's past participle form.

Past tense: A verb tense used to discuss completed past actions. All *regular* past tense verbs end in *–ed.* However, there are more than 100 *irregular* verbs (see The Writer's Resources).

Period: A punctuation mark [.] that is used to end a complete statement or is included in an abbreviation.

Personal pronouns: Those pronouns that refer to a person (*I/me, you, he/him, she/her, it, we/us,* and *they/them*). They are divided into three forms, depending on how they are used in a sentence. These forms are *subjective* (pronoun used as a subject), *objective* (pronoun used as an object), or *possessive* (pronoun indicating possession/ownership).

Personification: Giving human characteristics to nonhuman or inanimate objects (e.g., *The wind howled all through the night.*).

Phrasal verb: A two-word or three-word expression that combines a verb with another word, changing the meaning (e.g., *pick it up*).

Phrase: A group of related words missing a subject, verb, or both subject and verb. Phrases are used in sentences to complete thoughts or add descriptive detail; they may be restrictive or nonrestrictive (see Additional Punctuation Rules, Interrupters in The Writer's Resources). There are several types of phrases used as modifiers in sentences: *prepositional phrases, participial phrases, gerund phrases, infinitive phrases,* and *absolute phrases.*

Predicate: The part of the sentence containing the verb, making a statement or asking a question about the subject.

Prepositional phrase: A *preposition* connects a noun or pronoun to the rest of the sentence, often showing location or time. A *prepositional phrase* contains a preposition (e.g., *in, on, over, before, after,* etc.) and its object.

Present continuous (progressive) tense: A verb tense that discusses actions that are happening now or are planned for the future. This tense is formed by adding a form of the verb *to be* (*is, am, are*) with the verb + *ing*.

Present perfect tense: A verb tense used to describe an action or condition in the past that continues up to the present. The tense is formed by combining *has/have* + the past participle.

Present tense: A verb tense used to discuss habitual actions, facts, or conditions that are true of the present.

Pre-writing: The step in the writing process in which the writer thinks about the topic, purpose, and audience, and explores ideas for development through *brainstorming, clustering,* or *freewriting.*

Process analysis: An organizational structure that explains how to do something or how something works.

Pronoun: A word that takes the place of or refers to nouns. The word or words that the pronoun refers to are known as the *antecedent(s)* of the pronoun. Pronouns can be divided into several categories. The most common categories are *personal pronouns, relative pronouns, demonstrative pronouns, indefinite pronouns,* and *reflexive pronouns.*

Question mark: A punctuation mark [?] that ends direct questions.

Reflexive pronouns: The reflexive form adds *–self* or *–selves* to the pronoun and is used to indicate action performed to or on the antecedent.

Regular verb: A verb ending in *–ed* in the past tense or past participle, or forming its third person singular form by adding *–s* or *–es*.

Relative clause: A clause that functions like an adjective, beginning with a *relative pronoun* (*who, whom, which, that*).

Relative pronouns: Those pronouns used to introduce a qualifying or explanatory clause (*who, whom, which, that, whoever, whichever*).

Restrictive clause: A clause that is essential to identify a noun or to complete the meaning. This type of clause simply follows the noun or idea it is modifying. No commas are used to set off restrictive clauses.

Run-on sentence: A sentence containing two independent clauses with nothing that joins them together (a serious grammatical error).

Semicolon: A mark of punctuation [;] that usually joins two independent clauses or occasionally separates items in a series containing internal commas.

Sentence: A complete statement or question containing a subject and a verb, and expressing a complete thought.

Simile: A comparison using *like* or *as* (e.g., my love is *like a rose*).

Simple sentence: A group of words with a subject and a verb, expressing complete meaning.

Subject: The topic (who or what) about which a clause makes a statement or asks a question. Usually the subject is a noun or pronoun, and usually the subject precedes the verb.

Subject-verb agreement: Subjects and verbs in the present tense (as well as in the past and future tenses) should agree in number. Thus, singular subjects require verbs with singular endings, and plural subjects require verbs with plural endings.

Subordinating conjunction: A word that joins two clauses by making one clause less in importance and dependent on the second (independent) clause. (Examples: *although, after, because, while,* etc.) See The Writer's Resources for more information.

Subordination: Joining a dependent clause to an independent clause.

Synonym: A word with the same, or close to the same, meaning as another word.

Tense: The form of the verb that shows when in time an action occurred (present, past, future). See The Writer's Resources for more information.

Thesis statement: The sentence, usually included in the introduction, that states the main idea of the essay and often outlines the subtopics of the essay (*essay map*).

Topic sentence: A sentence stating the main idea of a paragraph.

Transitional word: A word explaining how or in what way two ideas are related. These are often *adverbial conjunctions* (see *Adverbial conjunction*).

Uncountable nouns: Nouns that represent an idea or concept that cannot be counted (e.g., water, air, fruit), and cannot be made plural.

Verb: A word indicating action, feeling, or being; verbs can be divided into three classes: *action verbs, linking verbs,* and *helping verbs* (see Chapter 2). Additionally, the form of the verb can indicate the time of the action: *present, past,* or *future* (also known as *tense*).

Text Credits

A.J. Jacobs, "Extremely Cool," *Entertainment Weekly*, 1996. Reprinted by permission of the author.

Bruce Catton, "Grant and Lee: A Study in Contrasts" from *The American Story*, Earl Schneck Miers, editor. Capitol Historical Society. Reprinted by permission of the United States Capitol Society.

Excerpt from "Deep Cold" from *The Rural Life* by Verlyn Klinkenborg. Copyright © 2003 by Verlyn Klinkenborg. By permission of Little, Brown and Company, Inc.

Excerpt from "Living on Tokyo Time" by Lynnika Butler from the *Utne Reader*, January/February 2003. Reprinted by permission of the author.

Excerpt from Shelby Steele, from *The Content of Our Character* by Shelby Steele. Copyright © 1990 by the author and reprinted by permission of the Carol Mann Agency.

William Raspberry, "The Handicap of Definition." © 1982 The Washington Post. All rights reserved. Used by permission and protected by the Copyright Laws of the United States. The printing, copying, redistribution, or retransmission of the Material without express written permission is prohibited.

Grace Suh, "The Eye of the Beholder." Copyright © 1992. Reprinted by permission of the author. First appeared in A Magazine, 1992.

Jan Harold Brunvand, "The Roommate's Death" from *The Vanishing Hitchhiker: American Urban Legends and Their Meanings* by Jan Harold Brunvand. Copyright © 1981 by Jan Harold Brunvand. Used by permission of W.W. Norton & Company, Inc.

Luis J. Rodriguez, "The Ice Cream Truck." From *Always Running–La Vida Loca, Gang Days In L.A.* by Luis J. Rodriguez. (Curbstone Press, 1993). Reprinted with permission of Curbstone Press. Distributed by Consortium.

Mary Ann Hogan, "Why We Carp and Harp." First appeared in the *Los Angeles Times*, March 10, 1992. Reprinted by permission of the author.

Nancy Masterson Sakamoto, "Conversational Ballgames" from *Polite Fictions*. Tokyo: Kinseido, Ltd., 982. © 1982 by Nancy Masterson Sakamoto. Reprinted by permission of the author.

Robert Keith Miller, "Discrimination Is a Virtue" from *Newsweek*, July 21, 1980. Reprinted by permission of the author.

Robert L. Forward, "Indistinguishable Magic" excerpted from *Indistinguishable Magic*. Baen Books, copyright © 1995. Reprinted by permission of Baen Books.

Russell Baker, "The Plot Against People," the *New York Times*, June 18, 1968. Copyright © 1968 by the New York Times. Reprinted with permission.

Timothy Gower, "Strive to Be Fit, Not Fanatical" from the *Los Angeles Times*, June 7, 1999. Copyright © 1999 by Timothy Gower. Reprinted by permission of the author.

Photo Credits

Page iv: © Fancy/Veer/Royalty-Free/Corbis; Page iv: Ed Betz/AP Images; Page viii: Bonnie S. Rauch/Super Stock, Inc.; Page ix: Carson Baldwin, Jr./Earth Scenes/Animals, Animals; Page x: © Jonathan Ernst/Reuters/Corbis; Page xi: Sandy King/The Image Bank/Getty Images; Page xiii: Dave Kramer/Index Stock Imagery; Page xiii: © Scot Frei/Corbis; Page 1: Erik Dreyer/Getty Images; Page 2: © Fancy/Veer/Royalty-Free/Corbis; Page 2: Jerry S. Mendoza/AP Images; Page 2: Rubberball/Jupiter Images; Page 2: Ed Lallo/Index Stock Imagery/Photolibrary; Page 20: © Jonathan Ernst/Reuters/Corbis; Page 48: Stock Image/Jupiter Images; Page 85: Carson Baldwin, Jr./Earth Scenes/Animals, Animals; Page 116: Hulton Archive/Getty Images; Page 133: © Fancy/Veer/Royalty-Free/Corbis; Page 157: Comstock/Creatas/Jupiter Images; Page 159: Frank Micelotta/Getty Images; Page 175: © Jeff Vanuga/Corbis; Page 177: Don Ryan/AP Images; Page 190: Sandy King/The Image Bank/Getty Images; Page 192: Jim Mone/AP Images; Page 203: Dave Kramer/Index Stock Imagery; Page 205: Ed Betz/AP Images; Page 217: © Kevin Fleming/Corbis; Page 217: Paul Warner/AP Images; Page 219: Monika Graff/The Image Works; Page 231: A. Ramey/Photo Edit, Inc. (www.photoeditinc.com); Page 233: © Tony Arruza/Corbis; Page 247: Bonnie S. Rauch/Super Stock, Inc.; Page 249: Justin Sullivan/Getty Images; Page 259: © Scot Frei/Corbis; Page 261: Ulrike Welsch/Photo Researchers, Inc.; Page 282: Walter Bibikow/Index Stock Imagery; Page 287: Stock Image/Super Stock, Inc.; Page 308: Kevin Mazur/Getty Images.

INDEX